Colonels in Blue —
Indiana, Kentucky
and Tennessee

ALSO BY ROGER D. HUNT

*Colonels in Blue — Michigan, Ohio and West Virginia:
A Civil War Biographical Dictionary* (McFarland, 2011)

Colonels in Blue — Indiana, Kentucky and Tennessee
A Civil War Biographical Dictionary

ROGER D. HUNT

McFarland & Company, Inc., Publishers
Jefferson, North Carolina, and London

LIBRARY OF CONGRESS CATALOGUING-IN-PUBLICATION DATA

Hunt, Roger D.
Colonels in blue : Indiana, Kentucky and Tennessee :
a Civil War biographical dictionary / Roger D. Hunt.
    p.   cm.
Includes bibliographical references and index.

ISBN 978-0-7864-7318-2
softcover : acid free paper ∞

1. United States—History—Civil War, 1861–1865—Biography—Dictionaries. 2. Indiana—History—Civil War, 1861–1865—Biography—Dictionaries. 3. Kentucky—History—Civil War, 1861–1865—Biography—Dictionaries. 4. Tennessee—History—Civil War, 1861–1865—Biography—Dictionaries. 5. United States. Army—Officers—History—Civil War, 1861–1865—Dictionaries. I. Title
E467.H8928 2014   355.0092'2—dc23   2013041033

BRITISH LIBRARY CATALOGUING DATA ARE AVAILABLE

© 2014 Roger D. Hunt. All rights reserved

No part of this book may be reproduced or transmitted in any form or by any means, electronic or mechanical, including photocopying or recording, or by any information storage and retrieval system, without permission in writing from the publisher.

On the cover: (*from left*) John Abram Hendricks (U.S. Military Academy Library); Sion St. Clair Bass (Massachusetts MOLLUS Collection, USAMHI); Daniel Weisiger Lindsey (The National Archives)

Manufactured in the United States of America

McFarland & Company, Inc., Publishers
Box 611, Jefferson, North Carolina 28640
www.mcfarlandpub.com

In memory of
Michael J. Winey,
military historian and
photo curator extraordinaire
(1941–2012)

TABLE OF CONTENTS

Acknowledgments

ix

Introduction

1

Indiana
Regiments 3
Biographies 16

Kentucky
Regiments 135
Biographies 140

Tennessee
Regiments 197
Biographies 200

Bibliography

225

Index of Names

243

Acknowledgments

Although I appreciate the contributions of all of the individuals in the following list, I want to mention a few whose contributions to this volume have been especially noteworthy. Craig Dunn, John Sickles and Mark Weldon have been generous in providing access to their outstanding collections of Indiana colonels. Everitt Bowles, Rick Brown, Rick Carlile, Henry Deeks, Dennis Keesee, Steve Meadow, and Jim Quinlan have been especially helpful in providing elusive photographs and valuable information. Randy Hackenburg, Dr. Richard Sommers and the late Mike Winey have provided ready access to the unparalleled photo archives of the U.S. Army Military History Institute during the past 30 years. Alan Aimone has been equally hospitable in providing access to the outstanding collections at the U.S. Military Academy Library.

Jill M. Abraham, National Archives, Washington, DC
Robert P. Addleman, Los Angeles, CA
Alan C. Aimone, U.S. Military Academy Library, West Point, NY
Michael Albanese, Kendall, NY
Robert L. Bailey, Roane County Heritage Commission, Kingston, TN
Gil Barrett, New Bern, NC
Richard A. Baumgartner, Huntington, WV
Nancy Bean, Montgomery, AL
Tim Beckman, Indianapolis, IN
Jon Bernard, Kilauea, Kauai, HI
Everitt Bowles, Woodstock, GA
Mike Brackin, Manchester, CT
Dave Broman, Howard County Historical Society, Kokomo, IN
Timothy R. Brookes, East Liverpool, OH
Rick Brown, Leesburg, VA
Paul J. Brzozowski, Fairfield, CT
David L. Callihan, Dryden, NY
Robert Cammaroto, Alexandria, VA
Nan J. Card, Rutherford B. Hayes Presidential Center, Fremont, OH
Richard F. Carlile, Dayton, OH
William H. Carr, Mason, MI
Allen Cebula, Chicago, IL
Steve Cotham, McClung Historical Collection, Knoxville, TN
Henry Deeks, Ashburnham, MA
Alice Duckworth, Arizona Capitol Museum, Phoenix, AZ
Craig Dunn, Kokomo, IN
Jacqueline T. Eubanks, Stuart, FL
Jerry Everts, Lambertville, MI
Jason Flahardy, University of Kentucky Archives, Lexington, KY
Heather Fox, The Filson Historical Society, Louisville, KY
Perry M. Frohne, Oshkosh, WI
John Fuller, Columbia, MD
Bryan Fuxa, Colorado Springs, CO
Ralph U. Gooding, Danbury, WI
John P. Gurnish, Mogadore, OH
Randy Hackenburg, Boiling Springs, PA
Thomas Harris, New York, NY
J. Michael Higgs, Cave Hill Cemetery, Louisville, KY
Scott N. Hilts, Arcade, NY
Michael A. Hogle, Okemos, MI
Kurt Holman, Perryville Battlefield State Historic Site, Perryville, KY
Geoff Hunt, The Texas Collection, Baylor University, Waco, TX
Anne Johnson, Des Moines, IA
Craig T. Johnson, Towson, MD
James A. Johnson, Wills Point, TX
Elizabeth H. Joyner, Vicksburg National Military Park, Vicksburg, MS
Alan Jutzi, The Huntington Library, San Marino, CA
Dennis M. Keesee, Westerville, OH
Jim Kettel, Boyd County Public Library, Ashland, KY

Acknowledgments

Jeff Kowalis, Orland Park, IL
Michael Kraus, Pittsburgh, PA
John W. Kuhl, Pittstown, NJ
Mary Beth Linne', National Archives, Washington, DC
Eric Lowman, Mentone, IN
Robert F. MacAvoy, Clark, NJ
Kalawakua Mayer, Dallas, TX
Michael J. McAfee, Newburgh, NY
Mike McCormick, Terre Haute, IN
Karina McDaniel, Tennessee State Library and Archives, Nashville, TN
Edward McGuire, New York State Library, Albany, NY
Sarah T. McNeive, Topeka, KS
Steven J. Meadow, Midland, MI
Mike Medhurst, Kansas City, MO
Marie Melchiori, Vienna, VA
Mary Michals, Abraham Lincoln Presidential Library, Springfield, IL
Franklin Miller, Jr., Gambier, OH
Leoneita C. Milner, Dallas, TX
Tom Molocea, North Lima, OH
Tom Mullusky, Gilder Lehrman Institute of American History, New York, NY
Jim Mundie, Kenner, LA
David M. Neville, Export, PA
Howard L. Norton, Vilonia, AR
Olaf, Berkeley, CA
Ronn Palm, Kittanning, PA
David K. Parks, Utica, MI
Ben Pauley, Zionsville, IN
Jan Perone, Abraham Lincoln Presidential Library, Springfield, IL
Robert Perry, Prestonsburg, KY
Nicholas P. Picerno, Bridgewater, VA
Sally R. Polhemus, McClung Historical Collection, Knoxville, TN
Susan Ponstein, Newcastle, OK
Clark Prather, Vista, CA
Marian Presswood, Benton, TN
James Quinlan, Alexandria, VA
Edmund J. Raus, Jr., Manassas, VA
Bryan Reed, Cleveland State Community College, Cleveland, TN
Miranda L. Fraley Rhodes, Tennessee State Museum, Nashville, TN
David L. Richards, Gettysburg, PA
Nancy Richey, Western Kentucky University, Bowling Green, KY
Jeffrey I. Richman, Brooklyn, NY
Robert L. Riddle, Lincoln, NE
Stephen B. Rogers, Ithaca, NY
Amelia Rudolph, Queens, NY
Paul Russinoff, Baltimore, MD
Donald K. Ryberg, Westfield, NY
Dale Schaefer, Elmwood Cemetery, Memphis, TN
Jody Schmidt, Elmwood Cemetery, Memphis, TN
Patrick A. Schroeder, Daleville, VA
Alan J. Sessarego, Gettysburg, PA
Nancy Sherbert, Kansas State Historical Society, Topeka, KS
John Sickles, Merrillville, IN
Richard S. Skidmore, Hanover, IN
Sam Small, Gettysburg, PA
Wes Small, Gettysburg, PA
Dr. Richard J. Sommers, U.S. Army Military History Institute, Carlisle, PA
Dale and Sharon Sternberg, Marshfield, WI
John A. Stovall, Dublin, TX
Larry M. Strayer, Dayton, OH
Karl E. Sundstrom, North Riverside, IL
Susan Sutton, Indiana Historical Society, Indianapolis, IN
David W. Taylor, Sylvania, OH
Daniel C. Toomey, Linthicum, MD
Ken C. Turner, Ellwood City, PA
Michael W. Waskul, Ypsilanti, MI
Mark Weldon, Fort Wayne, IN
Wesley W. Wilson, DePauw University Archives, Greencastle, IN
Michael J. Winey, Mechanicsburg, PA
Richard A. Wolfe, Bridgeport, WV
Mary Moore Young, San Antonio, TX
Buck Zaidel, Cromwell, CT
Dave Zullo, Lake Monticello, VA

I am also indebted to the staffs of the following libraries for their capable assistance:

Abraham Lincoln Presidential Library & Museum, Springfield, IL
Alexandrian Free Public Library, Mount Vernon, IN
Bartholomew County Library, Columbus, IN
Bedford Public Library, Bedford, IN
Boyd County Public Library, Ashland, KY
Civil War Library & Museum, Philadelphia, PA
Colorado Historical Society, Denver, CO
Connecticut State Library, Hartford, CT
Eastern Kentucky University Special Collections and Archives, Richmond, KY
Family History Library, Salt Lake City, UT
Filson Historical Society, Louisville, KY
Goshen Public Library, Goshen, IN
Huntington City–Township Public Library, Huntington, IN
The Huntington Library, San Marino, CA
Huntsville Madison County Public Library, Huntsville, AL
Indiana Historical Society, Indianapolis, IN
Indiana State Library, Indianapolis, IN
Jeffersonville Township Public Library, Jeffersonville, IN
Jonesborough–Washington County Library, Jonesborough, TN
Kansas State Historical Society, Topeka, KS
Kentucky Historical Society, Frankfort, KY

Acknowledgments

Kokomo Public Library, Kokomo, IN
La Porte County Public Library, La Porte, IN
Lawrenceburg Public Library, Lawrenceburg, IN
Library of Congress, Washington, DC
Madison–Jefferson County Public Library, Madison, IN
Maysville–Mason County Public Library, Maysville, KY
Minnesota Historical Society, St. Paul, MN
Mishawaka-Penn-Harris Public Library, Mishawaka, IN
Morrisson-Reeves Library, Richmond, IN
Mount Sterling–Montgomery County Public Library, Mount Sterling, KY
National Archives, Washington, DC
National Society Daughters of the American Revolution, Washington, DC
New Albany–Floyd County Public Library, New Albany, IN
New England Historic Genealogical Society, Boston, MA
New Jersey State Archives, Trenton, NJ
New York Genealogical and Biographical Society, New York, NY
The New-York Historical Society, New York, NY
New York State Library, Albany, NY
Ohio Genealogical Society, Mansfield, OH
Ohio Historical Society, Columbus, OH
Ottawa Public Library, Ottawa, KS
Paris–Bourbon County Library, Paris, KY
Peru Public Library, Peru, IN
Polk County Historical and Genealogical Society, Benton, TN
Rutherford B. Hayes Presidential Center, Fremont, OH
San Bernardino Public Library, San Bernardino, CA
San Diego Public Library, San Diego, CA
Santa Barbara Public Library, Santa Barbara, CA
Schaffer Library, Union College, Schenectady, NY
Southeast Tennessee Digital Archive, Cleveland, TN
Spokane Public Library, Spokane, WA
State Historical Society of Missouri, Columbia, MO
State Library of Iowa, Des Moines, IA
Tacoma Public Library, Tacoma, WA
Tennessee State Library and Archives, Nashville, TN
Tennessee State Museum, Nashville, TN
Tippecanoe County Public Library, Lafayette, IN
U.S. Army Military History Institute, Carlisle, PA
U.S. Military Academy Library, West Point, NY
University of Kentucky Special Collections and Archives, Lexington, KY
Vigo County Public Library, Terre Haute, IN
Wabash Carnegie Public Library, Wabash, IN
Warsaw Community Public Library, Warsaw, IN
Western Kentucky University, Special Collections Library, Bowling Green, KY
Western Reserve Historical Society, Cleveland, OH
Willard Library, Evansville, IN
Wisconsin Historical Society, Madison, WI

Introduction

At the beginning of the Civil War the Regular Army of the United States numbered only 1,098 officers and 15,304 enlisted men. Faced with this shortage of manpower in suppressing the escalating rebellion, President Abraham Lincoln issued a call for 75,000 militia for three months service on April 15, 1861, and then a call for 500,000 volunteers for three years service on July 22, 1861. These calls for troops and others issued later in the war specified that the various state governors would appoint the commanding officers of the regiments raised in their states.

Patriotic fervor throughout the Northern states resulted in spirited competition to complete the organization of regiments to meet the state quotas. In most cases the prospective commanders of these regiments were prominent citizens whose military background (if any) consisted of service in a local militia organization. In general the early war Union army colonels were known more for their patriotic enthusiasm than for their military competence. Many of them were more successful in convincing their fellow townsmen to enlist than they were in actually leading them into battle. Fortunately for the Union cause, the colonels who stayed in the service eventually acquired the necessary military skills or were replaced by subordinates who proved their capabilities on the field of battle.

This book is the fifth in a series of books containing photographs and biographical sketches of that diverse group of motivated citizens who attained the rank of colonel in the Union army, but failed to win promotion to brigadier general or brevet brigadier general. This volume presents the colonels who commanded regiments from Indiana, Kentucky, and Tennessee. Preceding the photographs and biographical sketches for each state is a breakdown by regiment of all the colonels who commanded regiments from that state, with the name of each colonel being followed by the dates of his service. Included in this breakdown are the colonels who were promoted beyond the rank of colonel, with their final rank indicated in bold letters. Those indicated as attaining the rank of brigadier general are covered in the book *Generals in Blue,* by Ezra J. Warner, while those attaining the rank of brevet brigadier general are covered in the book *Brevet Brigadier Generals in Blue,* by Roger D. Hunt and Jack R. Brown.

Some explanatory notes are necessary concerning the content of the biographical sketches:

1. The date associated with each rank may be the date when the colonel was commissioned or appointed or the date when he was mustered at that rank. Generally, the date of muster was used whenever available. The reader should be aware that these dates were often adjusted or corrected by the War Department during and after the war, so that

any hope of providing totally consistent dates is virtually impossible.

2. When the word "Colonel" is italicized, this indicates that the colonel was commissioned as colonel but never mustered as such.

3. Images not identified as to source are from the author's collection.

4. The following abbreviations are used in the text:

AAG	Assistant Adjutant General
ACM	Assistant Commissary of Musters
ACP	Appointment, Commission, and Personal
ADC	Aide-de-Camp
AIG	Assistant Inspector General
aka	Also Known As
AQM	Assistant Quartermaster
Brig.	Brigadier
Bvt.	Brevet
Capt.	Captain
CB	Commission Branch
Co.	County or Company
Col.	Colonel
CSA	Confederate States Army
DOW	Died of Wounds
GAR	Grand Army of the Republic
Gen.	General
GSW	Gun Shot Wound
KIA	Killed in Action
Lt.	Lieutenant
MOLLUS	Military Order of the Loyal Legion of the United States
NHDVS	National Home for Disabled Volunteer Soldiers
RQM	Regimental Quartermaster
Twp.	Township
U.S.	United States
USA	United States Army
USAMHI	United States Army Military History Institute
USCT	United States Colored Troops
USMA	United States Military Academy
USV	United States Volunteers
VRC	Veteran Reserve Corps
Vol.	Volume
VS	Volunteer Service

INDIANA

Regiments

1st Cavalry

Conrad Baker	Aug. 20, 1861	Mustered out Sept. 12, 1864

2nd Cavalry

John A. Bridgland	Nov. 1, 1861	Resigned March 22, 1862
Robert N. Hudson	April 5, 1862	Declined
Edward M. McCook	April 30, 1862	Promoted **Brig. Gen., USV,** April 27, 1864
James W. Stewart	March 1, 1864	Mustered out Oct. 4, 1864

3rd Cavalry

Scott Carter	Oct. 30, 1861	Resigned March 11, 1863
George H. Chapman	March 12, 1863	Promoted **Brig. Gen., USV,** July 21, 1864

4th Cavalry

Isaac P. Gray	Sept. 4, 1862	Resigned Feb. 11, 1863
Lawrence S. Shuler	Feb. 12, 1863	Resigned May 16, 1863
John A. Platter	May 17, 1863	Resigned Sept. 9, 1863
John T. Deweese	Sept. 10, 1863	Resigned March 11, 1864, **Bvt. Brig. Gen., USV**
Horace P. Lamson	March 12, 1864	Mustered out July 3, 1865

5th Cavalry

Robert R. Stewart	Oct. 18, 1862	Declined
Felix W. Graham	Dec. 10, 1862	Resigned Dec. 15, 1863
Thomas H. Butler	March 1, 1864	Mustered out June 27, 1865, **Bvt. Brig. Gen., USV**

6th Cavalry (Designation changed from 71st Infantry, Feb. 23, 1863)

James Biddle	Nov. 11, 1862	Mustered out June 27, 1865, **Bvt. Brig. Gen., USV**
Courtland C. Matson	July 1, 1865	Mustered out Sept. 15, 1865

7th Cavalry

John P. C. Shanks	Oct. 9, 1863	Mustered out Sept. 19, 1865, **Bvt. Brig. Gen., USV**
Thomas M. Browne	Oct. 10, 1865	Mustered out Feb. 18, 1866, **Bvt. Brig. Gen., USV**

8th Cavalry

Thomas J. Harrison	Aug. 29, 1861	Mustered out Feb. 17, 1865, **Bvt. Brig. Gen., USV**
Fielder A. Jones	March 1, 1865	Mustered out July 20, 1865, **Bvt. Brig. Gen., USV**

9th Cavalry

William S. McClure	Feb. 2, 1864	Declined
George W. Jackson	April 30, 1864	Resigned June 3, 1865
Eli Lilly	June 4, 1865	Mustered out Aug. 25, 1865

10th Cavalry

Thomas N. Pace	Feb. 15, 1864	Resigned March 16, 1865
George R. Swallow	June 8, 1865	Mustered out Aug. 31, 1865

11th Cavalry

Robert R. Stewart	Feb. 2, 1864	Resigned May 9, 1865
Abram Sharra	May 19, 1865	Mustered out Sept. 19, 1865

12th Cavalry

Edward Anderson	March 1, 1864	Mustered out Nov. 10, 1865

13th Cavalry

Gilbert M. L. Johnson	April 29, 1864	Mustered out Nov. 18, 1865, **Bvt. Brig. Gen.**, USV

1st Heavy Artillery (Designation changed from 21st Infantry, Feb. 1863)

John A. Keith	May 18, 1863	Resigned Feb. 2, 1865
Benjamin F. Hays	Feb. 3, 1865	Mustered out Jan. 10, 1866

6th Infantry (3 months)

Thomas T. Crittenden	April 27, 1861	To 6 IN Infantry (3 years), Later **Brig. Gen.**, USV

6th Infantry (3 years)

Thomas T. Crittenden	Sept. 20, 1861	Promoted **Brig. Gen.**, USV, April 28, 1862
Philemon P. Baldwin	May 17, 1862	KIA Sept. 19, 1863
Hagerman Tripp	Sept. 21, 1863	Discharged June 22, 1864

7th Infantry (3 months)

Ebenezer Dumont	April 27, 1861	To 7 IN Infantry (3 years), Later **Brig. Gen.**, USV

7th Infantry (3 years)

Ebenezer Dumont	Sept. 13, 1861	Promoted **Brig. Gen.**, USV, Sept. 3, 1861
James Gavin	Nov. 27, 1861	Resigned April 22, 1863
Ira G. Grover	April 23, 1863	Mustered out Sept. 20, 1864, **Bvt. Brig. Gen.**, USV

8th Infantry (3 months)

William P. Benton	April 27, 1861	To 8 IN Infantry (3 years), Later **Brig. Gen.**, USV

8th Infantry (3 years)

William P. Benton	Sept. 5, 1861	Promoted **Brig. Gen.**, USV, April 28, 1862
David Shunk	May 25, 1862	Died Feb. 21, 1865, **Bvt. Brig. Gen.**, USV
John R. Polk	Feb. 22, 1865	Mustered out Aug. 28, 1865

9th Infantry (3 months)

Robert H. Milroy	April 27, 1861	To 9 IN Infantry (3 years), Later **Brig. Gen.**, USV

9th Infantry (3 years)

Robert H. Milroy	Aug. 27, 1861	Promoted **Brig. Gen.**, USV, Sept. 3, 1861
Gideon C. Moody	Nov. 15, 1861	Mustered out Aug. 19, 1862
William H. Blake	Aug. 20, 1862	Resigned April 16, 1863
Isaac C. B. Suman	April 30, 1863	Mustered out Sept. 28, 1865, **Bvt. Brig. Gen.**, USV

10th Infantry (3 months)

Joseph J. Reynolds	April 25, 1861	Promoted **Brig. Gen.**, USV, May 17, 1861
Mahlon D. Manson	May 10, 1861	To 10 IN Infantry (3 years), Later **Brig. Gen.**, USV

10th Infantry (3 years)

Mahlon D. Manson	Sept. 18, 1861	Promoted **Brig. Gen.**, USV, March 24, 1862

William C. Kise	April 5, 1862	Discharged Nov. 17, 1862
William B. Carroll	Nov. 18, 1862	KIA Sept. 19, 1863
Marsh B. Taylor	Sept. 21, 1863	Mustered out Sept. 19, 1864

11th Infantry (3 months)

Lewis Wallace	April 25, 1861	To 11 IN Infantry (3 years), Later **Brig. Gen.** USV

11th Infantry (3 years)

Lewis Wallace	Aug. 31, 1861	Promoted **Brig. Gen., USV,** Sept. 3, 1861
George F. McGinnis	Sept. 3, 1861	Promoted **Brig. Gen., USV,** Nov. 29, 1862
Daniel Macauley	March 10, 1863	Mustered out July 26, 1865, **Bvt. Brig. Gen.,** USV

12th Infantry (1 year)

John M. Wallace	May 15, 1861	Resigned Aug. 6, 1861
William H. Link	Aug. 26, 1861	To 12 IN Infantry (3 years)

12th Infantry (3 years)

William H. Link	Aug. 18, 1862	DOW Sept. 20, 1862
Reuben Williams	Nov. 17, 1862	Mustered out June 8, 1865, **Bvt. Brig. Gen.,** USV

13th Infantry

Jeremiah C. Sullivan	June 19, 1861	Promoted **Brig. Gen., USV,** April 28, 1862
Robert S. Foster	April 30, 1862	Promoted **Brig. Gen., USV,** June 12, 1863
Cyrus J. Dobbs	July 17, 1863	Mustered out June 30, 1864
John H. Lawrence	June 1, 1865	Mustered out Sept. 5, 1865

14th Infantry

Nathan Kimball	June 7, 1861	Promoted **Brig. Gen., USV,** April 15, 1862
William Harrow	April 26, 1862	Promoted **Brig. Gen., USV,** Nov. 29, 1862
John Coons	Jan. 22, 1863	KIA May 12, 1864

15th Infantry

George D. Wagner	June 14, 1861	Promoted **Brig. Gen., USV,** Nov. 29, 1862
Gustavus A. Wood	March 9, 1863	Mustered out June 25, 1864

16th Infantry (1 year)

Pleasant A. Hackleman	May 20, 1861	Promoted **Brig. Gen., USV,** April 28, 1862
Thomas J. Lucas	May 6, 1862	To 16 IN Infantry (3 years), Later **Brig. Gen.,** USV

16th Infantry (3 years)

Thomas J. Lucas	May 27, 1862	Promoted **Brig. Gen., USV,** Nov. 10, 1864
Robert Conover	Feb. 20, 1865	Mustered out June 30, 1865

17th Infantry

Milo S. Hascall	June 12, 1861	Promoted **Brig. Gen., USV,** April 25, 1862
John T. Wilder	April 25, 1862	Resigned Oct. 4, 1864, **Bvt. Brig. Gen.,** USV
Jacob G. Vail	Nov. 18, 1864	Mustered out Aug. 8, 1865, **Bvt. Brig. Gen.,** USV

18th Infantry

Thomas Pattison	Aug. 16, 1861	Resigned June 3, 1862
Henry D. Washburn	July 15, 1862	Mustered out July 26, 1865, **Bvt. Brig. Gen.,** USV
Doil R. Bowden	July 27, 1865	Mustered out Aug. 28, 1865

19th Infantry

Solomon Meredith	July 29, 1861	Promoted **Brig. Gen., USV,** Oct. 6, 1862
Samuel J. Williams	Oct. 8, 1862	KIA May 6, 1864
John M. Lindley	May 13, 1864	Mustered out Oct. 19, 1864, **Bvt. Brig. Gen.,** USV

Indiana Regiments

20th Infantry

William L. Brown	July 22, 1861	KIA Aug. 29, 1862
John Van Valkenburg	Aug. 30, 1862	Discharged Feb. 10, 1863
John Wheeler	Feb. 21, 1863	KIA July 2, 1863
William C. L. Taylor	July 4, 1863	Mustered out Sept. 22, 1864
William Orr	Oct. 18, 1864	Mustered out May 15, 1865
Albert S. Andrews	May 16, 1865	Mustered out July 12, 1865

21st Infantry (Designation changed to 1st Heavy Artillery, Feb. 1863)

James W. McMillan	July 24, 1861	Promoted **Brig. Gen., USV**, Nov. 29, 1862

22nd Infantry

Jefferson C. Davis	Aug. 1, 1861	Promoted **Brig. Gen., USV**, Dec. 18, 1861
Michael Gooding	June 13, 1862	Resigned Feb. 7, 1864
William M. Wiles	Feb. 6, 1864	Mustered out Jan. 9, 1865
Thomas Shea	June 9, 1865	Mustered out July 24, 1865

23rd Infantry

William L. Sanderson	July 29, 1861	Resigned July 29, 1864
George S. Babbitt	Jan. 1, 1865	Mustered out July 23, 1865

24th Infantry

Alvin P. Hovey	July 31, 1861	Promoted **Brig. Gen., USV**, April 28, 1862
William T. Spicely	May 14, 1862	Mustered out July 21, 1865, **Bvt. Brig. Gen., USV**

25th Infantry

James C. Veatch	Aug. 19, 1861	Promoted **Brig. Gen., USV**, April 28, 1862
William H. Morgan	May 1, 1862	Resigned May 20, 1864, **Bvt. Brig. Gen., USV**
James S. Wright	Jan. 1, 1865	Mustered out July 17, 1865

26th Infantry

William M. Wheatley	Aug. 30, 1861	Resigned Sept. 27, 1862
John G. Clark	Sept. 28, 1862	Mustered out Sept. 28, 1865
Newton A. Logan	Oct. 10, 1865	Mustered out Jan. 15, 1866

27th Infantry

Silas Colgrove	Sept. 12, 1861	Mustered out Nov. 4, 1864, **Bvt. Brig. Gen., USV**

28th Infantry (See 1st Cavalry)

29th Infantry

John F. Miller	Aug. 27, 1861	Promoted **Brig. Gen., USV**, Jan. 5, 1864
David M. Dunn	March 1, 1864	Mustered out Sept. 27, 1864
Samuel O. Gregory	Feb. 25, 1865	Mustered out Dec. 2, 1865

30th Infantry

Sion S. Bass	Oct. 4, 1861	DOW April 14, 1862
Joseph B. Dodge	April 26, 1862	Mustered out Sept. 29, 1864
Henry W. Lawton	Feb. 10, 1865	Mustered out Nov. 25, 1865

31st Infantry

Charles Cruft	Sept. 20, 1861	Promoted **Brig. Gen., USV**, July 16, 1862
John Osborn	July 17, 1862	Resigned July 14, 1863
John T. Smith	July 27, 1863	Resigned March 12, 1865
James R. Hallowell	March 13, 1865	Mustered out Dec. 8, 1865

32nd Infantry

August Willich	Aug. 24, 1861	Promoted **Brig. Gen., USV**, July 17, 1862

Henry Von Trebra	July 18, 1862	Died Aug. 6, 1863
Francis Erdelmeyer	Aug. 8, 1863	Mustered out Sept. 7, 1864

33rd Infantry

John Coburn	Sept. 16, 1861	Mustered out Sept. 20, 1864, **Bvt. Brig. Gen., USV**
James E. Burton	May 4, 1865	Mustered out July 21, 1865

34th Infantry

Asbury E. Steele	Oct. 4, 1861	Resigned Jan. 14, 1862
Townsend Ryan	Jan. 15, 1862	Resigned June 14, 1862
Robert A. Cameron	June 15, 1862	Promoted **Brig. Gen., USV,** Aug. 11, 1863
Robert B. Jones	Dec. 1, 1863	Resigned March 20, 1865
Robert G. Morrison	March 21, 1865	Mustered out Feb. 3, 1866

35th Infantry

John C. Walker	Dec. 11, 1861	Discharged Aug. 6, 1862
Bernard F. Mullen	Aug. 7, 1862	Resigned May 29, 1864
Augustus G. Tassin	March 4, 1865	Mustered out Sept. 30, 1865, **Bvt. Brig. Gen., USV**

36th Infantry

William Grose	Oct. 23, 1861	Promoted **Brig. Gen., USV,** July 30, 1864
Oliver H. P. Carey	July 31, 1864	Mustered out Sept. 21, 1864

37th Infantry

George W. Hazzard	Oct. 17, 1861	Resigned March 5, 1862
Carter Gazlay	April 8, 1862	Dismissed Aug. 13, 1862
James S. Hull	Aug. 14, 1862	Mustered out Oct. 27, 1864

38th Infantry

Benjamin F. Scribner	Sept. 18, 1861	Resigned Aug. 21, 1864, **Bvt. Brig. Gen., USV**
Daniel F. Griffin	Aug. 22, 1864	Resigned Nov. 8, 1864, **Bvt. Brig. Gen., USV**
David H. Patton	May 20, 1865	Mustered out July 15, 1865

39th Infantry (See 8th Cavalry)

40th Infantry

William C. Wilson	Dec. 30, 1861	Resigned March 27, 1862
John W. Blake	April 5, 1862	Mustered out Feb. 10, 1865
Henry Leaming	May 1, 1865	Mustered out Dec. 21, 1865

41st Infantry (See 2nd Cavalry)

42nd Infantry

James G. Jones	Oct. 10, 1861	Mustered out Nov. 1, 1864
William T. B. McIntire	Oct. 11, 1864	Resigned Dec. 12, 1864
Gideon R. Kellams	April 10, 1865	Mustered out July 21, 1865

43rd Infantry

George K. Steele	Jan. 2, 1862	Resigned Jan. 16, 1862
William E. McLean	Jan. 16, 1862	Mustered out May 17, 1865
John C. Major	May 20, 1865	Mustered out Aug. 31, 1865

44th Infantry

Hugh B. Reed	Nov. 26, 1861	Resigned Nov. 26, 1862
William C. Williams	Nov. 27, 1862	Resigned May 12, 1863
Simeon C. Aldrich	July 27, 1863	Died Aug. 15, 1864
James F. Curtis	Dec. 1, 1864	Mustered out Sept. 14, 1865

45th Infantry (See 3rd Cavalry)
46th Infantry

Graham N. Fitch	Dec. 10, 1861	Resigned Aug. 5, 1862
Thomas H. Bringhurst	Aug. 6, 1862	Mustered out Sept. 4, 1865

47th Infantry

James R. Slack	Dec. 13, 1861	Promoted **Brig. Gen., USV,** Nov. 10, 1864
John A. McLaughlin	March 1, 1865	Mustered out Oct. 23, 1865

48th Infantry

Norman Eddy	Jan. 16, 1862	Resigned July 11, 1863
Edward J. Wood	July 12, 1863	Mustered out Jan. 15, 1865
Newton Bingham	May 1, 1865	Mustered out July 15, 1865

49th Infantry

John W. Ray	Nov. 21, 1861	Resigned Oct. 17, 1862
James Keigwin	Oct. 18, 1862	Mustered out Nov. 29, 1864
James Leeper	Dec. 1, 1864	Mustered out Sept. 13, 1865

50th Infantry

Cyrus L. Dunham	Dec. 25, 1861	Resigned Nov. 18, 1863
Samuel T. Wells	Nov. 19, 1863	Mustered out May 26, 1865

51st Infantry

Abel D. Streight	Dec. 12, 1861	Resigned March 16, 1865, **Bvt. Brig. Gen., USV**
David A. McHolland	March 17, 1865	Mustered out April 17, 1865
William N. Denny	June 1, 1865	Mustered out Dec. 13, 1865

52nd Infantry

James M. Smith	Feb. 1, 1862	Resigned June 4, 1862
Edward H. Wolfe	Sept. 19, 1862	Mustered out Jan. 31, 1865, **Bvt. Brig. Gen., USV**
Zalmon S. Main	May 27, 1865	Mustered out Sept. 10, 1865

53rd Infantry

Walter Q. Gresham	March 10, 1862	Promoted **Brig. Gen., USV,** Aug. 11, 1863
William Jones	Oct. 31, 1863	KIA July 22, 1864
Warner L. Vestal	Jan. 31, 1865	Mustered out July 21, 1865

54th Infantry (3 months)

John L. Mansfield	June 10, 1862	Resigned June 18, 1862
David Garland Rose	June 19, 1862	Mustered out Sept. 26, 1862

54th Infantry (1 year)

Fielding Mansfield	Nov. 17, 1862	Mustered out Dec. 8, 1863

55th Infantry (3 months)
Regiment not entitled to a colonel since it never attained full strength.

56th Infantry
Did not complete organization. Consolidated with 52nd Infantry.

57th Infantry

John W. T. McMullen	Oct. 18, 1861	Resigned March 6, 1862
Cyrus C. Hines	March 6, 1862	Resigned July 27, 1863
George W. Lennard	July 28, 1863	DOW May 14, 1864
Willis Blanche	June 24, 1864	Resigned May 1, 1865
John S. McGraw	May 2, 1865	Mustered out Dec. 14, 1865

58th Infantry

Henry M. Carr	Dec. 17, 1861	Resigned June 17, 1862
George P. Buell	June 24, 1862	Mustered out July 25, 1865, **Bvt. Brig. Gen., USV**

59th Infantry

Jesse I. Alexander	Feb. 11, 1862	Resigned Sept. 1, 1864
Jefferson K. Scott	Aug. 13, 1864	Mustered out April 10, 1865
Thomas A. McNaught	June 28, 1865	Mustered out July 17, 1865, **Bvt. Brig. Gen., USV**

60th Infantry

Richard Owen	Jan. 31, 1862	Resigned Nov. 20, 1863
Augustus Goelzer	April 19, 1864	Mustered out March 21, 1865

61st Infantry
and
62nd Infantry

Did not complete organization.

63rd Infantry

John S. Williams	Aug. 30, 1862	Resigned June 14, 1863
James McMannomy	July 1, 1863	Resigned Jan. 17, 1864
Israel N. Stiles	March 19, 1864	Mustered out June 21, 1865, **Bvt. Brig. Gen., USV**

64th Infantry

Did not complete organization.

65th Infantry

John W. Foster	Aug. 24, 1862	Resigned March 12, 1864
Thomas Johnson	March 12, 1864	Discharged Aug. 29, 1864
John W. Hammond	Sept. 7, 1864	Mustered out June 22, 1865

66th Infantry

DeWitt C. Anthony	Sept. 22, 1862	Resigned March 24, 1864, **Bvt. Brig. Gen., USV**
Roger Martin	March 25, 1864	Mustered out June 3, 1865

67th Infantry

Frank Emerson	Aug. 22, 1862	Resigned Sept. 10, 1864

68th Infantry

Edward A. King	Aug. 20, 1862	KIA Sept. 20, 1863
John S. Scobey	Sept. 21, 1863	Resigned Nov. 13, 1863
Harvey J. Espy	Nov. 14, 1863	Mustered out June 20, 1865

69th Infantry

William A. Bickle	Aug. 19, 1862	Resigned Oct. 24, 1862
Hermann J. Korff	Aug. 24, 1862	Temporary assignment
Thomas W. Bennett	Nov. 1, 1862	Mustered out Jan. 4, 1865, **Bvt. Brig. Gen., USV**
Oran Perry	April 13, 1865	Mustered out July 5, 1865

70th Infantry

Benjamin Harrison	Aug. 7, 1862	Mustered out June 8, 1865, **Bvt. Brig. Gen., USV**

71st Infantry (Designation changed to 6th Cavalry, Feb. 23, 1863)

James Biddle	Nov. 11, 1862	To 6th Cavalry, **Bvt. Brig. Gen., USV**

72nd Infantry

Abram O. Miller	Aug. 24, 1862	Mustered out June 26, 1865, **Bvt. Brig. Gen., USV**

Indiana Regiments

73rd Infantry

Gilbert Hathaway	Aug. 21, 1862	KIA May 2, 1863
Alfred B. Wade	July 6, 1864	Mustered out July 1, 1865

74th Infantry

Charles W. Chapman	Aug. 21, 1862	Resigned Nov. 26, 1863
Myron H. Baker	Nov. 27, 1863	KIA Aug. 5, 1864
Thomas Morgan	Jan. 1, 1865	Mustered out June 9, 1865

75th Infantry

John U. Pettit	Aug. 20, 1862	Resigned Oct. 24, 1862
Milton S. Robinson	Oct. 29, 1862	Resigned March 29, 1864, **Bvt. Brig. Gen., USV**
William O'Brien	April 1, 1864	Mustered out June 8, 1865

76th Infantry (30 days)

James Gavin	July 19, 1862	Temporary assignment

77th Infantry (See 4th Cavalry)

78th Infantry (60 days)

Regiment not entitled to a colonel since it never attained full strength.

79th Infantry

Frederick Knefler	Sept. 28, 1862	Mustered out June 7, 1865, **Bvt. Brig. Gen., USV**

80th Infantry

Charles Denby	Oct. 21, 1862	Resigned Jan. 17, 1863
Lewis Brooks	Jan. 18, 1863	Resigned Aug. 9, 1863
James L. Culbertson	Nov. 1, 1863	Resigned Jan. 26, 1864
Alfred Dale Owen	Jan. 27, 1864	Mustered out June 22, 1865

81st Infantry

William W. Caldwell	Aug. 30, 1862	Dismissed July 6, 1863
Horatio Woodbury	July 7, 1863	Declined
Ranna S. Moore	Oct. 12, 1863	Transferred to 13th Cavalry, June 24, 1864
Oliver P. Anderson	Jan. 1, 1865	Mustered out June 13, 1865

82nd Infantry

Morton C. Hunter	Sept. 20, 1862	Mustered out June 24, 1865, **Bvt. Brig. Gen., USV**

83rd Infantry

Benjamin J. Spooner	Nov. 6, 1862	Resigned April 28, 1865, **Bvt. Brig. Gen., USV**
George H. Scott	May 1, 1865	Mustered out June 2, 1865

84th Infantry

Nelson Trusler	Oct. 4, 1862	Resigned Oct. 19, 1863
Andrew J. Neff	Dec. 11, 1863	Resigned Sept. 7, 1864, **Bvt. Brig. Gen., USV**
Martin B. Miller	June 1, 1865	Mustered out June 14, 1865

85th Infantry

John P. Baird	Sept. 4, 1862	Resigned July 20, 1864
Alexander B. Crane	July 21, 1864	Mustered out June 12, 1865

86th Infantry

Orville S. Hamilton	Sept. 6, 1862	Resigned Jan. 13, 1863
George F. Dick	Jan. 14, 1863	Mustered out June 6, 1865, **Bvt. Brig. Gen., USV**

87th Infantry

Kline G. Shryock	Sept. 1, 1862	Resigned March 21, 1863
Newell Gleason	March 22, 1863	Mustered out June 10, 1865, **Bvt. Brig. Gen., USV**

88th Infantry

George Humphrey	Aug. 21, 1862	Resigned Oct. 17, 1863
Cyrus E. Briant	Oct. 18, 1863	Mustered out June 7, 1865

89th Infantry

Charles D. Murray	Aug. 28, 1862	Mustered out July 19, 1865

90th Infantry (See 5th Cavalry)

91st Infantry

John Mehringer	Oct. 20, 1863	Mustered out June 26, 1865, **Bvt. Brig. Gen., USV**

92nd Infantry

Did not complete organization. Consolidated with 93rd Infantry.

93rd Infantry

DeWitt C. Thomas	Oct. 21, 1862	Mustered out Aug. 10, 1865, **Bvt. Brig. Gen., USV**

94th Infantry

Did not complete organization.

95th Infantry

Did not complete organization.

96th Infantry

Did not complete organization. Consolidated with 99th Infantry.

97th Infantry

Robert F. Catterson	Nov. 25, 1862	Promoted **Brig. Gen., USV,** May 31, 1865
Aden G. Cavins	June 7, 1865	Mustered out June 9, 1865

98th Infantry

Did not complete organization. Consolidated with 100th Infantry.

99th Infantry

Alexander Fowler	Oct. 28, 1862	Mustered out Dec. 22, 1864
Josiah Farrar	May 2, 1865	Mustered out June 5, 1865

100th Infantry

Charles Case	Oct. 21, 1862	Declined
Sandford J. Stoughton	Nov. 29, 1862	Resigned Jan. 7, 1864
Albert Heath	Jan. 8, 1864	Resigned May 1, 1865
Ruel M. Johnson	May 2, 1865	Mustered out June 8, 1865

101st Infantry

William Garver	Sept. 6, 1862	Resigned May 30, 1863
Thomas Doan	May 31, 1863	Mustered out June 24, 1865

102nd Minute Men

Benjamin M. Gregory	July 10, 1863	Mustered out July 17, 1863

103rd Minute Men

Lawrence S. Shuler	July 10, 1863	Mustered out July 16, 1863

104th Minute Men
James Gavin | July 10, 1863 | Mustered out July 18, 1863

105th Minute Men
Kline G. Shryock | July 12, 1863 | Mustered out July 18, 1863

106th Minute Men
Isaac P. Gray | July 12, 1863 | Mustered out July 17, 1863

107th Minute Men
DeWitt C. Rugg | July 12, 1863 | Mustered out July 18, 1863

108th Minute Men
William C. Wilson | July 12, 1863 | Mustered out July 18, 1863

109th Minute Men
John R. Mahan | July 10, 1863 | Mustered out July 17, 1863

110th Minute Men
Graham N. Fitch | July 12, 1863 | Mustered out July 15, 1863

111th Minute Men
Robert Conover | July 13, 1863 | Mustered out July 15, 1863

112th Minute Men
Hiram F. Braxton | July 10, 1863 | Mustered out July 18, 1863

113th Minute Men
George W. Burge | July 10, 1863 | Mustered out July 16, 1863

114th Minute Men
Samuel Lambertson | July 9, 1863 | Mustered out July 21, 1863

115th Infantry
John R. Mahan | Aug. 17, 1863 | Mustered out Feb. 25, 1864

116th Infantry
William C. Kise | Sept. 4, 1863 | Mustered out March 2, 1864

117th Infantry
Thomas J. Brady | Oct. 4, 1863 | Mustered out Feb. 29, 1864, **Bvt. Brig. Gen., USV**

118th Infantry
George W. Jackson | Sept. 22, 1863 | Mustered out March 3, 1864

119th Infantry (See 7th Cavalry)

120th Infantry
Richard F. Barter | March 12, 1864 | Resigned Aug. 8, 1864
Allen W. Prather | Aug. 17, 1864 | Resigned Aug. 30, 1865
Reuben C. Kise | Sept. 9, 1865 | Mustered out Jan. 8, 1866, **Bvt. Brig. Gen., USV**

121st Infantry (See 9th Cavalry)

122nd Infantry
Did not complete organization. Consolidated with 120th Infantry.

123rd Infantry
John C. McQuiston | March 9, 1864 | Mustered out Aug. 25, 1865, **Bvt. Brig. Gen., USV**

124th Infantry
James Burgess	March 1, 1864	Resigned July 9, 1864
John M. Orr	July 10, 1864	Mustered out Aug. 31, 1865

125th Infantry (See 10th Cavalry)

126th Infantry (See 11th Cavalry)

127th Infantry (See 12th Cavalry)

128th Infantry
Richard P. DeHart	March 18, 1864	Resigned April 28, 1865, **Bvt. Brig. Gen., USV**
Jasper Packard	June 26, 1865	Mustered out April 10, 1866, **Bvt. Brig. Gen., USV**

129th Infantry
Charles Case	April 11, 1864	Resigned June 14, 1864
Charles A. Zollinger	June 15, 1864	Mustered out Aug. 29, 1865

130th Infantry
Charles S. Parrish	March 12, 1864	Mustered out Dec. 2, 1865, **Bvt. Brig. Gen., USV**

131st Infantry (See 13th Cavalry)

132nd Infantry
Samuel C. Vance	May 20, 1864	Mustered out Sept. 7, 1864

133rd Infantry
Robert N. Hudson	May 17, 1864	Mustered out Sept. 5, 1864

134th Infantry
James Gavin	May 23, 1864	Mustered out Sept. 2, 1864

135th Infantry
William C. Wilson	May 24, 1864	Mustered out Sept. 29, 1864

136th Infantry
John W. Foster	May 23, 1864	Mustered out Sept. 2, 1864

137th Infantry
Edward J. Robinson	May 27, 1864	Mustered out Sept. 21, 1864

138th Infantry
James H. Shannon	May 27, 1864	Mustered out Sept. 22, 1864

139th Infantry
George Humphrey	June 8, 1864	Mustered out Sept. 29, 1864

140th Infantry
Thomas J. Brady	Oct. 24, 1864	Mustered out July 11, 1865, **Bvt. Brig. Gen., USV**

141st Infantry
Did not complete organization. Consolidated with 140th Infantry.

142nd Infantry
John M. Comparet	Nov. 3, 1864	Dismissed Aug. 2, 1865

143rd Infantry
John F. Grill	Feb. 20, 1865	Mustered out Oct. 17, 1865

144th Infantry
George W. Riddle | March 7, 1865 | Mustered out Aug. 5, 1865

145th Infantry
Will A. Adams | Feb. 22, 1865 | Mustered out Jan. 21, 1866, **Bvt. Brig. Gen., USV**

146th Infantry
Merit C. Welsh | March 9, 1865 | Mustered out Aug. 31, 1865

147th Infantry
Milton Peden | March 11, 1865 | Mustered out Aug. 4, 1865

148th Infantry
Nicholas R. Ruckle | March 3, 1865 | Mustered out Sept. 5, 1865

149th Infantry
William H. Fairbanks | Feb. 22, 1865 | Mustered out Sept. 27, 1865

150th Infantry
Marsh B. Taylor | March 10, 1865 | Mustered out Aug. 5, 1865

151st Infantry
Joshua Healey | April 13, 1865 | Mustered out Sept. 19, 1865

152nd Infantry
Whedon W. Griswold | March 9, 1865 | Mustered out Aug. 30, 1865

153rd Infantry
Oliver H. P. Carey | March 1, 1865 | Mustered out Sept. 4, 1865

154th Infantry
Frank Wilcox | April 17, 1865 | Mustered out Aug. 4, 1865

155th Infantry
John M. Wilson | April 18, 1865 | Mustered out Aug. 4, 1865

156th Infantry
Regiment not entitled to a colonel since it never attained full strength.

Indiana Legion

1st Regiment (Posey County), Indiana Legion
Alvin P. Hovey | June 7, 1861 | Promoted **Brig. Gen., USV**
Enoch R. James | Aug. 30, 1861 | Resigned June 1862
John A. Mann | June 10, 1862 | Resigned Jan. 2, 1865

2nd Regiment (Vanderburgh County), Indiana Legion
James E. Blythe | June 7, 1861 | Promoted Brig. Gen., IN Legion
William E. Hollingsworth | Nov. 30, 1861 | Resigned May 1864
Victor Bisch | Sept. 20, 1864

3rd Regiment (Warrick and Gibson Counties), Indiana Legion
Daniel F. Bates | Sept. 26, 1861
Rufus R. Roberts | Nov. 22, 1861

4th Regiment (Spencer County), Indiana Legion
John W. Crooks | June 12, 1861 | Resigned March 1, 1864
William N. Walker | June 28, 1864 | Resigned Nov. 30, 1864

5th Regiment (Perry County), Indiana Legion

Charles H. Mason	June 6, 1861	Resigned Nov. 20, 1861
Charles T. Fournier	Jan. 2, 1862	Died April 28, 1865

6th Regiment (Harrison County), Indiana Legion

Thomas C. Slaughter	Sept. 24, 1861	Declined
Lewis Jordan	Sept. 25, 1861	

7th Regiment (Floyd County), Indiana Legion

Benjamin F. Scribner	June 8, 1861	**Bvt. Brig. Gen., USV**
William W. Tuley	Sept. 23, 1861	Resigned Sept. 1862
Edmund A. Maginness	Sept. 6, 1862	

8th Regiment (Clark and Scott Counties), Indiana Legion

James Keigwin	Aug. 30, 1861	Transferred to 49th Infantry
John N. Ingram	Sept. 6, 1861	Resigned Oct. 13, 1862
John F. Willey	Nov. 25, 1862	

9th Regiment (Jefferson County), Indiana Legion

John A. Hendricks	June 10, 1861	Transferred to 22nd Infantry
Samuel B. Sering	Aug. 29, 1861	

9th Regiment (Jennings County), Indiana Legion

Washington Malick	Aug. 1, 1861	Resigned June 16, 1862
Kennedy Brown	Aug. 6, 1862	

10th Regiment (Switzerland County), Indiana Legion

Oliver Ormsby	June 8, 1861
Harris Keeney	May 29, 1863

11th Regiment (Ohio County), Indiana Legion

Hugh T. Williams	Sept. 25, 1861

12th Regiment (Dearborn County), Indiana Legion

Zephaniah Heustis	Sept. 25, 1861	Resigned Sept. 1862
Joseph H. Burkam	Sept. 6, 1862	Resigned June 6, 1864
John A. Platter	Aug. 1, 1864	

Boone County Regiment, Indiana Legion

Benjamin M. Gregory	April 16, 1864	Transferred to 135th Infantry

City of Indianapolis Regiment, Indiana Legion

DeWitt C. Rugg	Aug. 14, 1863	Resigned Nov. 7, 1863
Samuel C. Vance	April 21, 1864	Transferred to 132nd Infantry

Crawford County Regiment, Indiana Legion

Horatio Woodbury	Oct. 4, 1861	Transferred to 81st Infantry
John T. Morgan	Sept. 8, 1862	Died March 13, 1863
Samuel M. Johnston	Aug. 1, 1863	

Delaware County Regiment, Indiana Legion

Jacob H. Koontz	Nov. 16, 1863

Hendricks County Regiment, Indiana Legion

Virgil H. Lyon	Oct. 20, 1863	Transferred to 9th Cavalry
Thomas Nichols	June 27, 1864	

Howard County Regiment, Indiana Legion

John M. Garrett	Sept. 21, 1863	Transferred to 11th Cavalry
Nathaniel P. Richmond	April 1, 1864	

Johnson County Regiment, Indiana Legion

Samuel Lambertson	Aug. 11, 1863

Marion County Regiment, Indiana Legion

William R. Wall	Aug. 15, 1863	Transferred to 9th Cavalry
Thomas Webb	June 27, 1864	

Monroe County Regiment, Indiana Legion

James B. Mulky	Sept. 24, 1861

Montgomery County Regiment, Indiana Legion

Sampson M. Houston	Oct. 16, 1863

Orange County Regiment, Indiana Legion

Charles D. Pearson	Sept. 13, 1861	Transferred to 49th Infantry

Parke County Regiment, Indiana Legion

Casper Budd	Oct. 10, 1862	Resigned Aug. 26, 1864

Vigo County Regiment, Indiana Legion

Harvey D. Scott	Aug. 15, 1863

Biographies

Simeon C. Aldrich

1 Lieutenant, Co. K, 44 IN Infantry, Nov. 22, 1861. Captain, Co. K, 44 IN Infantry, Dec. 10, 1861. GSW hand, Shiloh, TN, April 6, 1862. Lieutenant Colonel, 44 IN Infantry, Dec. 6, 1862. *Colonel,* 44 IN Infantry, July 27, 1863. Provost Marshal, Post of Chattanooga, TN, Nov.–Dec. 1863. Battle honors: Shiloh, Chickamauga.

Born: Oct. 14, 1816 Rockingham, VT

Died: Aug. 15, 1864 Pleasant Lake, IN (chronic diarrhea)

Occupation: Merchant and farmer

Offices/Honors: Sheriff of Steuben County, IN, 1851–53

Miscellaneous: Resided Pleasant Lake, Steuben Co., IN

Buried: Pleasant Lake Cemetery, Pleasant Lake, IN (Aldrich Circle)

References: *History of Steuben County, IN.* Chicago, IL, 1885. John H. Rerick. *The 44th Indiana Volunteer Infantry: History of Its Services in the War of the Rebellion.* LaGrange, IN, 1880. Pension File and Military Service File, National Archives. Letters Received, Volunteer Service Branch, Adju-

Simeon C. Aldrich (John H. Rerick. *The 44th Indiana Volunteer Infantry: History of Its Services in the War of the Rebellion.* LaGrange, Indiana, 1880).

Simeon C. Aldrich (Mark Weldon Collection).

tant General's Office, File 11886(VS)1885, National Archives. Audree S. Lewis. *Cemeteries of Steuben County, Indiana.* N.p., 1990.

Jesse Ianthus Alexander

Colonel, 59 IN Infantry, Feb. 11, 1862. Commanded 1 Brigade, 7 Division, 16 Army Corps, Department of the Tennessee, Dec. 22, 1862–Jan. 1, 1863. Commanded 1 Brigade, 7 Division, 17 Army Corps, Army of the Tennessee, April 12–May 2, 1863. Commanded 1 Brigade, 2 Division, 17 Army Corps, Army of the Tennessee, Sept. 14–Dec. 20, 1863. Commanded 1 Brigade, 3 Division, 15 Army Corps, Army of the Tennessee, Dec. 20, 1863–Feb. 4, 1864 and April 2–Sept. 1, 1864. Resigned Sept. 1, 1864, since "the condition of my family at home requires my presence." Battle honors: Island No. 10, Corinth, Jackson, Champion's Hill, Vicksburg, Missionary Ridge.

Born: Oct. 10, 1824 Gosport, IN
Died: May 30, 1871 Terre Haute, IN
Education: Graduated Indiana University, Bloomington, IN, 1845
Other Wars: Mexican War (Captain, Co. B, 4 IN Infantry)
Occupation: Lawyer and farmer
Offices/Honors: U.S. Collector of Internal Revenue, 1867–69. Indiana Senate, 1850–52, 1855, 1857.
Miscellaneous: Resided Gosport, Owen Co., IN; and Terre Haute, Vigo Co., IN
Buried: Gosport Cemetery, Gosport, IN
References: Rebecca A. Shepherd, Charles W.

Jesse Ianthus Alexander (The National Archives [BA-200]).

Calhoun, Elizabeth Shanahan-Shoemaker, and Alan F. January, editors. *A Biographical Directory of the Indiana General Assembly.* Vol. 1, 1816–1899. Indianapolis, IN, 1980. Theophilus A. Wylie. *Indiana University, Its History from 1820 to 1890.* Indianapolis, IN, 1890. Obituary, *Terre Haute Daily Express*, May 31, 1871. Pension File and Military Service File, National Archives. Stephen E. Towne, editor. *A Fierce, Wild Joy: The Civil War Letters of Colonel Edward J. Wood, 48th Indiana Volunteer Infantry Regiment.* Knoxville, TN, 2007.

Edward Anderson

Chaplain, 37 IL Infantry, Sept. 18, 1861. Resigned April 25, 1862, "in consequence of hurts received while in the army and which will require months in recovery, combined with conditions of my family which require my attendance on them." Colonel, 12 IN Cavalry, March 1, 1864. Commanded Post of Brownsboro, AL, July–Sept. 1864. Commanded Post of Tullahoma, TN, Nov. 1864. Commanded 2 Brigade, 4 Division, 20 Army Corps, District of Tennessee, Dec. 1864. Honorably mustered out, Nov. 10, 1865. Battle honors: Pea Ridge, Murfreesboro.

Born: Nov. 19, 1833 Boston, MA
Died: May 21, 1916 Quincy, MA
Education: Attended Phillips Academy, Andover, MA

Edward Anderson (courtesy The Excelsior Brigade, Alexandria, Virginia).

Edward Anderson (photograph by W. C. North's New Rooms, 211 Superior Street, Cleveland, Ohio; Roger D. Hunt Collection, USAMHI [RG98S-CWP160.28]).

Occupation: Congregational clergyman
Miscellaneous: Resided St. Joseph, Berrien Co., MI, 1858–60; Chicago, IL, 1860–64; Michigan City, La Porte Co., IN, 1864–68; Ashtabula, Ashtabula Co., OH, 1868–70; Jamestown, Chautauqua Co., NY, 1870–74; Quincy, Adams Co., IL, 1874–81; Toledo, Lucas Co., OH, 1881–84; Norwalk, Fairfield Co., CT, 1884–90; Danielson, Windham Co., CT, 1890–98; and Quincy, Norfolk Co., MA, 1898–1916
Buried: Forest Hills Cemetery, Jamaica Plain, MA (Narcissus Path, Lot 130)
References: *Who Was Who in America, 1897–1942.* Chicago, 1942. Obituary, *Boston Globe*, May 22, 1916. *History of Adams County, IL.* Chicago, IL, 1879. Pension File and Military Service File, National Archives. Letters Received, Volunteer Service Branch, Adjutant General's Office, File I227(VS) 1865, National Archives. Edward Anderson. *Camp Fire Stories: A Series of Sketches of the Union Army in the Southwest.* Chicago, IL, 1896. Michael A. Mullins. *The Fremont Rifles: A History of the 37th Illinois Veteran Volunteer Infantry.* Wilmington, NC, 1990.

Oliver P. Anderson

Private, Co. K, 81 IN Infantry, Aug. 29, 1862. 1 Sergeant, Co. K, 81 IN Infantry, Sept. 5, 1862. GSW right foot and taken prisoner, Stone's River, TN, Dec. 31, 1862. Paroled Jan. 2, 1863. 1 Lieutenant, Co. K, 81 IN Infantry, April 15, 1863. Captain, Co. K, 81 IN Infantry, June 18, 1863. GSW right thigh, Chickamauga, GA, Sept. 20, 1863. *Colonel,* 81 IN Infantry, Jan. 1, 1865. Lieutenant Colonel, 81 IN Infantry, Jan. 7, 1865. Anderson's muster as lieutenant colonel was the culmination of a lengthy period of discord among the officers of the regiment, some of whom resented the promotion of Anderson over Major Edward G. Mathey, who had led the regiment in recent battles but who was accused of disloyalty by other officers due to his open display of disrespect for President Lincoln. Honorably mustered out, June 13, 1865. Battle honors: Stone's River, Chickamauga, Atlanta Campaign, Franklin.
Born: Aug. 4, 1834 Ripley Co., IN
Died: March 2, 1921 Lebanon, KY
Occupation: Engineer before war. Grocer, mail carrier, and clerk after war.
Offices/Honors: Superintendent, Lebanon (KY) National Cemetery
Miscellaneous: Resided Troy, Perry Co., IN, 1865–83; New Albany, Floyd Co., IN; Jeffersonville, Clark Co., IN; and Lebanon, Marion Co., KY, 1906–21
Buried: Fairview Cemetery, New Albany, IN (Plat 11, Range 6, Lot 20)

Oliver P. Anderson (copy of image in the Craig Dunn Collection).

References: Pension File and Military Service File, National Archives. Obituary, *New Albany Daily Ledger*, March 3, 1921. George W. Morris. *History of the 81st Regiment of Indiana Volunteer Infantry in the Great War of the Rebellion, 1861 to 1865*. Louisville, KY, 1901.

Albert Shaw Andrews

Corporal, Co. B, 14 IN Infantry, June 7, 1861. Sergeant, Co. B, 14 IN Infantry, Oct. 16, 1861. 2 Lieutenant, Co. B, 14 IN Infantry, Nov. 21, 1861. 1 Lieutenant, Co. B, 14 IN Infantry, Nov. 1, 1862. GSW Morton's Ford, VA, Feb. 6, 1864. GSW left groin, Wilderness, VA, May 6, 1864. 1 Lieutenant, Co. F, 20 IN Infantry, June 6, 1864. 1 Lieutenant, Co. E, 20 IN Infantry, July 23, 1864. Captain, Co. E, 20 IN Infantry, Sept. 2, 1864. Captain, Co. B, 20 IN Infantry, Oct. 18, 1864. GSW left thigh, Boydton Plank Road, VA, Oct. 27, 1864. Lieuten-

Albert Shaw Andrews (C. Eppert, Photographer, No. 87 Main Street, Between Third and Fourth, Terre Haute, Indiana; courtesy Henry Deeks).

ant Colonel, 20 IN Infantry, Jan. 27, 1865. GSW elbow, Watkins' House, VA, March 25, 1865. Bvt. Colonel, USV, March 25, 1865, for gallant and efficient services in the battles before Petersburg, VA. *Colonel*, 20 IN Infantry, May 16, 1865. Honorably mustered out, July 12, 1865. Battle honors: Morton's Ford, Wilderness, Boydton Plank Road, Hatcher's Run, Petersburg Campaign.

Born: Aug. 8, 1841 Marshall, IL
Died: Oct. 21, 1870 Marshall, IL
Occupation: Clerk before war. Farmer and clerk after war.
Miscellaneous: Resided Terre Haute, Vigo Co., IN; and Marshall, Clark Co., IL
Buried: Marshall Cemetery, Marshall, IL
References: Pension File and Military Service File, National Archives. Elliott M. Andrews. *The Descendants of Lieutenant John Andrews*. Lee, ME, 1962. Letters Received, Volunteer Service Branch, Adjutant General's Office, File A84(VS)1865, National Archives. Alan D. Gaff. *On Many a Bloody Field: Four Years in the Iron Brigade*. Bloomington, IN, 1996. Nancy Niblack Baxter. *Gallant Fourteenth: The Story of an Indiana Civil War Regiment*. Traverse City, MI, 1980. Craig L. Dunn. *Harvestfields of Death: The 20th Indiana Volunteers of Gettysburg*. Carmel, IN, 1999.

George Seymour Babbitt

Captain, Co. D, 23 IN Infantry, July 29, 1861. Acting AAG, Staff of Brig. Gen. Walter Q. Gresham, Sept. 24, 1863–June 1864. Lieutenant Col-

George Seymour Babbitt (USAMHI [RG98S-CW P49.19]).

John Pearson Baird (Jefferson E. Brant. *History of the 85th Indiana Volunteer Infantry, Its Organization, Campaigns and Battles.* Bloomington, Indiana, 1902).

onel, 23 IN Infantry, Aug. 3, 1864. *Colonel,* 23 IN Infantry, Jan. 1, 1865. Honorably mustered out, July 23, 1865. Battle honors: Vicksburg, Atlanta Campaign.
  Born: Feb. 27, 1834 MI
  Died: Jan. 22, 1869 Coldwater, MI
  Education: Attended University of Michigan, Ann Arbor, MI
  Occupation: General ticket agent in the employ of the Louisville, New Albany & Chicago Railroad
  Miscellaneous: Resided New Albany, Floyd Co., IN; and Coldwater, Branch Co., MI
  Buried: Oak Grove Cemetery, Coldwater, MI (Old Plat, Lot 443)
  References: Obituary, *New Albany Daily Ledger,* March 5, 1869. Military Service File, National Archives. Matilda Gresham. *Life of Walter Quintin Gresham.* Chicago, IL, 1919. Isaac N. Demmon, editor. *General Catalogue of Officers and Students University of Michigan, 1837–1911.* Ann Arbor, MI, 1912.

John Pearson Baird

Colonel, 85 IN Infantry, Sept. 4, 1862. Taken prisoner, Thompson's Station, TN, March 5, 1863. Confined Libby Prison, Richmond, VA. Paroled April 12, 1863. Commanded Post of Franklin, TN, June 1863 and Sept. 1863. Commanded 2 Brigade, 1 Division, 11 Army Corps, Army of the Cumberland, March 25–April 16, 1864. Resigned July 20, 1864, due to physical disability, caused by "general mucous irritability involving the mucous membrane of the stomach and bowels, and of the bladder and urethra ... producing at intervals much inconvenience and the most intense suffering." Battle honors: Thompson's Station, Atlanta Campaign.
  Born: Jan. 5, 1830 Spencer Co., KY
  Died: March 7, 1881 Indianapolis, IN
  Education: Attended Franklin (IN) College. Graduated Indiana University Law School, Bloomington, IN, 1852.
  Occupation: Lawyer
  Offices/Honors: Indiana House of Representatives, 1859
  Miscellaneous: Resided Terre Haute, Vigo Co., IN, to 1876; and Indianapolis, IN, 1876–81
  Buried: Woodlawn Cemetery, Terre Haute, IN (Division 35, Block 5, Lot 38)
  References: Henry C. Bradsby. *History of Vigo County, IN.* Chicago, IL, 1891. Charles C. Oakey. *Greater Terre Haute and Vigo County Closing the First Century's History of City and County.* Chicago and New York, 1908. Obituary, *Terre Haute Daily Express,* March 9, 1881. Rebecca A. Shepherd, Charles W. Calhoun, Elizabeth Shanahan-Shoemaker, and Alan F. January, editors. *A Biographical Directory of the Indiana General Assembly.* Vol. 1, 1816–1899.

Indianapolis, IN, 1980. Military Service File, National Archives. Jefferson E. Brant. *History of the 85th Indiana Volunteer Infantry, Its Organization, Campaigns and Battles.* Bloomington, IN, 1902. Frank J. Welcher and Larry G. Ligget. *Coburn's Brigade: 85th Indiana, 33rd Indiana, 19th Michigan, and 22nd Wisconsin in the Western Civil War.* Carmel, IN, 1999. Letters Received, Volunteer Service Branch, Adjutant General's Office, File J120(VS)1865, National Archives.

Conrad Baker

Colonel, 1 IN Cavalry, Aug. 20, 1861. Commanded 4 Brigade, 1 Division, Army of the Southwest, July 1862. Commanded 1 Brigade, Cavalry Division, District of Eastern Arkansas, Department of the Missouri, Dec. 1862–Jan. 1863. Commanded 1 Brigade, 2 Cavalry Division, 13 Army Corps, Army of the Tennessee, Feb. 8–April 3, 1863. Acting Assistant Provost Marshal General, Indianapolis, IN, April 29, 1863–Aug. 17, 1864. Honorably mustered out, Sept. 12, 1864. Battle honors: Fredericktown, MO.

Born: Feb. 12, 1817 Franklin Co., PA
Died: April 28, 1885 Indianapolis, IN
Education: Attended Pennsylvania (now Gettysburg) College, Gettysburg, PA
Occupation: Lawyer
Offices/Honors: Indiana House of Representatives, 1845–46. Lieutenant Governor of Indiana, 1865–67. Governor of Indiana, 1867–73.
Miscellaneous: Resided Evansville, Vanderburgh Co., IN, to 1867; and Indianapolis, IN, 1867–85
Buried: Oak Hill Cemetery, Evansville, IN (Section 12, Lot 50)
References: Jacob Piatt Dunn. *Greater Indianapolis: The History, The Industries, The Institutions, and the People of a City of Homes.* Chicago, IL, 1910. *Pictorial and Biographical Memoirs of Indianapolis and Marion County, IN.* Chicago, IL, 1893. *A Biographical History of Eminent and Self-Made Men of the State of Indiana.* Cincinnati, OH, 1880. Obituary, *Indianapolis Journal,* April 29, 1885. John H. B. Nowland. *Sketches of Prominent Citizens of 1876.* Indianapolis, IN, 1877. *National Cyclopedia of American Biography.* Rebecca A. Shepherd, Charles W. Calhoun, Elizabeth Shanahan-Shoemaker, and Alan F. January, editors. *A Biographical Directory of the Indiana General Assembly.* Vol. 1, 1816–1899. Indianapolis, IN, 1980. Pension File and Military Service File, National Archives.

Myron H. Baker

Captain, Co. E, 74 IN Infantry, Aug. 8, 1862. Major, 74 IN Infantry, Aug. 20, 1862. Lieutenant Colonel, 74 IN Infantry, March 8, 1863. *Colonel,* 74 IN Infantry, Nov. 27, 1863. GSW forehead, Utoy Creek, GA, Aug. 5, 1864. Battle honors: Chickamauga, Missionary Ridge, Atlanta Campaign.

Conrad Baker (as governor of Indiana) (Indiana Historical Society, P0130 [Bass Photo Collection]).

Myron H. Baker (Mark Weldon Collection).

Born: March 14, 1837 Parma, Monroe Co., NY
Died: Aug. 5, 1864 KIA Utoy Creek, GA
Education: Attended Hillsdale (MI) College
Occupation: Lawyer
Miscellaneous: Resided Morenci, Lenawee Co., MI; and Goshen, Elkhart Co., IN
Buried: Old Morenci Cemetery, Morenci, MI
References: Will F. Peddycord. *History of the 74th Regiment Indiana Volunteer Infantry.* Warsaw, IN, 1913. Obituary, *Goshen Times*, Aug. 25, 1864. Military Service File, National Archives. Henry S. K. Bartholomew. *Pioneer History of Elkhart County, Indiana, with Sketches and Stories.* Goshen, IN, 1930. Arlan K. Gilbert. *Hillsdale Honor: The Civil War Experience.* Hillsdale, MI, 1994.

Philemon Prindle Baldwin

1 Lieutenant, Co. A, 6 IN Infantry (3 months), April 25, 1861. Captain, Co. A, 6 IN Infantry (3 months), May 2, 1861. Honorably mustered out, Aug. 2, 1861. Captain, Co. A, 6 IN Infantry (3 years), Sept. 12, 1861. Colonel, 6 IN Infantry, May 17, 1862. Commanded 3 Brigade, 2 Division, Right Wing, 14 Army Corps, Army of the Cumberland, Dec. 24, 1862–Jan. 9, 1863. Commanded 3 Brigade, 2 Division, 20 Army Corps, Army of the Cumberland, Jan. 9–27, 1863 and April 17–Sept. 19, 1863. GSW Chickamauga, GA, Sept. 19, 1863. Battle honors: Shiloh, Corinth, Stone's River, Chickamauga.
Born: Oct. 29, 1836 Clark Co., IN
Died: Sept. 19, 1863 KIA Chickamauga, GA
Occupation: Merchant dealing in agricultural implements
Miscellaneous: Resided Bethlehem, Clark Co., IN; and Madison, Jefferson Co., IN. Brother-in-law of Brig. Gen. Thomas T. Crittenden.
Buried: Chickamauga, GA (body never recovered). Cenotaph at Springdale Cemetery, Madison, IN.
References: Theodore C. Rose, compiler. *The Tousey Family in America.* Elmira, NY, 1916. Charles C. Baldwin. *The Baldwin Genealogy from 1500 to 1881.* Cleveland, OH, 1881. Obituary, *Madison Daily Evening Courier,* Sept. 26, 1863. Charles C. Briant. *History of the 6th Regiment Indiana Volunteer Infantry, of Both the Three Months' and Three Years' Services.* Indianapolis, IN, 1891. William H. Doll. *History of the 6th Regiment Indiana Volunteer Infantry in the Civil War, April 25, 1861, to September 22, 1864.* Columbus, IN, 1903. William Henry Smith, "The Sixth Indiana Regiment, Its Historical Record," *The Indianian,* Vol. 4, No. 5 (Oct. 1899). William Sumner Dodge. *History of the Old Second Division, Army of the Cumberland.* Chicago, IL, 1864. Pension File and Military Service File, National Archives. *Indiana at Chickamauga, 1863–*

Philemon Prindle Baldwin (Charles C. Briant. *History of the 6th Regiment Indiana Volunteer Infantry, of Both the Three Months' and Three Years' Services.* **Indianapolis, Indiana, 1891).**

1900. Report of Indiana Commissioners Chickamauga National Military Park. Indianapolis, IN, 1901.

Richard Fulton Barter

1 Lieutenant, Adjutant, 24 IN Infantry, July 31, 1861. Major, 24 IN Infantry, April 26, 1862. Lieutenant Colonel, 24 IN Infantry, May 14, 1862. Provost Marshal, Post of Helena, AR, Dec. 22, 1862–Feb. 11, 1863 and March 21–30, 1863. GSW left hand, Champion's Hill, MS, May 16, 1863. Resigned Nov. 27, 1863, being unfit for duty due to his wound. Colonel, 120 IN Infantry, March 12, 1864. Commanded 1 Brigade, 1 Division, 23 Army Corps, Army of the Ohio, April 10–Aug. 8, 1864 (brigade temporarily attached to 3 Division as 4 Brigade, June 9–Aug. 8, 1864). Resigned Aug. 8, 1864, since "my father died, leaving an estate the settlement of which requires my immediate presence." Battle honors: Shiloh, Champion's Hill, Atlanta Campaign.
Born: July 2, 1837 IN
Died: May 25, 1901 Mount Vernon, IN
Education: Attended Western Military Institute, Drennon Springs, KY. Attended Indiana University, Bloomington, IN.
Occupation: Farmer, stationer and U.S. War Department clerk

Miscellaneous: Resided Mount Vernon, Posey Co., IN; and Washington, DC
Buried: Bellefontaine Cemetery, Mount Vernon, IN
References: Pension File and Military Service File, National Archives. Obituary, *Mount Vernon Western Star,* May 30, 1901. *History of Posey County, IN.* Chicago, IL, 1886. Richard J. Fulfer. *A History of the Trials and Hardships of the 24th Indiana Volunteer Infantry.* Indianapolis, IN, 1913. Letters Received, Volunteer Service Branch, Adjutant General's Office, File B549(VS)1864, National Archives. William P. Leonard. *History and Directory of Posey County.* Evansville, IN, 1882.

Sion St. Clair Bass

Colonel, 30 IN Infantry, Oct. 4, 1861. GSW upper thigh, Shiloh, TN, April 7, 1862.
Born: Jan. 8, 1827 Salem, KY
Died: April 14, 1862 DOW Paducah, KY
Education: Attended Bartlett's College of Commerce, Cincinnati, OH
Occupation: Merchant and proprietor of iron foundry and machine shop
Miscellaneous: Resided Fort Wayne, Allen Co., IN; and Salem, Livingston Co., KY
Buried: Lindenwood Cemetery, Fort Wayne, IN (Section H, Lot 33)
References: *Colonel Sion S. Bass, 1827–1862.* Fort Wayne, IN, 1954. *Valley of the Upper Maumee River with Historical Account of Allen County and the City of Fort Wayne, Indiana.* Madison, WI, 1889. Bert J. Griswold. *The Pictorial History of Fort Wayne, IN.* Chicago, 1917. William Sumner Dodge.

Richard Fulton Barter (Tileston Bros., Photographists, No. 50 Main Street, Evansville, Indiana; Craig Dunn Collection).

Richard Fulton Barter (post-war) (The National Archives [BA-483]).

Sion St. Clair Bass (Mark Weldon Collection).

Sion St. Clair Bass (Massachusetts MOLLUS Collection, USAMHI [Vol. 130, p. 6658]).

History of the Old Second Division, Army of the Cumberland. Chicago, IL, 1864. David Stevenson. *Indiana's Roll of Honor.* Indianapolis, IN, 1864. Military Service File, National Archives. John W. Coons, compiler. *Indiana at Shiloh.* Indianapolis, IN, 1904.

Daniel Francis Bates

Colonel 3 IN Legion (Warrick and Gibson Counties), Sept. 26, 1861.

Born: Jan. 13, 1826 IN
Died: Dec. 25, 1876 Evansville, IN
Occupation: Farmer and produce broker
Miscellaneous: Resided Yankeetown, Warrick Co., IN; and Newburgh, Warrick Co., IN
Buried: Bates Hill Cemetery, Yankeetown, IN
References: Obituary, *Evansville Journal,* Dec. 26, 1876. Glenn A. Black. *Down Through the Years: A History of Newburgh Lodge No. 174, F. & A. M., Newburgh, IN.* Franklin, IN, 1955. *Report of Major General Love of the Indiana Legion.* Indianapolis, IN, 1863. *Operations of the Indiana Legion and Minute Men, 1863–4. Documents Presented to the General Assembly, with the Governor's Message, Jan. 6, 1865.* Indianapolis, IN, 1865. John P. Etter. *The Indiana Legion: A Civil War Militia.* Carmel, IN, 2006.

William A. Bickle

Colonel, 69 IN Infantry, Aug. 19, 1862. Resigned Oct. 24, 1862, "in consequence of ill health.... Having no military experience, I presume the service will sustain no loss by my withdrawal."

Born: Feb. 16, 1819 Rockbridge Co., VA
Died: March 11, 1898 Richmond, IN
Education: Attended Miami University, Oxford, OH
Occupation: Lawyer and judge
Miscellaneous: Resided Richmond, Wayne Co., IN
Buried: Earlham Cemetery, Richmond, IN (Section 6, Lots 36–37)
References: Military Service File, National Archives. *History of Wayne County, IN.* Chicago, IL, 1884. Obituary, *Richmond Evening Item,* March 11, 1898. Henry C. Fox. *Memoirs of Wayne County and the City of Richmond, IN.* Madison, WI, 1912. Carolyn S. Bridge. *These Men Were Heroes Once: The 69th Indiana Volunteer Infantry.* West Lafayette, IN, 2005. Donald E. Thompson, compiler. *Indiana Authors and Their Books, 1967–1980.* Crawfordsville, IN, 1981.

Newton Bingham

1 Sergeant, Co. F, 48 IN Infantry, Dec. 12, 1861. 2 Lieutenant, Co. G, 48 IN Infantry, Aug. 1, 1862. Captain, Co. G, 48 IN Infantry, Aug. 10, 1863. Major, 48 IN Infantry, March 1, 1865. Lieutenant Colonel, 48 IN Infantry, April 1, 1865. *Colonel,* 48 IN Infantry, May 1, 1865. Honorably mustered out, July 15, 1865. Battle honors: Iuka, Corinth, Champion's Hill, Vicksburg, Campaign of the Carolinas.

Born: March 6, 1841 St. Joseph Co., IN
Died: Nov. 25, 1868 Mishawaka, IN
Occupation: Painter before war. Dry goods merchant after war.

Newton Bingham (Craig Dunn Collection).

Offices/Honors: Postmaster of Mishawaka, IN, 1867–68

Miscellaneous: Resided Mishawaka, St. Joseph Co., IN

Buried: City Cemetery, Mishawaka, IN (Lot 269 or Lot 156, unmarked)

References: Pension File and Military Service File, National Archives. Obituary, *St. Joseph Valley Register,* Dec. 3, 1868. Obituary, *South Bend National Union,* Nov. 28, 1868. David Parsons Holton and Mrs. Frances K. (Forward) Holton. *Winslow Memorial. Family Records of Winslows and Their Descendants in America, with the English Ancestry as Far as Known.* Kenelm Winslow. New York, 1877–88.

Victor Bisch

Captain, Vanderburgh Greys, 2 IN Legion (Vanderburgh County), Aug. 9, 1861. Major, Paymaster, 1 Brigade, 2 Division, IN Legion, Sept. 18, 1862. Colonel, 2 IN Legion (Vanderburgh County), Sept. 20, 1864.

Born: 1830? France

Died: Jan. 8, 1895 Evansville, IN

Occupation: Lawyer and notary public

Offices/Honors: Auditor, Vanderburgh Co., IN, 1862–70

Miscellaneous: Resided Evansville, Vanderburgh Co., IN

Buried: Oak Hill Cemetery, Evansville, IN (Section 31, Lot 43)

References: Obituary, *Evansville Journal,* Jan. 11, 1895. *History of Vanderburgh County, IN.* Madison, WI, 1889. Interment Records, Oak Hill Cemetery, Evansville, IN. John P. Etter. *The Indiana Legion: A Civil War Militia.* Carmel, IN, 2006.

John Wesley Blake

Captain, Co. C, 10 IN Infantry (3 months), April 25, 1861. Resigned June 13, 1861. Brigade Major, Staff of Brig. Gen. William S. Rosecrans, June–July 1861. Captain, Co. K, 10 IN Infantry (3 years), Aug. 29, 1861. Lieutenant Colonel, 40 IN Infantry, Dec. 10, 1861. Colonel, 40 IN Infantry, April 5, 1862. GSW left arm, Stone's River, TN, Dec. 31, 1862. Taken prisoner and paroled, LaVergne, TN, Jan. 1, 1863. Exchanged May 7, 1863. While awaiting exchange, he was acquitted by court-martial, Feb. 17, 1863, of charges preferred by his personal enemy, Brig. Gen. George D. Wagner, alleging drunkenness at Stone's River. Commanded 2 Brigade, 2 Division, 4 Army Corps, Army of the Cumberland, July 10–25 and Sept. 30–Oct. 10, 1864. Honorably mustered out, Feb. 10, 1865. Battle honors: Rich Mountain, Shiloh, Perryville, Stone's River, Atlanta Campaign (Kenesaw Mountain, Peach Tree Creek).

John Wesley Blake (Metropolitan Photograph Gallery, 53 College Street, Nashville, Tennessee, J. H. Van Stavoren, Proprietor).

Born: June 17, 1822 Hampton, Adams Co., PA

Died: April 9, 1909 Indianapolis, IN

Education: Graduated Hanover (IN) College, 1848

Occupation: Lawyer, real estate agent and pension attorney

Offices/Honors: Judge of Common Pleas Court, 1852–56. Indiana House of Representatives, 1857.

Miscellaneous: Resided Frankfort, Clinton Co., IN; Lafayette, Tippecanoe Co., IN; and Indianapolis, IN. Brother of Colonel William H. Blake (9 IN).

Buried: Crown Hill Cemetery, Indianapolis, IN (Section 1, Lot 69)

References: Pension File and Military Service File, National Archives. Obituary, *Indianapolis Star,* April 10, 1909. Rebecca A. Shepherd, Charles W. Calhoun, Elizabeth Shanahan-Shoemaker, and Alan F. January, editors. *A Biographical Directory of the Indiana General Assembly.* Vol. 1, 1816–1899. Indianapolis, IN, 1980. Jacob Piatt Dunn. *Greater Indianapolis: The History, The Industries, The Institutions, and the People of a City of Homes.* Chicago, IL, 1910. *History of Clinton County, IN.* Chicago,

IL, 1886. Joseph Claybaugh. *History of Clinton County, IN.* Indianapolis, IN, 1913. Letters Received, Volunteer Service Branch, Adjutant General's Office, File I141(VS)1863, National Archives. James Birney Shaw. *History of the 10th Regiment Indiana Volunteer Infantry, Three Months and Three Years Organizations.* Lafayette, IN, 1912. Jack Zinn. *The Battle of Rich Mountain.* Parsons, WV, 1971.

William Howard Blake

Captain, Co. B, 9 IN Infantry (3 months), April 25, 1861. Honorably mustered out, Aug. 2, 1861. Major, 9 IN Infantry (3 years), Sept. 5, 1861. Lieutenant Colonel, 9 IN Infantry, Nov. 15, 1861. Colonel, 9 IN Infantry, Aug. 20, 1862. Resigned April 16, 1863, due to disability caused by a hydrocele of the right testicle. Battle honors: Shiloh, Corinth, Stone's River.

Born: Jan. 22, 1826 Hampton, Adams Co., PA
Died: Oct. 25, 1882 Guadalajara, Mexico
Education: Attended Indiana University, Bloomington, IN
Occupation: Western adventurer and lawyer before war. Farmer, miner and college professor in Mexico after war.
Offices/Honors: U.S. Consul, Manzanillo, Mexico, 1864–67
Miscellaneous: Resided Frankfort, Clinton Co., IN; Michigan City, La Porte Co., IN, before war; Manzanillo and Guadalajara, Mexico, after war. Brother of Colonel John W. Blake (40 IN).
Buried: Panteon de Belen Cemetery, Guadalajara, Mexico

William Howard Blake (Walter & Heuck's Gallery, Successors to Porter, 106 Fourth St., Cincinnati, Ohio; Craig Dunn Collection).

References: *Proceedings of the 8th Annual Reunion of the 9th Indiana Veteran Volunteer Infantry Association, Held at Logansport, IN, August 26–27, 1891.* Military Service File, National Archives. Dispatches from U.S. Consuls in Manzanillo, Mexico, National Archives.

Willis Blanche

Captain, Co. G, 57 IN Infantry, Dec. 17, 1861. Major, 57 IN Infantry, Feb. 12, 1863. GSW left hand, Missionary Ridge, TN, Nov. 25, 1863. Lieutenant Colonel, 57 IN Infantry, May 15, 1864. *Colonel,* 57 IN Infantry, June 24, 1864. Shell wound left thigh, Nashville, TN, Dec. 16, 1864. Resigned May 1, 1865, due to disability from wounds. Battle honors: Missionary Ridge, Atlanta Campaign, Nashville.

Willis Blanche (U.S. Military Academy Library).

Born: May 24, 1825 Ross Co., OH
Died: Sept. 13, 1892 Kokomo, IN
Occupation: Farmer
Offices/Honors: Indiana House of Representatives, 1867. Sheriff of Howard Co., IN, 1872–74.
Miscellaneous: Resided Kokomo, Howard Co., IN; and Centre Township, Howard Co., IN
Buried: Crown Point Cemetery, Kokomo, IN (Section 1, Lot 160)
References: Pension File and Military Service File, National Archives. Obituary, *Kokomo Gazette Tribune,* Sept. 13, 1892. Kingman Brothers, compilers. *Combination Atlas Map of Howard County, IN.* Chicago, IL, 1877. *A Biographical History of*

Eminent and Self-Made Men of the State of Indiana. Cincinnati, OH, 1880. Charles Blanchard, editor. *Counties of Howard and Tipton, Indiana. Historical and Biographical.* Chicago, IL, 1883. Rebecca A. Shepherd, Charles W. Calhoun, Elizabeth Shanahan-Shoemaker, and Alan F. January, editors. *A Biographical Directory of the Indiana General Assembly.* Vol. 1, 1816–1899. Indianapolis, IN, 1980. Asbury L. Kerwood. *Annals of the 57th Regiment Indiana Volunteers, Marches, Battles, and Incidents of Army Life.* Dayton, OH, 1868.

James E. Blythe

Colonel, 2 IN Legion (Vanderburgh County), June 7, 1861. Brig. Gen., 1 Brigade, 2 Division, IN Legion, Nov. 1, 1861.
Born: Nov. 8, 1819 Lexington, KY
Died: July 4, 1864 Evansville, IN
Education: Attended Transylvania University, Lexington, KY. Graduated Hanover (IN) College, 1838.
Occupation: Lawyer
Offices/Honors: Indiana House of Representatives, 1847 and 1859
Miscellaneous: Resided Evansville, Vanderburgh Co., IN
Buried: Oak Hill Cemetery, Evansville, IN (Section 18, Lot 44)
References: Obituary, *Evansville Daily Journal*, July 6, 1864. Rebecca A. Shepherd, Charles W. Calhoun, Elizabeth Shanahan-Shoemaker, and Alan F. January, editors. *A Biographical Directory of the Indiana General Assembly.* Vol. 1, 1816–1899. Indianapolis, IN, 1980. *General Catalogue of the Alumni of Hanover College, 1833–1883.* Hanover, IN, 1883. *Report of Major General Love of the Indiana Legion.* Indianapolis, IN, 1863. John P. Etter. *The Indiana Legion: A Civil War Militia.* Carmel, IN, 2006.

Doil R. Bowden

1 Sergeant, Co. B, 18 IN Infantry, Aug. 16, 1861. 1 Lieutenant, Co. B, 18 IN Infantry, Sept. 3, 1862. Captain, Co. B, 18 IN Infantry, Feb. 12, 1863. GSW right thigh, Cedar Creek, VA, Oct. 19, 1864. Colonel, 18 IN Infantry, July 27, 1865. Honorably mustered out, Aug. 28, 1865. Battle honors: Pea Ridge, Vicksburg Campaign, Winchester, Cedar Creek.
Born: July 29, 1839 near Mount Olive, Martin Co., IN
Died: Sept. 15, 1905 Bedford, IN
Occupation: Drug store clerk before war. Merchant and mail carrier after war.
Miscellaneous: Resided Bedford, Lawrence Co., IN
Buried: Green Hill Cemetery, Bedford, IN (Section 2, Lot 7)
References: Pension File and Military Service File, National Archives. Obituary, *Bedford Daily Mail*, Sept. 15, 1905. *History of Lawrence, Orange and Washington Counties, IN.* Chicago, IL, 1884.

Doil R. Bowden (Craig Dunn Collection).

Hiram Francis Braxton

2 Lieutenant, Co. A, 24 IN Infantry, July 31, 1861. Resigned Dec. 23, 1862, "unconditional and immediate." In forwarding his resignation, Colonel William T. Spicely commented, "Please see that this resignation is accepted. It is unnecessary for me to give you reasons why I desire this. You are sufficiently apprised of his conduct and deportment as an officer." Colonel, 112 IN Minute Men, July 10, 1863. Honorably mustered out, July 18, 1863. Captain, Co. H, 117 IN Infantry, Aug. 16, 1863. Honorably mustered out, Feb. 24, 1864. Battle honors: Shiloh.
Born: Oct. 1, 1836 Paoli, IN
Died: May 20, 1881 Ellettsville, IN
Education: Graduated Hanover (IN) College, 1857
Occupation: Clerk before war. Grocer and farmer after war.
Miscellaneous: Resided Paoli, Orange Co., IN; Bedford, Lawrence Co., IN; and Ellettsville, Monroe Co., IN, after 1869
Buried: Ellettsville Methodist Cemetery, Ellettsville, IN
References: Pension File and Military Service File, National Archives. *General Catalogue of the Alumni of Hanover College, 1833–1883.* Hanover, IN, 1883. Letters Received, Volunteer Service Branch, Adjutant General's Office, File B1376(VS)1864, National Archives. Myron A. Munson. *The Munson Record, 1637–1887: A Genealogical and Biographical*

Account of Captain Thomas Munson and His Descendants. New Haven, CT, 1895.

Cyrus E. Briant

Captain, Co. D, 88 IN Infantry, Aug. 11, 1862. Lieutenant Colonel, 88 IN Infantry, Dec. 6, 1862. *Colonel,* 88 IN Infantry, Oct. 18, 1863. Commanded Right Wing, 1 Brigade, 1 Division, 14 Army Corps, Army of the Cumberland, Jan.–April 1865. Honorably mustered out, June 7, 1865. Bvt. Colonel, USV, March 13, 1865, for meritorious services. Battle honors: Stone's River, Lookout Mountain, Missionary Ridge, Dalton, Atlanta Campaign, Savannah Campaign, Campaign of the Carolinas.

Born: March 2, 1829 Birmingham, Erie Co., OH

Died: Aug. 21, 1906 Huntington, IN

Occupation: Lumber manufacturer

Offices/Honors: Indiana House of Representatives, 1887, 1889

Miscellaneous: Resided New Haven, Allen Co., IN, to 1870; and Huntington, Huntington Co., IN, after 1870

Buried: Mount Hope Cemetery, Huntington, IN (Section O, Lot 14)

Cyrus E. Briant (photograph by Wm. Dunckleburg, Nos. 2 and 3 Phoenix Block, Calhoun Street, Fort Wayne, Indiana; Mark Weldon Collection).

References: *Biographical Memoirs of Huntington County, IN.* Chicago, IL, 1901. Will Cumback and J. B. Maynard, editors. *Men of Progress Indiana.* Indianapolis, IN, 1899. George I. Reed, editor. *Encyclopedia of Biography of Indiana.* Chicago, IL, 1895. *Memorial Record of Northeastern Indiana.* Chicago, IL, 1896. *History of Huntington County, IN, from the Earliest Time to the Present.* Chicago, IL, 1887. Obituary, *Fort Wayne Journal-Gazette,* Aug. 22, 1906. Obituary, *Huntington Daily News-Democrat,* Aug. 22, 1906. Rebecca A. Shepherd, Charles W. Calhoun, Elizabeth Shanahan-Shoemaker, and Alan F. January, editors. *A Biographical Directory of the Indiana General Assembly.* Vol. 1, 1816–1899. Indianapolis, IN, 1980. Pension File and Military Service File, National Archives. *History 88th Indiana Volunteers Infantry. Engagements, Chronology, Roster.* Fort Wayne, IN, 1895.

John Alexander Bridgland

Colonel, 2 IN Cavalry, Nov. 1, 1861. Suffering from dyspepsia and "passing large quantities of blood from his bowels," he resigned March 22, 1862, since "my very enfeebled condition, joined with the assurance of my medical advisors, that severe exercise or violent excitement would certainly cause a return of my disease has forced on me the melancholy and painful conviction that I cannot hope for a great while, if ever, to be able to perform the duties of my position efficiently."

Born: Dec. 3, 1826 Lynchburg, VA

Died: July 29, 1890 Fairland, Shelby Co., IN

Occupation: Wholesale tobacco merchant and dealer in horses

Offices/Honors: U.S. Consul, Havre, France, 1873–81

Miscellaneous: Resided Richmond, Wayne Co., IN; Indianapolis, IN; and New York City, NY

Buried: Earlham Cemetery, Richmond, IN (Section 3, Lot 56)

References: *Society of the Army of the Cumberland. Twenty-First Reunion, Toledo, OH, 1890.* Cincinnati, OH, 1891. Obituary, *Richmond Evening Item,* July 31, 1890. Obituary, *Indianapolis Journal,* July 31, 1890. Military Service File, National Archives. John C. Power, editor. *Directory and Soldiers' Register of Wayne County, IN.* Richmond, IN, 1865.

Thomas Hall Bringhurst

Major, 46 IN Infantry, Nov. 25, 1861. Lieutenant Colonel, 46 IN Infantry, May 25, 1862. Colonel, 46 IN Infantry, Aug. 6, 1862. Commanded 3 Division, 13 Army Corps, Department of the Gulf, April 9–27, 1864. Commanded 1 Brigade, 3 Division, 13 Army Corps, Department of the Gulf, April 27–May 24, 1864. Honorably mustered out,

Sept. 4, 1865. Battle honors: Vicksburg Campaign (Port Gibson, Champion's Hill), Jackson Campaign, Red River Campaign.

Born: Aug. 20, 1819 Philadelphia, PA

Died: May 23, 1899 Logansport, IN

Other Wars: Mexican War (Corporal, Co. G, 1 IN Infantry)

Occupation: Newspaper editor to 1870. Engaged later in the manufacture of spokes and other wooden materials for wagons and carriages.

Offices/Honors: Special Agent, U.S. Post Office Department, 1869–76

Miscellaneous: Resided Logansport, Cass Co., IN

Buried: Mount Hope Cemetery, Logansport, IN (Section 13, Lot 1032)

References: Josiah G. Leach. *History of the Bringhurst Family with Notes on the Clarkson, De-Peyster, and Boude Families.* Philadelphia, PA, 1901. Obituary, *Logansport Daily Journal,* May 24, 1899. *Biographical and Genealogical History of Cass, Miami, Howard and Tipton Counties, IN.* Chicago, IL, 1898. *A Biographical History of Eminent and Self-Made Men of the State of Indiana.* Cincinnati, OH, 1880. Thomas B. Helm, editor. *History of Cass County, IN.* Chicago, IL, 1886. J. Robert T. Craine, compiler. *The Ancestry and Posterity of Matthew Clarkson (1664–1702).* N.p., 1971. *History of the 46th Regiment Indiana Volunteer Infantry, September 1861–September 1865.* Logansport, IN, 1888. Pension File and Military Service File, National

Above: Thomas Hall Bringhurst (Ewing & Black, Photographers, Ground Floor, Broadway, Logansport, Indiana; Craig Dunn Collection). *Below:* Thomas Hall Bringhurst (seated second from right, with officers of the 46th Indiana Infantry).

Archives. Letters Received, Volunteer Service Branch, Adjutant General's Office, File L687(VS) 1862, National Archives.

Lewis Brooks

Captain, Co. C, 14 IN Infantry, June 2, 1861. Resigned May 8, 1862. Lieutenant Colonel, 80 IN Infantry, Sept. 4, 1862. Colonel, 80 IN Infantry, Jan. 18, 1863. Predisposed to phthisis and suffering from frequent attacks of fever, he resigned Aug. 9, 1863, "immediate and unconditional in consequence of continued ill health." Battle honors: Cheat Mountain, Perryville.

Born: Oct. 30, 1835 Martin Co., IN
Died: March 18, 1913 Center Twp., Martin Co., IN
Occupation: Merchant before war. Farmer after war.
Offices/Honors: Martin County Commissioner two terms, Martin County Treasurer two terms, and Martin County Auditor one term
Miscellaneous: Resided Loogootee, Martin Co., IN, to 1872; and Shoals, Martin Co., IN, after 1872
Buried: Brooks Cemetery, Mount Pleasant, Martin Co., IN
References: Obituary, *Martin County Tribune*, March 21, 1913. Pension File and Military Service File, National Archives. Lewis Brooks. *Lewis Brooks, Soldier and Citizen.* N.p., 1907. Thomas J. Brooks, compiler. *The Brooks and Houghton Families Descended from Hannah Chute Poor.* N.p., 1909. James T. Rogers. *Col. Lewis Brooks: A Tribute.* N.p., 1915. Nancy Niblack Baxter. *Gallant Fourteenth: The Story of an Indiana Civil War Regiment.* Traverse City, MI, 1980. Letters Received, Volunteer Service Branch, Adjutant General's Office, File B173(VS) 1865, National Archives. *History of Lawrence and Monroe Counties, Indiana. Their People, Industries and Institutions.* Indianapolis, IN, 1914.

Kennedy Brown

Captain, Scipio Guards, 9 IN Legion (Jennings County), June 3, 1861. Major, 9 IN Legion, July 23, 1861. Colonel, 9 IN Legion, Aug. 6, 1862.

Kennedy Brown (post-war) (*Biographical Record of Bartholomew and Jackson Counties, Indiana.* Indianapolis, Indiana, 1904).

Born: May 4, 1817 near Donegal, Ireland
Died: Nov. 8, 1890 near Scipio, IN
Occupation: Farmer
Miscellaneous: Resided Scipio, Jennings Co., IN
Buried: Reddington Cemetery, Reddington, Jackson Co., IN
References: *Biographical Record of Bartholomew and Jackson Counties, IN.* Indianapolis, IN, 1904. Obituary, *Columbus Daily Herald,* Nov. 8, 1890. Pension File, National Archives. Margaret Read

Lewis Brooks (copy of image in the Craig Dunn Collection).

MacDonald. *Scipio, Indiana: Threads from the Past.* Fairfield, WA, 1988. *Report of Major General Love of the Indiana Legion.* Indianapolis, IN, 1863. *Operations of the Indiana Legion and Minute Men, 1863–4. Documents Presented to the General Assembly, with the Governor's Message, Jan. 6, 1865.* Indianapolis, IN, 1865. John P. Etter. *The Indiana Legion: A Civil War Militia.* Carmel, IN, 2006.

William Lyons Brown

Colonel, 20 IN Infantry, July 22, 1861. Described by Brig. Gen. Philip Kearny as, "Brave, skillful, a disciplinarian, full of energy, and a charming gentleman." GSW left temple, Groveton, VA, Aug. 29, 1862. Battle honors: Seven Days' Campaign (Glendale), Groveton.

Born: Nov. 19, 1817 St. Clairsville, OH
Died: Aug. 29, 1862 KIA Groveton, VA
Other Wars: Mexican War (1 Lieutenant, 1 IN Infantry)
Occupation: Merchant and banker
Miscellaneous: Resided Logansport, Cass Co., IN
Buried: Ninth Street Cemetery, Logansport, IN (Lot 4)
References: Jehu Z. Powell, editor. *History of Cass County, IN.* Chicago and New York, 1913. Craig L. Dunn. *Harvestfields of Death: The 20th Indiana Volunteers of Gettysburg.* Carmel, IN, 1999.

William Lyons Brown (William N. Pickerill, comp. *Indiana at the Fiftieth Anniversary of the Battle of Gettysburg.* Indianapolis, Indiana, 1913).

Pension File and Military Service File, National Archives. David Stevenson. *Indiana's Roll of Honor.* Indianapolis, IN, 1864. *The War of the Rebellion: A Compilation of the Official Records of the Union and Confederate Armies.* (Series 1, Vol. 12, Part 2, p. 417). Washington, DC, 1885. William N. Pickerill, compiler. *Indiana at the Fiftieth Anniversary of the Battle of Gettysburg.* Indianapolis, IN, 1913.

Casper Budd

Colonel, Parke County Regiment, IN Legion, Oct. 10, 1862. Resigned Aug. 26, 1864.

Born: Nov. 16, 1805 Lycoming Co., PA
Died: May 9, 1894 near Waveland, IN
Occupation: Farmer
Offices/Honors: Indiana House of Representatives, 1863
Miscellaneous: Resided Howard Twp., Parke Co., IN; and Waveland, Montgomery Co., IN
Buried: Waveland Presbyterian Cemetery, Waveland, IN
References: Hiram W. Beckwith. *History of Vigo and Parke Counties, Together with Historic Notes on the Wabash Valley.* Chicago, IL, 1880. Alfred T. Andreas. *Atlas Map of Parke County, IN.* Chicago, IL, 1874. Obituary, *Rockville Republican,* May 16, 1894. Rebecca A. Shepherd, Charles W. Calhoun, Elizabeth Shanahan-Shoemaker, and Alan F. January,

William Lyons Brown (Craig Dunn Collection).

Casper Budd.

editors. *A Biographical Directory of the Indiana General Assembly.* Vol. 1, 1816–1899. Indianapolis, IN, 1980. Obituary, *Indianapolis Sentinel,* May 12, 1894. John P. Etter. *The Indiana Legion: A Civil War Militia.* Carmel, IN, 2006.

George W. Burge

Captain, Co. E, 27 IN Infantry, Sept. 1, 1861. Major, 27 IN Infantry, July 27, 1862. GSW head, Cedar Mountain, VA, Aug. 9, 1862. Resigned Feb. 9, 1863, since "I deem myself incompetent to discharge the duties necessarily imposed on me ... on account of the limited education which I received in my youthful days, having never received an education which suited me for said position." Colonel, 113 IN Minute Men, July 10, 1863. Honorably mustered out July 16, 1863. Battle honors: Cedar Mountain.
 Born: Oct. 5, 1829 Wheeling, WV
 Died: May 1, 1899 Topeka, KS
 Occupation: Carpenter and builder
 Miscellaneous: Resided Washington, Daviess Co., IN; Rockport, Spencer Co., IN; and Topeka, Shawnee Co., KS, after 1870
 Buried: Topeka Cemetery, Topeka, KS (Section 38, Lot 39)
 References: Pension File and Military Service File, National Archives. Obituary, *Topeka Daily Capital,* May 3, 1899. Wilbur D. Jones, Jr. *Giants in the Cornfield: The 27th Indiana Infantry.* Shippensburg, PA, 1997. Edmund R. Brown. *The 27th Indiana Volunteer Infantry in the War of the Rebellion.* Monticello, IN, 1899.

George W. Burge (Rick Brown Collection).

James Burgess

Captain, Co. A, 7 IN Infantry (3 months), April 25, 1861. Honorably mustered out, Aug. 2, 1861. Lieutenant Colonel, 70 IN Infantry, Aug. 9, 1861. Colonel, 124 IN Infantry, March 1, 1864. Resigned July 9, 1864, being "unfitted for field service" due to "hypertrophy of the heart." Battle honors: Atlanta Campaign (Rocky Face Ridge, Resaca).
 Born: Aug. 1, 1826 Springfield, OH
 Died: Feb. 20, 1912 Topeka, KS
 Occupation: Tanner and merchant before war. Farmer and postal superintendent after war.
 Offices/Honors: Deputy Clerk, Hendricks Co., IN, 1852–60. Indiana House of Representatives, 1861. Kansas House of Representatives, 1874. Register of Deeds, Shawnee Co., KS, 1886–90.
 Miscellaneous: Resided Danville, Hendricks Co., IN, before war; Indianapolis, IN; and Soldier Twp. and Topeka, Shawnee Co., KS, after 1868

Buried: Topeka Cemetery, Topeka, KS (Section 76, Lot 70)

References: James L. King, editor. *History of Shawnee County, Kansas, and Representative Citizens.* Chicago, IL, 1905. Pension File and Military Service File, National Archives. Obituary, *Topeka State Journal*, Feb. 21, 1912. Rebecca A. Shepherd, Charles W. Calhoun, Elizabeth Shanahan-Shoemaker, and Alan F. January, editors. *A Biographical Directory of the Indiana General Assembly.* Vol. 1, 1816–1899. Indianapolis, IN, 1980. James Sutherland. *Biographical Sketches of the Members of the Forty-First General Assembly of the State of Indiana with That of the State Officers and Judiciary.* Indianapolis, IN, 1861. Samuel Merrill. *The 70th Indiana Volunteer Infantry in the War of the Rebellion.* Indianapolis, IN, 1900.

Joseph Hayes Burkam

Captain, Dearborn Guards, 12 IN Legion (Dearborn County), Aug. 12, 1862. Colonel, 12 IN Legion (Dearborn County), Sept. 6, 1862. Resigned June 6, 1864. Battle honors: Morgan's Ohio Raid.

Born: June 19, 1838 Dearborn Co., IN
Died: Dec. 24, 1912 Cincinnati, OH
Occupation: Capitalist and lumber dealer
Miscellaneous: Resided Lawrenceburg, Dearborn Co., IN; and Cincinnati, OH
Buried: Greendale Cemetery, Lawrenceburg, IN (Section B, Lots 82–83)
References: *History of Dearborn, Ohio and Switzerland Counties, Indiana, from Their Earliest Settlement.* Chicago, IL, 1885. Obituary, *Lawrenceburg Register*, Dec. 26, 1912. John P. Etter. *The Indiana Legion: A Civil War Militia.* Carmel, IN, 2006. *Report of Major General Love of the Indiana Legion.* Indianapolis, IN, 1863. *Operations of the Indiana Legion and Minute Men, 1863–4. Documents Presented to the General Assembly, with the Governor's Message, Jan. 6, 1865.* Indianapolis, IN, 1865. Death notice, *Cincinnati Enquirer*, Dec. 25, 1912.

James Ellis Burton

Captain, Co. H, 33 IN Infantry, Sept. 16, 1861. Taken prisoner, Thompson's Station, TN, March 5, 1863. Confined Libby Prison, Richmond, VA. Paroled May 5, 1863. GSW left thigh, Kenesaw Mountain, GA, June 22, 1864. Lieutenant Colonel, 33 IN Infantry, Oct. 1, 1864. Colonel, 33 IN Infantry, May 4, 1865. Commanded 2 Brigade, 2 Division, 14 Army Corps, Army of the Cumberland, June 1865. Honorably mustered out, July 21, 1865. Battle honors: Atlanta Campaign (Kenesaw Mountain), Savannah Campaign, Campaign of the Carolinas (Averasborough, Bentonville).

James Ellis Burton.

Born: Sept. 23, 1824 Mount Tabor, IN
Died: Sept. 28, 1900 Gosport, IN
Occupation: Merchant and livestock speculator before war. Farmer after war.
Miscellaneous: Resided Martinsville, Morgan Co., IN
Buried: Liberty Church Cemetery, near Mount Tabor, Monroe Co., IN
References: Pension File and Military Service File, National Archives. John R. McBride. *History of the 33rd Indiana Veteran Volunteer Infantry.* Indianapolis, IN, 1900. Obituary, *Martinsville Republican*, Oct. 4, 1900. Charles Blanchard, editor. *Counties of Morgan, Monroe and Brown, Indiana. Historical and Biographical.* Chicago, IL, 1884. Frank J. Welcher and Larry G. Ligget. *Coburn's Brigade: 85th Indiana, 33rd Indiana, 19th Michigan, and 22nd Wisconsin in the Western Civil War.* Carmel, IN, 1999.

William Wallace Caldwell

Captain, Ellsworth Zouaves, 8 IN Legion (Clark and Scott Counties), June 12, 1861. Captain, Co. B, 23 IN Infantry, July 27, 1861. Resigned March 28, 1862, due to "bronchitis which cannot be treated in the field." Colonel, 81 IN Infantry, Aug. 30, 1862. Commanded 32 Brigade, 9 Division, 3 Army Corps, Army of the Ohio, Sept.–Oct. 1862. Commanded 3 Brigade, 1 Division, 20 Army Corps, Army of the Cumberland, Jan. 9–March 9, 1863 and April 5–May 15, 1863. Having expressed himself "opposed to many acts of the President on proper occasions and in a manner becoming an officer," he was dismissed July 6, 1863, "by direction of the President of the United States, ... for uttering disloyal sentiments." Even though the allegations against him were based entirely on the statements of a clique of disaffected officers, whom he had ordered before a Board of Examination, and were contradicted by emphatic statements of support from his superior officers, including Major General Rosecrans, his appeals for revocation of his dismissal were consistently denied, with Judge Advocate General Joseph Holt commenting, "The presence of an officer in the army entertaining and defiantly expressing sentiments so shamefully disloyal as these cannot be productive of other than the worst results." Battle honors: Perryville, Tullahoma Campaign (Liberty Gap).

Oliver Hazard Perry Carey and family (Craig Dunn Collection).

Born: Aug. 3, 1834 Portsmouth, OH
Died: Nov. 2, 1891 Chicago, IL
Occupation: Insurance agent
Offices/Honors: Postmaster, Jeffersonville, IN, 1858–61
Miscellaneous: Resided Jeffersonville, Clark Co., IN, to 1869; Indianapolis, IN, 1869–76; and Chicago, IL, after 1876
Buried: Walnut Ridge Cemetery, Jeffersonville, IN (Wathen's Reserve)
References: Pension File and Military Service File, National Archives. Obituary, *Jeffersonville Evening News,* Nov. 3, 1891. Letters Received, Volunteer Service Branch, Adjutant General's Office, File J389(VS)1863, National Archives. Lewis C. Baird. *Baird's History of Clark County, IN.* Indianapolis, IN, 1909. Sidney Elizabeth Lyon, editor. *Lyon Memorial: Families of Connecticut and New Jersey.* Detroit, MI, 1907. George W. Morris. *History of the 81st Regiment of Indiana Volunteer Infantry in the Great War of the Rebellion, 1861 to 1865.* Louisville, KY, 1901. Alfred T. Andreas. *History of Chicago from the Earliest Period to the Present Time.* Chicago, IL, 1886. Death notice, *Chicago Daily Tribune,* Nov. 4, 1891.

Oliver Hazard Perry Carey

1 Lieutenant, Co. K, 8 IN Infantry (3 months), April 22, 1861. Captain, Co. K, 8 IN Infantry, April 23, 1861. Honorably mustered out, Aug. 6, 1861. Captain, Co. H, 8 IN Infantry (3 years), Aug. 20, 1861. Lieutenant Colonel, 36 IN Infantry, Aug. 30, 1861. GSW left ankle, Chickamauga, GA, Sept. 19, 1863. *Colonel,* 36 IN Infantry, July 31, 1864. Honorably mustered out, Sept. 21, 1864. Private, Co. D, 153 IN Infantry, Feb. 13, 1865. Captain, Co. D, 153 IN Infantry, Feb. 18, 1865. Colonel, 153 IN Infantry, March 1, 1865. Commanded 1 Brigade, 2 Division, Department of Kentucky, March 23–June 14, 1865. Honorably mustered out, Sept. 4, 1865. Battle honors: Shiloh, Corinth, Chickamauga, Dalton, Atlanta Campaign.

Born: Feb. 26, 1819 Connersville, IN
Died: June 19, 1889 Marion, IN

Oliver Hazard Perry Carey (post-war) (*A Biographical History of Eminent and Self-Made Men of the State of Indiana.* Cincinnati, Ohio, 1880).

Other Wars: Mexican War (1 Lieutenant, 4 IN Infantry)

Occupation: Livery operator and mail contractor before war. Farmer after war.

Offices/Honors: Indiana House of Representatives, 1877, 1879

Miscellaneous: Resided Marion, Grant Co., IN

Buried: IOOF (now Estates of Serenity) Cemetery, Marion, IN (Block 2, Lot 36)

References: *A Biographical History of Eminent and Self-Made Men of the State of Indiana.* Cincinnati, OH, 1880. George Hazzard. *Hazzard's History of Henry County, IN, 1822–1906. Military Edition.* New Castle, IN, 1906. *History of Grant County, IN.* Chicago, IL, 1886. Pension File and Military Service File, National Archives. Letters Received, Volunteer Service Branch, Adjutant General's Office, File C1928(VS)1863, National Archives. William Grose. *The Story of the Marches, Battles and Incidents of the 36th Regiment Indiana Volunteer Infantry.* New Castle, IN, 1891. Rebecca A. Shepherd, Charles W. Calhoun, Elizabeth Shanahan-Shoemaker, and Alan F. January, editors. *A Biographical Directory of the Indiana General Assembly.* Vol. 1, 1816–1899. Indianapolis, IN, 1980. Seth C. Cary. *John Cary, The Plymouth Pilgrim.* Boston, MA, 1911.

Henry Montgomery Carr

Captain, Co. G, 11 IN Infantry (3 months), April 22, 1861. Honorably mustered out, Aug. 4, 1861. Captain, Co. G, 11 IN Infantry (3 years), Aug. 24, 1861. Lieutenant Colonel, 58 IN Infantry, Oct. 22, 1861. Colonel, 58 IN Infantry, Dec. 16, 1861. Commanded 21 Brigade, 6 Division, Department of the Ohio, Jan.–March 1862. Resigned June 17, 1862, in anticipation of charges being preferred against him for allowing "a couple of army wagons belonging to the 58th Indiana to haul sutler's goods from Pittsburg Landing to Corinth, MS." Captain, Co. B, 72 IN Infantry, Aug. 9, 1862. Major, 72 IN Infantry, Oct. 18, 1862. Acting AIG, 4 Division, 14 Army Corps, Army of the Cumberland, April–Sept. 8, 1863. Resigned June 28, 1864, due to "chronic diarrhea ... combined with ... a great disorder of the nerve functions that seems to originate in the disordered condition of the digestive apparatus." Battle honors: Chickamauga, Meridian Expedition, Atlanta Campaign.

Born: Aug. 1, 1829 Crawfordsville, IN

Died: March 18, 1884 Louisville, KY

Occupation: Lawyer and school teacher before war. Lawyer and pension claim agent after war.

Miscellaneous: Resided Crawfordsville, Montgomery Co., IN; and Louisville, KY

Buried: Cave Hill Cemetery, Louisville, KY (Section A, Lot 558)

References: Pension File and Military Service File, National Archives. Obituary, *Louisville Commercial,* March 19, 1884. Obituary, *Louisville Courier-Journal,* March 19, 1884. Letters Received, Volunteer Service Branch, Adjutant General's Office, File C709(VS)1862, National Archives. Gilbert R. Stormont, compiler. *History of the 58th Regiment of Indiana Volunteer Infantry, Its Organization, Campaigns and Battles, from 1861 to 1865.* Princeton, IN, 1895. Benjamin F. Magee. *History of the 72nd Indiana Volunteer Infantry of the Mounted Lightning Brigade.* Lafayette, IN, 1882.

William B. Carroll

Captain, Co. E, 10 IN Infantry, Sept. 18, 1861. Major, 10 IN Infantry, Aug. 11, 1862. Lieutenant Colonel, 10 IN Infantry, Aug. 16, 1862. Colonel, 10 IN Infantry, Nov. 18, 1862. GSW right side, Chickamauga, GA, Sept. 19, 1863. Battle honors: Mill Springs, Corinth, Perryville, Tullahoma Campaign, Chickamauga.

Born: March 3, 1831 MD

William B. Carroll (James Birney Shaw. *History of the 10th Regiment Indiana Volunteer Infantry, Three Months and Three Years Organizations.* Lafayette, Indiana, 1912).

Died: Sept. 19, 1863 KIA Chickamauga, GA
Occupation: Printer
Miscellaneous: Resided Lafayette, Tippecanoe Co., IN
Buried: Greenbush Cemetery, Lafayette, IN (Division 5, Lot 327)
References: Pension File and Military Service File, National Archives. Obituary, *Lafayette Daily Courier*, Sept. 24, 1863. *Report of the Adjutant General of the State of Indiana*. Indianapolis, IN, 1865. Vol. 1, p. 385. James Birney Shaw. *History of the 10th Regiment Indiana Volunteer Infantry, Three Months and Three Years Organizations*. Lafayette, IN, 1912. *Indiana at Chickamauga, 1863–1900. Report of Indiana Commissioners Chickamauga National Military Park*. Indianapolis, IN, 1901.

Scott Carter

Lieutenant Colonel, 1 IN Cavalry, July 20, 1861. Colonel, 3 IN Cavalry, Oct. 30, 1861. Placed under arrest by Brig. Gen. Alfred Pleasanton, Sept. 5, 1862, for "Disobedience of Orders," but not brought to trial, he finally resigned March 11, 1863, since "my health has become so much impaired by exposure while in the service as to be unable to discharge the duties of my position."
Born: April 19, 1820 Culpeper Co., VA
Died: Jan. 13, 1898 Vevay, IN
Education: Attended Transylvania University, Lexington, KY
Other Wars: Mexican War (Captain, Co. D, 3 IN Infantry)
Occupation: Lawyer and judge
Offices/Honors: Judge of Common Pleas Court, 1869–73
Miscellaneous: Resided Vevay, Switzerland Co., IN. As described in 1885, "His head is massive, the forehead broad and high, and crowned by a luxuriant growth of snow-white hair, while his long, flowing beard and tall, well-proportioned figure, makes him at once dignified and imposing."
Buried: Vevay Cemetery, Vevay, IN
References: *A Biographical History of Eminent and Self-Made Men of the State of Indiana*. Cincinnati, OH, 1880. Obituary, *Vevay Reveille*, Jan. 20, 1898. Pension File and Military Service File, National Archives. *History of Dearborn, Ohio and Switzerland Counties, Indiana, from Their Earliest Settlement*. Chicago, IL, 1885. Letters Received, Volunteer Service Branch, Adjutant General's Office, File P910(VS)1862, National Archives. Elias W. H. Beck, "Letters of a Civil War Surgeon," *Indiana Magazine of History*, Vol. 27, No. 2 (June 1931). William N. Pickerill. *History of the 3rd Indiana Cavalry*. Indianapolis, IN, 1906.

Charles Case

1 Lieutenant, Adjutant, 44 IN Infantry, Nov. 26, 1861. Acting Brigade Commissary, Staff of Colonel (later Brig. Gen.) Charles Cruft, 3 Brigade, 4 Division, Army of the Tennessee, Jan.–March 1862. Major, 3 IN Cavalry, April 16, 1862. Resigned July 19, 1862, on account of chronic diarrhea. Colonel, 100 IN Infantry, Oct. 21, 1862 (declined). Colonel, 129 IN Infantry, April 11, 1864. Resigned June 14, 1864, due to "chronic diarrhea, producing extreme emaciation and prolapse of the rectum." Battle honors: Fort Donelson, Atlanta Campaign (Resaca).
Born: Dec. 21, 1817 Austinburg, Ashtabula Co., OH
Died: June 30, 1883 Brighton, Washington Co., IA
Occupation: Lawyer
Offices/Honors: U.S. House of Representatives, 1857–61
Miscellaneous: Resided Fort Wayne, Allen Co., IN; and Washington, DC
Buried: Congressional Cemetery, Washington, DC (Range 67, Site 287)
References: Peggy Seigel, "Charles Case: A Radical Republican in the Irrepressible Conflict," *Indiana Magazine of History*, Vol. 107, No. 4 (Dec. 2011). James L. Harrison, compiler. *Biographical Directory of the American Congress, 1774–1949*. Washington, DC, 1950. Obituary, *Fort Wayne Daily Gazette*, July 2, 1883. Obituary, *Fort Wayne Daily*

Charles Case (U.S. House of Representatives, 1859) (McClees' Gallery of Photographic Portraits of the Senators, Representatives & Delegates of the Thirty-Fifth Congress, Library of Congress [LC-DIG-ppmsca-26789]).

Charles Case (U.S. House of Representatives) (Frederick Hill Meserve. Historical Portraits, A Part of the Collection of Americana of Frederick Hill Meserve. New York City, 1913–1915; courtesy New York State Library).

Sentinel, July 2, 1883. John H. Rerick. *The 44th Indiana Volunteer Infantry: History of Its Services in the War of the Rebellion.* LaGrange, IN, 1880. Military Service File, National Archives. *Valley of the Upper Maumee River with Historical Account of Allen County and the City of Fort Wayne, Indiana.* Madison, WI, 1889.

Aden Gainey Cavins

Captain, Co. E, 59 IN Infantry, Dec. 26, 1861. Major, 97 IN Infantry, Nov. 1, 1862. Lieutenant Colonel, 97 IN Infantry, Nov. 19, 1862. *Colonel,* 97 IN Infantry, June 7, 1865. Honorably mustered out, June 9, 1865. Battle Honors: Jackson, Missionary Ridge, Atlanta Campaign (Resaca, Dallas, Kenesaw Mountain, Atlanta), Campaign of the Carolinas.

Born: Oct. 24, 1827 Lawrence Co., IN
Died: Nov. 14, 1906 Bloomfield, IN
Education: Attended Indiana Asbury (now DePauw) University, Greencastle, IN. Graduated Indiana University Law School, Bloomington, IN, 1850.
Occupation: Lawyer
Offices/Honors: Nebraska House of Representatives, 1860–61

Aden Gainey Cavins (Indiana Asbury University, 1849) (DePauw University Archives and Special Collections).

Aden Gainey Cavins (post-war) (*History of Greene and Sullivan Counties, Indiana.* Chicago, Illinois, 1884).

Miscellaneous: Resided Bloomfield, Greene Co., IN; and Nebraska City, Otoe Co., NE, 1858–61

Buried: Grandview Cemetery, Bloomfield, IN

References: *Biographical Memoirs of Greene County, IN, with Reminiscences of Pioneer Days.* Indianapolis, IN, 1908. *History of Greene and Sullivan Counties, IN.* Chicago, IL, 1884. Obituary, *Bloomfield News,* Nov. 16, 1906. Pension File and Military Service File, National Archives. *War Letters of Aden G. Cavins Written to His Wife Matilda Livingston Cavins.* Evansville, IN, 1907. Obituary Circular, Whole No. 218, Indiana MOLLUS. Theophilus A. Wylie. *Indiana University, Its History from 1820 to 1890.* Indianapolis, IN, 1890. Letters Received, Volunteer Service Branch, Adjutant General's Office, File C1131(VS)1865, National Archives.

Charles Warner Chapman

Captain, Co. A, 74 IN Infantry, July 28, 1862. Colonel, 74 IN Infantry, Aug. 21, 1862. Commanded 2 Brigade, 3 Division, 14 Army Corps, Army of the Cumberland, March 6–April 27, 1863 and Sept. 20–Oct. 10, 1863. Seriously injured, Chickamauga, GA, Sept. 19, 1863, when his mortally wounded horse fell upon him breaking his arm

Charles Warner Chapman (Will F. Peddycord. *History of the 74th Regiment Indiana Volunteer Infantry.* Warsaw, Indiana, 1913).

and shoulder. Resigned Nov. 26, 1863, due to chronic diarrhea, which during the past four weeks "has become so severe that I have been totally unfit for any kind of duty." Battle honors: Chickamauga.

Born: Sept. 19, 1826 Richmond, IN

Died: April 7, 1889 Warsaw, IN

Education: Attended Indiana Asbury (now DePauw) University, Greencastle, IN

Occupation: Lumber merchant, mill operator and lawyer

Offices/Honors: Indiana House of Representatives, 1861. U.S. Register in Bankruptcy, District of Indiana, 1868–72. Indiana Senate, 1865, 1873, 1875.

Miscellaneous: Resided Warsaw, Kosciusko Co., IN

Buried: Oakwood Cemetery, Warsaw, IN (Block 4, Lot 12)

References: *A Biographical History of Eminent and Self-Made Men of the State of Indiana.* Cincinnati, OH, 1880. George I. Reed, editor. *Encyclopedia of Biography of Indiana.* Chicago, IL, 1895. Kingman Brothers, compilers. *Combination Atlas Map of Kosciusko County, IN.* Chicago, IL, 1879. Lemuel W. Royse. *A Standard History of Kosciusko County, IN.* Chicago, IL, 1919. Obituary, *Warsaw Daily Times,* April 9, 1889. Rebecca A. Shepherd, Charles W. Calhoun, Elizabeth Shanahan-Shoemaker, and Alan F. January, editors. *A Biographical*

Charles Warner Chapman (Webster & Bro., Photographic Gallery, Louisville, Kentucky; Roger D. Hunt Collection, USAMHI [RG98S-CWP 160.33]).

Directory of the Indiana General Assembly. Vol. 1, 1816–1899. Indianapolis, IN, 1980. Will F. Peddycord. *History of the 74th Regiment Indiana Volunteer Infantry.* Warsaw, IN, 1913. Military Service File, National Archives.

John Gilkeson Clark

Major, 26 IN Infantry, Aug. 19, 1861. Lieutenant Colonel, 26 IN Infantry, July 1, 1862. Colonel, 26 IN Infantry, Sept. 28, 1862. Commanded 1 Brigade, 2 Division, Army of the Frontier, Department of the Missouri, Nov. 24, 1862–Jan. 1863 and Feb.–March 1863. Commanded 2 Division, Army of the Frontier, Department of the Missouri, Jan. 1863. Commanded 1 Brigade, 2 Division, 13 Army Corps, Department of the Gulf, Oct.–Dec. 1863. Commanded Post of Donaldsonville, LA, July 1864 and Dec. 1864. Commanded Post of Thibodeaux, LA, Jan.–Feb. 1865. Commanded Post of Macon, MS, June–July 1865. Honorably mustered out, Sept. 28, 1865. Battle honors: Prairie Grove.

Born: Feb. 21, 1836 Pleasant Green, Frederick Co., VA

Died: Dec. 28, 1910 Frankfort, IN

Occupation: Commission merchant and railroad executive

Offices/Honors: Treasurer, Clinton Co., IN, 1867–71

Miscellaneous: Resided Clarks Hill, Tippecanoe Co., IN; Jefferson, Clinton Co., IN; and Frankfort, Clinton Co., IN

Buried: Green Lawn Cemetery, Frankfort, IN (Monument E Section, Lot 306)

References: Pension File and Military Service File, National Archives. Obituary, *Frankfort News,* Dec. 28, 1910. Obituary Circular, Whole No. 278, Indiana MOLLUS. *History of Clinton County, IN.* Chicago, IL, 1886.

John Marcellus Comparet

Captain, Co. C, 15 IN Infantry, June 6, 1861. Major, 15 IN Infantry, Oct. 29, 1862. Lieutenant Colonel, 15 IN Infantry, March 9, 1863. Detached in command of 51 IN Infantry, Nov. 6, 1863–May 30, 1864. Honorably mustered out, June 25, 1864. Colonel, 142 IN Infantry, Nov. 3, 1864. Commanded Post of Nashville, TN, July 1865. Dismissed Aug. 2, 1865, for failing to obey orders from Major Gen. Stoneman to "break up certain gambling houses in the City of Nashville, and to arrest the United States officers found in the said gambling houses." The disability resulting from his dismissal was removed, Nov. 20, 1865, "in consideration of his general good character as a soldier during the war," and also because the list identifying the gambling houses was "so vague as to be useless without the assistance of a guide." Battle honors: Stone's River.

Born: Aug. 6, 1835 Fort Wayne, IN

Died: Feb. 19, 1908 Blanco, TX

Occupation: Millwright and machinist

Offices/Honors: Postmaster, Blanco, TX, 1873–79, 1889–93, and 1897–1907

Miscellaneous: Resided Fort Wayne, Allen Co., IN; Fredericksburg, Gillespie Co., TX; and Blanco, Blanco Co., TX, 1872–1908

Buried: Blanco Cemetery, Blanco, TX (Section 2D, Row 43)

References: Pension File and Military Service File, National Archives. Letters Received, Volunteer Service Branch, Adjutant General's Office, File T1061(VS)1865, National Archives. Obituary, *Fort Wayne News,* March 9, 1908. Edward M. Burns. *Historical Sketch of the Organization and Service of the 15th Regiment Indiana Volunteers.* Valparaiso, IN, 1889. William R. Hartpence. *History of the 51st Indiana Veteran Volunteer Infantry.* Cincinnati, OH, 1894. *Valley of the Upper Maumee River with Historical Account of Allen County and the City of Fort Wayne, Indiana.* Madison, WI, 1889. Death notice, *San Antonio Express,* Feb. 21, 1908.

Robert Conover

1 Lieutenant, Adjutant, 16 IN Infantry (1 year), May 14, 1861. Acting ADC, Staff of Brig. Gen. John J. Abercrombie, March–April 1862. Honorably mustered out, May 14, 1862. 1 Lieutenant, Adjutant, 16 IN Infantry (3 years), May 27, 1862. Acting

John Gilkeson Clark (Abraham Lincoln Presidential Library & Museum).

AAG, Staff of Brig. Gen. Stephen G. Burbridge, 1 Brigade, 10 Division, 13 Army Corps, Army of the Tennessee, March 6–July 4, 1863. Resigned July 4, 1863, in order to "improve my situation ... in one of the new regiments about to be formed in my state." Colonel, 111 IN Minute Men, July 13, 1863. Honorably mustered out, July 15, 1863. Major, 16 IN Infantry, July 15, 1863. Lieutenant Colonel, 16 IN Infantry, Oct. 10, 1864. Commanded Post of Thibodeaux, LA, Dec. 1864. *Colonel,* 16 IN Infantry, Feb. 20, 1865. Honorably mustered out, June 30, 1865. Battle honors: Champion's Hill.

Born: May 14, 1839 Shelbyville, IN
Died: Sept. 21, 1872 Savannah, MO
Occupation: Grocer before war. Clothing merchant and real estate agent after war.
Offices/Honors: Sheriff, Andrew Co., MO, 1870–72
Miscellaneous: Resided Shelbyville, Shelby Co., IN; and Fillmore, Andrew Co., MO, 1865–72
Buried: City Cemetery, Savannah, MO (Section 1 South)
References: Obituary, *Andrew County Republican,* Sept. 27, 1872. Military Service File, National Archives. *Shelby County in the Civil War.* Shelbyville, IN, 1961.

John Coons

Captain, Co. G, 14 IN Infantry, June 7, 1861. Lieutenant Colonel, 14 IN Infantry, Aug. 11, 1862. GSW left shoulder, Antietam, MD, Sept. 17, 1862. Colonel, 14 IN Infantry, Jan. 22, 1863. Commanded 1 Brigade, 3 Division, 2 Army Corps, Army of the Potomac, Feb.–March 1863. Commanded 3 Brigade, 3 Division, 2 Army Corps, Army of the Potomac, July 17–Aug. 15, 1863. GSW Spotsylvania, VA, May 12, 1864. Battle honors: Cheat Mountain, Antietam, Chancellorsville, Gettysburg, Bristoe Station, Mine Run, Wilderness, Spotsylvania.

Born: 1828? Knox Co., IN
Died: May 12, 1864 KIA Spotsylvania, VA
Occupation: Lawyer
Miscellaneous: Resided Vincennes, Knox Co., IN
Buried: Greenlawn Cemetery, Vincennes, IN
References: Military Service File, National Archives. Obituary, *Vincennes Weekly Western Sun,* June 10, 1864. Nancy Niblack Baxter. *Gallant Fourteenth: The Story of an Indiana Civil War Regiment.* Traverse City, MI, 1980. Edmund J. Raus, Jr. *A Generation on the March: The Union Army at Gettysburg.* Gettysburg, PA, 1996. Theodore T. Scribner. *Indiana's Roll of Honor.* Indianapolis, IN, 1866.

Alexander Baxter Crane

Captain, Co. C, 85 IN Infantry, Aug. 20, 1862. Lieutenant Colonel, 85 IN Infantry, Sept. 4, 1862. Taken prisoner, Thompson's Station, TN, March 5, 1863. Confined Libby Prison, Richmond, VA. Paroled May 5, 1863. *Colonel,* 85 IN Infantry, July

Alexander Baxter Crane (post-war) (Jefferson E. Brant. *History of the 85th Indiana Volunteer Infantry, Its Organization, Campaigns and Battles.* Bloomington, Indiana, 1902).

John Coons (William N. Pickerill, comp. *Indiana at the Fiftieth Anniversary of the Battle of Gettysburg.* Indianapolis, Indiana, 1913).

21, 1864. Commanded 2 Brigade, 3 Division, 20 Army Corps, Army of the Cumberland, Oct. 30–Nov. 11, 1864. Honorably mustered out, June 12, 1865. Battle honors: Thompson's Station, Atlanta Campaign (Peach Tree Creek), Savannah Campaign, Campaign of the Carolinas.
   Born: April 23, 1833 Berkley, Bristol Co., MA
   Died: April 16, 1930 Scarsdale, NY
   Education: Graduated Amherst (MA) College, 1854
   Occupation: Lawyer
   Offices/Honors: District Attorney, Vigo Co., IN, 1857–59
   Miscellaneous: Resided Terre Haute, Vigo Co., IN, to 1865; New York City, NY, 1865–73; Scarsdale, Westchester Co., NY, after 1873
   Buried: Churchyard of St. James the Less, Scarsdale, NY
   References: Obituary, *New York Times,* April 17, 1930. Pension File and Military Service File, National Archives. William L. Montague, editor. *Biographical Record of the Alumni of Amherst College, During Its First Half Century, 1821–1871.* Amherst, MA, 1883. D. Hamilton Hurd, compiler. *History of Bristol County, MA.* Philadelphia, PA, 1883. Letters Received, Volunteer Service Branch, Adjutant General's Office, File C649(VS)1863, National Archives. Jefferson E. Brant. *History of the 85th Indiana Volunteer Infantry, Its Organization, Campaigns and Battles.* Bloomington, IN, 1902. Frank J. Welcher and Larry G. Ligget. *Coburn's Brigade: 85th Indiana, 33rd Indiana, 19th Michigan, and 22nd Wisconsin in the Western Civil War.* Carmel, IN, 1999.

John Wilson Crooks

Colonel, 4 IN Legion (Spencer County), June 12, 1861. Resigned March 1, 1864.
   Born: Oct. 6, 1817 IL
   Died: May 1, 1864 Rockport, IN
   Other Wars: Mexican War (Captain, Co. E, 4 IN Infantry)
   Occupation: Physician
   Offices/Honors: Treasurer, Spencer Co., IN, 1860–64
   Miscellaneous: Resided Rockport, Spencer Co., IN
   Buried: Sunset Hill Cemetery, Rockport, IN (Section 6)
   References: Pension File, National Archives. *History of Warrick, Spencer and Perry Counties, IN.* Chicago, IL, 1885. John P. Etter. *The Indiana Legion: A Civil War Militia.* Carmel, IN, 2006. *Report of Major General Love of the Indiana Legion.* Indianapolis, IN, 1863. Bess V. Ehrmann. *Back Trails of Indiana.* New York City, NY, 1943.

James Lowery Culbertson

Captain, Co. C, 80 IN Infantry, Aug. 15, 1862. Major, 80 IN Infantry, Jan. 18, 1863. Lieutenant Colonel, 80 IN Infantry, March 14, 1863. Colonel, 80 IN Infantry, Nov. 1, 1863. Suffering from "frequent attacks of hemorrhage of the lungs with a strong predisposition to consumption," he resigned Jan. 26, 1864, "my health being such that I cannot do my country nor myself justice by remaining."
   Born: April 4, 1828 Bedford, IN
   Died: Nov. 18, 1911 Edwardsport, IN
   Occupation: Farmer before war. Lawyer and dry goods merchant after war.
   Offices/Honors: Commissioner, Knox Co., IN, 1854–60
   Miscellaneous: Resided Edwardsport, Knox Co., IN
   Buried: Edwardsport Town Cemetery, Edwardsport, IN
   References: Pension File and Military Service File, National Archives. Obituary, *Vincennes Capital,* Nov. 20, 1911. F. C. Hardacre, compiler. *Historical Atlas of Knox County, IN.* Vincennes, IN, 1903.

James Lowery Culbertson (standing right with officers of the 80th Indiana Infantry, including Colonel Lewis Brooks seated left, Major John W. Tucker seated right, and Adjutant Alfred D. Owen standing left) (Indiana Historical Society, P0415 [Indiana Carte-de-Visite Collection]).

James F. Curtis

2 Lieutenant, Co. I, 44 IN Infantry, Nov. 22, 1861. Captain, Co. I, 44 IN Infantry, Oct. 18, 1862. GSW left hand, Chickamauga, GA, Sept. 19, 1863. Major, 44 IN Infantry, Aug. 23, 1864. Lieutenant

James F. Curtis (as Captain, 44 Indiana Infantry, seated right, with Major Joseph C. Hodges, seated left, Adjutant Samuel E. Smith, standing left, and 1 Lieutenant David S. Belknap, standing right) (Mark Weldon Collection).

Colonel, 44 IN Infantry, Sept. 28, 1864. Colonel, 44 IN Infantry, Dec. 1, 1864. Commanded 2 Brigade, 1 Separate Division, District of the Etowah, Department of the Cumberland, April 1865 and June 1865. Commanded Post of Chattanooga, TN, June 1865. Honorably mustered out, Sept. 14, 1865. Battle honors: Shiloh, Chickamauga.

Born: Aug. 8, 1838 Kingsville, Ashtabula Co., OH

Died: Sept. 16, 1875 Petoskey, MI

Occupation: Jeweler before war. Dry goods merchant after war.

Miscellaneous: Resided Elkhart, Elkhart Co., IN; and Petoskey, Emmet Co., MI

Buried: Grace Lawn Cemetery, Elkhart, IN (Block E, Lot 13, unmarked)

References: Pension File and Military Service File, National Archives. Obituary, *Goshen Times,* Sept. 23, 1875. John H. Rerick. *The 44th Indiana Volunteer Infantry: History of Its Services in the War of the Rebellion.* LaGrange, IN, 1880.

Charles Denby

Lieutenant Colonel, 42 IN Infantry, Sept. 30, 1861. GSW mouth, Perryville, KY, Oct. 8, 1862. Colonel, 80 IN Infantry, Oct. 21, 1862. Suffering "habitually in riding with a very severe cramp in my left leg," he resigned Jan. 17, 1863, "on the ground of physical disability." Battle honors: Perryville.

Born: June 16, 1830 Mount Joy, Botetourt Co., VA

Died: Jan. 13, 1904 Jamestown, NY

Education: Attended Georgetown (DC) College. Graduated Virginia Military Institute, Lexington, VA, 1850.

Occupation: Lawyer

Offices/Honors: Indiana House of Representatives, 1857. U.S. Minister to China, 1885–98.

Miscellaneous: Resided Evansville, Vanderburgh Co., IN. Son-in-law of Colonel Graham N. Fitch (46 IN Infantry).

Buried: Oak Hill Cemetery, Evansville, IN (Section 25, Lot 54)

References: *Dictionary of American Biography.* Obituary, *Evansville Courier,* Jan. 14, 1904. *National Cyclopedia of American Biography.* Joseph P. Elliott. *History of Evansville and Vanderburgh County, IN.* Evansville, IN, 1897. *History of Vanderburgh County, IN.* Madison, WI, 1889. *A Biographical History of Eminent and Self-Made Men of the State of Indiana.* Cincinnati, OH, 1880. Obituary Circular, Whole No. 180, Indiana MOLLUS. Military Service File, National Archives. Spillard F. Horrall. *History of the 42nd Indiana Volunteer Infantry.*

Charles Denby (photograph by Webster & Bro., Louisville, KY).

Chicago, IL, 1892. Jennings C. Wise. *The Military History of the Virginia Military Institute from 1839 to 1865.* Lynchburg, VA, 1915. Rebecca A. Shepherd, Charles W. Calhoun, Elizabeth Shanahan-Shoemaker, and Alan F. January, editors. *A Biographical Directory of the Indiana General Assembly.* Vol. 1, 1816–1899. Indianapolis, IN, 1980. Obituary, *New York Times*, Jan. 14, 1904.

William N. Denny

1 Lieutenant, Co. G, 14 IN Infantry, June 7, 1861. Captain, Co. E, 51 IN Infantry, Feb. 23, 1862. Taken prisoner, near Rome, GA, May 3, 1863. Confined Libby Prison, Richmond, VA; Macon, GA; and Camp Sorghum, Columbia, SC. Escaped Feb. 15, 1865. Major, 51 IN Infantry, Nov. 6, 1864. Lieutenant Colonel, 51 IN Infantry, March 17, 1865. *Colonel,* 51 IN Infantry, June 1, 1865. Honorably mustered out, Dec. 13, 1865. Battle honors: Streight's Raid.

Born: May 12, 1836 Bruceville, Knox Co., IN
Died: Jan. 29, 1915 Council Bluffs, IA
Education: Attended Vincennes (IN) University
Occupation: Deputy county clerk before war. Farmer after war.
Offices/Honors: Postmaster, Vincennes, IN, 1869–82
Miscellaneous: Resided Vincennes, Knox Co., IN; Neosho, Newton Co., MO; and Council Bluffs, Pottawattamie Co., IA, after 1901
Buried: Greenlawn Cemetery, Vincennes, IN
References: *History of Knox and Daviess Counties, IN.* Chicago, IL, 1886. Obituary, *Vincennes Capital,* Jan. 30 and Feb. 2, 1915. Pension File and Military Service File, National Archives. Letters Received, Volunteer Service Branch, Adjutant General's Office, File D598(VS)1865, National Archives. Obituary, *Omaha Morning World-Herald*, Jan. 30, 1915. William R. Hartpence. *History of the 51st Indiana Veteran Volunteer Infantry.* Cincinnati, OH, 1894. Nancy Niblack Baxter. *Gallant Fourteenth: The Story of an Indiana Civil War Regiment.* Traverse City, MI, 1980. George E. Greene. *History of Old Vincennes and Knox County, IN.* Chicago, IL, 1911.

Thomas Doan

Captain, Co. H, 12 IN Infantry (1 year), May 15, 1861. Honorably mustered out, May 19, 1862. Captain, Co. I, 101 IN Infantry, Aug. 11, 1862. Lieutenant Colonel, 101 IN Infantry, Sept. 6, 1862. *Colonel,* 101 IN Infantry, May 31, 1863 (Since he was actually performing the duties of colonel on the date he was commissioned, his record was amended in 1885 to show him mustered in as of that date.) Commanded 2 Brigade, 3 Division, 14 Army

Thomas Doan (Godshaw & Flexner, Photographers, Bee Hive Gallery, 309 Main Street, Louisville, Kentucky; Rick Brown Collection).

Thomas Doan (Godshaw & Flexner, Photographers, Bee Hive Gallery, 309 Main Street, Louisville, Kentucky; Roger D. Hunt Collection, USAMHI [RG98S-CWP80.63]).

Corps, Army of the Cumberland, Jan. 1–April 3, 1865. Bvt. Colonel, USV, March 13, 1865, for gallant and meritorious services. Honorably mustered out, June 24, 1865. Battle honors: Chickamauga, Missionary Ridge, Atlanta Campaign (Resaca, Kenesaw Mountain, Peach Tree Creek), Savannah Campaign, Campaign of the Carolinas.
Born: Dec. 28, 1826 Wilmington, OH
Died: Aug. 2, 1865 Marion, IN
Occupation: Lawyer
Miscellaneous: Resided Marion, Grant Co., IN. First cousin of Bvt. Brig. Gen. Azariah W. Doan.
Buried: IOOF (now Estates of Serenity) Cemetery, Marion, IN (Block 4, Lot 9)
References: Pension File and Military Service File, National Archives. Alfred A. Doane, compiler. *The Doane Family*. Boston, MA, 1902. Letters Received, Volunteer Service Branch, Adjutant General's Office, File D563(VS)1864, National Archives. Ralph D. Kirkpatrick. *Local History and Genealogy Abstracts from Marion, Indiana Newspapers, 1865–1870*. Bowie, MD, 2001.

Cyrus Johnson Dobbs

2 Lieutenant, Co. A, 11 IN Infantry (3 months), April 25, 1861. Captain, Co. A, 13 IN Infantry, June 19, 1861. Major, 13 IN Infantry, Oct. 25, 1861. GSW left wrist, Kernstown, VA, March 23, 1862. Lieutenant Colonel, 13 IN Infantry, May 10, 1862. Colonel, 13 IN Infantry, July 17, 1863. Commanded

Cyrus Johnson Dobbs (Massachusetts MOLLUS Collection, USAMHI [Vol. 53, p. 2640]).

1 Brigade, 2 Provisional Division, District of Florida, Department of the South, March–April 1864. Honorably mustered out, June 30, 1864. Lieutenant Colonel, 3 U.S. Veteran Volunteer Infantry, Jan. 18, 1865. Honorably mustered out, May 7, 1866. Battle honors: Rich Mountain, Kernstown, Siege of Suffolk, Siege of Fort Wagner, Bermuda Hundred.
Born: Oct. 9, 1833 Wayne Co., OH
Died: Jan. 17, 1885 Indianapolis, IN
Education: Attended Ohio Wesleyan University, Delaware, OH
Occupation: Saddler before war. Superior court bailiff and Deputy U.S. Marshal after war.
Miscellaneous: Resided Indianapolis, Marion Co., IN
Buried: Fairmount Cemetery, Jackson, OH (Old Section, Lot 86, unmarked)
References: *A Biographical History of Eminent and Self-Made Men of the State of Indiana*. Cincinnati, OH, 1880. Pension File and Military Service File, National Archives. Obituary, *Jackson (OH) Standard*, Jan. 29, 1885. Obituary, *Indianapolis Journal*, Jan. 18, 1885. Letters Received, Volunteer Service Branch, Adjutant General's Office, File D915(VS)1864, National Archives.

Joseph B. Dodge

Lieutenant Colonel, 30 IN Infantry, Sept. 12, 1861. Colonel, 30 IN Infantry, April 26, 1862. Commanded 2 Brigade, 2 Division, Right Wing, 14 Army Corps, Army of the Cumberland, Dec. 31, 1862–Jan. 9, 1863. Commanded 2 Brigade, 2 Division, 20 Army Corps, Army of the Cumberland, Jan. 9–May 18, 1863 and June 29–Oct. 9, 1863. Honorably mustered out, Sept. 29, 1864. Battle honors: Shiloh, Stone's River, Chickamauga.
Born: June 3, 1830 Starkey's Corners, Yates Co., NY
Died: July 7, 1891 Warsaw, IN
Education: Attended Genesee Wesleyan Seminary, Lima, NY
Occupation: School teacher and collection agent before war. Farmer, real estate agent, and insurance agent after war.
Offices/Honors: Treasurer of Kosciusko Co., IN, 1856–60
Miscellaneous: Resided Warsaw, Kosciusko Co., IN
Buried: Oakwood Cemetery, Warsaw, IN (Block 19, Lot 13)
References: *Biographical and Historical Record of Kosciusko County, IN*. Chicago, IL, 1887. Pension File and Military Service File, National Archives. Obituary, *Warsaw Daily Times*, July 13, 1891. Kingman Brothers, compilers. *Combination Atlas Map of Kosciusko County, IN*. Chicago, IL, 1879. William

Cyrus Livingston Dunham

Colonel, 50 IN Infantry, Dec. 25, 1861. Taken prisoner and paroled, Munfordville, KY, Sept. 17, 1862. Commanded 2 Brigade, District of Jackson, 16 Army Corps, Army of the Tennessee, Dec. 18, 1862–March 18, 1863. Commanded Post of New Albany, IN, July–Oct. 1863. Resigned Nov. 18, 1863, on account of physical disability due to "enfeebled constitutional powers, accompanied with chronic rheumatism of the hips, interfering with locomotion, and chronic diarrhea of six months standing." Battle honors: Munfordville, Parker's Cross Roads.

Born: Jan. 16, 1817 Dryden, Tompkins Co., NY
Died: Nov. 21, 1877 Jeffersonville, IN
Occupation: Lawyer and judge
Offices/Honors: Indiana House of Representatives, 1846–48 and 1865. U.S. House of Representatives, 1849–55. Indiana Secretary of State, 1859–61.
Miscellaneous: Resided Salem, Washington Co., IN; New Albany, Floyd Co., IN; and Jeffersonville, Clark Co., IN, 1871–77
Buried: Walnut Ridge Cemetery, Jeffersonville, IN (Section C, Lot 87)
References: William W. Woollen. *Biographical and Historical Sketches of Early Indiana*. Indianapolis, IN, 1883. Obituary, *Jeffersonville Evening News*, Nov. 21, 1877. James L. Harrison, compiler. *Biog-*

Joseph B. Dodge (*Indiana at Chickamauga, 1863–1900. Report of Indiana Commissioners Chickamauga National Military Park*. Indianapolis, Indiana, 1901).

Joseph B. Dodge (William Sumner Dodge. *History of the Old Second Division, Army of the Cumberland*. Chicago, Illinois, 1864).

Sumner Dodge. *History of the Old Second Division, Army of the Cumberland*. Chicago, IL, 1864. *Indiana at Chickamauga, 1863–1900. Report of Indiana Commissioners Chickamauga National Military Park*. Indianapolis, IN, 1901.

Cyrus Livingston Dunham (The National Archives [BA-482]).

raphical Directory of the American Congress, 1774–1949. Washington, DC, 1950. Obituary, *Louisville Commercial*, Nov. 22, 1877. Pension File and Military Service File, National Archives. Rebecca A. Shepherd, Charles W. Calhoun, Elizabeth Shanahan-Shoemaker, and Alan F. January, editors. *A Biographical Directory of the Indiana General Assembly*. Vol. 1, 1816–1899. Indianapolis, IN, 1980. Letters Received, Volunteer Service Branch, Adjutant General's Office, File D443(VS)1862, National Archives. Burton D. Myers. *Trustees and Officers of Indiana University, 1820 to 1950*. Bloomington, IN, 1951. *History of the Ohio Falls Cities and Their Counties*. Cleveland, OH, 1882.

David Maxwell Dunn

Lieutenant Colonel, 9 IN Infantry (3 months), April 27, 1861. Honorably mustered out, July 29, 1861. Lieutenant Colonel, 29 IN Infantry, Aug. 27, 1861. Nominated as Brig. Gen., U.S. Volunteers, Nov. 29, 1862. Nomination withdrawn, Feb. 12, 1863. Taken prisoner, Stone's River, TN, Dec. 31, 1862. Confined at Atlanta, GA, and Richmond, VA. Paroled May 5, 1863. Dismissed Sept. 30, 1863, for reported intoxication while on picket duty. Dismissal revoked upon Major General Rosecrans' testimony as to his "past gallantry and good services" and the statement of Colonel Philip Sidney Post (59 IL Infantry), "If Col. Dunn was intoxicated, he had a most remarkably sober way of showing it." Colonel, 29 IN Infantry, March 1, 1864. Honorably mustered out, Sept. 27, 1864. Battle honors: Shiloh, Stone's River, Tullahoma Campaign (Liberty Gap), Chickamauga.

Born: Nov. 18, 1818 Hanover, IN
Died: Aug. 20, 1889 Washington, DC
Education: Graduated Hanover (IN) College, 1839
Other Wars: Mexican War (2 Lieutenant, Co. G, 1 IN Infantry)
Occupation: Lawyer, banker and railroad president before war. U.S. diplomatic service after war.
Offices/Honors: Indiana House of Representatives, 1855. U.S. Consul, Charlottetown, Prince Edward Island, 1871–83. U.S. Consul, Valparaiso, Chile, 1883–86.
Miscellaneous: Resided Logansport, Cass Co., IN; and Washington, DC. Brother of Bvt. Brig. Gen. William McKee Dunn.
Buried: Oak Hill Cemetery, Washington, DC (Lot 452 East)
References: William Sumner Dodge. *History of the Old Second Division, Army of the Cumberland*. Chicago, IL, 1864. Obituary, *Logansport Daily Journal*, Aug. 22, 1889. Rebecca A. Shepherd, Charles W. Calhoun, Elizabeth Shanahan-Shoemaker, and Alan F. January, editors. *A Biographical Directory of the Indiana General Assembly*. Vol. 1, 1816–1899. Indianapolis, IN, 1980. Obituary, *Washington Post*, Aug. 23, 1889. Military Service File, National Archives. Letters Received, Volunteer Service Branch, Adjutant General's Office, File D1024 (VS)1863, National Archives. *General Catalogue of the Alumni of Hanover College, 1833–1883*. Hanover, IN, 1883.

Norman Eddy

Colonel, 48 IN Infantry, Jan. 16, 1862. GSW right forearm, Iuka, MS, Sept. 19, 1862. Commanded 1 Brigade, 7 Division, Left Wing, 16 Army Corps, Army of the Tennessee, Jan. 1–Jan. 20, 1863. Commanded 1 Brigade, 7 Division, 17 Army Corps, Army of the Tennessee, Jan. 20–Feb. 5, 1863. Resigned July 11, 1863, since "I am no longer able to bear the hardships of the field," due to "atrophy of the right arm in consequence of a bullet wound ... and vertigo and great debility from sunstroke." Battle honors: Iuka, Siege of Vicksburg.

Born: Dec. 10, 1810 Scipio, NY
Died: Jan. 28, 1872 Indianapolis, IN
Education: Graduated University of Pennsylvania Medical School, Philadelphia, PA, 1835
Occupation: Physician (to 1847) and lawyer (after 1847)
Offices/Honors: Indiana Senate, 1849–52. U.S. House of Representatives, 1853–55. U.S. Collector of Internal Revenue, 9th District, Indiana, 1865–69. Indiana Secretary of State, 1871–72.
Miscellaneous: Resided Mishawaka, St. Joseph

David Maxwell Dunn (P. S. Ryder, Photographist, 25 and 28 N. Pennsylvania St., Indianapolis, Indiana; Craig Dunn Collection).

Norman Eddy (The National Archives [BA-862]).

Co., IN; and South Bend, St. Joseph Co., IN, after 1847
Buried: City Cemetery, South Bend, IN (Section 2 West, Lot 20, Block 1)
References: *History of St. Joseph County, IN.* Chicago, IL, 1880. Pension File and Military Service File, National Archives. Obituary, *St. Joseph Valley Register*, Feb. 1, 1872. *South Bend and the Men Who Have Made It.* South Bend, IN, 1901. Ruth S. D. Eddy, compiler. *The Eddy Family in America.* Boston, MA, 1930. James L. Harrison, compiler. *Biographical Directory of the American Congress, 1774–1949.* Washington, DC, 1950. Rebecca A. Shepherd, Charles W. Calhoun, Elizabeth Shanahan-Shoemaker, and Alan F. January, editors. *A Biographical Directory of the Indiana General Assembly.* Vol. 1, 1816–1899. Indianapolis, IN, 1980. *Who Was Who in America: Historical Volume, 1607–1896.* Chicago, IL, 1963. Stephen E. Towne, editor. *A Fierce, Wild Joy: The Civil War Letters of Colonel Edward J. Wood, 48th Indiana Volunteer Infantry Regiment.* Knoxville, TN, 2007.

Frank Emerson

Colonel, 67 IN Infantry, Aug. 22, 1862. Taken prisoner and paroled, Munfordville, KY, Sept. 17, 1862. GSW left thigh, Arkansas Post, AR, Jan. 11, 1863. Commanded 1 Brigade, 4 Division, 13 Army Corps, Army of the Gulf, March 27–April 8, 1864. GSW left hip and taken prisoner, Sabine Cross Roads, LA, April 8, 1864. Paroled June 16, 1864. Resigned Sept. 10, 1864, "on account of physical disability from wounds received in action." Battle honors: Munfordville, Arkansas Post, Sabine Cross Roads.
Born: Feb. 28, 1815 Haverhill, NH
Died: Jan. 26, 1894 Brownstown, IN
Education: Graduated Dartmouth College, Hanover, NH, 1838
Other Wars: Mexican War (2 Lieutenant, 3 U.S. Dragoons)
Occupation: Lawyer and judge
Offices/Honors: Indiana Senate, 1851–52. Treasurer, Jackson Co., IN, 1852–56. Judge of Common Pleas Court, 1856–60 and 1868–73. Judge of Circuit Court, 1873.
Miscellaneous: Resided Brownstown, Jackson Co., IN
Buried: Fairview Cemetery, Brownstown, IN
References: *A Biographical History of Eminent and Self-Made Men of the State of Indiana.* Cincinnati, OH, 1880. *Biographical Record of Bartholomew and Jackson Counties, IN.* Indianapolis, IN, 1904. *History of Jackson County, IN.* Chicago, IL, 1886. Obituary, *Brownstown Banner*, Feb. 1, 1894. Pension File and Military Service File, National Archives. Letters Received, Volunteer Service Branch, Adjutant General's Office, File E446(VS)1864, National Archives. Rebecca A. Shepherd, Charles W. Calhoun, Elizabeth Shanahan-Shoemaker, and Alan F. January, editors. *A Biographical Directory of the Indiana General Assembly.* Vol. 1, 1816–1899. Indianapolis, IN, 1980. Charles Henry Pope, compiler. *The Haverhill Emersons.* Boston, MA, 1913. Reuben B. Scott. *The History of the 67th Regiment Indiana Infantry Volunteers, War of the Rebellion.* Bedford, IN, 1892.

Francis Erdelmeyer

Sergeant, Co. E, 11 IN Infantry (3 months), April 25, 1861. Honorably mustered out, Aug. 4, 1861. Captain, Co. A, 32 IN Infantry, Aug. 24, 1861. Lieutenant Colonel, 32 IN Infantry, Oct. 20, 1862. *Colonel,* 32 IN Infantry, Aug. 8, 1863. Commanded 1 Brigade, 2 Division, 20 Army Corps, Army of the Cumberland, Sept. 19–Oct. 9, 1863. Honorably mustered out, Sept. 7, 1864. Battle honors: Shiloh, Stone's River, Chickamauga, Missionary Ridge, Atlanta Campaign.
Born: Nov. 2, 1835 Hernsheim, Hessen-Darmstadt, Germany
Died: Oct. 16, 1926 Indianapolis, IN
Occupation: Upholsterer before war. Engaged in retail drug business after war.
Offices/Honors: Treasurer, Marion Co., IN, 1869–71
Miscellaneous: Resided Indianapolis, IN
Buried: Crown Hill Cemetery, Indianapolis, IN (Section 12, Lot 35)
References: Jacob Piatt Dunn. *Greater Indi-*

Francis Erdelmeyer (photograph by E. & J. Bruening, Indianapolis, Indiana; Adolph Metzner Photograph Album, Library of Congress [LC-USZ62-129680]).

anapolis: The History, the Industries, the Institutions, and the People of a City of Homes. Chicago, IL, 1910. *Commemorative Biographical Record of Prominent and Representative Men of Indianapolis and Vicinity.* Chicago, IL, 1908. Pension File and Military Service File, National Archives. Obituary, *Indianapolis News*, Oct. 19, 1926. Joseph R. Reinhart, editor. *August Willich's Gallant Dutchmen: Civil War Letters from the 32nd Indiana Infantry.* Kent, OH, 2006. James Barnett, "Willich's Thirty-Second Indiana Volunteers," *Cincinnati Historical Society Bulletin*, Vol. 37, No. 1 (Spring 1979). Michael A. Peake. *Blood Shed in This War: Civil War Illustrations by Captain Adolph Metzner, 32nd Indiana.* Indianapolis, IN, 2010.

Harvey (aka Henry) Jefferson Espy

2 Lieutenant, Co. F, 68 IN Infantry, July 22, 1862. Captain, Co. F, 68 IN Infantry, Aug. 12, 1862. Taken prisoner and paroled, Munfordville, KY, Sept. 17, 1862. GSW Hoover's Gap, TN, June 25, 1863. GSW right arm, Chickamauga, GA, Sept. 19, 1863. Major, 68 IN Infantry, Sept. 21, 1863. Lieutenant Colonel, 68 IN Infantry, Nov. 14,

Harvey (aka Henry) Jefferson Espy (kansasmemory.org, Kansas State Historical Society).

1863. *Colonel*, 68 IN Infantry, Nov. 14, 1863. Stunned by shell explosion, Missionary Ridge, TN, Nov. 25, 1863. Commanded 3 Brigade, Provisional Division, Army of the Cumberland, Dec. 19–23, 1864. Honorably mustered out, June 20, 1865. Battle honors: Tullahoma Campaign (Hoover's Gap), Chickamauga, Missionary Ridge, Nashville.

Born: March 20, 1831 Ripley, OH (or Erie Co., OH)
Died: April 14, 1868 Springdale, KS
Other Wars: Private, Co. B and K, 1 U.S. Dragoons, 1852–57
Occupation: Lawyer and farmer
Miscellaneous: Resided Council Grove, Morris Co., KS; and Napoleon, Ripley Co., IN, before war. Resided Springdale, Leavenworth Co., KS, after war.
Buried: Place of burial unknown
References: Pension File and Military Service File, National Archives. Rita Espy Kuhbander and William G. Espy. *The Espy-Espey Genealogy Book.* Baltimore, MD, 1987. Florence M. Espy. *History and Genealogy of the Espy Family in America.* Fort Madison, IA, 1905. Letters Received, Commission Branch, Adjutant General's Office, File E391(CB) 1865, National Archives. Edwin W. High. *History of the 68th Regiment Indiana Volunteer Infantry, 1862–1865.* N.p., 1902.

William Henry Fairbanks

Private, Co. C, 11 IN Infantry (3 months), April 23, 1861. Honorably mustered out, Aug. 4, 1861. 1 Lieutenant, Co. E, 31 IN Infantry, Sept. 3, 1861. Acting AAG, Staff of Colonel (later Brig. Gen.) Charles Cruft, Dec. 1861–Feb. 1862. Captain, Co. E, 31 IN Infantry, Jan. 3, 1862. Shell wound head, Shiloh, TN, April 6, 1862. Acting AAG, Staff of Brig. Gen. Charles Cruft, Aug. 1862–Oct. 1863. Major, 31 IN Infantry, Sept. 6, 1863. Acting AIG, 1 Division, 4 Army Corps, Army of the Cumberland, Nov. 1863–Sept. 1864. Lieutenant Colonel, 31 IN Infantry, June 26, 1864. Resigned Sept. 23, 1864, since "I have heretofore been of the universal impression that at the expiration of three years from the date of my first muster I could be honorably mustered out, and have under such belief made every arrangement with my business that now demands my attention." Colonel, 149 IN Infantry, Feb. 22, 1865. Commanded Post of Decatur, District of Northern Alabama, April–Sept. 1865. Honorably mustered out, Sept. 27, 1865. Battle honors: Fort Donelson, Shiloh, Stone's River, Chickamauga, Atlanta Campaign.

Born: Aug. 12, 1839 Terre Haute, IN
Died: Dec. 18, 1908 on train en route to Terre Haute, IN
Occupation: Bookkeeper before war. Following an active career in the mining and smelting business after the war, he became a wholesale grocer and provision dealer.
Miscellaneous: Resided Terre Haute, Vigo Co., IN, to 1866 and 1897–1908; St. Louis, MO, 1866–68; Springfield, Greene Co., MO, 1868–72; and Joplin, Jasper Co., MO, 1872–97
Buried: Highland Lawn Cemetery, Terre Haute, IN (Section 3, Lot 442)
References: Obituary Circular, Whole No. 252, Indiana MOLLUS. *History of Jasper County, MO.* Des Moines, IA, 1883. Charles C. Oakey. *Greater Terre Haute and Vigo County Closing the First Century's History of City and County.* Chicago and New York, 1908. Obituary, *Terre Haute Tribune,* Dec. 19, 1908. Pension File and Military Service File, National Archives. Lorenzo S. Fairbanks. *Genealogy of the Fairbanks Family in America, 1633–1897.* Boston, MA, 1897. Letters Received, Volunteer Service Branch, Adjutant General's Office, File F186(VS)1865, National Archives. John Thomas Smith. *A History of the 31st Regiment of Indiana Volunteer Infantry in the War of the Rebellion.* Cincinnati, OH, 1900.

Josiah Farrar

Captain, Co. D, 99 IN Infantry, Aug. 19, 1862. Lieutenant Colonel, 99 IN Infantry, May 1, 1865.

Josiah Farrar (Daniel R. Lucas. *New History of the 99th Indiana Infantry.* Rockford, Illinois, 1900).

Colonel, 99 IN Infantry, May 2, 1865. Honorably mustered out, June 5, 1865. Battle honors: Dalton, Atlanta Campaign, Campaign of the Carolinas.

Born: Sept. 25, 1826 near Depauville, Jefferson Co., NY
Died: March 20, 1909 Peru, IN
Occupation: Lawyer
Offices/Honors: Mayor of Peru, IN, 1867–68
Miscellaneous: Resided Peru, Miami Co., IN
Buried: Mount Hope Cemetery, Peru, IN (Section B, Lot 56)
References: Charles W. Taylor. *Biographical Sketches and Review of the Bench and Bar of Indiana.* Indianapolis, IN, 1895. *History of Miami County, Indiana.* Chicago, IL, 1887. Obituary, *Peru Daily Chronicle,* March 20, 1909. Daniel R. Lucas. *New History of the 99th Indiana Infantry.* Rockford, IL, 1900. Pension File and Military Service File, National Archives. Letters Received, Volunteer Service Branch, Adjutant General's Office, File P1180(VS) 1866, National Archives.

Graham Newell Fitch

Colonel, 46 IN Infantry, Dec. 10, 1861. Commanded 2 Brigade, 3 Division, Army of the Mississippi, March–April 1862. Based on reports (which he denied) that he had murdered in cold

Eminent and Self-Made Men of the State of Indiana. Cincinnati, OH, 1880. James L. Harrison, compiler. *Biographical Directory of the American Congress, 1774–1949.* Washington, DC, 1950. Obituary, *Logansport Daily Journal,* Nov. 30, 1892. Kingman Brothers, compilers. *Combination Atlas Map of Cass County, IN.* Chicago, IL, 1878. Rebecca A. Shepherd, Charles W. Calhoun, Elizabeth Shanahan-Shoemaker, and Alan F. January, editors. *A Biographical Directory of the Indiana General Assembly.* Vol. 1, 1816–1899. Indianapolis, IN, 1980. Roscoe C. Fitch, compiler. *History of the Fitch Family, 1400–1930.* Haverhill, MA, 1930. Military Service File, National Archives. *History of the 46th Regiment Indiana Volunteer Infantry, September 1861–September 1865.* Logansport, IN, 1888.

John Watson Foster

Major, 25 IN Infantry, Aug. 19, 1861. Lieutenant Colonel, 25 IN Infantry, May 1, 1862. Colonel, 65 IN Infantry, Aug. 24, 1862. Commanded Post of Henderson, KY, District of Western Kentucky, Department of the Ohio, March–May 1863. Commanded 2 Brigade, 4 Division, 23 Army Corps, Army of the Ohio, Aug. 28–Oct. 17, 1863. Commanded 4 Brigade, 4 Division, 23 Army Corps, Army of the Ohio, Oct.17–Nov. 3, 1863. Com-

Graham Newell Fitch (U.S. House of Representatives, 1859) (McClees' Gallery of Photographic Portraits of the Senators, Representatives & Delegates of the Thirty-Fifth Congress, Library of Congress [LC-DIG-ppmsca-26779]).

blood two peaceful citizens during an expedition up the White River (AR) in June 1862, the Confederate War Department issued an order labeling him a felon and promising retaliation against his troops, if captured. Resigned Aug. 5, 1862, due to "a small inguinal hernia, which was so aggravated by a fall of my horse ... as not only to subject me to unceasing pain since, but to completely disable me from further service in the saddle without that lengthened rest and treatment which cannot be had within the time of an ordinary furlough." Colonel, 110 IN Minute Men, July 12, 1863. Honorably mustered out, July 15, 1863. Battle honors: New Madrid, Fort Pillow, Memphis, White River Expedition.

Born: Dec. 5, 1810 LeRoy, NY
Died: Nov. 29, 1892 Logansport, IN
Education: Attended Middlebury Academy, Wyoming, NY, and Geneva (NY) College
Occupation: Physician
Offices/Honors: Indiana House of Representatives, 1836–37 and 1839–40. U.S. House of Representatives, 1849–53. U.S. Senate, 1857–61.
Miscellaneous: Resided Logansport, Cass Co., IN. Father-in-law of Colonel Charles Denby (80 IN Infantry).
Buried: Mount Hope Cemetery, Logansport, IN (Section 13, Lot 152)
References: *Biographical and Genealogical History of Cass, Miami, Howard and Tipton Counties, IN.* Chicago, IL, 1898. *A Biographical History of*

John Watson Foster (John W. Coons, comp. *Indiana at Shiloh.* Indianapolis, Indiana, 1904).

manded 2 Division, Cavalry Corps, Army of the Ohio, Nov. 1863–Feb. 1864. Resigned March 12, 1864, "on account of the peculiar situation of my business and family affairs imperatively requiring my attention." Colonel, 136 IN Infantry, May 23, 1864. Honorably mustered out, Sept. 2, 1864. Battle honors: Fort Donelson, Shiloh, East Tennessee Campaign, Knoxville Campaign.

Born: March 2, 1836 Pike Co., IN
Died: Nov. 15, 1917 Washington, DC
Education: Graduated Indiana University, Bloomington, IN, 1855. Attended Harvard Law School, Cambridge, MA.
Occupation: Lawyer, newspaper editor, and diplomat
Offices/Honors: U.S. Minister to Mexico, 1873–80. U.S. Minister to Russia, 1880–81. U.S. Minister to Spain, 1883–85. U.S. Secretary of State, 1892–93.
Miscellaneous: Resided Evansville, Vanderburgh Co., IN, to 1873; and Washington, DC. Grandfather of U.S. Secretary of State John Foster Dulles.
Buried: Oak Hill Cemetery, Evansville, IN (Section 19, Lot 55)
References: *Dictionary of American Biography. National Cyclopedia of American Biography.* Daniel W. Snepp. *John W. Foster: Evansville's Distinguished Citizen.* N.p., 1975. George I. Reed, editor. *Encyclopedia of Biography of Indiana.* Chicago, IL, 1895. Joseph P. Elliott. *A History of Evansville and Vanderburgh County, IN.* Evansville, IN, 1897. Obituary, *New York Times,* Nov. 16, 1917. Military Service File, National Archives. John W. Foster. *War Stories for My Grandchildren.* Washington, DC, 1918. John W. Foster. *Diplomatic Memoirs.* Boston and New York, 1909.

Charles Theodore Fournier

Captain, Deutscher Jager, 5 IN Legion (Perry County), Aug. 13, 1861. Lieutenant Colonel, 5 IN Legion, Nov. 7, 1861. Colonel 5 IN Legion (Perry County), Jan. 2, 1862. Battle honors: Morgan's Ohio Raid.

Born: Feb. 11, 1830 France
Died: April 28, 1865 Cannelton, IN
Occupation: Brewer
Miscellaneous: Resided Cannelton, Perry Co., IN
Buried: Place of burial unknown
References: Obituary, *New Albany Daily Ledger,* May 5, 1865. *Report of Major General Love of the Indiana Legion.* Indianapolis, IN, 1863. *Operations of the Indiana Legion and Minute Men, 1863–4. Documents Presented to the General Assembly, with the Governor's Message, Jan. 6, 1865.* Indianapolis, IN, 1865. John P. Etter. *The Indiana Legion: A Civil War Militia.* Carmel, IN, 2006. Thomas J. De la Hunt. *Perry County: A History.* Indianapolis, IN, 1916.

Alexander Fowler

Captain, Co. B, 15 IN Infantry, June 14, 1861. Major, 15 IN Infantry, Oct. 21, 1861. Colonel, 99 IN Infantry, Oct. 28, 1862. Commanded 3 Brigade, 4 Division, 15 Army Corps, Army of the Tennessee, Aug. 20–Sept. 20, 1863 and Jan. 27–March 12, 1864. Commanded 3 Brigade, 2 Division, 15 Army Corps, Army of the Tennessee, Sept. 28–Nov. 2, 1864. Honorably mustered out Dec. 22, 1864. Battle honors: Jackson Campaign, Atlanta Campaign.

Born: June 10, 1822 Granville, Licking Co., OH
Died: March 17, 1907 Springfield, MO
Other Wars: Mexican War (Sergeant, Co. F, 1 U.S. Infantry). Lost right thumb by accidental explosion of powder horn.
Occupation: Carpenter before war. Lumber dealer and farmer after war.

Alexander Fowler (James Bonney, Photographer, South Bend, Indiana; Roger D. Hunt Collection, USAMHI [RG98S-CWP207.11]).

Miscellaneous: Resided South Bend, St. Joseph Co., IN, to 1868; Fort Scott, Bourbon Co., KS; Bronson, Bourbon Co., KS; and Springfield, Greene Co., MO, after 1900

Buried: Hazelwood Cemetery, Springfield, MO (Lot 305)

References: Daniel R. Lucas. *New History of the 99th Indiana Infantry.* Rockford, IL, 1900. Obituary, *Springfield Daily Leader,* March 20, 1907. Pension File and Military Service File, National Archives. Letters Received, Volunteer Service Branch, Adjutant General's Office, File F1014(VS)1864, National Archives.

John M. Garrett

Corporal, Co. G, 9 IN Infantry (3 months), April 24, 1861. Honorably mustered out, July 29, 1861. 2 Lieutenant, Co. G, 13 MO State Militia Cavalry, April 14, 1862. Resigned July 15, 1862, for "personal reasons." 1 Lieutenant, Co. H, 106 IN Minute Men, July 10, 1863. Honorably mustered out, July 17, 1863. Captain, Howard Guards, Howard County Regiment, IN Legion, July 31, 1863. Colonel, Howard County Regiment, IN Legion, Sept. 21, 1863. Captain, Co. E, 11 IN Cavalry, Dec. 23, 1863. Resigned Feb. 20, 1865, on account of disability due to "chronic ulceration of the bowels accompanied with diarrhea and great general debility."

Born: Nov. 18, 1833 Wayne Co., IN
Died: Sept. 2, 1911 Indianapolis, IN
Occupation: Carriage maker
Miscellaneous: Resided Kokomo, Howard Co., IN; Muncie, Delaware Co., IN; Columbus, Bartholomew Co., IN; and Indianapolis, IN
Buried: Crown Hill Cemetery, Indianapolis, IN (Section F, Lot 4417)
References: Pension File and Military Service File, National Archives. Obituary, *Indianapolis Star,* Sept. 4, 1911. John P. Etter. *The Indiana Legion: A Civil War Militia.* Carmel, IN, 2006.

William Garver

Colonel, 101 IN Infantry, Sept. 6, 1862. Resigned May 30, 1863, due to "general functional derangement of vital organs rendering him wholly unfit for the duties of his office."

Born: July 19, 1816 near Hamilton, Butler Co., OH
Died: June 14, 1895 Noblesville, IN
Occupation: Lawyer and farmer
Offices/Honors: Indiana Senate, 1848–51. Judge of Common Pleas Court, 1864–73. Indiana House of Representatives, 1877.
Miscellaneous: Resided Noblesville, Hamilton Co., IN.
Buried: Riverside Cemetery, Noblesville, IN

William Garver (post-war) (Thomas B. Helm. *History of Hamilton County, Indiana.* Chicago, Illinois, 1880).

References: *Portrait and Biographical Record of Madison and Hamilton Counties, IN.* Chicago, IL, 1893. Thomas B. Helm. *History of Hamilton County, IN.* Chicago, IL, 1880. *A Biographical History of Eminent and Self-Made Men of the State of Indiana.* Cincinnati, OH, 1880. Obituary, *Noblesville Democrat,* June 21, 1895. Rebecca A. Shepherd, Charles W. Calhoun, Elizabeth Shanahan-Shoemaker, and Alan F. January, editors. *A Biographical Directory of the Indiana General Assembly.* Vol. 1, 1816–1899. Indianapolis, IN, 1980. Pension File and Military Service File, National Archives. Joe H. Burgess. *Hamilton County and the Civil War.* N.p., 1967.

James Gavin

1 Lieutenant, Adjutant, 7 IN Infantry (3 months), April 26, 1861. Honorably mustered out, Aug. 25, 1861. Lieutenant Colonel, 7 IN Infantry (3 years), Sept. 13, 1861. Colonel, 7 IN Infantry, Nov. 27, 1861. Temporarily assigned as *Colonel,* 76 IN Infantry (30 days), July 19, 1862, while at home on leave. GSW right breast, 2nd Bull Run, VA, Aug. 30, 1862. Nominated as Brig. Gen., U.S. Volunteers, Nov. 29, 1862. Nomination withdrawn, Feb. 12, 1863. Commanded 2 Brigade, 1 Division, 1 Army Corps, Army of the Potomac, Nov. 20–Dec. 22, 1862 and Jan. 18–March 26, 1863. Still suffering from the effects of his wound, he resigned April 22, 1863, due to "the situation of a complicated busi-

James Gavin (copy of image in Richard S. Skidmore Collection, a gift from the late Mary Selch).

ness neglected for two years..." and "domestic misfortunes which imperatively require immediate and constant personal attention." Colonel, 104 IN Minute Men, July 10, 1863. Honorably mustered out, July 18, 1863. Colonel, 134 IN Infantry, May 23, 1864. Honorably mustered out, Sept. 2, 1864. Battle honors: Port Republic, 2nd Bull Run, Fredericksburg, Morgan's Ohio Raid.

Born: March 31, 1830 Butler Co., OH
Died: July 4, 1873 Cincinnati, OH
Occupation: Lawyer
Offices/Honors: County Clerk, Decatur Co., IN, 1864–67
Miscellaneous: Resided Greensburg, Decatur Co., IN; and Cincinnati, OH
Buried: South Park Cemetery, Greensburg, IN (Old Ground, Section 2, Lot 149)
References: *A Biographical History of Eminent and Self-Made Men of the State of Indiana.* Cincinnati, OH, 1880. Obituary, *The Decatur Press*, July 12, 1873. Lewis A. Harding, editor. *History of Decatur County, Indiana, Its People, Industries and Institutions.* Indianapolis, IN, 1915. *Atlas of Decatur County, Indiana.* Chicago, 1882. Pension File and Military Service File, National Archives. Letters Received, Volunteer Service Branch, Adjutant General's Office, File G960(VS)1862, National Archives. Orville Thomson. *From Philippi to Appomattox: Narrative of the Service of the 7th Indiana Infantry in the War for the Union.* N.p., 1904. John P. Etter. *The Indiana Legion: A Civil War Militia.* Carmel, IN, 2006.

Carter Gazlay

Lieutenant Colonel, 37 IN Infantry, Sept. 20, 1861. Colonel, 37 IN Infantry, April 8, 1862. Dismissed Aug. 13, 1862, having been found guilty of conduct unbecoming an officer and a gentleman, for selling "to one Henry Eastman a pair of horses and 22 bales of cotton that had been stolen."

Born: June 15, 1828 Patriot, IN
Died: July 7, 1909 Iola, KS
Occupation: Lawyer
Miscellaneous: Resided Lawrenceburg, Dearborn Co., IN, before war; Cincinnati, OH, 1862–92; Pratt, Pratt Co., KS, 1892–1904; Iola, Allen Co., KS, 1904–09
Buried: Patriot Cemetery, Patriot, Switzerland Co., IN
References: Pension File and Military Service File, National Archives. Obituary, *Vevay Reveille*, July 15, 1909. Thomas P. Lowry. *Tarnished Eagles: The Courts-Martial of Fifty Union Colonels and Lieutenant Colonels.* Mechanicsburg, PA, 1997. Letters Received, Volunteer Service Branch, Adjutant General's Office, File G1012(VS)1862, National Archives. Court-martial Case Files, 1809–1894, File KK-194, National Archives. Wanda L. Morford. *Switzerland County, Indiana, Cemetery Inscriptions, 1817–1985.* Cincinnati, OH, 1986. George H. Puntenney. *History of the 37th Regiment of Indiana Infantry Volunteers.* Rushville, IN, 1896. Obituary, *Cincinnati Enquirer*, July 8, 1909.

Augustus Goelzer

Captain, Co. G, 60 IN Infantry, Feb. 20, 1862. Lieutenant Colonel, 60 IN Infantry, Nov. 11, 1863. *Colonel,* 60 IN Infantry, April 19, 1864. Commanded Post of Thibodeaux, District of LaFourche, LA, July–Oct. 1864. Honorably mustered out, March 21, 1865. Battle honors: Arkansas Post, Red River Campaign.

Born: Sept. 29, 1827 Berlin, Germany
Died: May 11, 1889 Scranton, MS
Occupation: Served in Prussian army before coming to America in 1853. Later engaged in mercantile business.
Miscellaneous: Resided Haubstadt, Gibson Co., IN; Fort Branch, Gibson Co., IN; Mobile, AL; and Scranton (now Pascagoula), Jackson Co., MS
Buried: Greenwood Cemetery, Pascagoula, MS (South Section)
References: Research files of Robert A. Goelzer, Jr., courtesy of John A. Stovall. Military Service

File, National Archives. Else Martin. *Cemeteries of Jackson County, Mississippi; A Requiem*. Pascagoula, MS, 2008. Letters Received, Colored Troops Branch, Adjutant General's Office, File G8(CT)1863, National Archives. Obituary, *Mobile Daily Register*, May 19, 1889.

Michael Gooding

Captain, Co. A, 22 IN Infantry, Aug. 15, 1861. Major, 22 IN Infantry, May 10, 1862. Colonel, 22 IN Infantry, June 13, 1862. Commanded 1 Brigade, 4 Division, Army of the Mississippi, Aug. 12–Sept. 26, 1862. Commanded 30 Brigade, 9 Division, 3 Army Corps, Army of the Ohio, Sept.–Nov. 1862. Wounded and taken prisoner, Perryville, KY, Oct. 8, 1862. Paroled Oct. 9, 1862. While under arrest and awaiting trial "for complicity in woman stealing" and allowing "the said woman ... dressed in men's clothing to ride in the rear of his regiment through the streets of Knoxville, TN, thereby exciting the laughter and derision of all beholders ... to the great disgrace of the command and the service," he resigned Feb. 7, 1864, claiming "chronic diarrhea and soreness of the lungs for the last 18 months." Major Gen. Gordon Granger accepted his resignation "for the benefit of the service," with the added comment, "He has never been either useful nor ornamental to the service." Battle honors: Perryville, Stone's River, Tullahoma Campaign, Missionary Ridge.

Born: 1830? Prussia

Michael Gooding (Indiana Historical Society, P0310 [Indiana Civil War Carte de Visite Portraits]).

Died: Nov. 29, 1864 Murfreesboro, TN (disease of stomach and bowels)

Occupation: Brewer

Miscellaneous: Resided Vernon, Jennings Co., IN

Buried: Garland Brook Cemetery, Columbus, IN (Section 28, Lot 281)

References: Pension File and Military Service File, National Archives. *Souvenir and Official Program 19th Annual Encampment, Department of Indiana, GAR and Auxiliary Societies, Columbus, IN, May 17–20, 1898*. Louisville, KY, 1898. Letters Received, Volunteer Service Branch, Adjutant General's Office, Files L456(VS)1863 and O56(VS)1864, National Archives. Randolph V. Marshall. *An Historical Sketch of the 22nd Regiment Indiana Volunteers, from Its Organization to the Close of the War, Its Battles, Its Marches, and Its Hardships, Its Brave Officers and Its Honored Dead*. Madison, IN, 1884.

Felix William Graham

Captain, Co. G, 3 IN Cavalry, Sept. 10, 1861. Resigned April 9, 1862, due to "extreme debility resulting from a severe attack of typhoid fever." Captain, Co. F, 5 IN Cavalry, Aug. 30, 1862. Major, 5 IN Cavalry, Oct. 2, 1862. Colonel, 5 IN Cavalry, Dec. 10, 1862. Commanded 2 Brigade, 4 Division, 23 Army Corps, Army of the Ohio, Aug. 21–28, 1863. Commanded 2 Brigade, 2 Division, Cavalry Corps, Army of the Ohio, Nov.–Dec. 1863. Resigned Dec. 15, 1863, "to devote my attention to the comfort and well-being of my family," since "my wife is very ill ... and unable to give

Michael Gooding (courtesy Ralph U. Gooding).

any attention to a large family of children who absolutely need it." Battle honors: Knoxville Campaign.
Born: July 19, 1831 Johnson Co., IN
Died: April 9, 1902 Macon, GA
Occupation: Farmer and trader
Miscellaneous: Resided Franklin, Johnson Co., IN; Clermont, Marion Co., IN; Stewartsville, DeKalb Co., MO; Pendleton, Madison Co., IN; Anderson, Madison Co., IN; Columbus, Bartholomew Co., IN; and Indianapolis, IN
Buried: Crown Hill Cemetery, Indianapolis, IN (Section 9, Lot 880)
References: Pension File and Military Service File, National Archives. Obituary, *Indianapolis Sentinel*, April 10, 1902. Obituary, *Indianapolis Journal*, April 10, 1902. John Graham. *Our Graham Family History*. Woodbridge, VA, 1992. Washington L. Sanford. *History of 14th Illinois Cavalry and the Brigades to Which It Belonged*. Chicago, IL, 1898. *Annual Reunion of the Fifth Indiana Cavalry Association*. Indianapolis, IN, 1883–1919.

Isaac Pusey Gray

Colonel, 4 IN Cavalry, Sept. 4, 1862. "Suffering from chronic gastritis, with corresponding disease of the liver and kidneys, together with hemorrhoids," he resigned Feb. 11, 1863. Colonel, 106 IN Minute Men, July 12, 1863. Honorably mustered out, July 17, 1863. Captain, Union City Guards, Randolph Battalion, IN Legion, Aug. 8, 1863. Resigned Nov. 16, 1863. Battle honors: Morgan's Ohio Raid.
Born: Oct. 18, 1828 Chester Co., PA
Died: Feb. 14, 1895 Mexico City, Mexico
Occupation: Dry goods merchant before war. Lawyer, grain merchant, and politician after war.
Offices/Honors: Indiana Senate, 1869 and 1871. Lieutenant Governor of Indiana, 1877–80. Governor of Indiana, 1880–81, 1885–89. U.S. Minister to Mexico, 1893–95.
Miscellaneous: Resided Union City, Randolph Co., IN, to 1885; and Indianapolis, IN, after 1885.
Buried: Union City Cemetery, Union City, IN
References: *Dictionary of American Biography*. George I. Reed, editor. *Encyclopedia of Biography of Indiana*. Chicago, IL, 1895. Pension File and Military Service File, National Archives. Rebecca A. Shepherd, Charles W. Calhoun, Elizabeth Shanahan-Shoemaker, and Alan F. January, editors. *A Biographical Directory of the Indiana General Assembly*. Vol. 1, 1816–1899. Indianapolis, IN, 1980. *A Biographical History of Eminent and Self-Made Men of the State of Indiana*. Cincinnati, OH, 1880. *A Portrait and Biographical Record of Delaware and Randolph Counties, IN*. Chicago, IL, 1894. Will Cumback and J. B. Maynard, editors. *Men of Progress, Indiana*. Indianapolis, IN, 1899. Richard J. Reid. *Fourth Indiana Cavalry: A History*. Olaton, KY, 1994. *Operations of the Indiana Legion and Minute Men, 1863-4. Documents Presented to the General Assembly, with the Governor's Message, Jan. 6, 1865*. Indianapolis, IN, 1865.

Benjamin Moore Gregory

Captain, Zionsville Union Guards, Boone County Regiment, IN Legion, June 17, 1861. Captain, Co. F, 10 IN Infantry, Sept. 2, 1861. Major, 10 IN Infantry, May 20, 1862. Suffering from intermittent fever, he resigned July 13, 1862, since "my health is not sufficiently good to endure longer the exposure of camp life; and my business at home requires my personal supervision to prevent large sacrifices." Colonel, 102 IN Minute Men, July 10, 1863. Honorably mustered out, July 17, 1863. Colonel, Boone County Regiment, IN Legion, April 16, 1864. Major, 135 IN Infantry, May 25, 1864. Honorably mustered out, Sept. 29, 1864. Battle honors: Mill Springs, Morgan's Ohio Raid.
Born: Nov. 23, 1829 Burns, Allegany Co., NY
Died: July 15, 1899 Zionsville, IN
Occupation: Hardware merchant
Miscellaneous: Resided Zionsville, Boone Co., IN
Buried: Crown Hill Cemetery, Indianapolis, IN (Section 21, Lot 78)

Isaac Pusey Gray (as governor of Indiana) (George I. Reed, ed. *Encyclopedia of Biography of Indiana*. Chicago, Illinois, 1895).

Benjamin Moore Gregory (post-war) (Samuel Harden and D. Spahr, comps. *Early Life and Times in Boone County, Indiana*. Indianapolis, Indiana, 1887).

References: *Portrait and Biographical Record of Boone and Clinton Counties, IN*. Chicago, IL, 1895. Obituary, *Lebanon Pioneer*, July 20, 1899. Kenyon Stevenson. *A History of the William Carroll Family of Allegany County, NY*. York, PA, 1929. Samuel Harden and D. Spahr, compilers. *Early Life and Times in Boone County, Indiana*. Indianapolis, IN, 1887. Military Service File, National Archives. James Birney Shaw. *History of the 10th Regiment Indiana Volunteer Infantry, Three Months and Three Years Organizations*. Lafayette, IN, 1912. Obituary, *Indianapolis Sentinel*, July 16, 1899. *Operations of the Indiana Legion and Minute Men, 1863–4. Documents Presented to the General Assembly, with the Governor's Message, Jan. 6, 1865*. Indianapolis, IN, 1865.

Samuel Oscar Gregory

Private, Co. F, 9 IN Infantry (3 months), April 24, 1861. Honorably mustered out, July 29, 1861. 2 Lieutenant, Co. C, 29 IN Infantry, Aug. 27, 1861. Captain, Co. F, 29 IN Infantry, Dec. 1, 1863. Captain, Co. C, 29 IN Infantry, May 17, 1864. Lieutenant Colonel, 29 IN Infantry, Nov. 1, 1864. Colonel, 29 IN Infantry, Feb. 25, 1865. Honorably mustered out, Dec. 2, 1865. Battle honors: Stone's River.
Born: Jan. 20, 1843 La Porte, IN
Died: April 26, 1899 San Francisco, CA
Occupation: Farmer before war. Manufacturer

Samuel Oscar Gregory (T. M. Schleier, Photographer, Cor. Union and Cherry Sts., and 27 Public Square, Nashville, Tennessee; Craig Dunn Collection).

of wagon wheels, fruit grower, Post Office clerk, and manufacturer's agent after war.
Miscellaneous: Resided La Porte, La Porte Co., IN, and Chicago, IL, to 1875; Alma, Santa Clara Co., CA, and San Francisco, CA, after 1875
Buried: San Francisco National Cemetery, San Francisco, CA (George H. Thomas Post Plot, Grave 278)
References: Pension File and Military Service File, National Archives. H. S. Foote, editor. *Pen Pictures from the Garden of the World, or Santa Clara County, CA*. Chicago, IL, 1888. Obituary, *San Francisco Call*, April 27, 1899. Obituary, *San Francisco Chronicle*, April 27, 1899. Grant Gregory, compiler. *Ancestors and Descendants of Henry Gregory*. Provincetown, MA, 1938.

John Frederick Grill

Captain, Co. C, 24 IN Infantry, July 2, 1861. Major, 24 IN Infantry, May 14, 1862. Acting AIG, Staff of Brig. Gen. Alvin P. Hovey, 12 Division, 13 Army Corps, Army of the Tennessee, May–July 1863. Lieutenant Colonel, 24 IN Infantry, Jan. 27, 1864. Honorably mustered out, Dec. 31, 1864. Colonel, 143 IN Infantry, Feb. 20, 1865. Commanded 5 Sub-District, District of Middle Tennessee, and

John Frederick Grill (copy of image in the Craig Dunn Collection).

Post of Clarksville, TN, June–Sept. 1865. Honorably mustered out, Oct. 17, 1865. Battle honors: Vicksburg Campaign, Jackson Campaign.
Born: Sept. 11, 1821 Offenbach, Bavaria, Germany
Died: April 6, 1880 Evansville, IN
Occupation: Tanner, produce merchant, and grocer
Miscellaneous: Resided Evansville, Vanderburgh Co., IN
Buried: Oak Hill Cemetery, Evansville, IN (Section 8, Lot 50)
References: Pension File and Military Service File, National Archives. Joseph P. Elliott. *History of Evansville and Vanderburgh County, IN.* Evansville, IN, 1897. Obituary, *Tagliche Evansville Union,* April 7, 1880. Richard J. Fulfer. *A History of the Trials and Hardships of the 24th Indiana Volunteer Infantry.* Indianapolis, IN, 1913.

Whedon Wyllys Griswold

1 Lieutenant, Co. H, 30 IN Infantry, Sept. 15, 1861. Captain, Co. H, 30 IN Infantry, Feb. 2, 1863. GSW head, Lovejoy's Station, GA, Sept. 2, 1864. Major, 30 IN Infantry, Dec. 3, 1864. Colonel, 152 IN Infantry, March 9, 1865. Commanded 1 Brigade, 3 Division, Army of the Shenandoah, June–July 1865. Honorably mustered out, Aug. 30, 1865. Battle honors: Atlanta Campaign (Lovejoy's Station).
Born: Dec. 28, 1829 Norfolk, CT
Died: Jan. 23, 1893 Chanute, KS
Occupation: Lawyer before war. Lawyer and real estate, loan and insurance agent after war.

Whedon Wyllys Griswold (copy of image in the Craig Dunn Collection).

Whedon Wyllys Griswold (photograph by J. A. Shoaff's Art Gallery, No. 8 Cor. Main & Calhoun, Fort Wayne, Indiana; Mark Weldon Collection).

Offices/Honors: County Recorder, DeKalb Co., IN, 1855–59. Auditor, DeKalb Co., IN, 1866–70. Auditor, Stevens Co., MN, 1874–82.
Miscellaneous: Resided Auburn, DeKalb Co.,

IN, to 1872; Morris, Stevens Co., MN, 1872–91; Chanute, Neosho Co., KS, 1891–93

Buried: Elmwood Cemetery, Chanute, KS

References: Pension File and Military Service File, National Archives. *Illustrated Album of Biography of Pope and Stevens Counties, MN.* Chicago, IL, 1888. Warren Upham and Mrs. Rose Barteau Dunlap, compilers. *Minnesota Biographies, 1655–1912. Minnesota Historical Society Collections, Vol. 14.* St. Paul, MN, 1912. Letters Received, Volunteer Service Branch, Adjutant General's Office, File A1414(VS)1865, National Archives. Obituary, *Morris Sun*, Feb. 2, 1893. *History of DeKalb County, IN.* Indianapolis, IN, 1914. Edna W. Townsend, compiler and editor. *Griswold Family: England-America.* Middleboro, MA, 1978.

James Reed Hallowell

Private, Co. C, 11 IN Infantry (3 months), April 23, 1861. Honorably mustered out, Aug. 4, 1861. 2 Lieutenant, Co. I, 31 IN Infantry, Sept. 5, 1861. 1 Lieutenant, Co. I, 31 IN Infantry, Jan. 7, 1862. GSW right hip and right arm, Fort Donelson, TN, Feb. 15, 1862. Captain, Co. I, 31 IN Infantry, April 10, 1862. Acting AAG, 1 Brigade, 1 Division, 4 Army Corps, Army of the Cumberland, May 22–August 8, 1864. Major, 31 IN Infantry, Sept. 24, 1864. Lieutenant Colonel, 31 IN Infantry, Sept. 25, 1864. *Colonel*, 31 IN Infantry, March 13, 1865. Bvt. Colonel, USV, March 13, 1865, for gallant and meritorious services during the war. Honorably mustered out, Dec. 8, 1865. Battle honors: Fort Donelson, Stone's River, Chickamauga, Nashville.

Born: Dec. 27, 1841 Montgomery Co., PA

Died: June 24, 1898 Crawfordsville, IN

James Reed Hallowell (post-war) (*The United States Biographical Dictionary.* Kansas Volume. Chicago and Kansas City, 1879).

Education: Attended Indiana Asbury (now De-Pauw) University, Greencastle, IN

Occupation: Miller before war. Lawyer after war.

Offices/Honors: Kansas House of Representatives, 1876. Kansas Senate, 1877–79. U.S. District Attorney, 1879–85.

Miscellaneous: Resided Bellmore, Parke Co., IN, before war; Rockville, Parke Co., IN, 1866–1869; Baxter Springs, Cherokee Co., KS, 1871–77; Columbus, Cherokee Co., KS, 1877–89; and Wichita, Sedgwick Co., KS, after 1889

Buried: Oak Hill Cemetery, Crawfordsville, IN (Section 10, Lot 112)

References: *The United States Biographical Dictionary.* Kansas Volume. Chicago and Kansas City, 1879. Obituary Circular, Whole No. 200, Kansas MOLLUS. Obituary, *Crawfordsville Daily Argus News*, June 25, 1898. Pension File and Military Service File, National Archives. John Thomas Smith. *A History of the 31st Regiment of Indiana Volunteer Infantry in the War of the Rebellion.* Cincinnati, OH, 1900. Nathaniel T. Allison. *History of Cherokee County, Kansas, and Representative Citizens.* Chicago, IL, 1904. Letters Received, Volunteer Service Branch, Adjutant General's Office, File H352(VS)1870, National Archives.

Orville S. Hamilton

Colonel, 86 IN Infantry, Sept. 6, 1862. Relieved from command prior to the battle of Stone's River due to his inability to execute basic regimental movements, he resigned Jan. 13, 1863, citing "the

James Reed Hallowell (Hall & Co.'s Photograph Gallery, Cor. College & Cedar Sts., Nashville, Tennessee).

health of my family, my pecuniary embarrassments at home, and my inexperience in military matters." In accepting his resignation, Brig. Gen. Samuel Beatty commented, "This officer is wholly incompetent to command and an acceptance will be a benefit to the service. His officers refuse to go into action under his command." Battle honors: Stone's River.

Born: March 11, 1819 Fleming Co., KY
Died: Sept. 29, 1877 Lebanon, IN
Occupation: Lawyer
Offices/Honors: Indiana House of Representatives, 1859
Miscellaneous: Resided Lebanon, Boone Co., IN
Buried: Cedar Hill Cemetery, Lebanon, IN
References: James A. Barnes, James R. Carnahan, and Thomas H. B. McCain. *The 86th Regiment Indiana Volunteer Infantry. A Narrative of Its Services in the Civil War of 1861–1865.* Crawfordsville, IN, 1895. Obituary, *Lebanon Patriot,* Oct. 4, 1877. Pension File and Military Service File, National Archives. Rebecca A. Shepherd, Charles W. Calhoun, Elizabeth Shanahan-Shoemaker, and Alan F. January, editors. *A Biographical Directory of the Indiana General Assembly.* Vol. 1, 1816–1899. Indianapolis, IN, 1980.

John W. Hammond

1 Lieutenant, Co. E, 65 IN Infantry, Aug. 13, 1862. Captain, Co. K, 65 IN Infantry, May 2, 1863. Acting AAG, 2 Division, Cavalry Corps, Army of

John W. Hammond (copy of image in the Craig Dunn Collection).

John W. Hammond (F. W. Knight, Photographer, Henderson, Kentucky; John Sickles Collection).

the Ohio, Feb.–March, 1864. Lieutenant Colonel, 65 IN Infantry, Sept. 6, 1864. *Colonel,* 65 IN Infantry, Sept. 7, 1864. Honorably mustered out, June 22, 1865. Battle honors: Franklin, Campaign of the Carolinas.

Born: Aug. 31, 1840 Boonville, IN
Died: April 11, 1904 Oskaloosa, IA
Education: Attended Iowa Wesleyan College, Mount Pleasant, IA
Occupation: Miller before war. Lawyer, manufacturer and banker after war.
Miscellaneous: Resided Ottumwa, Wapello Co., IA, to 1867 and 1880–85; Prairie City, Jasper Co., IA, 1867–80; New Sharon, Mahaska Co., IA; and Oskaloosa, Mahaska Co., IA
Buried: Forest Cemetery, Oskaloosa, IA (Section 48, Lot 1)
References: Pension File and Military Service File, National Archives. Obituary, *Oskaloosa Herald,* April 14, 1904.

Gilbert Hathaway

Colonel, 73 IN Infantry, Aug. 21, 1862. GSW heart, Blount's Plantation, AL, May 2, 1863. Battle honors: Stone's River, Streight's Raid (Blount's Plantation).

Gilbert Hathaway (Wm. M. Scott, Photographer, La Porte, Indiana; John Sickles Collection).

Born: Jan. 8, 1813 Sag Harbor, NY
Died: May 2, 1863 KIA Blount's Plantation, AL
Education: Attended Kenyon College, Gambier, OH
Occupation: Lawyer
Miscellaneous: Resided La Porte, La Porte Co., IN
Buried: Pine Lake Cemetery, La Porte, IN
References: George I. Reed, editor. *Encyclopedia of Biography of Indiana*. Chicago, IL, 1895. *History of the 73rd Indiana Volunteers in the War of 1861–65*. Washington, DC, 1909. Elizabeth S. Versailles, compiler. *Hathaways of America*. Northampton, MA, 1970. David Stevenson. *Indiana's Roll of Honor*. Indianapolis, IN, 1864. Pension File and Military Service File, National Archives. Mattie Liston-Griswold, compiler. *Tracy Genealogy: Ancestors and Descendants of Thomas Tracy of Lenox, Massachusetts*. Kalamazoo, MI, 1900. Jasper Packard. *History of La Porte County, Indiana, and Its Townships, Towns and Cities*. La Porte, IN, 1876.

Benjamin F. Hays

Major, 21 IN Infantry, July 24, 1861. GSW foot, Baton Rouge, LA, Aug. 5, 1862. Lieutenant Colonel, 1 IN Heavy Artillery, May 18, 1863. Colonel, 1 IN Heavy Artillery, Feb. 3, 1865. Commanded Dis-

Gilbert Hathaway (Wm. M. Scott, Photographer, La Porte, Indiana; Richard F. Carlile Collection).

Benjamin F. Hays (photograph by A. D. Lytle, Main Street, Baton Rouge, Louisiana; Craig Dunn Collection).

trict of South Alabama, Department of Alabama, July–Dec. 1865. Honorably mustered out, Jan. 10, 1866. Battle honors: Baton Rouge, Mobile Campaign.
Born: Sept. 4, 1826 Greene Co., TN
Died: Jan. 14, 1872 Gosport, IN
Other Wars: Mexican War (2 Lieutenant, Co. B, 4 IN Infantry)
Occupation: Merchant
Offices/Honors: Indiana House of Representatives, 1867
Miscellaneous: Resided Gosport, Owen Co., IN
Buried: Gosport Cemetery, Gosport, IN
References: Pension File and Military Service File, National Archives. Rebecca A. Shepherd, Charles W. Calhoun, Elizabeth Shanahan-Shoemaker, and Alan F. January, editors. *A Biographical Directory of the Indiana General Assembly.* Vol. 1, 1816–1899. Indianapolis, IN, 1980. Letters Received, Volunteer Service Branch, Adjutant General's Office, File H1752(VS)1863, National Archives. Charles Blanchard, editor. *Counties of Clay and Owen, Indiana. Historical and Biographical.* Chicago, IL, 1884. Phillip E. Faller. *The Indiana Jackass Regiment in the Civil War: A History of the 21st Infantry/1st Heavy Artillery Regiment, with a Roster.* Jefferson, NC, 2013.

George Whitfield Hazzard

Captain, 4 U.S. Artillery, July 6, 1859. Colonel, 37 IN Infantry, Oct. 17, 1861. In arrest upon various charges attributed to his "great tyranny to his troops," he resigned March 5, 1862, having been recalled to his Regular Army command. Commanded Artillery, 1 Division, 2 Army Corps, Army of the Potomac, April–June 1862. Shell wound leg, White Oak Swamp, VA, June 30, 1862. Battle honors: Peninsular Campaign (Fair Oaks, White Oak Swamp).
Born: Aug. 31, 1825 Seaford, DE
Died: Aug. 14, 1862 DOW Baltimore, MD
Education: Graduated U.S. Military Academy, West Point, NY, 1847
Other Wars: Mexican War (2 Lieutenant, 4 U.S. Artillery)
Occupation: Regular Army (Captain, 4 U.S. Artillery)
Miscellaneous: Resided Brookville, Franklin Co., IN
Buried: New Cathedral Cemetery, Baltimore, MD (Section H, Lot 278)
References: Cullum File, U.S. Military Academy Library. Pension File and Military Service File, National Archives. George H. Puntenney. *History of the 37th Regiment of Indiana Infantry Volunteers.* Rushville, IN, 1896. George W. Cullum.

George Whitfield Hazzard (U.S. Military Academy Library).

Biographical Register of the Officers and Graduates of the U.S. Military Academy. Third Edition. Boston and New York, 1891. "A Tyrannous Colonel Rebuked," *New York Daily Tribune,* Feb. 19, 1862.

Joshua Healey

Corporal, Co. G, 9 IN Infantry (3 months), April 24, 1861. Honorably mustered out, July 29, 1861. Captain, Co. G, 9 IN Infantry (3 years), Aug. 29, 1861. Major, 128 IN Infantry, April 19, 1864. Acting AIG, 3 Brigade, 3 Division, 23 Army Corps, Army of the Ohio, Aug. 29–Sept. 12, 1864. Acting AIG, Staff of Brig. Gen. Thomas H. Ruger, 1 Division, 23 Army Corps, Jan.–March 1865. Colonel, 151 IN Infantry, April 13, 1865. Honorably mustered out, Sept. 19, 1865. Battle honors: Atlanta Campaign (Resaca), Campaign of the Carolinas (Kinston).
Born: Nov. 18, 1838 Beauharnois Co., Quebec, Canada
Died: Jan. 2, 1880 Goodland, IN
Occupation: School teacher and farmer before war. Printer and newspaper publisher after war.
Miscellaneous: Resided Logansport, Cass Co., IN; Rensselaer, Jasper Co., IN; and Goodland, Newton Co., IN
Buried: Weston Cemetery, Rensselaer, IN
References: Louis H. Hamilton and William Darroch, editors. *Standard History of Jasper and Newton Counties, IN.* Chicago and New York, 1916. *Biographical History of Tippecanoe, White, Jasper, Newton, Benton, Warren and Pulaski Counties, IN.* Chicago, IL, 1899. Pension File and Military

Joshua Healey (Archibald Gracie. *The Truth About Chickamauga*. Boston and New York, 1911).

Joshua Healey (Donald W. Healey Collection, USAMHI [RG98S-CWP18.77]).

Service File, National Archives. Obituary, *Indianapolis Daily Sentinel*, Jan. 7, 1880. Letters Received, Volunteer Service Branch, Adjutant General's Office, File I201(VS)1865, National Archives.

Albert Heath

1 Sergeant, Co. C, 9 IN Infantry (3 months), April 24, 1861. Honorably mustered out, July 29, 1861. Captain, Co. I, 44 IN Infantry, Nov. 10, 1861. GSW leg, Shiloh, TN, April 6, 1862. Lieutenant Colonel, 100 IN Infantry, Oct. 18, 1862. Shell wound left side of chest, Missionary Ridge, TN, Nov. 25, 1863. *Colonel,* 100 IN Infantry, Jan. 8, 1864. Resigned May 1, 1865, due to physical disability from wounds received in action. Battle honors: Shiloh, Jackson Campaign, Missionary Ridge, Atlanta Campaign (Resaca, Jonesborough, Lovejoy's Station).

Born: 1826? Erie Co., NY

Died: Sept. 19, 1887 Indian Diggings, El Dorado Co., CA

Occupation: Lawyer and mine operator

Miscellaneous: Resided Middlebury, Elkhart Co., IN, before war; Santa Cruz, Santa Cruz Co., CA; San Francisco, CA; and Volcano, Amador Co., CA, after war

Buried: Volcano Cemetery, Volcano, CA

References: Pension File and Military Service File, National Archives. Eli J. Sherlock. *Memorabilia of the Marches and Battles in Which the 100th Regiment of Indiana Infantry Volunteers Took an Ac-*

Albert Heath (Schwing & Rudd, Photographers, Army of the Cumberland; Mark Weldon Collection).

Albert Heath (copy of image in the Craig Dunn Collection).

John Abram Hendricks (U.S. Military Academy Library).

tive Part, War of the Rebellion, 1861–5. Kansas City, MO, 1896. John H. Rerick. *The 44th Indiana Volunteer Infantry: History of Its Services in the War of the Rebellion.* LaGrange, IN, 1880. Obituary, *Placerville Mountain Democrat,* Sept. 24, 1887. Henry S. K. Bartholomew. *Pioneer History of Elkhart County, Indiana, with Sketches and Stories.* Goshen, IN, 1930.

John Abram Hendricks

Colonel, 9 IN Legion (Jefferson County), June 10, 1861. Lieutenant Colonel, 22 IN Infantry, Aug. 15, 1861. GSW Pea Ridge, AR, March 7, 1862. Battle honors: Pea Ridge.
Born: March 7, 1823 Madison, IN
Died: March 7, 1862 KIA Pea Ridge, AR
Education: Attended Hanover (IN) College. Graduated Indiana University, Bloomington, IN, 1843.
Other Wars: Mexican War (Captain, 16 U.S. Infantry)
Occupation: Lawyer
Miscellaneous: Resided Madison, Jefferson Co., IN. Son of former Indiana Governor William Hendricks.
Buried: Fairmount Cemetery, Madison, IN
References: Theodore T. Scribner. *Indiana's Roll of Honor.* Indianapolis, Ind., 1866. Obituary, *Madison Daily Evening Courier,* March 18, 1862. Pension File and Military Service File, National Archives. *Souvenir and Official Program 19th Annual Encampment, Department of Indiana, GAR and Auxiliary Societies, Columbus, IN, May 17–20, 1898.* Louisville, KY, 1898. Randolph V. Marshall. *An Historical Sketch of the 22nd Regiment Indiana Volunteers, from Its Organization to the Close of the War, Its Battles, Its Marches, and Its Hardships, Its Brave Officers and Its Honored Dead.* Madison, IN, 1884. Theophilus A. Wylie. *Indiana University, Its History from 1820 to 1890.* Indianapolis, IN, 1890. *A Genealogical and Biographical Record of Decatur County, IN.* Chicago, IL, 1900.

Zephaniah Heustis

Colonel, 12 IN Legion (Dearborn County), Sept. 25, 1861. Resigned Sept. 1862.
Born: May 19, 1824 Manchester, Dearborn Co., IN
Died: March 18, 1892 Lawrenceburg, IN
Occupation: Railroad conductor and superintendent
Miscellaneous: Resided Lawrenceburg, Dearborn Co., IN
Buried: Greendale Cemetery, Lawrenceburg, IN (Section A, Lots 47–49–50, unmarked)
References: Obituary, *Lawrenceburg Register,* March 24, 1892. Obituary of wife, Elizabeth (Steele) Heustis, *Lawrenceburg Register,* July 17, 1879. Archibald Shaw, editor. *History of Dearborn County, IN.* Indianapolis, IN, 1915. Cemetery records, Greendale Cemetery, Lawrenceburg, IN. John P. Etter. *The Indiana Legion: A Civil War Militia.* Carmel, IN, 2006.

Cyrus Cooke Hines

Sergeant, Co. H, 11 IN Infantry (3 months), April 24, 1861. Captain, ADC, Staff of Brig. Gen. Thomas A. Morris, June 18, 1861. Major, 24 IN Infantry, July 31, 1861. Colonel, 57 IN Infantry, March 6, 1862. Shell wound right thigh, Stone's River, TN, Dec. 31, 1862. Resigned July 27, 1863, on account of physical disability "which the surgeons pronounce permanent." Battle honors: Shiloh, Stone's River.

Born: Dec. 10, 1830 Sandy Hill (now Hudson Falls), NY
Died: June 6, 1901 Indianapolis, IN
Education: Attended Uxbridge (MA) Academy
Occupation: Lawyer and judge
Offices/Honors: Circuit court judge, 1866–70
Miscellaneous: Resided Indianapolis, Marion Co., IN; and New York City, NY, after 1885
Buried: Crown Hill Cemetery, Indianapolis, IN (Section 7, Lot 1)
References: Pension File and Military Service File, National Archives. Charles W. Taylor. *Biographical Sketches and Review of the Bench and Bar of Indiana.* Indianapolis, IN, 1895. Obituary, *Indianapolis Sentinel,* June 7, 1901. Asbury L. Kerwood. *Annals of the 57th Regiment Indiana Volunteers, Marches, Battles, and Incidents of Army Life.* Dayton, OH, 1868.

Cyrus Cooke Hines (post-war) (Charles W. Taylor. *Biographical Sketches and Review of the Bench and Bar of Indiana.* Indianapolis, Indiana, 1895).

William E. Hollingsworth

Lieutenant Colonel, 2 IN Legion (Vanderburgh County), Sept. 28, 1861. Colonel, 2 IN Legion (Vanderburgh County), Nov. 30, 1861. Resigned May 1864. Captain, Co. F, 136 IN Infantry, May 21, 1864. Honorably mustered out, Sept. 2, 1864.

Born: June 2, 1822 Simpsonville, Shelby Co., KY
Died: March 14, 1892 Evansville, IN

William E. Hollingsworth (post-war) (Obituary, *Evansville Courier,* March 15, 1892).

Occupation: Wholesale queensware merchant
Miscellaneous: Resided Evansville, Vanderburgh Co., IN
Buried: Oak Hill Cemetery, Evansville, IN (Section 35, Lot 3)
References: Obituary, *Evansville Courier,* March 15, 1892. Obituary, *Evansville Journal,* March 15, 1892. Pension File, National Archives. J. Adger Stewart. *Descendants of Valentine Hollingsworth, Sr.* Louisville, KY, 1925. *History of Vanderburgh County, IN.* Madison, WI, 1889. *Report of Major General Love of the Indiana Legion.* Indianapolis, IN, 1863. John P. Etter. *The Indiana Legion: A Civil War Militia.* Carmel, IN, 2006.

Sampson McMillan Houston

Colonel, Montgomery County Regiment, IN Legion, Oct. 16, 1863.

Born: July 14, 1826 Scioto Co., OH
Died: Nov. 4, 1903 Irvington, IN
Education: Attended Wabash College, Crawfordsville, IN
Occupation: Farmer and stock raiser before war. Christian Church evangelist, brick manufacturer, contractor, real estate agent, and county court judge after war.
Miscellaneous: Resided Crawfordsville, Montgomery Co., IN, to 1873; Irvington, Marion Co., IN, 1873–84 and 1898–1903; and Springfield, Greene Co., MO, 1884–98
Buried: Crown Hill Cemetery, Indianapolis, IN (Section 27, Lot 129)
References: *Pictorial and Genealogical Record of Greene County, MO.* Chicago, IL, 1893. Obituary, *Indianapolis Journal,* Nov. 5, 1903. John P. Etter. *The Indiana Legion: A Civil War Militia.* Carmel, IN, 2006.

Robert Noble Hudson

Colonel, ADC, Staff of Major Gen. John C. Fremont, Sept. 20–Nov. 19, 1861. Colonel, Additional ADC, March 31, 1862. *Colonel,* 2 IN Cavalry, April 5, 1862. Declined. Provost Marshal, Staff of Major Gen. John C. Fremont, April 21–June 28, 1862. Resigned Aug. 26, 1863, "to enable me to take a command in the Indiana Legion." Colonel, 133 IN Infantry, May 17, 1864. Honorably mustered out, Sept. 5, 1864.
Born: Nov. 7, 1819 Brookville, IN
Died: Aug. 30, 1889 Terre Haute, IN
Education: Graduated Indiana Asbury (now DePauw) University, Greencastle, IN, 1844
Occupation: Lawyer and newspaper editor
Offices/Honors: Indiana House of Representatives, 1851–52, 1855
Miscellaneous: Resided Terre Haute, Vigo Co., IN
Buried: Highland Lawn Cemetery, Terre Haute, IN (Section 3, Lot 142)
References: Hiram W. Beckwith. *History of Vigo and Parke Counties, Together with Historic Notes on the Wabash Valley.* Chicago, IL, 1880. Obituary, *Terre Haute Express,* Aug. 31, 1889. Mike McCormick, "Wabash Valley Profiles: Robert N. Hudson," *Terre Haute Tribune-Star,* Sept. 18, 1999. Pension File, National Archives. Letters Received, Commission Branch, Adjutant General's Office, File H330(CB)1863, National Archives. Rebecca A. Shepherd, Charles W. Calhoun, Elizabeth Shanahan-Shoemaker, and Alan F. January, editors. *A Biographical Directory of the Indiana General Assembly.* Vol. 1, 1816–1899. Indianapolis, IN, 1980. Charles A. Martin, editor. *DePauw University: Alumnal Register of Officers, Faculties and Graduates, 1837–1900.* Greencastle, IN, 1901. William Raimond Baird. *Betas of Achievement.* New York City, NY, 1914.

James Standiford Hull

Major, 37 IN Infantry, Oct. 17, 1861. Lieutenant Colonel, 37 IN Infantry, April 26, 1862. Colonel, 37 IN Infantry, Aug. 14, 1862. GSW left hip, passing through the pelvis and into the right hip, Stone's River, TN, Dec. 31, 1862. Honorably mustered out, Oct. 27, 1864. Battle honors: Stone's River, Tullahoma Campaign.
Born: Aug. 12, 1821 North Bend, Hamilton Co., OH
Died: Dec. 19, 1876 Elgin, IL (killed by improper dosage of drugs at insane asylum)
Occupation: Farmer before war. Storekeeper after war.
Offices/Honors: Indiana Senate, 1861
Miscellaneous: Resided Elrod, Ripley Co., IN; and Moore's Hill, Dearborn Co., IN, before war; Nashville, TN; and Chicago, IL, after war
Buried: Rosehill Cemetery, Chicago, IL (Section G, Lot 258)
References: Lewis W. Hicks, compiler. *The Biographical Record of the Class of 1870 Yale College.*

Robert Noble Hudson (photograph by Charles D. Fredricks & Co. "Specialite," 587 Broadway, New York).

Boston, MA, 1911. Pension File and Military Service File, National Archives. James Sutherland. *Biographical Sketches of the Members of the Forty-First General Assembly of the State of Indiana with That of the State Officers and Judiciary.* Indianapolis, IN, 1861. Rebecca A. Shepherd, Charles W. Calhoun, Elizabeth Shanahan-Shoemaker, and Alan F. January, editors. *A Biographical Directory of the Indiana General Assembly.* Vol. 1, 1816–1899. Indianapolis, IN, 1980. George H. Puntenney. *History of the 37th Regiment of Indiana Infantry Volunteers.* Rushville, IN, 1896. Obituary, *Chicago Daily Tribune*, Dec. 23, 1876. Obituary, *Nashville Daily American*, Dec. 22, 1876. Letters Received, Volunteer Service Branch, Adjutant General's Office, File H317(VS)1870, National Archives.

George Humphrey

Major, 12 IN Infantry (1 year), May 15, 1861. Lieutenant Colonel, 12 IN Infantry, Aug. 26, 1861. Honorably mustered out, May 19, 1862. Colonel, 88 IN Infantry, Aug. 21, 1862. GSW right shoulder, Stone's River, TN, Jan. 3, 1863. His regiment being much reduced in strength (not requiring a colonel) and his business having been destroyed by fire, he resigned Oct. 17, 1863, since "my personal attention is demanded ... in order to enable me to save anything out of the wreck left me by the fire." Colonel, 139 IN Infantry, June 8, 1864. Honorably mustered out, Sept. 29, 1864. Battle honors: Perryville, Stone's River, Tullahoma Campaign, Chickamauga.

Born: Feb. 2, 1825 Irvine, Ayrshire, Scotland
Died: Aug. 4, 1886 Fort Wayne, IN
Other Wars: Mexican War (2 Lieutenant, Co. E, 1 IN Infantry)
Occupation: Carpenter and builder
Miscellaneous: Resided Fort Wayne, Allen Co., IN. Brother-in-law of Bvt. Brig. Gen. Judson D. Bingham.
Buried: Lindenwood Cemetery, Fort Wayne, IN (Section B, Lot 75)
References: Thomas B. Helm, editor. *History of Allen County, IN.* Chicago, IL, 1880. Obituary, *Fort Wayne Daily Gazette*, Aug. 5, 1886. Pension File and Military Service File, National Archives. Bert J. Griswold. *The Pictorial History of Fort Wayne, Indiana.* Chicago, IL, 1917. Moses D. Gage. *From Vicksburg to Raleigh; or, A Complete History of the 12th Regiment Indiana Volunteer Infantry.* Chicago, IL, 1865. *History 88th Indiana Volunteers Infantry. Engagements, Chronology, Roster.* Fort Wayne, IN, 1895.

John Nelson Ingram

Captain, Clark Guards, 8 IN Legion (Clark and Scott Counties), June 10, 1861. Resigned July 24, 1861. Colonel, 8 IN Legion (Clark and Scott Counties), Sept. 6, 1861. Having neglected his business, he resigned Oct. 13, 1862, "to avoid financial embarrassment."

Born: Nov. 29, 1825 Jefferson Co., IN
Died: Oct. 30, 1908 Jeffersonville, IN
Other Wars: Mexican War (Private, Co. G, 3 IN Infantry)
Occupation: Tanner and cemetery superintendent
Miscellaneous: Resided Jeffersonville, Clark Co., IN
Buried: Walnut Ridge Cemetery, Jeffersonville, IN (Section A, Lot 10)
References: Obituary, *Jeffersonville Evening News*, Oct. 30, 1908. *Biographical and Historical Souvenir for the Counties of Clark, Crawford, Harrison, Floyd, Jefferson, Jennings, Scott, and Washington, IN.* Chicago, IL, 1889. Lewis C. Baird. *Baird's History of Clark County, IN.* Indianapolis, IN, 1909. John P. Etter. *The Indiana Legion: A Civil War Militia.* Carmel, IN, 2006. *History of the Ohio Falls Cities and Their Counties.* Cleveland, OH, 1882.

George Washington Jackson

2 Lieutenant, Co. C, 34 IN Infantry, Sept. 16, 1861. Acting ADC, Staff of Colonel (later Brig. Gen.) Jacob Ammen, 10 Brigade, 4 Division, Department of the Ohio, Dec. 25, 1861–March 23, 1862. 1 Lieutenant, Co. C, 34 IN Infantry, April

George Humphrey (Mark Weldon Collection).

George Washington Jackson (John Sickles Collection).

George Washington Jackson (Craig Dunn Collection).

14, 1862. Captain, Co. C, 34 IN Infantry, May 12, 1862. Commanded Pioneer Corps, 12 Division, 13 Army Corps, Army of the Tennessee, March 26–July 1863. Colonel, 118 IN Infantry, Sept. 22, 1863. Commanded 2 Brigade, Left Wing, Forces in East Tennessee, Department of the Ohio, Nov.–Dec. 1863. Honorably mustered out, March 3, 1864. Colonel, 9 IN Cavalry, April 30, 1864. Commanded Post of Pulaski, TN, District of Northern Alabama, Department of the Cumberland, Sept. 1864. Severely injured left arm and left breast when thrown from his horse, Franklin, TN, Dec. 17, 1864. Commanded 1 Brigade, 7 Division, Cavalry Corps, Military Division of the Mississippi, Feb. 3–March 18, 1865. Commanded Cavalry Forces, District of Vicksburg, Department of Mississippi, March 28–May 1865. Being "extremely anxious to get out of the service" to attend to private business, he resigned June 3, 1865, "the war being comparatively at an end." Battle honors: Vicksburg Campaign (Port Gibson, Champion's Hill), Knoxville Campaign, Nashville Campaign.

Born: Aug. 11, 1831 VA
Died: Feb. 8, 1912 Fairland, Shelby Co., IN
Occupation: Druggist before war. Farmer and lumber dealer after war.
Miscellaneous: Resided Huntington, Huntington Co., IN, before war; Wentzville, St. Charles Co., MO; Brunswick, Chariton Co., MO; Pierce City, Lawrence Co., MO; Wellington, Sumner Co., KS; and Winfield, Cowley Co., KS, after war
Buried: Union Cemetery, Winfield, KS (Block T)
References: Pension File and Military Service File, National Archives. *History of Saline County, MO*. St. Louis, MO, 1881. Obituary, *Shelbyville Democrat*, Feb. 8, 1912. Letters Received, Volunteer Service Branch, Adjutant General's Office, File I692(VS)1863, National Archives. Daniel W. Comstock. *Ninth Cavalry. 121st Regiment Indiana Volunteers*. Richmond, IN, 1890. Obituary, *Winfield Daily Courier*, Feb. 12, 1912. Obituary, *Indianapolis Star*, Feb. 9, 1912.

Enoch Randolph James

Colonel, 1 IN Legion (Posey County), Aug. 30, 1861. Resigned June 1862.
Born: July 4, 1800 Bardstown, KY
Died: Aug. 11, 1863 Mount Vernon, IN
Occupation: Merchant and banker
Offices/Honors: Indiana Senate, 1847–52
Miscellaneous: Resided Mount Vernon, Posey Co., IN. Father-in-law of Brig. Gen. William Harrow. Father-in-law of Brig. Gen. Alvin P. Hovey.
Buried: Old North Cemetery, Mount Vernon, IN
References: *History of Posey County, IN*. Chicago, IL, 1886. Obituary, *Evansville Daily Journal*, Aug. 14, 1863. Rebecca A. Shepherd, Charles W. Calhoun, Elizabeth Shanahan-Shoemaker, and Alan F. January, editors. *A Biographical Directory of the Indiana General Assembly*. Vol. 1, 1816–1899. Indianapolis, IN, 1980. William P. Leonard. *History

and Directory of Posey County. Evansville, IN, 1882. Darlene McConnell. *Posey Troops, 1861–1865. An Indiana Border County in the Great Rebellion.* Mount Vernon, IN, 1999.

Ruel Milton Johnson

Captain, Co. D, 100 IN Infantry, Aug. 22, 1862. Major, 100 IN Infantry, Sept. 5, 1863. Picket officer, Staff of Brig. Gen. William Harrow, 4 Division, 15 Army Corps, Army of the Tennessee, July 16–22, 1864. Taken prisoner near Atlanta, GA, July 22, 1864. Confined at Charleston, SC. Exchanged, Sept. 28, 1864. *Colonel,* 100 IN Infantry, May 2, 1865. Lieutenant Colonel, 100 IN Infantry, May 16, 1865. Honorably mustered out, June 8, 1865. Battle honors: Jackson Campaign, Missionary Ridge, Atlanta Campaign (Resaca, Dallas, Atlanta), Savannah Campaign, Campaign of the Carolinas.

Born: June 5, 1836 Harbor Creek Twp., Erie Co., PA

Died: Nov. 12, 1901 Goshen, IN

Education: Graduated University of Michigan, Ann Arbor, MI, 1858

Occupation: Lawyer

Offices/Honors: Medal of Honor, Chattanooga,

Ruel Milton Johnson (J. H. Young, Photographer, Cor. Baltimore and Charles Sts., Baltimore, Maryland; Roger D. Hunt Collection, USAMHI [RG98S-CWP160.34]).

TN, Nov. 25, 1863. "While in command of the regiment, bravely exposed himself to the fire of the enemy, encouraging and cheering his men."

Miscellaneous: Resided Goshen, Elkhart Co., IN; Elkhart, Elkhart Co., IN; Santa Fe, NM, 1886–88; and Las Vegas, San Miguel Co., NM, 1888–90

Buried: Oakridge Cemetery, Goshen, IN (East Section, Lot 539)

References: *Pictorial and Biographical Memoirs of Elkhart and St. Joseph Counties, Indiana.* Chicago, IL, 1893. Obituary, *Goshen Weekly Democrat,* Nov. 13, 1901. Charles W. Taylor. *Biographical Sketches and Review of the Bench and Bar of Indiana.* Indianapolis, IN, 1895. Obituary Circular, Whole No. 147, Indiana MOLLUS. Pension File and Military Service File, National Archives. Eli J. Sherlock. *Memorabilia of the Marches and Battles in Which the 100th Regiment of Indiana Infantry Volunteers Took an Active Part, War of the Rebellion, 1861–5.* Kansas City, MO, 1896. George Lang, Raymond L. Collins, and Gerard F. White, compilers. *Medal of Honor Recipients, 1863–1994.* New York City, NY, 1995.

Ruel Milton Johnson (J. H. Young, Photographer, Cor. Baltimore and Charles Sts., Baltimore, Maryland; Roger D. Hunt Collection, USAMHI [RG98S-CWP80.62]).

Thomas Johnson

Captain, Co. K, 24 IN Infantry, July 31, 1861. Resigned March 14, 1862, "in consequence of continued and severe indisposition (chronic diarrhea) which has rendered me unfit for service nearly one half my time." Lieutenant Colonel, 65 IN Infantry, Aug. 16, 1862. Colonel, 65 IN Infantry, March 12, 1864. Honorably discharged, Aug. 29, 1864, on account of physical disability due to "phthisis pulmonalis." Battle honors: East Tennessee Campaign.

Born: June 3, 1830 Gibson Co., IN
Died: June 29, 1882 Topeka, KS
Occupation: Merchant, insurance agent, and U.S. Land Office clerk
Miscellaneous: Resided Hazleton, Gibson Co., IN; Washington, Daviess Co., IN; and Topeka, Shawnee Co., KS, after 1871
Buried: Oak Grove Cemetery, Washington, IN (Section O)
References: Pension File and Military Service File, National Archives. Obituary, *Topeka Daily Capital*, June 30, 1882. Obituary, *Daviess County Democrat*, July 1, 1882. Letters Received, Volunteer Service Branch, Adjutant General's Office, File J617(VS)1864, National Archives.

Samuel M. Johnston

Captain, Ohio Township Greys, Crawford County Regiment, IN Legion, Sept. 12, 1861. Captain, Co. H, 49 IN Infantry, Nov. 20, 1861. Resigned Feb. 14, 1863, since "I have been an invalid for over three months and unfit for duty." Colonel, Crawford County Regiment, IN Legion, Aug. 1, 1863.

Born: 1833? IN
Died: Jan. 13, 1904 Evansville, IN
Occupation: Farmer and river pilot
Miscellaneous: Resided Fredonia, Crawford Co., IN, to 1882; Cannelton, Perry Co., IN, 1882–1902; and Evansville, Vanderburgh Co., IN, 1902–04
Buried: Old Cliff Cemetery, Cannelton, IN (Section 6)
References: Pension File and Military Service File, National Archives. Obituary, *Evansville Journal-News*, Jan. 13, 1904. Obituary, *Cannelton Enquirer*, Jan. 16, 1904. Letters Received, Volunteer Service Branch, Adjutant General's Office, File 12002(VS)1885, National Archives. Doris Byrd Leistner. *Crawford County Indiana Civil War Veterans*. New Albany, IN, 2005.

James Garrard Jones

Colonel, 42 IN Infantry, Oct. 10, 1861. Commanded 14 Brigade, 5 Division, Department of the Ohio, Jan. 12–March 18, 1862. Commanded 17 Brigade, 3 Division, 1 Army Corps, Army of the Ohio, Oct. 14–Nov. 5, 1862. Commanded 17 Brigade, 3 Division, Center, 14 Army Corps, Army of the Cumberland, Nov. 5–Dec. 26, 1862. Assistant Superintendent of Volunteer Recruiting Service, Indianapolis, IN, June 21, 1863–Aug. 20, 1864. Acting Assistant Provost Marshal General, Indianapolis, IN, Aug. 20–Oct. 10, 1864. Honorably mustered out, Nov. 1, 1864. Battle honors: Perryville.

James Garrard Jones (courtesy Susan Ponstein; image copied by Tim Beckman).

Born: July 3, 1814 Paris, KY
Died: April 5, 1872 Evansville, IN
Occupation: Lawyer and judge
Offices/Honors: Mayor of Evansville, IN, 1847–53. Attorney General of Indiana, 1859–61. Judge of 15th Judicial Circuit, 1869–70.
Miscellaneous: Resided Evansville, Vanderburgh Co., IN. In his *Memoirs*, Brig. Gen. John Beatty made the following derogatory remark concerning Colonel Jones, " He can not manage a regiment, and not even his best friends have any confidence in his military capacity."
Buried: Oak Hill Cemetery, Evansville, IN (Section 13, Lot 34)
References: Pension File and Military Service File, National Archives. Obituary, *Evansville Daily Journal*, April 8, 1872. Edward White, editor. *Evansville and Its Men of Mark*. Evansville, IN, 1873. *History of Vanderburgh County, IN*. Madison,

WI, 1889. Letters Received, Volunteer Service Branch, Adjutant General's Office, File J422(VS) 1862, National Archives. Spillard F. Horrall. *History of the 42nd Indiana Volunteer Infantry.* Chicago, IL, 1892. John Beatty. *The Citizen-Soldier; or, Memoirs of a Volunteer.* Cincinnati, OH, 1879. http://freepages.history.rootsweb.ancestry.com/~indiana42nd/JAMES_G_JONES_BIO.htm.

Robert Barclay Jones

Captain, Co. F, 34 IN Infantry, Sept. 5, 1861. Major, 34 IN Infantry, June 15, 1862. Commanded Post of New Madrid (MO), District of Mississippi, Department of the Mississippi (and later Department of the Tennessee), June 14–Nov. 1862. Commanded Post of Island No. 10 (TN), District of Columbus, Department of the Tennessee, Dec. 1862–Jan. 16, 1863. Lieutenant Colonel, 34 IN Infantry, June 18, 1863. Colonel, 34 IN Infantry, Dec. 1, 1863. Commanded U.S. Forces, Lake Pontchartrain (LA), Defenses of New Orleans, Department of the Gulf, June 25–Dec. 17, 1864. Commanded Post of Brazos Santiago (TX), Department of the Gulf, Jan. 16–March 20, 1865. Resigned March 20, 1865, "because my regiment is reduced below the minimum number of a regiment of volunteers and

Robert Barclay Jones.

is not entitled to an officer of the rank of colonel." Battle honors: Vicksburg Campaign (Champion's Hill), Jackson Campaign.

Born: July 27, 1826 Montgomery Co., OH
Died: July 25, 1866 Marion, IN
Occupation: Lawyer and civil engineer
Offices/Honors: County surveyor, Grant Co., IN, 1852–54. County clerk, Grant Co., IN, 1856–61.
Miscellaneous: Resided Marion, Grant Co., IN
Buried: IOOF (now Estates of Serenity) Cemetery, Marion, IN (Block 1, Lot 18)
References: Kingman Brothers, compilers. *Combination Atlas Map of Grant County, IN.* Chicago, IL, 1877. *History of Grant County, IN.* Chicago, IL, 1886. Military Service File, National Archives. Letters Received, Volunteer Service Branch, Adjutant General's Office, File J817(VS)1863, National Archives.

William Jones

Lieutenant Colonel, 53 IN Infantry, Feb. 24, 1862. *Colonel,* 53 IN Infantry, Oct. 31, 1863. GSW both thighs and shell wound head, Atlanta, GA, July 22, 1864. Battle honors: Siege of Corinth (Hatchie Bridge), Meridian Expedition, Atlanta Campaign (Atlanta).

Born: 1803? Vincennes, IN
Died: July 22, 1864 KIA Atlanta, GA
Occupation: Merchant and farmer
Offices/Honors: Indiana House of Representatives, 1838–41
Miscellaneous: Resided Gentryville, Spencer Co., IN, where young Abraham Lincoln clerked in his store in 1829
Buried: Marietta National Cemetery, Marietta, GA (Section A, Grave 1091)

Robert Barclay Jones (Roger D. Hunt Collection, USAMHI [RG98S-CWP207.9]).

William Jones (Ida M. Tarbell. "Abraham Lincoln: Indiana Reminiscences of Lincoln," *McClure's Magazine*, Vol. 6, No. 1 [December 1895]).

References: Rebecca A. Shepherd, Charles W. Calhoun, Elizabeth Shanahan-Shoemaker, and Alan F. January, editors. *A Biographical Directory of the Indiana General Assembly.* Vol. 1, 1816–1899. Indianapolis, IN, 1980. "Hon. William Jones," *Rockport Weekly Democrat*, Feb. 19, 1876. Pension File and Military Service File, National Archives. Garland A. Haas. *To the Mountain of Fire and Beyond: The 53rd Indiana Regiment from Corinth to Glory.* Carmel, IN, 1997. Bess V. Ehrmann. *The Missing Chapter in the Life of Abraham Lincoln.* Chicago, IL, 1938. Ray E. Boomhower. "Destination Indiana: Col. William Jones: Friend of Lincoln," *Traces of Indiana and Midwestern History*, Vol. 4, No. 4 (Fall 1992).

Lewis Jordan

Colonel, 6 IN Legion (Harrison County), Sept. 25, 1861. Battle honors: Morgan's Ohio Raid (Corydon).
Born: March 14, 1792 Shenandoah Co., VA
Died: July 5, 1873 Corydon, IN
Other Wars: War of 1812 (Private, Captain Richard Proctor's Co., Virginia Militia)
Occupation: Tanner
Offices/Honors: Postmaster, Corydon, IN, 1844–45 and 1856–58
Miscellaneous: Resided Corydon, Harrison Co., IN. Father-in-law of Colonel Thomas C. Slaughter (6 IN Legion).

Lewis Jordan (Howard & Davies, Photographers, No. 26 and 28 West Washington Street, Indianapolis, Indiana; Rick Brown Collection).

Buried: Cedar Hill Cemetery, Corydon, IN (Plat 1, Row 12, Grave 225)
References: F. A. Bulleit, compiler. *Illustrated Atlas and History of Harrison County, Indiana.* Corydon, IN, 1906. Obituary, *Corydon Democrat*, July 7, 1873. Interment Records, Cedar Hill Cemetery, Corydon, IN. Arville L. Funk. *The Morgan Raid in Indiana and Ohio (1863).* Corydon, IN, 1978. *Report of Major General Love of the Indiana Legion.* Indianapolis, IN, 1863. *Operations of the Indiana Legion and Minute Men, 1863–4. Documents Presented to the General Assembly, with the Governor's Message, Jan. 6, 1865.* Indianapolis, IN, 1865. John P. Etter. *The Indiana Legion: A Civil War Militia.* Carmel, IN, 2006.

Harris Keeney

1 Lieutenant, Co. C, 54 IN Infantry (3 months), June 10, 1862. Honorably mustered out, Sept. 11, 1862. Colonel, 10 IN Legion (Switzerland County), May 29, 1863.
Born: April 20, 1818 Delaware Co., NY
Died: Jan. 15, 1872 New Florence, MO
Occupation: Blacksmith
Offices/Honors: Sheriff of Switzerland Co., IN, 1855–59
Miscellaneous: Resided Vevay, Switzerland Co., IN, before war; and New Florence, Montgomery Co., MO, after war

Buried: New Florence Cemetery, New Florence, MO

References: Pension File, National Archives. Obituary, *Vevay Reveille*, Jan. 27, 1872. *History of Dearborn, Ohio and Switzerland Counties, Indiana, from Their Earliest Settlement.* Chicago, IL, 1885. *Operations of the Indiana Legion and Minute Men, 1863–4. Documents Presented to the General Assembly, with the Governor's Message, Jan. 6, 1865.* Indianapolis, IN, 1865. John P. Etter. *The Indiana Legion: A Civil War Militia.* Carmel, IN, 2006.

James Keigwin

Colonel, 8 IN Legion (Clark and Scott Counties), Aug. 30, 1861. Lieutenant Colonel, 49 IN Infantry, Nov. 21, 1861. Colonel, 49 IN Infantry, Oct. 18, 1862. Commanded 1 Brigade, 9 Division, 13 Army Corps, Army of the Tennessee, May 19–July 28, 1863. Commanded 3 Brigade, 1 Division, 13 Army Corps, Army of the Tennessee, July 28–Aug. 7, 1863. Commanded 3 Brigade, 1 Division, 13 Army Corps, Department of the Gulf, Aug. 7–15, 1863 and Dec. 23, 1863–Feb. 28, 1864. Commanded 2 Brigade, 1 Division, 13 Army Corps, Department of the Gulf, May 23–June 11, 1864. Commanded 1 Division, Military District of Kentucky, Department of the Ohio, Oct. 1864. Honorably mustered out, Nov. 29, 1864. Battle honors: Chickasaw Bluffs, Vicksburg Campaign (Port Gibson, Champion's Hill, Vicksburg), Jackson Campaign, Red River Campaign.

Born: Oct. 18, 1829 Jeffersonville, IN
Died: Aug. 25, 1904 Louisville, KY
Occupation: Brick manufacturer and contractor
Offices/Honors: Indiana Senate, 1871. Superintendent, Cave Hill National Cemetery, Louisville, KY, 1891–1904.
Miscellaneous: Resided Jeffersonville, Clark Co., IN; and Louisville, KY
Buried: Cave Hill National Cemetery, Louisville, KY (Section B, Grave 4285)
References: Obituary, *Jeffersonville Evening News*, Aug. 25, 1904. Obituary, *Louisville Courier-Journal*, Aug. 26, 1904. Pension File and Military Service File, National Archives. Lewis C. Baird. *Baird's History of Clark County, IN.* Indianapolis, IN, 1909. Rebecca A. Shepherd, Charles W. Calhoun, Elizabeth Shanahan-Shoemaker, and Alan F. January, editors. *A Biographical Directory of the Indiana General Assembly.* Vol. 1, 1816–1899. Indianapolis, IN, 1980. Letters Received, Volunteer Service Branch, Adjutant General's Office, File I585(VS)1863, National Archives. John P. Etter. *The Indiana Legion: A Civil War Militia.* Carmel, IN, 2006.

John Alexander Keith

Lieutenant Colonel, 21 IN Infantry, July 23, 1861. GSW right shoulder, Baton Rouge, LA, Aug. 5, 1862. Colonel, 1 IN Heavy Artillery, May 18, 1863. Accused of "speculating in veterans and new recruits while on duty as a recruiting officer," he resigned Feb. 2, 1865, due to physical disability since "my wound has never ceased discharging, and at times I am almost unfitted for any duty." Battle honors: Baton Rouge.

Born: May 29, 1832 Germantown, Mason Co., KY
Died: Dec. 10, 1910 Columbus, IN
Occupation: Lawyer
Miscellaneous: Resided Columbus, Bartholomew Co., IN
Buried: City Cemetery, Columbus, IN (Irwin Addition, Lot 59)
References: *A Biographical History of Eminent and Self-Made Men of the State of Indiana.* Cincinnati, OH, 1880. Pension File and Military Service File, National Archives. Obituary, *Columbus Evening Republican,* Dec. 12, 1910. Dianne Brummett and Donna Kuhlman, editors. *City Cemetery Records of Columbus, IN.* Columbus, IN, 1991. Letters Received, Volunteer Service Branch, Adjutant General's Office, File H533(VS)1863, National

James Keigwin (Relief portrait, Vicksburg National Military Park).

John Alexander Keith (photograph by A. D. Lytle, Main Street, Baton Rouge, Louisiana; Craig Dunn Collection).

Archives. Phillip E. Faller. *The Indiana Jackass Regiment in the Civil War: A History of the 21st Infantry/1st Heavy Artillery Regiment, with a Roster.* Jefferson, NC, 2013.

Gideon R. Kellams

1 Lieutenant, Co. H, 42 IN Infantry, Sept. 30, 1861. Captain, Co. H, 42 IN Infantry, March 14, 1863. Major, 42 IN Infantry, Nov. 1, 1864. Lieutenant Colonel, 42 IN Infantry, Dec. 13, 1864. Bvt. Colonel, USV, March 13, 1865, for meritorious services. Colonel, 42 IN Infantry, April 10, 1865. Honorably mustered out, July 21, 1865. Battle honors: Atlanta Campaign, Savannah Campaign, Campaign of the Carolinas (Bentonville).
Born: June 6, 1828 near Gentryville, IN
Died: Jan. 19, 1902 Gentryville, IN
Occupation: Lawyer and farmer
Miscellaneous: Resided Gentryville, Spencer Co., IN
Buried: Garden of Memory Cemetery, Gentryville, IN
References: Pension File and Military Service File, National Archives. Obituary, *Rockport Journal,* Jan. 24, 1902. Spillard F. Horrall. *History of the 42nd Indiana Volunteer Infantry.* Chicago, IL, 1892. *History of Warrick, Spencer and Perry Counties, IN.* Chicago, IL, 1885.

Edward Augustine King

Lieutenant Colonel, 19 U.S. Infantry, May 14, 1861. Colonel, 68 IN Infantry, Aug. 20, 1862. Taken prisoner and paroled, Munfordville, KY, Sept. 17, 1862. Colonel, 6 U.S. Infantry, Aug. 1, 1863. Commanded 2 Brigade, 4 Division, 14 Army Corps, Army of the Cumberland, Aug. 2–Sept. 20, 1863. GSW head, Chickamauga, GA, Sept. 20, 1863. Battle honors: Munfordville, Chickamauga.
Born: April 3, 1814 Cambridge, NY
Died: Sept. 20, 1863 KIA Chickamauga, GA
Other Wars: Texas War for Independence. Mexican War (Captain, 15 U.S. Infantry).
Occupation: Lawyer
Offices/Honors: Postmaster, Dayton, OH, 1853–61
Miscellaneous: Resided Dayton, Montgomery Co., OH. Uncle of the wife of Major Gen. Thomas J. Wood.
Buried: Woodland Cemetery, Dayton, OH (Section 68, Lot 177)
References: *Biographical Cyclopedia and Portrait Gallery with an Historical Sketch of the State of Ohio.* Vol. 3. Cincinnati, OH, 1884. Cameron H. King. *The King Family of Suffield, CT.* San Francisco, CA, 1908. Augustus W. Drury. *History of the City of Dayton and Montgomery County, Ohio.* Chicago and Dayton, 1909. John F. Edgar. *Pioneer Life in Dayton and Vicinity, 1796–1840.* Dayton, OH, 1896. Edwin W. High. *History of the 68th Regiment Indiana Volunteer Infantry, 1862–1865.* N.p., 1902. *Indiana at Chickamauga, 1863–1900. Report of Indiana Commissioners Chickamauga National Military Park.* Indianapolis, IN, 1901. *A Genealogy of the King Family.* Buffalo, NY, 1930. Pension File and Military Service File, National Archives. Death

Gideon R. Kellams (Spillard F. Horrall. *History of the 42nd Indiana Volunteer Infantry.* Chicago, Illinois, 1892).

Edward Augustine King (photograph by Webster & Bro., Louisville, Kentucky; courtesy Everitt Bowles).

William Coalbaugh Kise (James Birney Shaw. *History of the 10th Regiment Indiana Volunteer Infantry, Three Months and Three Years Organizations.* Lafayette, Indiana, 1912).

report, *Cincinnati Daily Commercial*, Sept. 30, 1863.

William Coalbaugh Kise

Captain, Co. I, 10 IN Infantry (3 months), April 25, 1861. Honorably mustered out, Aug. 2, 1861. Lieutenant Colonel, 10 IN Infantry (3 years), Sept. 18, 1861. Colonel, 10 IN Infantry, April 5, 1862. Discharged for disability, Nov. 17, 1862, due to "diarrhea of three months standing, and which has at times assumed a grave character." Colonel, 116 IN Infantry, Sept. 4, 1863. Honorably mustered out, March 2, 1864. Battle honors: Mill Springs, Perryville, Morgan's Ohio Raid, East Tennessee Campaign.

Born: Jan. 30, 1815 Fayette Co., KY
Died: Sept. 10, 1884 Lebanon, IN
Other Wars: Mexican War (2 Lieutenant, Co. F, 5 IN Infantry)
Occupation: Lawyer and farmer
Offices/Honors: Circuit court clerk, Boone Co., IN, 1851–59
Miscellaneous: Resided Lebanon, Boone Co., IN. Father of Bvt. Brig. Gen. Reuben C. Kise.
Buried: Oak Hill Cemetery, Lebanon, IN (Section 10, Lot 49)
References: Samuel Harden and D. Spahr, compilers. *Early Life and Times in Boone County, Indiana.* Indianapolis, IN, 1887. Obituary, *Lebanon Patriot*, Sept. 11, 1884. Kingman Brothers, compilers. *Combination Atlas Map of Boone County, IN.* Chicago, IL, 1878. Pension File and Military Service File, National Archives. Letters Received, Volunteer Service Branch, Adjutant General's Office, File K485(VS)1863, National Archives. James Birney Shaw. *History of the 10th Regiment Indiana Volunteer Infantry, Three Months and Three Years Organizations.* Lafayette, IN, 1912. Leander M. Crist. *History of Boone County, IN.* Indianapolis, IN, 1914.

Jacob Harvey Koontz

Captain, Co. A, 111 IN Minute Men, July 10, 1863. Honorably mustered out, July 15, 1863. Captain, Yorktown Guards, Delaware County Regiment, IN Legion, Aug. 8, 1863. Colonel, Delaware County Regiment, IN Legion, Nov. 16, 1863.

Born: Dec. 27, 1827 Fayette Co., IN
Died: Sept. 15, 1908 Mount Pleasant Twp., Delaware Co., IN
Occupation: Dry goods merchant, farmer, and mill operator
Offices/Honors: Indiana House of Representatives, 1877

Jacob Harvey Koontz (post-war) (Thomas B. Helm. *History of Delaware County, Indiana.* Chicago, Illinois, 1881).

Miscellaneous: Resided Yorktown, Delaware Co., IN
Buried: Beech Grove Cemetery, Muncie, IN (Block 26, Lot 4)
References: Thomas B. Helm. *History of Delaware County, IN.* Chicago, IL, 1881. *A Biographical History of Eminent and Self-Made Men of the State of Indiana.* Cincinnati, OH, 1880. Rebecca A. Shepherd, Charles W. Calhoun, Elizabeth Shanahan-Shoemaker, and Alan F. January, editors. *A Biographical Directory of the Indiana General Assembly.* Vol. 1, 1816–1899. Indianapolis, IN, 1980. Frank D. Haimbaugh, editor. *History of Delaware County, IN.* Indianapolis, IN, 1924. General W. H. Kemper, editor. *A Twentieth Century History of Delaware County, IN.* Chicago, IL, 1908. Lowell L. Koontz. *History of the Descendants of John Koontz.* Parsons, WV, 1979. *Operations of the Indiana Legion and Minute Men, 1863–4. Documents Presented to the General Assembly, with the Governor's Message, Jan. 6, 1865.* Indianapolis, IN, 1865.

Hermann Jacob Korff

Lieutenant Colonel, 10 OH Infantry (3 months), May 6, 1861. Lieutenant Colonel, 10 OH Infantry (3 years), June 4, 1861. Discharged Dec. 12, 1861, "having been absent without leave for 20 days or more and having rendered no reports to his regiment." He requested a reconsideration of his discharge, but, upon an adverse report from Gen. Buell, the War Department declined to act upon his request. Nevertheless he continued his battle for reinstatement, reporting himself for duty on numerous occasions. In response to an order from Major Gen. Lewis Wallace, he reported to Lexington, KY, where by virtue of an order from Major Gen. Cassius M. Clay, he assumed command as *Colonel,* 69 IN Infantry, Aug. 24, 1862, in the absence of Colonel William A. Bickle, who was still recruiting for his regiment in Indiana. Taken prisoner and paroled, Richmond, KY, Aug. 30, 1862. Lieutenant Colonel, 1 Regiment, U.S. Paroled Forces, Camp Chase, OH, Oct. 24, 1862. Exchanged Nov. 8, 1862. When he applied in December 1862 for pay and recognition for his services as colonel, he was informed that "his service was rendered without competent authority and gave him no military status. ... He was not subject to orders and was not, in any sense, under General Wallace's command. Colonel Korff knew he was not in the Army. His going to Kentucky was purely voluntary on his part. ... It is not shown that any such services were performed as entitled him to pay under the law." Battle honors: Carnifex Ferry, Richmond.

Born: Sept. 9, 1824 Hamm, Germany
Died: July 31, 1882 Chicago, IL
Occupation: Journalist and agent
Miscellaneous: Resided Cincinnati, OH; and Chicago, IL
Buried: Wunders Cemetery, Chicago, IL
References: Pension File and Military Service File, National Archives. Letters Received, Volunteer Service Branch, Adjutant General's Office, File W14(VS)1862, National Archives. Frank Moore, editor. *The Rebellion Record: A Diary of American Events.* Fifth Volume. New York City, NY, 1864. Carolyn S. Bridge. *These Men Were Heroes Once: The 69th Indiana Volunteer Infantry.* West Lafayette, IN, 2005. D. Warren Lambert. *When the Ripe Pears Fell: The Battle of Richmond, Kentucky.* Richmond, KY, 1995. http://trees.ancestry.com/tree/1090618/person/-1999648652.

Samuel Lambertson

Captain, Co. F, 7 IN Infantry, Sept. 13, 1861. Resigned Oct. 31, 1862, "physically incapacitated from attending to my duties, owing to my advanced age (50 years) and the exposure of an arduous winter campaign in the mountains of Western Virginia." Colonel, 114 IN Minute Men, July 9, 1863. Honorably mustered out, July 21, 1863. Colonel, Johnson County Regiment, IN Legion, Aug. 11, 1863.

Born: June 15, 1815 PA
Died: Dec. 23, 1888 Southport, IN
Occupation: Merchant tailor
Miscellaneous: Resided Franklin, Johnson Co., IN; Adams, Decatur Co., IN; and Southport, Marion Co., IN

Samuel Lambertson (post-war) (*Atlas of Johnson County, Indiana.* Chicago, Illinois, 1881).

Buried: Greenlawn Cemetery, Franklin, IN (Pine Section, Lot 101)
References: *Atlas of Johnson County, Indiana.* Chicago, IL, 1881. Pension File and Military Service File, National Archives. A. B. Hayes and Sam D. Cox. *History of the City of Lincoln, Nebraska.* Lincoln, NE, 1889. Obituary, *Franklin Republican,* Dec. 28, 1888.

Horace P. Lamson

Private, Co. L, 2 IN Cavalry, Sept. 25, 1861. Sergeant Major, 2 IN Cavalry, Oct. 1, 1861. Sergeant, Co. L, 2 IN Cavalry, Feb. 1, 1862. 1 Lieutenant, Adjutant, 4 IN Cavalry, Aug. 5, 1862. Major, 4 IN Cavalry, April 24, 1863. Commanded Post of Camp Nelson, KY, Jan. 20–March 1864. Lieutenant Colonel, 4 IN Cavalry, March 12, 1864. *Colonel,* 4 IN Cavalry, March 12, 1864. Commanded 2 Brigade, 1 Division, Cavalry Corps, Department of the Cumberland, May 26–July 21, 1864 and July 30–Oct. 29, 1864. Commanded 2 Brigade, 1 Division, Cavalry Corps, Military Division of the Mississippi, May 1865. Honorably mustered out, July 3, 1865. Battle honors: Atlanta Campaign, Wilson's Raid.
Born: Oct. 7, 1833 Centreville, IN
Died: March 8, 1900 Washington, DC
Occupation: Cabinet maker, undertaker and U.S. Pension Office clerk
Offices/Honors: Coroner, Kosciusko Co., IN, 1878–79
Miscellaneous: Resided Centreville, Wayne Co., IN; Warsaw, Kosciusko Co., IN; and Washington, DC, after 1882

Buried: Arlington National Cemetery, Arlington, VA (Section 1, Lot 347)
References: Pension File and Military Service File, National Archives. Obituary, *Washington National Tribune,* March 29, 1900. Obituary, *Warsaw Daily Times,* March 13, 1900. "Col. Lamson Paralyzed," *Washington Morning Times,* June 25, 1897. Kingman Brothers, compilers. *Combination Atlas Map of Kosciusko County, IN.* Chicago, IL, 1879. Richard J. Reid. *Fourth Indiana Cavalry: A History.* Olaton, KY, 1994.

John Henry Lawrence

Sergeant, Co. D, 13 IN Infantry, June 19, 1861. 2 Lieutenant, Co. D, 13 IN Infantry, Dec. 7, 1861. Accidental GSW right breast, Suffolk, Va., Sept. 30, 1862. 1 Lieutenant, Co. D, 13 IN Infantry, Sept. 11, 1863. Captain, Co. B, 13 IN Infantry, June 20, 1864. GSW Chaffin's Farm, VA, Sept. 29, 1864. Major, 13 IN Infantry, Dec. 1, 1864. Bvt. Lieutenant Colonel, USV, March 13, 1865, for gallant and meritorious conduct at the storming of Fort Fisher, NC. Lieutenant Colonel, 13 IN Infantry, May 1, 1865. Colonel, 13 IN Infantry, June 1, 1865. Commanded Post of Goldsboro, NC, July 1865. Honorably mustered out, Sept. 5, 1865. Battle honors: Richmond Campaign (Chaffin's Farm), Fort Fisher.
Born: Nov. 14, 1843 Madison, IN
Died: April 29, 1904 Carthage, MO
Occupation: Printer before war. U.S. Internal Revenue Bureau clerk, music store proprietor, and commercial salesman after war.

John Henry Lawrence (copy of image in the Craig Dunn Collection).

John Henry Lawrence (Gorgas & Mulvey, Photographers, Madison, Indiana; Indiana Historical Society, P0471 [Oskaloosa M. Smith Photograph Album]).

Miscellaneous: Resided Madison, Jefferson Co., IN; Washington, DC; St. Louis, MO; and Carthage, Jasper Co., MO
Buried: Park Cemetery, Carthage, MO (Block 27, Lot 32)
References: Obituary, *Carthage Evening Press*, April 29, 1904. Pension File and Military Service File, National Archives. Letters Received, Volunteer Service Branch, Adjutant General's Office, File Z18(VS)1865, National Archives.

Henry Ware Lawton

Sergeant, Co. E, 9 IN Infantry (3 months), April 24, 1861. Honorably mustered out, July 29, 1861. 1 Lieutenant, Co. A, 30 IN Infantry, Aug. 20, 1861. Captain, Co. A, 30 IN Infantry, May 17, 1862. Acting AIG, 3 Brigade, 1 Division, 4 Army Corps, Army of the Cumberland, Aug. 24–Dec. 6, 1864. Lieutenant Colonel, 30 IN Infantry, Nov. 15, 1864. *Colonel*, 30 IN Infantry, Feb. 10, 1865. Bvt. Colonel, USV, March 13, 1865, for gallant and meritorious services during the war. Honorably mustered out, Nov. 25, 1865. Battle honors: Atlanta Campaign, Franklin, Nashville.

Born: March 17, 1843 Manhattan, Lucas Co., OH
Died: Dec. 19, 1899 KIA San Mateo, Luzon, Philippine Islands
Other Wars: Major General, USV, Philippine War
Education: Attended Harvard Law School, Cambridge, MA
Occupation: Regular Army (Colonel, Inspector General, July 7, 1898)
Offices/Honors: Medal of Honor, Atlanta, GA, Aug. 3, 1864. "Led a charge of skirmishers against the enemy rifle pits and stubbornly and successfully resisted two determined attacks of the enemy to retake the works."
Miscellaneous: Resided Fort Wayne, Allen Co., IN; and Washington, DC
Buried: Arlington National Cemetery, Arlington, VA (Section 2, Lot 841)
References: Steven L. Ossad, "Henry Ware Lawton: Flawed Giant and Hero of Four Wars," *Army History: The Professional Bulletin of Army History*, PB 20–06–1 (No. 63), Winter 2007. *Major General Henry W. Lawton of Fort Wayne, Indiana*. Fort Wayne, IN, 1954. *National Cyclopedia of American Biography. Dictionary of American Biography.* Obituary, *New York Tribune*, Dec. 20, 1899. Robert S. Robertson, "Address Delivered Before the Lawton Memorial Meeting," *Addresses, Memorials, and Sketches*. Published by The Maumee Valley Pioneer Association. Toledo, OH, 1900. *Society of the Army*

Henry Ware Lawton (*Indiana at Chickamauga, 1863–1900. Report of Indiana Commissioners Chickamauga National Military Park.* Indianapolis, Indiana, 1901).

Henry Ware Lawton (as Major General, 1899) (Frederick Hill Meserve. Historical Portraits, A Part of the Collection of Americana of Frederick Hill Meserve. New York City, 1913–1915; courtesy New York State Library).

of the Cumberland. Twenty-Eighth Reunion, Detroit, MI, Sept. 26 and 27, 1899. Cincinnati, OH, 1900. Richard F. Snow, "American Characters: Henry Ware Lawton," *American Heritage*, Vol. 33, No. 3 (April/May 1982). Military Service File, National Archives. George Lang, Raymond L. Collins, and Gerard F. White, compilers. *Medal of Honor Recipients, 1863–1994*. New York City, NY, 1995.

Henry Leaming

1 Lieutenant, Co. C, 40 IN Infantry, Nov. 6, 1861. Captain, Co. C, 40 IN Infantry, Dec. 6, 1861. Major, 40 IN Infantry, July 12, 1862. Lieutenant Colonel, 40 IN Infantry, April 26, 1864. *Colonel*, 40 IN Infantry, May 1, 1865. Commanded Post of Texana, TX, Oct.–Nov. 1865. Honorably mustered out, Dec. 21, 1865. Battle honors: Stone's River, Atlanta Campaign (Kenesaw Mountain), Franklin, Nashville.

Born: Nov. 25, 1825 Philadelphia, PA
Died: March 23, 1899 Lafayette, IN
Education: Attended University of Pennsylvania, Philadelphia, PA (Class of 1844)
Occupation: Merchant before war. U.S. Internal Revenue storekeeper, insurance agent, railway mail clerk, and farmer after war.
Miscellaneous: Resided Lafayette, Tippecanoe Co., IN; and Romney, Tippecanoe Co., IN
Buried: Romney Cemetery, Romney, IN
References: *Biographical Record and Portrait Album of Tippecanoe County, IN.* Chicago, IL, 1888. Obituary, *Lafayette Morning Journal*, March 24, 1899. Pension File and Military Service File, National Archives. Mabel Vohland. *Christopher and Esther Leaming and Their Descendants*. Gibbon, NE, 1977. *University of Pennsylvania: Biographical Catalogue of the Matriculates of the College*. Philadelphia, PA, 1894.

James Leeper

Captain, Co. D, 49 IN Infantry, Nov. 11, 1861. Shell wound right groin, Vicksburg, MS, May 19, 1863. Major, 49 IN Infantry, Nov. 30, 1864. Lieutenant Colonel, 49 IN Infantry, Dec. 1, 1864. *Colonel*, 49 IN Infantry, Dec. 1, 1864. Honorably mustered out, Sept. 13, 1865. Battle honors: Vicksburg Campaign (Vicksburg).

Born: 1829? Natchitoches, LA
Died: May 26, 1872 Jeffersonville, IN
Occupation: River pilot and State Prison guard
Miscellaneous: Resided Charlestown, Clark Co., IN; and Jeffersonville, Clark Co., IN
Buried: Eastern Cemetery, Jeffersonville, IN
References: Pension File and Military Service File, National Archives. Obituary, *Louisville Courier-Journal*, May 28, 1872. Lewis C. Baird. *Baird's History of Clark County, IN*. Indianapolis, IN, 1909. Letters Received, Volunteer Service Branch, Adjutant General's Office, File 339(VS)1878, National Archives.

George Washington Lennard

1 Lieutenant, Adjutant, 36 IN Infantry, Sept. 30, 1861. Acting ADC, Staff of Brig. Gen. Thomas J. Wood, 6 Division, Army of the Ohio, Oct. 24, 1861–Dec. 22, 1862. 1 Lieutenant, Co. H, 36 IN Infantry, April 25, 1862. 1 Lieutenant, Co. E, 36 IN Infantry, May 14, 1862. 1 Lieutenant, Co. C, 36 IN Infantry, June 13, 1862. 1 Lieutenant, Co. A, 36 IN Infantry, Nov. 1862. Lieutenant Colonel, 57 IN Infantry, Dec. 2, 1862. GSW right leg, Stone's River, TN, Dec. 31, 1862. *Colonel*, 57 IN Infantry, July 28, 1863. Provost Marshal, Post of Chattanooga, TN, Sept. 17–Oct. 1863. Shell wound right knee, Resaca, GA, May 14, 1864. Battle honors: Shiloh, Corinth, Perryville, Stone's River, Missionary Ridge, Atlanta Campaign (Resaca).

Born: March 5, 1825 near Newark, OH
Died: May 14, 1864 DOW Resaca, GA
Education: Graduated Cincinnati (OH) Eclec-

George Washington Lennard (photograph by Davies & Merritt, 26 & 28 West Washington St., Indianapolis, Indiana).

tic Medical Institute, 1850. Graduated Cincinnati (OH) Law School, 1855.
Occupation: Lawyer, physician, and newspaper editor
Miscellaneous: Resided New Castle, Henry Co., IN
Buried: South Mound Cemetery, New Castle, IN
References: George Hazzard. *Hazzard's History of Henry County, Indiana, 1822–1906. Military Edition.* New Castle, IN, 1906. Obituary, *New Castle Courier,* June 2, 1864. Asbury L. Kerwood. *Annals of the 57th Regiment Indiana Volunteers, Marches, Battles, and Incidents of Army Life.* Dayton, OH, 1868. Pension File and Military Service File, National Archives. Paul Hubbard and Christine Lewis, editors, " 'Give Yourself No Trouble About Me': The Shiloh Letters of George W. Lennard," *Indiana Magazine of History,* Vol. 76, No. 1 (March 1980).

Eli Lilly

2 Lieutenant, Co. E, 21 IN Infantry, July 24, 1861. Resigned Dec. 9, 1861. Captain, 18 Battery, Indiana Light Artillery, Aug. 4, 1862. Major, 9 IN Cavalry, April 4, 1864. Taken prisoner Sulphur Branch Trestle, AL, Sept. 25, 1864. Paroled Nov. 15,

Eli Lilly (John Sickles Collection).

1864. Lieutenant Colonel, 9 IN Cavalry, Dec. 28, 1864. *Colonel,* 9 IN Cavalry, June 4, 1865. Honorably mustered out, Aug. 25, 1865. Battle honors: Tullahoma Campaign (Hoover's Gap), Chickamauga, Sulphur Branch Trestle.
Born: July 8, 1838 Baltimore, MD
Died: June 6, 1898 Indianapolis, IN

Eli Lilly (seated right, with Colonel George W. Jackson) (Indiana Historical Society, P0310 [Indiana Civil War Carte de Visite Portraits]).

Education: Attended Indiana Asbury (now DePauw) University, Greencastle, IN
Occupation: Drug manufacturer and philanthropist
Miscellaneous: Resided Greencastle, Putnam Co., IN; Paris, Edgar Co., IL; and Indianapolis, IN
Buried: Crown Hill Cemetery, Indianapolis, IN (Section 13, Lot 19)
References: George I. Reed, editor. *Encyclopedia of Biography of Indiana.* Chicago, IL, 1895. Obituary, *Indianapolis Journal,* June 7, 1898. *National Cyclopedia of American Biography.* Jacob Piatt Dunn. *Greater Indianapolis: The History, The Industries, The Institutions, and the People of a City of Homes.* Chicago, IL, 1910. Obituary Circular, Whole No. 106, Indiana MOLLUS. David J. Bodenhamer and Robert G. Barrows, editors. *The Encyclopedia of Indianapolis.* Bloomington, IN, 1994. Military Service File, National Archives. John W. Rowell. *Yankee Artillerymen: Through the Civil War with Eli Lilly's Indiana Battery.* Knoxville, TN, 1975. Daniel W. Comstock. *Ninth Cavalry. 121st Regiment Indiana Volunteers.* Richmond, IN, 1890.

William Hardy Link

Lieutenant Colonel, 12 IN Infantry (1 year), May 15, 1861. Colonel, 12 IN Infantry, Aug. 26, 1861. Honorably mustered out, May 19, 1862. Colonel, 12 IN Infantry (3 years), Aug. 18, 1862. GSW right thigh, Richmond, KY, Aug. 30, 1862. Taken prisoner and paroled, Richmond, KY, Aug. 30, 1862. Battle honors: Richmond.
Born: March 2, 1821 Rockbridge Co., VA
Died: Sept. 20, 1862 DOW Richmond, KY
Other Wars: Mexican War (Captain, Co. I, 2 OH Infantry; and Major, 5 OH Infantry)
Occupation: Cooper
Miscellaneous: Resided Circleville, Pickaway Co., OH; and Fort Wayne, Allen Co., IN
Buried: Lindenwood Cemetery, Fort Wayne, IN (Section B, Lot 46)
References: David Stevenson. *Indiana's Roll of Honor.* Indianapolis, IN, 1864. Paxson R. Link. *The Link Family.* Paris, IL, 1951. Pension File and Military Service File, National Archives. Moses D. Gage. *From Vicksburg to Raleigh; or, A Complete History of the 12th Regiment Indiana Volunteer Infantry.* Chicago, IL, 1865. Sally C. Hogan, editor. *General Reub Williams's Memories of Civil War Times.* Westminster, MD, 2006.

Newton A. Logan

Captain, Co. G, 26 IN Infantry, Aug. 30, 1861. Taken prisoner, Stirling's Plantation, Bayou Fordoche, near Morganza, LA, Sept. 29, 1863. Confined Camp Ford, Tyler, TX. Paroled July 22, 1864. Major, 26 IN Infantry, Jan. 12, 1865. Lieutenant Colonel, 26 IN Infantry, March 11, 1865. Commanded Post of Macon, MS, Aug. 1865. *Colonel,* 26 IN Infantry, Oct. 10, 1865. Commanded Post of Columbus, MS, Oct. 1865. Honorably mustered out, Jan. 15, 1866. Battle honors: Vicksburg, Stirling's Plantation.
Born: March 24, 1836 Parke Co., IN
Died: June 27, 1919 Frankfort, IN
Occupation: Farmer, mill operator, and house painter
Offices/Honors: Indiana House of Representatives, 1889
Miscellaneous: Resided Jefferson, Clinton Co., IN; Monticello, White Co., IN; Michigantown, Clinton Co., IN; and Frankfort, Clinton Co., IN
Buried: Brandon Cemetery, Michigan Twp., Clinton Co., IN
References: Pension File and Military Service File, National Archives. Obituary, *Frankfort Crescent-News,* June 30, 1919. Rebecca A. Shepherd, Charles W. Calhoun, Elizabeth Shanahan-Shoemaker, and Alan F. January, editors. *A Biographical Directory of the Indiana General Assembly.* Vol. 1, 1816–1899. Indianapolis, IN, 1980. Joseph Claybaugh. *History of Clinton County, IN.* Indianapolis, IN, 1913.

Virgil H. Lyon

Corporal, Co. A, 7 IN Infantry (3 months), April 24, 1861. Honorably mustered out, Aug. 2,

William Hardy Link (photograph by Whitehurst Gallery, 434 Pennsylvania Avenue, Washington, DC; Library of Congress, [LC-DIG-cwpb-070 23]).

Virgil H. Lyon (John Sickles Collection).

1861. 1 Lieutenant, Co. B, 7 IN Infantry (3 years), Sept. 13, 1861. Resigned Oct. 1, 1862, "suffering from rheumatic pains in the legs and back," caused by "the excessive marching and exposure to which I have been subjected for the last sixteen months." Captain, Plainfield Guards, Hendricks County Regiment, IN Legion, March 21, 1863. Lieutenant Colonel, 103 IN Minute Men, July 10, 1863. Honorably mustered out, July 17, 1863. Colonel, Hendricks County Regiment, IN Legion, Oct. 20, 1863. Captain, Co. I, 9 IN Cavalry, Jan. 9, 1864. Major, 9 IN Cavalry, March 8, 1864. Lieutenant Colonel, 9 IN Cavalry, Aug. 26, 1865. Honorably mustered out, Aug. 28, 1865.

Born: May 6, 1836 Belleville, IN
Died: Sept. 12, 1879 Plainfield, IN
Occupation: Commercial traveler for wholesale clothing house
Miscellaneous: Resided Plainfield, Hendricks Co., IN
Buried: Maple Hill Cemetery, Plainfield, IN (Division B, Block 6, Lot 7)
References: Obituary, *Hendricks County Union*, Sept. 18, 1879. Obituary, *Indianapolis Daily Sentinel*, Sept. 13, 1879. Pension File and Military Service File, National Archives. Letters Received, Volunteer Service Branch, Adjutant General's Office, File L943(VS)1865, National Archives. Daniel W. Comstock. *Ninth Cavalry. 121st Regiment Indiana Volunteers*. Richmond, IN, 1890.

Edmund Ayres Maginness

2 Lieutenant, Anderson Rifles, 7 IN Legion (Floyd County), May 30, 1861. Colonel, 7 IN Legion (Floyd County), Sept. 6, 1862.

Born: Aug. 24, 1832 West Chester, PA
Died: Nov. 7, 1905 New Albany, IN
Education: Attended Dickinson College, Carlisle, PA (Class of 1852)
Occupation: Engaged in drug business in partnership with Bvt. Brig. Gen. Benjamin F. Scribner. In later years glass works superintendent and business manager for a Louisville newspaper.
Miscellaneous: Resided New Albany, Floyd Co., IN
Buried: Fairview Cemetery, New Albany, IN (Plat 11, Range 4, Lot 16)
References: Obituary, *New Albany Daily Ledger*, Nov. 7, 1905. George Leffingwell Reed, editor. *Alumni Record Dickinson College*. Carlisle, PA, 1905. *Report of Major General Love of the Indiana Legion*. Indianapolis, IN, 1863.

John Riley Mahan

Lieutenant Colonel, 14 IN Infantry, June 7, 1861. Resigned Feb. 1, 1862, since "I am physically unable to perform the duties of the position" and "my life is continually endangered by remaining in the service." Lieutenant Colonel, 55 IN Infantry, June 16, 1862. Honorably mustered out, Dec. 20, 1862. Colonel, 109 IN Minute Men, July 10, 1863. Honorably mustered out, July 17, 1863. Colonel, 115 IN Infantry, Aug. 17, 1863. Commanded 1 Brigade, Left Wing, Forces of East Tennessee, Department of the Ohio, Sept. 20, 1863–Jan. 11, 1864. Honor-

Virgil H. Lyon (as Corporal, 7 Indiana Infantry, 1861) (Craig Dunn Collection).

John Riley Mahan (Rick Brown Collection).

Zalmon Smith Main (photograph by Runnion's Art Gallery, Opposite Glenn's Block, Indianapolis, Indiana).

ably mustered out, Feb. 25, 1864. Battle honors: Richmond, Knoxville Campaign.
Born: Feb. 7, 1824 near Flemingsburg, KY
Died: Jan. 3, 1894 Greencastle, IN
Occupation: Farmer and trader
Offices/Honors: Sheriff, Putnam Co., IN, 1858–60
Miscellaneous: Resided Greencastle, Putnam Co., IN, and Indianapolis, IN
Buried: Forest Hill Cemetery, Greencastle, IN (Soldier Section, Block 6, Range 9, Lot 14)
References: Pension File and Military Service File, National Archives. Obituary, *Greencastle Banner Times,* Jan. 4, 1894. *Biographical and Historical Record of Putnam County, IN.* Chicago, IL, 1887. Jesse W. Weik. *Weik's History of Putnam County, IN.* Indianapolis, IN, 1910. Barbara A. Smith, compiler. *The Civil War Letters of Col. Elijah H. C. Cavins, 14th Indiana.* Owensboro, KY, 1981. *Operations of the Indiana Legion and Minute Men, 1863-4. Documents Presented to the General Assembly, with the Governor's Message, Jan. 6, 1865.* Indianapolis, IN, 1865.

Zalmon Smith Main

Captain, Co. A, 52 IN Infantry, Jan. 4, 1862. Dismissed March 7, 1862, for "disobedience of orders, allowing a citizen to send arms and clothing home from Fort Donelson, contrary to General Grant's order." He, however, stayed with the regiment, and ignorant of the dismissal, Governor Morton commissioned him as major and then as lieutenant colonel. Major, 52 IN Infantry, May 14, 1862. Lieutenant Colonel, 52 IN Infantry, June 5, 1862. "Under the peculiar circumstances of the case," his dismissal was revoked, Nov. 6, 1863, and he was "allowed to remain in the service of the United States as of the rank to which he has been promoted." Colonel, 52 IN Infantry, May 27, 1865. Honorably mustered out, Sept. 10, 1865. Battle honors: Corinth, Tupelo, Nashville, Mobile Campaign.

Zalmon Smith Main.

Born: Aug. (or April) 2, 1833 Liberty, NY
Died: Oct. 13, 1867 Hankins, NY
Occupation: Civil engineer and bridge builder
Miscellaneous: Resided Lawrenceburg, Dearborn Co., IN; Lancaster, Fairfield Co., OH; and Hankins, Sullivan Co., NY
Buried: Overlook Cemetery, Damascus, PA
References: Cyrus H. Brown, compiler. *Genealogical Record of Nathaniel Babcock, Simeon Main, Isaac Miner, Ezekiel Main*. Boston, MA, 1909. Nancy Porter Childress. *The Main Tree II: The Descendants of John Main of North Yarmouth, ME*. Phoenix, AZ, 1995. Pension File and Military Service File, National Archives. Letters Received, Volunteer Service Branch, Adjutant General's Office, File M2619(VS)1863, National Archives. John Y. Simon, editor. *The Papers of Ulysses S. Grant*. Volume 4: January 8–March 31, 1862. Carbondale, IL, 1972. "Letters from Civil War Soldiers to a Relative in Sullivan County, 1862–1866," *The Observer: A Publication of the Sullivan County Historical Society*, Vol. 21, No. 1 (Jan.–Feb. 2001) and Vol. 23, Issue 1 (Jan.–Feb. 2003).

John Crittenden Major

Captain, Co. A, 43 IN Infantry, Aug. 20, 1861. Major, 43 IN Infantry, March 7, 1862. Lieutenant Colonel, 43 IN Infantry, Oct. 4, 1862. Colonel, 43 IN Infantry, May 20, 1865. Honorably mustered out, Aug. 31, 1865. Battle honors: Helena, Little Rock.
Born: Aug. 27, 1831 Franklin Co., KY
Died: Aug. 18, 1920 Bagdad, KY
Education: Attended Kentucky Military Institute, near Frankfort, KY. Graduated Bartlett's Commercial College, Cincinnati, OH, 1854.

John Crittenden Major (copy of image in the Craig Dunn Collection).

John Crittenden Major (post-war) (*History of Montana, 1739–1885*. Chicago, Illinois, 1885).

Occupation: Carpenter, building contractor, and architect
Offices/Honors: County clerk, Clay Co., IN, 1860
Miscellaneous: Resident of Bowling Green, Clay Co., IN; Helena, Lewis and Clark Co., MT; and Bagdad, Shelby Co., KY
Buried: Bagdad Cemetery, Bagdad, KY
References: *History of Montana, 1739–1885*. Chicago, IL, 1885. Pension File and Military Service File, National Archives. Obituary, *The Shelby News*, Aug. 26, 1920. Letters Received, Volunteer Service Branch, Adjutant General's Office, File M3644(VS)1864, National Archives. William E. McLean. *The 43rd Regiment of Indiana Volunteers. An Historic Sketch of Its Career and Services*. Terre Haute, IN, 1903. William Travis. *A History of Clay County, IN*. New York and Chicago, 1909.

Washington Malick

Colonel, 9 IN Legion (Jennings County), Aug. 1, 1861. Resigned June 16, 1862.
Born: Sept. 14, 1807 Greene Co., TN
Died: March 25, 1882
Occupation: Methodist clergyman and woolen manufacturer
Offices/Honors: Indiana House of Representatives, 1855
Miscellaneous: Resided North Vernon, Jennings Co., IN; and Lovett, Jennings Co., IN
Buried: Hopewell Cemetery, near Lovett, IN

References: Rebecca A. Shepherd, Charles W. Calhoun, Elizabeth Shanahan-Shoemaker, and Alan F. January, editors. *A Biographical Directory of the Indiana General Assembly.* Vol. 1, 1816–1899. Indianapolis, IN, 1980. Naomi K. Sexton. *The Hoosier Journal of Ancestry: Jennings County Special.* No. 1–3. Little York, IN, 1987–92.

John Albert Mann

Lieutenant Colonel, 1 IN Legion (Posey County), Aug. 30, 1861. Colonel, 1 IN Legion (Posey County), June 10, 1862. Resigned Jan. 2, 1865. Battle honors: Morgan's Ohio Raid.
Born: June 3, 1823 Eckelsheim, Hesse-Darmstadt, Germany
Died: Feb. 15, 1884 Dallas, TX
Occupation: Dry goods merchant
Miscellaneous: Resided Mount Vernon, Posey Co., IN; and Dallas, TX, 1878–84
Buried: Greenwood Cemetery, Dallas, TX (Block 13)
References: Obituary, *Evansville Daily Journal,* Feb. 16, 1884. Obituary, *Norton's Union Intelligencer (Dallas, TX),* Feb. 20, 1884. Obituary, *Fort Worth Daily Gazette,* Feb. 16, 1884. *Report of Major General Love of the Indiana Legion.* Indianapolis, IN, 1863. *Operations of the Indiana Legion and Minute Men, 1863–4. Documents Presented to the General Assembly, with the Governor's Message, Jan. 6, 1865.* Indianapolis, IN, 1865. John P. Etter. *The Indiana Legion: A Civil War Militia.* Carmel, IN, 2006.

Fielding Mansfield

Major, 54 IN Infantry (3 months), June 14, 1862. Honorably mustered out, Sept. 26, 1862. Colonel, 54 IN Infantry (1 year), Nov. 17, 1862. Honorably mustered out, Dec. 8, 1863. Battle honors: Chickasaw Bluffs, Vicksburg Campaign.
Born: Dec. 23, 1841 Lexington, KY
Died: Dec. 17, 1914 Ferguson, MO
Education: Attended University of Wisconsin, Madison, WI
Occupation: Salesman before war. Match manufacturer and newspaper correspondent after war.
Offices/Honors: Two terms as St. Louis Jury Commissioner
Miscellaneous: Resided Madison, Jefferson Co., IN; Cincinnati, OH, 1864–66; St. Louis, MO, 1866–1903; Ferguson, St. Louis Co., MO, 1903–14. Son of Colonel John Lutz Mansfield (54 IN Infantry).
Buried: Bellefontaine Cemetery, St. Louis, MO (Block 35, Lot 3502)
References: Pension File and Military Service File, National Archives. Obituary, *St. Louis Globe Democrat,* Dec. 19, 1914. Letters Received, Volunteer Service Branch, Adjutant General's Office, File W2051(VS)1863, National Archives. W. J. Maxwell, compiler. *The Catalogue of the Phi Delta Theta Fraternity.* Eighth Edition. New York City, NY, 1918.

John Lutz Mansfield (born Johann B. Lutz)

Brig. Gen., 3 Brigade, IN Legion, Sept. 10, 1861. Colonel, 54 IN Infantry (3 months), June 10, 1862. Resigned June 18, 1862. Major Gen., 1 Division, IN Legion, July 30, 1864. Honorably mustered out, Nov. 1, 1865. Battle honors: Morgan's Ohio Raid.
Born: Jan. 6, 1803 Braunschweig, Germany
Died: Sept. 20, 1876 Mansfield, IL
Education: Attended universities at Gottingen and Heidelberg, Germany
Occupation: Educator, college professor and civil engineer
Offices/Honors: President, Transylvania University, Lexington, KY, 1830–32 and 1834–35. Indiana House of Representatives, 1859. Indiana Senate, 1863.
Miscellaneous: Resided Lexington, Fayette Co., KY; Madison, Jefferson Co., IN, 1858–66; Indianapolis, IN, 1866–70; and Mansfield, Piatt Co., IL, 1870–76. Father of Colonel Fielding Mansfield (54 IN Infantry).
Buried: Mansfield Cemetery, Mansfield, IL (Section 1, Row 17½)

John Lutz Mansfield (The Filson Historical Society, Louisville, Kentucky [PC13.0006]).

References: Rebecca A. Shepherd, Charles W. Calhoun, Elizabeth Shanahan-Shoemaker, and Alan F. January, editors. *A Biographical Directory of the Indiana General Assembly.* Vol. 1, 1816–1899. Indianapolis, IN, 1980. Emma C. Piatt. *History of Piatt County, Illinois.* Chicago, IL, 1883. Theodore Stein. *Historical Sketch of the German-English Independent School of Indianapolis.* Indianapolis, IN, 1913. Obituary, *Piatt County Herald,* Sept. 27, 1876. John P. Etter. *The Indiana Legion: A Civil War Militia.* Carmel, IN, 2006. *Report of Major General Love of the Indiana Legion.* Indianapolis, IN, 1863. *Operations of the Indiana Legion and Minute Men, 1863–4. Documents Presented to the General Assembly, with the Governor's Message, Jan. 6, 1865.* Indianapolis, IN, 1865.

Roger Martin

Major, 53 IN Infantry, Feb. 24, 1862. Resigned April 23, 1862, "in consequence of bad health," following a bout with mumps. Lieutenant Colonel, 66 IN Infantry, Aug. 17, 1862. *Colonel,* 66 IN Infantry, March 25, 1864. Commanded 1 Brigade, 4 Division, 15 Army Corps, Army of the Tennessee, Sept. 22–Oct. 19, 1864. Honorably mustered out, June 3, 1865. Battle honors: Atlanta Campaign (Resaca, Atlanta), Allatoona, Savannah Campaign, Campaign of the Carolinas.

Born: June 22, 1805 County Kerry, Ireland
Died: Jan. 17, 1873 Mitchell, IN
Occupation: Shoemaker into his middle years. Employed later as road master for New Albany & Salem Railroad Company and purchasing agent for Louisville, New Albany & Chicago Railroad Company.
Miscellaneous: Resided Salem, Washington Co., IN; and Mitchell, Lawrence Co., IN
Buried: Crown Hill Cemetery, Salem, IN
References: Pension File and Military Service File, National Archives. Obituary, *New Albany Ledger-Standard,* Jan. 18, 1873. *History of Lawrence, Orange and Washington Counties, IN.* Chicago, IL, 1884. *History of Lawrence and Monroe Counties, Indiana. Their People, Industries and Institutions.* Indianapolis, IN, 1914. Letters Received, Volunteer Service Branch, Adjutant General's Office, File P507(VS)1867, National Archives.

Charles Holland Mason

Colonel, 5 IN Legion (Perry County), June 6, 1861. Resigned Nov. 20, 1861.

Born: Aug. 9, 1827 Walpole, NH
Died: June 11, 1894 Vinita, OK
Occupation: Lawyer, judge and newspaper editor
Offices/Honors: Judge of Common Pleas Court, 1861–63 and 1870–72. United States Commissioner, 1st Judicial District, Indian Territory, 1890–94.
Miscellaneous: Resided Cannelton, Perry Co., IN; Rockport, Spencer Co., IN; and Vinita, Craig Co., OK, 1890–94
Buried: Fairview Cemetery, Vinita, OK (Block 6, Lot 13)
References: *A Biographical History of Eminent and Self-Made Men of the State of Indiana.* Cincinnati, OH, 1880. *History of Warrick, Spencer and Perry Counties, IN.* Chicago, IL, 1885. Thomas J. De La Hunt. *Perry County: A History.* Indianapolis, IN, 1916. Obituary, *Vinita Indian Chieftain,* June 14, 1894.

Courtland Cushing Matson

2 Lieutenant, Co. K, 16 IN Infantry (1 year), May 15, 1861. Detailed as Acting Signal Officer, Oct. 1861–May 1862. Honorably mustered out, May 23, 1862. 1 Lieutenant, Adjutant, 71 IN Infantry, July 19, 1862. Lieutenant Colonel, 71 IN Infantry, Dec. 13, 1862. Taken prisoner, Muldraugh's Hill, KY, Dec. 28, 1862. Paroled Jan. 10, 1863. Lieutenant Colonel, 6 IN Cavalry, Feb. 23, 1863. Commanded Post of Mount Sterling, KY, Sept.–Oct. 1863. Taken prisoner, Jug Tavern, near Atlanta, GA, Aug. 3, 1864. Confined Camp Asylum, Columbia, SC. Paroled March 3, 1865. *Colonel,* 6 IN Cavalry, July 1, 1865. Honorably mustered out, Sept. 15, 1865. Battle honors: Atlanta Campaign.

Born: April 25, 1841 Brookville, IN
Died: Sept. 4, 1915 Chicago, IL

Roger Martin (Massachusetts MOLLUS Collection, USAMHI [Vol. 73, p. 3645]).

Courtland Cushing Matson.

Education: Graduated Indiana Asbury (now DePauw) University, Greencastle, IN, 1862
Occupation: Lawyer
Offices/Honors: U.S. House of Representatives, 1881–89
Miscellaneous: Resided Greencastle, Putnam Co., IN

Buried: Forest Hill Cemetery, Greencastle, IN (Soldier Section, Block 7, Range 7, Lot 5)
References: Jesse W. Weik. *Weik's History of Putnam County, IN.* Indianapolis, IN, 1910. Will Cumback and J. B. Maynard, editors. *Men of Progress. Indiana.* Indianapolis, IN, 1899. Pension File and Military Service File, National Archives. James L. Harrison, compiler. *Biographical Directory of the American Congress, 1774–1949.* Washington, DC, 1950. Obituary, *Chicago Daily Tribune,* Sept. 5, 1915. Letters Received, Volunteer Service Branch, Adjutant General's Office, File M917(VS)1865, National Archives. *National Cyclopedia of American Biography.* J. Willard Brown. *The Signal Corps, U.S.A., in the War of the Rebellion.* Boston, MA, 1896.

William Simrall McClure

Captain, Co. E, 3 IN Cavalry, Aug. 22, 1861. Major, 3 IN Cavalry, Nov. 1, 1862. Commanded 1 Brigade, 1 Division, Cavalry Corps, Army of the Potomac, June 9, 1863. Discharged March 9, 1864, "to enable him to accept a commission as colonel of another regiment." Colonel, 9 IN Cavalry, Feb. 2, 1864 (Declined). Battle honors: Beverly Ford, Brandy Station, Gettysburg, Mine Run.
Born: April 6, 1834 Madison, IN
Died: Jan. 12, 1900 Madison, IN
Occupation: Steamboat agent and produce commission merchant
Miscellaneous: Resided Madison, Jefferson Co., IN

Courtland Cushing Matson (U.S. House of Representatives, 1881) (photograph by C. M. Bell, Washington, DC).

William Simrall McClure (Brady's National Photographic Portrait Galleries, Broadway & Tenth St., New York).

Buried: Springdale Cemetery, Madison, IN

References: Obituary, *Madison Courier,* Jan. 12, 1900. Pension File and Military Service File, National Archives. Letters Received, Volunteer Service Branch, Adjutant General's Office, File M627(VS) 1864, National Archives. William N. Pickerill. *History of the 3rd Indiana Cavalry.* Indianapolis, IN, 1906. http://trees.ancestry.com/tree/15478846/person/269005268.

John S. McGraw

Captain, Co. B, 57 IN Infantry, Dec. 5, 1861. GSW forehead, Missionary Ridge, TN, Nov. 25, 1863. Major, 57 IN Infantry, May 15, 1864. Lieutenant Colonel, 57 IN Infantry, May 2, 1865. *Colonel,* 57 IN Infantry, May 2, 1865. Honorably mustered out, Dec. 14, 1865. Battle honors: Stone's River, Missionary Ridge, Nashville.

Born: July 13, 1827 Philadelphia, PA

Died: Aug. 26, 1909 Philadelphia, PA

Occupation: Blacksmith and carriage maker

Miscellaneous: Resided Richmond, Wayne Co., IN

Buried: Earlham Cemetery, Richmond, IN (Section 5, Lot 28)

References: Pension File and Military Service File, National Archives. *Biographical and Genealogical History of Wayne, Fayette, Union, and Franklin Counties, Indiana.* Chicago, IL, 1899. Obituary, *Richmond Evening Item,* Aug. 27, 1909. Asbury L. Kerwood. *Annals of the 57th Regiment Indiana Volunteers, Marches, Battles, and Incidents of Army Life.* Dayton, OH, 1868. John C. Power, editor. *Directory and Soldiers' Register of Wayne County, IN.* Richmond, IN, 1865.

David Armstrong McHolland

Captain, Co. B, 51 IN Infantry, Dec. 10, 1861. Major, 51 IN Infantry, April 25, 1863. Taken prisoner, May 3, 1863, near Rome, GA. Confined Libby Prison, Richmond, VA; Macon, GA; Charleston, SC; Camp Asylum, Columbia, SC; and Charlotte, NC. Lieutenant Colonel, 51 IN Infantry, July 1, 1863. Paroled March 1, 1865. *Colonel,* 51 IN Infantry, March 17, 1865. Honorably mustered out, April 17, 1865. Battle honors: Streight's Raid.

Born: Dec. 15, 1827 Owen Co., IN

Died: April (or March) 10, 1877 Chillicothe, MO

Other Wars: Mexican War (Drummer, Co. B, 4 IN Infantry)

Occupation: Blacksmith before war. Farmer, lumberyard worker, and grain merchant after war.

Miscellaneous: Resided Kent Station, Newton Co., IN; Wheeling, Livingston Co., MO, 1865–73; and Chillicothe, Livingston Co., MO, 1873–77

Buried: Wheeling Cemetery, Wheeling, MO

References: Pension File and Military Service File, National Archives. Letters Received, Volunteer Service Branch, Adjutant General's Office, File M899(VS)1865, National Archives. William R. Hartpence. *History of the 51st Indiana Veteran Vol-*

John S. McGraw (photograph by Watson & Estell, Main Street, Richmond, Indiana; U.S. Military Academy Library).

David Armstrong McHolland.

unteer Infantry. Cincinnati, OH, 1894. Charles Blanchard, editor. *Counties of Clay and Owen, Indiana. Historical and Biographical.* Chicago, IL, 1884. http://trees.ancestry.com/tree/17161688/person/538989107.

William T. B. McIntire

Captain, Co. I, 42 IN Infantry, Sept. 28, 1861. Major, 42 IN Infantry, Oct. 21, 1862. Lieutenant Colonel, 42 IN Infantry, July 2, 1863. *Colonel,* 42 IN Infantry, Oct. 11, 1864. Resigned Dec. 12, 1864, since "My father died a few months ago leaving his estate in an unsettled condition." Battle honors: Tullahoma Campaign, Chickamauga, Lookout Mountain, Missionary Ridge, Atlanta Campaign.

Born: July 31, 1827 Petersburg, IN
Died: Nov. 22, 1904 Portland, OR
Occupation: Clerk, boardinghouse keeper, and grocer
Miscellaneous: Resided Petersburg, Pike Co., IN; St. Cloud, Stearns Co., MN; Minneapolis, MN; and Portland, Multnomah Co., OR
Buried: Grand Army of the Republic Cemetery, Portland, OR (Section 5, Lot 11)
References: Pension File and Military Service File, National Archives. Spillard F. Horrall. *History of the 42nd Indiana Volunteer Infantry.* Chicago, IL, 1892. Death Notice, *Portland Morning Oregonian,* Nov. 24, 1904.

John Alexander McLaughlin

1 Lieutenant, Co. K, 11 IN Infantry (3 months), April 25, 1861. Honorably mustered out, Aug. 2, 1861. Captain, Co. A, 47 IN Infantry, Oct. 10, 1861. Major, 47 IN Infantry, April 12, 1862. Lieutenant Colonel, 47 IN Infantry, Oct. 22, 1862. Commanded 1 Brigade, 1 Division, Reserve Corps, Military Division of West Mississippi, Feb. 4–18, 1865. Commanded 1 Brigade, 1 Division, 13 Army Corps, Military Division of West Mississippi, Feb. 18–24, 1865 and May–June 1865. *Colonel,* 47 IN Infantry, March 1, 1865. Commanded Post of Shreveport, LA, July 9–31, 1865. Honorably mustered out, Oct. 23, 1865. Battle honors: Yazoo Pass Expedition, Vicksburg Campaign (Port Gibson, Champion's Hill), Jackson Campaign, Mobile.

Born: Sept. 27, 1826 Indianapolis, IN
Died: April 15, 1890 Topeka, KS
Other Wars: Mexican War (1 Sergeant, Co. D, 4 IN Infantry)
Occupation: Gunsmith and dealer in firearms
Miscellaneous: Resided Indianapolis, IN; and Topeka, Shawnee Co., KS, after 1868
Buried: Topeka Cemetery, Topeka, KS (Section 27, Lot 1)
References: Alfred T. Andreas. *History of the State of Kansas.* Chicago, IL, 1883. Pension File and

John Alexander McLaughlin (Craig Dunn Collection).

Military Service File, National Archives. McLaughlin-Jordan Family Papers, 1841–1915 (Collection SC 1030), Indiana Historical Society, Indianapolis, IN. Obituary, *Topeka State Journal,* April 18, 1890. David Williamson. *The 47th Indiana Volunteer Infantry: A Civil War History.* Jefferson, NC, 2012.

William Edward McLean

Lieutenant Colonel, 43 IN Infantry, Sept. 27, 1861. Colonel, 43 IN Infantry, Jan. 16, 1862. Sick but unable to obtain a furlough, he submitted his resignation, May 12, 1862, due to "bad health and general disability caused by exposure in the miasmatic swamps of the Mississippi," expecting that the resignation would be held until he returned from a brief leave of absence. Through a misunderstanding, however, his resignation was, during his absence, approved and forwarded by brigade commander, Colonel Graham N. Fitch. The War Department quickly removed the disability resulting from his resignation, allowing Governor Morton to recommission him, June 25, 1862. The order accepting his resignation was eventually revoked, Nov. 17, 1866. Commanded 1 Brigade, 13 Division, 13 Army Corps, District of Eastern Arkansas, June 12–July 28, 1863. Commanded 1 Brigade, 13 Division, 16 Army Corps, District of Eastern Arkansas, July 28–Aug. 4, 1863. Commanded 2 Division, Arkansas Expedition, 16 Army

William Edward McLean (C. Eppert, Photographer, No. 87 Main Street, Between Third and Fourth, Terre Haute, Indiana).

Corps, Aug. 4–Sept. 6, 1863. Commanded 1 Brigade, 3 Division, Army of Arkansas, Department of the Missouri, Sept. 7, 1863–Jan. 6, 1864. Commanded 1 Brigade, 3 Division, 7 Army Corps, Department of Arkansas, Jan. 6–March 12, 1864. Commanded 2 Brigade, 3 Division, 7 Army Corps, Department of Arkansas, March 12–May 11, 1864. Commanded Post of Little Rock, AR, May 14–June 3, 1864. Honorably mustered out, May 17, 1865. Battle honors: Helena, Camden Expedition (Marks' Mills, Jenkins' Ferry).
Born: Oct. 12, 1832 Frederick, MD
Died: Nov. 2, 1906 Terre Haute, IN
Education: Graduated Indiana University, Bloomington, IN, 1849
Occupation: Lawyer and newspaper editor
Offices/Honors: Indiana Senate, 1857, 1859, 1893, and 1895. Indiana House of Representatives, 1861 and 1867. Deputy Commissioner, U.S. Pension Bureau, 1885–89.
Miscellaneous: Resided Terre Haute, Vigo Co., IN; and Washington, DC
Buried: Highland Lawn Cemetery, Terre Haute, IN (Section 3, Lot 137)
References: Charles C. Oakey. *Greater Terre Haute and Vigo County Closing the First Century's History of City and County.* Chicago and New York, 1908. Henry C. Bradsby. *History of Vigo County, IN.* Chicago, IL, 1891. Obituary, *Terre Haute Tribune,* Nov. 3, 1906. Rebecca A. Shepherd, Charles W. Calhoun, Elizabeth Shanahan-Shoemaker, and Alan F. January, editors. *A Biographical Directory of the Indiana General Assembly.* Vol. 1, 1816–1899. Indianapolis, IN, 1980. Obituary Circular, Whole No. 220, Indiana MOLLUS. Hiram W. Beckwith. *History of Vigo and Parke Counties, Together with Historic Notes on the Wabash Valley.* Chicago, IL, 1880. Pension File and Military Service File, National Archives. Letters Received, Volunteer Service Branch, Adjutant General's Office, File I119(VS) 1862, National Archives. William E. McLean. *The 43rd Regiment of Indiana Volunteers. An Historic Sketch of Its Career and Services.* Terre Haute, IN, 1903. James Sutherland. *Biographical Sketches of the Members of the Forty-First General Assembly of the State of Indiana with That of the State Officers and Judiciary.* Indianapolis, IN, 1861. Theophilus A. Wylie. *Indiana University, Its History from 1820 to 1890.* Indianapolis, IN, 1890.

James McMannomy

2 Lieutenant, Co. H, 63 IN Infantry, Aug. 11, 1862. Lieutenant Colonel, 63 IN Infantry, Sept. 1, 1862. Colonel, 63 IN Infantry, July 1, 1863. Resigned Jan. 17, 1864, "on account of physical disability of long standing."
Born: March 5, 1824 Kingston, Ross Co., OH
Died: July 20, 1906 Covington, IN
Other Wars: Mexican War (2 Lieutenant, Co. D, 1 IN Infantry)
Occupation: Farmer
Miscellaneous: Resided Covington, Fountain Co., IN
Buried: Prescott Grove Cemetery, Covington, IN
References: Thomas A. Clifton, editor. *Past and Present of Fountain and Warren Counties, Indiana.* Indianapolis, IN, 1913. Pension File and Military Service File, National Archives. Hiram W. Beckwith. *History of Fountain County, Together with Historic Notes on the Wabash Valley.* Chicago, IL, 1881. Obituary, *Covington Republican,* July 27, 1906. *Portrait and Biographical Record of Montgomery, Parke and Fountain Counties, IN.* Chicago, IL, 1893. Mary Blair Immel, compiler, "Family Records of Civil War Colonel, Gold Rusher, Horse Thief Detective, and Prosperous Farmer, James McMannomy," *The Hoosier Genealogist,* Vol. 44, No. 1 (Spring 2004).

John William Thomas McMullen

Colonel, 57 IN Infantry, Oct. 18, 1861. Resigned March 6, 1862, since the regiment "needs a man better skilled in the science and art of war than myself."

Born: Jan. 1, 1826 Orange Co., VA
Died: Oct. 18, 1906 Lafayette, IN
Occupation: Methodist clergyman
Miscellaneous: Resided Richmond, Wayne Co., IN; and Lafayette, Tippecanoe Co., IN
Buried: Springvale Cemetery, Lafayette, IN (Section 27, Lot 77)
References: Obituary, *Lafayette Morning Journal*, Oct. 19, 1906. *Biographical Record and Portrait Album of Tippecanoe County, IN.* Chicago, IL, 1888. Richard P. DeHart, editor. *Past and Present of Tippecanoe County, IN.* Indianapolis, IN, 1909. Obituary Circular, Whole No. 221, Indiana MOLLUS. Pension File and Military Service File, National Archives. Asbury L. Kerwood. *Annals of the 57th Regiment Indiana Volunteers, Marches, Battles, and Incidents of Army Life.* Dayton, OH, 1868. J. J. Lamb, "The 'Preacher Regiment' from Indiana: The 57th Indiana Infantry," *Civil War: The Magazine of the Civil War Society*, Vol. 12 (March 1988).

Martin Boots Miller

Captain, Co. E, 84 IN Infantry, Aug. 17, 1862. Major, 84 IN Infantry, Dec. 1, 1864. Lieutenant Colonel, 84 IN Infantry, April 13, 1865. *Colonel, 84 IN Infantry, June 1, 1865.* Honorably mustered out, June 14, 1865. Battle honors: Chickamauga, Atlanta Campaign.

Born: March 15, 1833 Ward Twp., Randolph Co., IN
Died: Nov. 30, 1903 Decatur, IN
Education: Attended Indiana Asbury (now DePauw) University, Greencastle, IN. Attended Miami University, Oxford, OH.
Occupation: Lawyer and U.S. Pension Bureau examiner
Miscellaneous: Resided Winchester, Randolph Co., IN; Rockford, Winnebago Co., IL; Washington, DC; and Decatur, Adams Co., IN
Buried: Fountain Park Cemetery, Winchester, IN
References: Obituary, *Winchester Herald*, Dec. 9, 1903. Ebenezer Tucker. *History of Randolph County, IN.* Chicago, IL, 1882. Pension File and Military Service File, National Archives. *The Alumni and Former Student Catalogue of Miami University, 1809–1892.* Oxford, OH, 1892.

Gideon Curtis Moody

Captain, Co. G, 9 IN Infantry (3 months), April 24, 1861. Honorably mustered out, July 29, 1861. Captain, 19 U.S. Infantry, May 14, 1861. Lieutenant Colonel, 9 IN Infantry (3 years), Aug. 28, 1861. Colonel, 9 IN Infantry, Nov. 15, 1861. Mustered out as colonel, Aug. 19, 1862, by order of Major

Gideon Curtis Moody (post-war) (Doane Robinson. *History of South Dakota*. Logansport, Indiana, 1904).

Gen. Don Carlos Buell, who, in requesting authority from the War Department, explained, "It is absolutely necessary for the good of the regiment and the service." Commissary of Musters, Staff of Major Gen. George H. Thomas, Sept. 1863–March 1864. Resigned Regular Army commission, March 16, 1864, since "my private interests imperatively demand my attention at once. I cannot support myself and my family comfortably on the pay I receive." Battle honors: Shiloh, Chickamauga.

Born: Oct. 16, 1832 Cortland, NY
Died: March 17, 1904 Los Angeles, CA
Occupation: Lawyer and judge
Offices/Honors: Indiana House of Representatives, 1861. Dakota Territory House of Representatives, 1867–68, 1869–70 (Speaker) and 1874–75 (Speaker). Associate Justice, Dakota Territory Supreme Court, 1878–83. U.S. Senate, 1889–91.
Miscellaneous: Resided New Albany, Floyd Co., IN, 1852–58; Rensselaer, Jasper Co., IN, 1858–64; Yankton, Dakota Territory, 1864–79; Deadwood, Lawrence Co., SD, 1879–1900; and Los Angeles, CA, 1900–04
Buried: Hollywood Forever Cemetery, Los Angeles, CA (Section 12, Lot 118)
References: Doane Robinson. *History of South Dakota*. Logansport, IN, 1904. *National Cyclopedia of American Biography*. George W. Kingsbury. *History of Dakota Territory*. Chicago, IL, 1915. Obitu-

ary, *Los Angeles Daily Times,* March 18, 1904. Larry Pressler. *U.S. Senators from the Prairie.* Vermillion, SD, 1982. Pension File and Military Service File, National Archives. Rebecca A. Shepherd, Charles W. Calhoun, Elizabeth Shanahan-Shoemaker, and Alan F. January, editors. *A Biographical Directory of the Indiana General Assembly.* Vol. 1, 1816–1899. Indianapolis, IN, 1980. *Proceedings of the 18th Annual Reunion of the 9th Indiana Veteran Volunteer Infantry Association, Held at Logansport, IN, October 7–8, 1904.* Letters Received, Commission Branch, Adjutant General's Office, File M279(CB)1864, National Archives. James Sutherland. *Biographical Sketches of the Members of the Forty-First General Assembly of the State of Indiana with That of the State Officers and Judiciary.* Indianapolis, IN, 1861. Charles F. Ritter and Jon L. Wakelyn. *American Legislative Leaders, 1850–1910.* Westport, CT, 1989.

Ranna Stevens Moore

Captain, Co. F, 81 IN Infantry, Aug. 22, 1862. *Colonel,* 81 IN Infantry, Oct. 12, 1863. Major, 13 IN Cavalry, June 24, 1864. Lieutenant Colonel, 13 IN Cavalry, Aug. 29, 1865. Honorably mustered out, Nov. 18, 1865.

Born: Oct. 28, 1838 Wilmington, Dearborn Co., IN

Died: Jan. 28, 1909 North Platte, NE

Occupation: Methodist clergyman

Miscellaneous: Resided Corydon, Harrison Co., IN; Indianapolis, IN, 1865–66; Brighton, Macoupin Co., IL (1870); Bois D'Arc, Montgomery Co., IL (1880); Inavale, Webster Co., NE; Hayes Center, Hayes Co., NE; and North Platte, Lincoln Co., NE

Buried: North Platte Cemetery, North Platte, NE

References: Pension File and Military Service File, National Archives. Obituary, *North Platte Semi-Weekly Tribune,* Jan. 29, 1909.

John T. Morgan

Colonel, Crawford County Regiment, IN Legion, Sept. 8, 1862.

Born: Sept. 14, 1817 Crawford Co., IN

Died: March 13, 1863 Leavenworth, IN

Occupation: Flour mill operator and carpenter

Miscellaneous: Resided Leavenworth, Crawford Co., IN

Buried: Cedar Hill Cemetery, Leavenworth, IN

References: Obituary, *New Albany Daily Ledger,* March 16, 1863. Doris Byrd Leistner. *Crawford County Indiana Civil War Veterans.* New Albany, IN, 2005. *Report of Major General Love of the Indiana Legion.* Indianapolis, IN, 1863.

Thomas Morgan

Captain, Co. K, 74 IN Infantry, Aug. 18, 1862. Taken prisoner and paroled, Munfordville, KY, Sept. 17, 1862. Major, 74 IN Infantry, July 28,

Thomas Morgan (copy of image in the Craig Dunn Collection).

Thomas Morgan (photograph by Morse's Gallery of the Cumberland, 25 Cedar St., opposite the Commercial Hotel, Nashville, Tennessee; Mark Weldon Collection).

1864. Lieutenant Colonel, 74 IN Infantry, Sept. 1, 1864. *Colonel,* 74 IN Infantry, Jan. 1, 1865. Honorably mustered out, June 9, 1865. Battle honors: Munfordville, Atlanta Campaign (Kenesaw Mountain, Jonesborough).
Born: May 26, 1821 Monmouthshire, Wales
Died: Sept. 21, 1915 Dixon, IL
Occupation: Builder and contractor
Miscellaneous: Resided Warsaw, Kosciusko Co., IN; and Dixon, Lee Co., IL, 1874–1915
Buried: Oakwood Cemetery, Dixon, IL (Lot 1252)
References: *Portrait and Biographical Record of Lee County, IL.* Chicago, IL, 1892. Pension File and Military Service File, National Archives. Obituary, *Dixon Evening Telegraph,* Sept. 22, 1915. Will F. Peddycord. *History of the 74th Regiment Indiana Volunteer Infantry.* Warsaw, IN, 1913. Letters Received, Volunteer Service Branch, Adjutant General's Office, File M2684(VS)1865, National Archives.

Robert Gilbert Morrison

Captain, Co. G, 34 IN Infantry, Sept. 23, 1861. Major, 34 IN Infantry, June 18, 1863. Lieutenant Colonel, 34 IN Infantry, Dec. 1, 1863. *Colonel,* 34 IN Infantry, March 21, 1865. Charged with misconduct at Palmetto Ranch, TX, May 13, 1865, he was acquitted of all charges, Sept. 5, 1865, following a lengthy trial. Commanded Separate Brigade, Western District of Texas, Department of Texas, Sept. 9–Dec. 14, 1865. Honorably mustered out, Feb. 3, 1866. Battle honors: Vicksburg Campaign, Palmetto Ranch.
Born: Jan. 6, 1838 Caledonia Co., VT
Died: Oct. 17, 1902 St. Johns, MI
Occupation: Dry goods merchant, grocer, and physician
Miscellaneous: Resided Roanoke, Huntington Co., IN, to 1872; Fort Wayne, Allen Co., IN, 1872–77; Allegan, Allegan Co., MI, 1879–85; Midland, Midland Co., MI, 1885–87; and St. Johns, Clinton Co., MI
Buried: Mount Rest Cemetery, St. Johns, MI
References: Pension File and Military Service File, National Archives. Letters Received, Volunteer Service Branch, Adjutant General's Office, File M3045(VS)1865, National Archives. Obituary, *Washington National Tribune,* Nov. 20, 1902. Jeffrey W. Hunt. *The Last Battle of the Civil War: Palmetto Ranch.* Austin, TX, 2002.

James Boleyn Mulky

Captain, Hoosier Greys, Monroe County Regiment, IN Legion, June 6, 1861. Colonel, Monroe County Regiment, IN Legion, Sept. 24, 1861. Major, 55 IN Infantry, June 11, 1862. Honorably mustered out, Sept. 9, 1862. Provost Marshal, 3rd District of Indiana, April 5–Oct. 31, 1865.
Born: Oct. 4, 1826 Crawford Co., IN
Died: Nov. 28, 1903 Bloomington, IN
Education: Graduated Indiana University, Bloomington, IN, 1859
Other Wars: Mexican War (Private, Co. A, 2 IN Infantry)
Occupation: Lawyer
Buried: Rose Hill Cemetery, Bloomington, IN
References: Charles Blanchard, editor. *Counties of Morgan, Monroe and Brown, Indiana. Historical and Biographical.* Chicago, IL, 1884. Obituary, *Bloomington Evening World,* Nov. 30, 1903. Pension File, National Archives. Theophilus A. Wylie. *Indiana University: Its History from 1820 to 1890.* Indianapolis, IN, 1890.

Bernard Francis Mullen

Lieutenant Colonel, 35 IN Infantry, May 22, 1862. Colonel, 35 IN Infantry, Aug. 7, 1862. GSW right thigh, Stone's River, TN, Jan. 2, 1863. Commanded Post of Madison, IN, June–Sept. 1863. Resigned May 29, 1864, "by reason of physical disability," due to "general debility and severe lung symptoms." Battle honors: Stone's River,

Robert Gilbert Morrison (photograph by J. A. Sheldon, 101 Canal St., New Orleans; Mark Weldon Collection).

Bernard Francis Mullen ("One Day a Year for the Sons of Erin; First Indianapolis Observance in 1864," *Indianapolis News*, March 11, 1922).

Morgan's Ohio Raid, Lookout Mountain, Missionary Ridge.
Born: March 4, 1825 Manayunk, PA
Died: Feb. 3, 1879 Indianapolis, IN
Other Wars: Mexican War (Assistant Surgeon, 5 IN Infantry)
Occupation: Physician
Miscellaneous: Resided Napoleon, Ripley Co., IN, to 1861; Madison, Jefferson Co., IN, 1861–1871; Terre Haute, Vigo Co., IN, after 1871
Buried: St. Joseph's Cemetery, Terre Haute, IN (unmarked)
References: Pension File and Military Service File, National Archives. Andrew Mullen. *Col. Bernard F. Mullen, Commander of the 35th Indiana Volunteers, 1st Irish Regiment, Civil War.* Celina, OH, 1968. Obituary, *Terre Haute Daily Express,* Feb. 4, 1879. Obituary, *Indianapolis Sentinel,* Feb. 3, 1879. General W. H. Kemper. *A Medical History of the State of Indiana.* Chicago, IL, 1911. Letters Received, Volunteer Service Branch, Adjutant General's Office, File M967(VS)1864, National Archives. Col. Bernard F. Mullen Family Materials, 1834–1893 (Collection SC 2807), Indiana Historical Society, Indianapolis, IN. "One Day a Year for the Sons of Erin; First Indianapolis Observance in 1864," *Indianapolis News,* March 11, 1922. William L. Burton. *Melting Pot Soldiers: The Union's Ethnic Regiments.* Ames, IA, 1988.

Charles Dennis Murray

Lieutenant Colonel, 20 IN Infantry, July 22, 1861. Claiming that the regiment was demoralized due to the bad temper and strict discipline of Colonel Brown, he resigned Nov. 23, 1861, for reasons "such as forbid me to have any further connection with the regiment." Colonel, 89 IN Infantry, Aug. 28, 1862. Taken prisoner and paroled, Munfordville, KY, Sept. 17, 1862. Commanded 1 Brigade, District of Memphis, 16 Army Corps, Army of the Tennessee, Jan. 12–March 31, 1863. Commanded 1 Brigade, 5 Division (District of Memphis), 16 Army Corps, Army of the Tennessee, March 31, 1863–Jan. 25, 1864. Commanded 1 Brigade, 3 Division, 16 Army Corps, Army of the Tennessee, May 31–Sept. 14, 1864. Having failed to report his address monthly while serving on several military commissions in Indiana, he was dismissed, April 18, 1865, for "evading duty and absence without leave." Dismissal revoked, April 28, 1865, upon positive evidence of his assignment to duty on the commissions. Commanded 1 Brigade, 2 Division, 16 Army Corps, Department of the Gulf, June 30–July 19, 1865. Honorably mustered out, July 19, 1865. Battle honors: Munfordville, Meridian Expedition, Red River Campaign (Fort DeRussy, Pleasant Hill), Tupelo.
Born: July 4, 1818 Greensburg, KY
Died: Aug. 8, 1873 Kokomo, IN
Occupation: Lawyer and newspaper editor
Offices/Honors: Indiana House of Representatives, 1849–50, 1855. Indiana Senate, 1857, 1859.
Miscellaneous: Resided Kokomo, Howard Co., IN; and Princeton, Bureau Co., IL, 1865–69
Buried: Crown Point Cemetery, Kokomo, IN (Section 1, Lot 7)
References: Rebecca A. Shepherd, Charles W. Calhoun, Elizabeth Shanahan-Shoemaker, and Alan F. January, editors. *A Biographical Directory of the Indiana General Assembly.* Vol. 1, 1816–1899. Indianapolis, IN, 1980. Pension File and Military Service File, National Archives. Obituary, *Kokomo Weekly Tribune,* Aug. 12, 1873. Craig L. Dunn. *Harvestfields of Death: The 20th Indiana Volunteers of Gettysburg.* Carmel, IN, 1999. Letters Received, Volunteer Service Branch, Adjutant General's Office, File I54(VS)1862, National Archives. "Howard County's Ranking Civil War Soldiers," *Kokomo Tribune,* Centennial Edition, Oct. 30, 1950. Jackson Morrow. *History of Howard County, IN.* Indianapolis, IN, 1910. Hervey Craven. *A Brief History of the 89th Indiana Volunteer Infantry.* Wabash, IN, 1899.

Charles Dennis Murray (seated third from left, with members of the Military Commission for the conspiracy trial of Lambdin P. Milligan and others: seated left to right, Ambrose A. Stevens, William E. McLean, Murray, Reuben Williams, Ansel D. Wass, and Albert Heath; standing left to right, Silas Colgrove, Thomas J. Lucas, Thomas W. Bennett, Benjamin J. Spooner, Richard P. DeHart, and Henry L. Burnett) (Craig Dunn Collection).

Thomas Nichols

Captain, Danville Cavalry, Hendricks County Regiment, IN Legion, Aug. 8, 1863. Colonel, Hendricks County Regiment, IN Legion, June 27, 1864.

Born: Nov. 5, 1803 near Bardstown, Nelson Co., KY

Died: Nov. 22, 1895 Danville, IN

Other Wars: Black Hawk War

Occupation: Carpenter, merchant, and farmer

Offices/Honors: Sheriff of Hendricks Co., IN, 1828–32, 1844–48, and 1860–64. Indiana House of Representatives, 1833–34 and 1836–37.

Buried: Danville South Cemetery, Danville, IN (Section A, Row 14)

References: *A Portrait and Biographical Record of Boone, Clinton and Hendricks Counties, IN.* Chicago, IL, 1895. *History of Hendricks County, IN.* Chicago, IL, 1885. Rebecca A. Shepherd, Charles W. Calhoun, Elizabeth Shanahan-Shoemaker, and Alan F. January, editors. *A Biographical Directory of the Indiana General Assembly.* Vol. 1, 1816–1899. Indianapolis, IN, 1980. Obituary, *Danville Republican,* Nov. 28, 1895.

Thomas Nichols (post-war) (*A Portrait and Biographical Record of Boone, Clinton and Hendricks Counties, Indiana.* Chicago, Illinois, 1895).

William O'Brien

Captain, Co. D, 12 IN Infantry (1 year), May 14, 1861. Honorably mustered out, May 19, 1862. 1 Lieutenant, Adjutant, 75 IN Infantry, July 18, 1862. Lieutenant Colonel, 75 IN Infantry, Aug. 20, 1862. GSW right forearm, Chickamauga, GA, Sept. 20, 1863. *Colonel,* 75 IN Infantry, April 1, 1864. Shell wound right hand, Peach Tree Creek, GA, July 20, 1864. Bvt. Colonel, USV, March 13, 1865, for gallantry and good conduct as commander of his regiment during the past year, and for especial gallantry at the battle of Peach Tree Creek, Georgia. Commanded 2 Brigade, Cruft's Provisional Division, Army of the Cumberland, April 1865. Honorably mustered out, June 8, 1865. Battle honors: Chickamauga, Atlanta Campaign (Peach Tree Creek).

Born: May 31, 1839 Marion Co., IN
Died: Oct. 3, 1875 Santa Barbara, CA
Education: Attended Indiana Asbury (now DePauw) University, Greencastle, IN
Occupation: Lawyer
Offices/Honors: Indiana Senate, 1873
Miscellaneous: Resided Noblesville, Hamilton Co., IN, to 1873; and Santa Barbara, CA
Buried: Santa Barbara Cemetery, Santa Barbara, CA (Montecito Section, Lot 78)
References: Obituary, *Santa Barbara Weekly Press,* Oct. 9, 1875. Rebecca A. Shepherd, Charles W. Calhoun, Elizabeth Shanahan-Shoemaker, and Alan F. January, editors. *A Biographical Directory of the Indiana General Assembly.* Vol. 1, 1816–1899. Indianapolis, IN, 1980. Pension File and Military Service File, National Archives. David B. Floyd. *History of the 75th Regiment of Indiana Infantry Volunteers, Its Organization, Campaigns, and Battles (1862–65).* Philadelphia, PA, 1893. Joe H. Burgess. *Hamilton County and the Civil War.* N.p., 1967.

Oliver Ormsby

Colonel, 10 IN Legion (Switzerland County), June 8, 1861.

Born: Nov. 29, 1828 Louisville, KY
Died: March 5, 1870 Vevay, IN (drowned in Ohio River)
Occupation: Lawyer
Offices/Honors: Clerk of county courts, 1856–62
Miscellaneous: Resided Vevay, Switzerland Co., IN
Buried: Place of burial unknown
References: Oliver O. Page. *A Short Account of the Family of Ormsby of Pittsburgh.* Albany, NY, 1892. Death Notice, *Vevay Reveille,* March 10, 1870. Obituary, *Vevay Reveille,* March 17, 1870. Perret Dufour. *The Swiss Settlement of Switzerland County, IN.* Indianapolis, IN, 1925. John P. Etter. *The Indiana Legion: A Civil War Militia.* Carmel, IN, 2006.

John M. Orr

Captain, Co. E, 16 IN Infantry (1 year), May 14, 1861. Honorably mustered out, May 23, 1862. Captain, Co. A, 16 IN Infantry (3 years), July 14, 1862. Major, 16 IN Infantry, Aug. 17, 1862. Lieutenant Colonel, 16 IN Infantry, Nov. 17, 1862. Shell wound head, Arkansas Post, AR, Jan. 12, 1863. Resigned April 2, 1863, due to wound, which "has impaired my hearing so much that it renders me totally unfit to perform the duties involved upon me as a field officer." Captain, Co. A, 124 IN Infantry, Dec. 26, 1863. Lieutenant Colonel, 124 IN Infantry, March 8, 1864. Colonel, 124 IN Infantry, July 10, 1864. Commanded 1 Brigade, 1 Division, 23 Army Corps, Department of the Ohio, Dec. 29, 1864–Feb. 2, 1865. Commanded 1 Brigade, 1 Division, 23 Army Corps, Department of North Carolina, Feb. 25–March 14, 1865 and May 18–June 27, 1865. Honorably mustered out, Aug. 31, 1865. Battle honors: Richmond, Arkansas Post, Atlanta Campaign, Franklin, Nashville, Campaign of the Carolinas (Kinston).

Born: 1829 Montgomery Co., OH
Died: Sept. 27, 1865 Connersville, IN (committed suicide by pistol shot to head)

William O'Brien.

John M. Orr.

John M. Orr (Mark Weldon Collection).

Occupation: Farmer and carriage painter
Miscellaneous: Resided Troy, Miami Co., OH; and Connersville, Fayette Co., IN
Buried: City Cemetery, Connersville, IN (Section 4W, Lot 89)
References: Pension File and Military Service File, National Archives. Obituary, *Connersville Weekly Times,* Sept. 28, 1865. Letters Received, Volunteer Service Branch, Adjutant General's Office, File O655(VS)1863, National Archives.

William Orr

2 Lieutenant, Co. K, 19 IN Infantry, July 29, 1861. 1 Lieutenant, Co. K, 19 IN Infantry, Aug. 23, 1862. GSW left breast, Antietam, MD, Sept. 17, 1862. Captain, Co. K, 19 IN Infantry, Sept. 18, 1862. Major, 19 IN Infantry, Aug. 4, 1864. Colonel, 20 IN Infantry, Oct. 18, 1864. Honorably mustered out, May 15, 1865. Battle honors: Antietam, Chancellorsville, North Anna, Petersburg Campaign.
Born: Sept. 15, 1838 Delaware Co., IN
Died: Jan. 14, 1867
Occupation: Lawyer

William Orr (Craig Dunn Collection).

Miscellaneous: Resided Selma, Delaware Co., IN; and Muncie, Delaware Co., IN
Buried: Orr Cemetery, near Selma, IN
References: Pension File and Military Service File, National Archives. *A Portrait and Biographical Record of Delaware and Randolph Counties, IN.* Chicago, IL, 1894. Craig L. Dunn. *Iron Men, Iron Will: The Nineteenth Indiana Regiment of the Iron Brigade.* Indianapolis, IN, 1995. Letters Received, Volunteer Service Branch, Adjutant General's Office, File O476(VS)1865, National Archives.

John Osborn

Lieutenant Colonel, 31 IN Infantry, Sept. 20, 1861. Colonel, 31 IN Infantry, July 17, 1862. Resigned July 14, 1863, since "I am 53 years of age, and my health so much impaired that I do not feel

able to longer discharge the duties of the office." Battle honors: Fort Donelson, Shiloh, Corinth, Stone's River.
Born: Sept. 1809 Maysville, KY
Died: June 11, 1887 Greencastle, IN
Other Wars: Mexican War (Captain, Co. D, 2 IN Infantry; GSW left knee, Buena Vista)
Occupation: Dry goods merchant and lawyer
Offices/Honors: Indiana House of Representatives, 1839–40. Clay County Auditor, 1850–59. Postmaster, Greencastle, IN, 1866–74.
Miscellaneous: Resided Bowling Green, Clay Co., IN, to 1861; and Greencastle, Putnam Co., IN
Buried: Forest Hill Cemetery, Greencastle, IN (Upper Circle, Block 6, Range 4, Lot 3)
References: Obituary, *Greencastle Banner,* June 16, 1887. Obituary, *Greencastle Times,* June 16, 1887. Rebecca A. Shepherd, Charles W. Calhoun, Elizabeth Shanahan-Shoemaker, and Alan F. January, editors. *A Biographical Directory of the Indiana General Assembly.* Vol. 1, 1816–1899. Indianapolis, IN, 1980. Pension File and Military Service File, National Archives. John Thomas Smith. *A History of the 31st Regiment of Indiana Volunteer Infantry in the War of the Rebellion.* Cincinnati, OH, 1900. Charles Blanchard, editor. *Counties of Clay and Owen, Indiana. Historical and Biographical.* Chicago, IL, 1884.

Alfred Dale Owen

Sergeant, Co. I, 15 IN Infantry, June 14, 1861. Discharged for disability, Aug. 29, 1861, due to rheumatism of the chest. 1 Lieutenant, Co. B, 60 IN Infantry, Nov. 16, 1861. Resigned July 22, 1862. 1 Lieutenant, Adjutant, 80 IN Infantry, Sept. 4, 1862. Taken prisoner and paroled, Perryville, KY, Oct. 8, 1862. Lieutenant Colonel, 80 IN Infantry, Nov. 1, 1863. *Colonel,* 80 IN Infantry, Jan. 27, 1864. Honorably mustered out, June 22, 1865. Battle honors: Perryville, Atlanta Campaign (Resaca), Franklin, Nashville, Campaign of the Carolinas.
Born: Oct. 16, 1840 New Harmony, IN
Died: Feb. 23, 1903 Mount Vernon, IN
Education: Attended Western Military Institute, Nashville, TN
Occupation: Merchant and bank cashier
Offices/Honors: Posey County Auditor, 1875–83. Mayor of Mount Vernon, IN, 1898–1900.
Miscellaneous: Resided New Harmony, Posey Co., IN; and Mount Vernon, Posey Co., IN. Nephew of Colonel Richard Owen (60 IN Infantry). Son of the noted geologist David Dale Owen.
Buried: Maple Hill Cemetery, New Harmony, IN
References: Obituary Circular, Whole No. 164, Indiana MOLLUS. *History of Posey County, IN.*

Alfred Dale Owen (Craig Dunn Collection).

Chicago, IL, 1886. Obituary, *Evansville Journal-News,* Feb. 23, 1903. Pension File and Military Service File, National Archives. John C. Leffel, editor. *History of Posey County, IN.* Chicago, IL, 1913.

Richard Owen

Lieutenant Colonel, 15 IN Infantry, June 14, 1861. Resigned Dec. 31, 1861, to accept promotion. Colonel, 60 IN Infantry, Jan. 31, 1862. Commanded Camp Morton Prison, Indianapolis, IN, Feb.–June, 1862. Taken prisoner and paroled, Munfordville, KY, Sept. 17, 1862. Commanded 1 Brigade, 10 Division, 13 Army Corps, Army of the Tennessee, July 8–Aug. 17, 1863. Commanded 1 Brigade, 4 Division, 13 Army Corps, Department of the Gulf, Sept. 7–Nov. 20, 1863. Resigned Nov. 20, 1863, in order to accept professorship at Indiana University. Battle honors: Cheat Mountain, Munfordville, Arkansas Post, Vicksburg Campaign, Jackson Campaign, Operations in the Teche Country (Bayou Bourbeau).
Born: Jan. 6, 1810 Braxfield House, near New Lanark, Scotland
Died: March 24, 1890 New Harmony, IN
Other Wars: Mexican War (Captain, 16 U.S. Infantry)
Occupation: Geologist and college professor
Offices/Honors: Professor of Natural Science and Chemistry, Indiana University, 1864–79
Miscellaneous: Resided New Harmony, Posey

Co., IN; and Bloomington, Monroe Co., IN, 1864–79. Brother of social reformer Robert Dale Owen and of geologist David Dale Owen. Uncle of Colonel Alfred D. Owen (80 IN Infantry).

Buried: Maple Hill Cemetery, New Harmony, IN

References: Victor Lincoln Albjerg. *Richard Owen Scotland 1810–Indiana 1890.* Lafayette, IN, 1946. *A Biographical History of Eminent and Self-Made Men of the State of Indiana.* Cincinnati, OH, 1880. *National Cyclopedia of American Biography. History of Posey County, IN.* Chicago, IL, 1886. Obituary, *New York Times,* March 26, 1890. Military Service File, National Archives. Hattie Lou Winslow and Joseph R. H. Moore. *Camp Morton, 1861–1865, Indianapolis Prison Camp.* Indianapolis, IN, 1940. Theophilus A. Wylie. *Indiana University, Its History from 1820 to 1890.* Indianapolis, IN, 1890. Theodore T. Scribner. *Indiana's Roll of Honor.* Indianapolis, IN, 1866. Edward White, editor. *Evansville and Its Men of Mark.* Evansville, IN, 1873.

Thomas Newsom Pace

Captain, Co. G, 1 IN Cavalry, Aug. 20, 1861. Major, 1 IN Cavalry, Jan. 3, 1863. Lieutenant Colonel, 1 IN Cavalry, May 1, 1863. Colonel, 10 IN Cavalry, Feb. 15, 1864. Commanded Post of Pulaski, TN, Oct.–Nov. 1864. Resigned March 16, 1865, since "my agent has recently died, which leaves my business in a very critical condition ... and unless I can give this matter my immediate and personal attention my losses will be much greater than I am able to bear." Battle honors: Helena, Pine Bluff.

Born: Aug. 17, 1831 near Burkesville, Cumberland Co., KY

Died: Feb. 5, 1919 Shenandoah, IA

Occupation: Dry goods and tobacco commission merchant

Offices/Honors: Postmaster of Shenandoah, IA, 1889–93

Miscellaneous: Resided Millersburg and Boonville, Warrick Co., IN, to 1868; Evansville, Vanderburgh Co., IN, 1868–74; Shenandoah, Page Co., IA, after 1874

Buried: Rose Hill Cemetery, Shenandoah, IA (Original Addition, Section 1, Lot 63)

References: *Biographical History of Page County, Iowa.* Chicago, IL, 1890. Pension File and Military Service File, National Archives. Obituary, *Shenandoah World,* Feb. 6, 1919. Letters Received, Volunteer Service Branch, Adjutant General's Office, File P1105(VS) 1864, National Archives.

Thomas Pattison

Captain, Aurora Union Artillery, 12 IN Legion (Dearborn County), June 5, 1861. Colonel, 18 IN Infantry, Aug. 16, 1861. Commanded 2 Division, Army of Southwest Missouri, Department of the Missouri, Dec. 1861–Jan. 1862. Commanded 1 Brigade, 3 Division, Army of Southwest Missouri, Department of the Missouri, March 1862. Commanded Post of Batesville, AR, May 1862. Resigned June 3, 1862, due to "the

Richard Owen (seated center, with officers of the 60th Indiana Infantry, including Chaplain William H. Carter, seated left, Quartermaster John J. Palmer, seated right, Captain Henry F. Fitton, standing left, and 1st Lieutenant Eugene F. Owen, standing right) (Ronn Palm Collection).

Thomas Pattison (dedicatory sheet music).

indirect censure thrown on me by the promotion of several of my juniors through the influence of Indiana politicians," in addition to "the ill health of my wife and my own affliction of prolapsis ani." Battle honors: Pea Ridge.

Born: May 2, 1815 County Armagh, Ireland
Died: Dec. 13, 1896 Chicago, IL
Occupation: Railroad surveyor and civil engineer. Assessor in Chicago Municipal Water Department in later years.
Miscellaneous: Resided Versailles, Ripley Co., IN; Aurora, Dearborn Co., IN; Cincinnati, OH; and Chicago, IL, after 1869
Buried: Spring Grove Cemetery, Cincinnati, OH (Section 53, Lot 133)
References: Obituary, *Chicago Daily Tribune*, Dec. 14, 1896. Obituary, *Chicago Daily Inter Ocean*, Dec. 15, 1896. Pension File and Military Service File, National Archives. Alfred T. Andreas. *History of Chicago from the Earliest Period to the Present Time.* Chicago, IL, 1886.

David Henry Patton

Corporal, Co. H, 38 IN Infantry, Sept. 18, 1861. Sergeant, Co. H, 38 IN Infantry, Dec. 1, 1862. Sergeant Major, 38 IN Infantry, Aug. 16, 1863. 1 Lieutenant, Co. H, 38 IN Infantry, June 5, 1864. Captain, Co. H, 38 IN Infantry, July 31, 1864. Lieutenant Colonel, 38 IN Infantry, May 5, 1865. Colonel, 38 IN Infantry, May 20, 1865. Honorably mustered out, July 15, 1865. Battle honors: Perryville, Stone's River, Atlanta Campaign (Jonesborough), Campaign of the Carolinas (Bentonville).

Born: Nov. 26, 1837 Flemingsburg, KY
Died: Jan. 17, 1914 Otterbein, IN
Education: Attended Waveland (IN) Collegiate Institute. Graduated Chicago (IL) Medical College, 1867.
Occupation: Physician
Offices/Honors: U.S. House of Representatives, 1891–93
Miscellaneous: Resided Waveland, Montgomery Co., IN, to 1867; Remington, Jasper Co., IN, 1867–93; and Woodward, Woodward Co., OK
Buried: Remington Cemetery, Remington, IN
References: William H. Powell, editor. *Officers of the Army and Navy (Volunteer) Who Served in the Civil War.* Philadelphia, PA, 1893. *Counties of Warren, Benton, Jasper and Newton, Indiana. Historical and Biographical.* Chicago, IL, 1883. Obituary, *Jasper County Democrat,* Jan. 24, 1914. Pension File and Military Service File, National Archives. James L. Harrison, compiler. *Biographical Directory of the American Congress, 1774–1949.* Washington, DC, 1950. Obituary Circular, Whole No. 323, Indiana MOLLUS. Henry F. Perry. *History of the 38th Regiment Indiana Volunteer Infantry.* Palo Alto, CA, 1906. James H. Royalty. *History of the Town of Remington and Vicinity.* Logansport, IN, 1894.

David Henry Patton (post-war) (James H. Royalty. *History of the Town of Remington and Vicinity.* Logansport, Indiana, 1894).

Charles Dewey Pearson

Colonel, Orange County Regiment, IN Legion, Sept. 13, 1861. Surgeon, 49 IN Infantry, Nov. 21, 1861. Resigned Feb. 7, 1862, due to disability from an attack of pneumonia. Assistant Surgeon, 82 IN Infantry, Aug. 14, 1862. Surgeon, 82 IN Infantry, Sept. 20, 1862. Suffering from "nervous prostration terminating in muscular and articular rheumatism," he resigned May 14, 1863, "satisfied that camp life and the fare incident thereto did not agree with me."

Born: April 12, 1820 Paoli, IN
Died: Feb. 14, 1890 Indianapolis, IN
Education: Attended Transylvania University, Lexington, KY. Attended Indiana Asbury (now DePauw) University, Greencastle, IN, and awarded honorary M.D. degree, 1852. Graduated Cincinnati (OH) College of Physicians and Surgeons, 1859. Graduated New York University Medical College, 1878.
Occupation: Physician and medical college professor. Also engaged in developing kaolin mines in Lawrence Co., IN.
Offices/Honors: Professor of Obstetrics, Central College of Physicians and Surgeons, Indianapolis, IN, 1879–86
Miscellaneous: Resided Orleans, Orange Co., IN, before war; and Indianapolis, IN, after war
Buried: Crown Hill Cemetery, Indianapolis, IN (Section 14, Lot 93)
References: *A Biographical History of Eminent and Self-Made Men of the State of Indiana*. Cincinnati, IN, 1880. Obituary, *Indianapolis Journal*, Feb. 15, 1890. Obituary Circular, Whole No. 21, Indiana MOLLUS. Lisabeth M. Holloway. *Medical Obituaries: American Physicians' Biographical Notices in Selected Medical Journals Before 1907*. New York and London, 1981. General William H. Kemper. *A Medical History of the State of Indiana*. Chicago, IL, 1911. Pension File, National Archives. Letters Received, Volunteer Service Branch, Adjutant General's Office, File D659(VS)1862, National Archives.

Milton Peden

1 Lieutenant, Co. K, 36 IN Infantry, Oct. 24, 1861. Captain, Co. K, 36 IN Infantry, April 26, 1862. Topographical Engineer, Staff of Colonel William Grose, 3 Brigade, 2 Division, Left Wing, 14 Army Corps, Army of the Cumberland, Dec. 1862. GSW right thigh, Stone's River, TN, Dec. 31, 1862. Provost Marshal, Staff of Colonel William Grose, 3 Brigade, 2 Division, 21 Army Corps, Army of the Cumberland, Aug. 3–Oct. 9, 1863. Provost Marshal, Staff of Brig. Gen. William Grose, 3 Brigade, 1 Division, 4 Army Corps, Army of the

Milton Peden (photograph by Andrews & Gordon Star Gallery, 33 West Washington Street, Near the Palmer House, Indianapolis, Indiana).

Cumberland, Oct. 10, 1863–Aug. 22, 1864. Honorably mustered out, Sept. 21, 1864. Colonel, 147 IN Infantry, March 11, 1865. Honorably mustered out, Aug. 4, 1865. Battle honors: Stone's River, Chickamauga.

Born: March 20, 1823 Claysville, Washington Co., PA
Died: Jan. 21, 1908 Knightstown, IN
Occupation: Farmer and millwright before war. Stove and tinware merchant after war.
Offices/Honors: Indiana House of Representatives, 1855. Indiana Senate, 1865.
Miscellaneous: Resided Knightstown, Henry Co., IN
Buried: Glencove Cemetery, Knightstown, IN
References: George Hazzard. *Hazzard's History of Henry County, IN, 1822–1906. Military Edition*. New Castle, IN, 1906. Obituary, *Knightstown Banner*, Jan. 24, 1908. Biographical sketch, *Knightstown Banner*, Jan. 31, 1908. Obituary Circular, Whole No. 241, Indiana MOLLUS. Pension File and Military Service File, National Archives. William Grose. *The Story of the Marches, Battles and Incidents of the 36th Regiment Indiana Volunteer Infantry*. New Castle, IN, 1891. Rebecca A. Shepherd, Charles W. Calhoun, Elizabeth Shanahan-Shoemaker, and Alan F. January, editors. *A Biographical Directory of the Indiana General Assembly*. Vol. 1, 1816–1899.

Indianapolis, IN, 1980. Norma Paden Heskett Locke, Elona Paden Bruce, Merrill Paden, Elsie Paden Beavers, Esther Paden Birk Osborn. *Peden-Paden Family History.* Wichita, KS, 2003. Letters Received, Volunteer Service Branch, Adjutant General's Office, File P169(VS)1863, National Archives.

Oran Perry

Private, Co. B, 16 IN Infantry (1 year), April 23, 1861. Sergeant Major, 16 IN Infantry, May 14, 1861. Honorably mustered out, May 23, 1862. 1 Lieutenant, Adjutant, 69 IN Infantry, Aug. 14, 1862. GSW leg, Richmond, KY, Aug. 30, 1862. Taken prisoner and paroled, Richmond, KY, Aug. 30, 1862. Lieutenant Colonel, 69 IN Infantry, March 13, 1863. GSW arm, Thompson's Hill, MS, May 1, 1863. Bvt. Colonel, USV, March 26, 1865, for faithful and meritorious services during the campaign against the city of Mobile and its defenses. GSW head, Fort Blakely, AL, April 9, 1865. *Colonel,* 69 IN Infantry, April 13, 1865. Honorably mustered out, July 5, 1865. Battle honors: Richmond, Vicksburg Campaign (Thompson's Hill), Jackson Campaign, Mobile Campaign (Fort Blakely).

Oran Perry (post-war) (Andrew W. Young. *History of Wayne County, Indiana.* Cincinnati, Ohio, 1872).

Born: Feb. 1, 1838 Liberty, IN
Died: Nov. 30, 1929 Indianapolis, IN
Occupation: Cashier for auction firm before war. Proprietor of Richmond Plow Works, 1867–73. Railroad freight agent in later years.
Offices/Honors: Quartermaster General of Indiana, 1902–05. Adjutant General of Indiana, 1905–10. Superintendent of Indiana Soldiers and Sailors Monument, 1918–29.
Miscellaneous: Resided Richmond, Wayne Co., IN, to 1874; and Indianapolis, IN
Buried: Earlham Cemetery, Richmond, IN (Section 1, Lot 260)
References: Oran Perry. *Recollections of the Civil War.* Second Edition. Indianapolis, IN, 1928. Obituary, *Richmond Item,* Dec. 1, 1929. Jacob P. Dunn. *Indiana and Indianans.* Chicago and New York, 1919. Andrew W. Young. *History of Wayne County, Indiana.* Cincinnati, OH, 1872. Carolyn S. Bridge. *These Men Were Heroes Once: The 69th Indiana Volunteer Infantry.* West Lafayette, IN, 2005. Military Service File, National Archives. John C. Power, editor. *Directory and Soldiers' Register of Wayne County, IN.* Richmond, IN, 1865.

Oran Perry (photograph by Watson & Estell, Main Street, Richmond, Indiana; courtesy Henry Deeks).

John Upfold Pettit

Colonel, 75 IN Infantry, Aug. 20, 1862. Resigned Oct. 24, 1862, since "bad health ... which has unfitted me for such service and which promises slow amendment, if any, leaves me no choice."
Born: Sept. 11, 1820 Fabius, NY

John Upfold Pettit (U.S. House of Representatives, 1859) (McClees' Gallery of Photographic Portraits of the Senators, Representatives & Delegates of the Thirty-Fifth Congress, Library of Congress [LC-DIG-ppmsca-26790]).

John Andrew Platter (copy of image in the Craig Dunn Collection).

Died: March 21, 1881 Wabash, IN
Education: Attended Hamilton College, Clinton, NY. Graduated Union College, Schenectady, NY, 1839.
Occupation: Lawyer and judge
Offices/Honors: Indiana House of Representatives, 1844–45 and 1865 (Speaker). U.S. Consul, Maranham, Brazil, 1850–53. U.S. House of Representatives, 1855–61.
Miscellaneous: Resided Wabash, Wabash Co., IN
Buried: Falls Cemetery, Wabash, IN (Original Part, Lot 486)
References: *A Biographical History of Eminent and Self-Made Men of the State of Indiana.* Cincinnati, IN, 1880. Thomas B. Helm. *History of Wabash County, IN.* Chicago, IL, 1884. Rebecca A. Shepherd, Charles W. Calhoun, Elizabeth Shanahan-Shoemaker, and Alan F. January, editors. *A Biographical Directory of the Indiana General Assembly.* Vol. 1, 1816–1899. Indianapolis, IN, 1980. John H. Stephens. *History of Miami County Illustrated.* Peru, IN, 1896. Charles F. Ritter and Jon L. Wakelyn. *American Legislative Leaders, 1850–1910.* Westport, CT, 1989. Military Service File, National Archives. Obituary, *New York Times,* March 23, 1881. David B. Floyd. *History of the 75th Regiment of Indiana Infantry Volunteers, Its Organization, Campaigns, and Battles (1862–65).* Philadelphia, PA, 1893.

John Andrew Platter

Captain, Co. I, 16 IN Infantry (1 year), May 14, 1861. Honorably mustered out, May 23, 1862. Captain, Co. B, 4 IN Cavalry, Aug. 4, 1862. Major, 4 IN Cavalry, Sept. 4, 1862. GSW head, Slatersville, KY, Nov. 24, 1862. Lieutenant Colonel, 4 IN Cavalry, Feb. 12, 1863. Colonel, 4 IN Cavalry, May 17, 1863. Resigned Sept. 9, 1863, due to "spasms and partial paralysis of the left side and confusion of his intellect," caused by his head wound. Colonel, 12 IN Legion (Dearborn County), Aug. 1, 1864. Battle honors: Tullahoma Campaign.
Born: Nov. 13, 1831 Ripley Co., IN
Died: June 27, 1867 Aurora, IN
Occupation: Plasterer before war. Auctioneer and insurance agent after war.
Miscellaneous: Resided Aurora, Dearborn Co., IN
Buried: Riverview Cemetery, Aurora, IN (Section E, Lot 22)
References: The Rev. David Edwin Platter. *A History of the Platter Family from About Year 1600 to the Present Time.* Cleveland, OH, 1919. Obituary, *Lawrenceburg Democratic Register,* July 4, 1867. Obituary, *Aurora Commercial,* June 29, 1867. Interment Records, Riverview Cemetery, Aurora, IN. Military Service File, National Archives. Richard J. Reid. *Fourth Indiana Cavalry: A History.* Olaton, KY, 1994. *Operations of the Indiana Legion and Minute Men, 1863–4. Documents Presented to the General Assembly, with the Governor's Message, Jan. 6, 1865.* Indianapolis, IN, 1865.

John Robert Polk

Private, Co. K, 8 IN Infantry (3 months), April 23, 1861. Honorably mustered out, Aug. 6, 1861.

Captain, Co. F, 8 IN Infantry (3 years), Aug. 20, 1861. Major, 8 IN Infantry, Nov. 26, 1864. Lieutenant Colonel, 8 IN Infantry, Nov. 27, 1864. *Colonel,* 8 IN Infantry, Feb. 22, 1865. Honorably mustered out, Aug. 28, 1865. Battle honors: Vicksburg Campaign, Shenandoah Valley Campaign.

Born: Oct. 11, 1832 New Castle, IN
Died: Oct. 21, 1875 Wabash, IN
Occupation: Clerk in dry goods store and later in the office of the County Auditor
Offices/Honors: Wabash County Auditor, 1866–74
Miscellaneous: Resided Wabash, Wabash Co., IN
Buried: Falls Cemetery, Wabash, IN (Original Part, Lot 334)
References: Obituary, *Wabash Plain Dealer,* Oct. 28, 1875. Clarkson W. Weesner, editor. *History of Wabash County, Indiana.* Chicago and New York, 1914. Pension File and Military Service File, National Archives. Letters Received, Volunteer Service Branch, Adjutant General's Office, File P1751(VS)1865, National Archives.

Allen Wiley Prather

1 Lieutenant, Co. B, 6 IN Infantry (3 months), April 25, 1861. Honorably mustered out, Aug. 2, 1861. 1 Lieutenant, Co. C, 6 IN Infantry (3 years), Aug. 20, 1861. Captain, Co. C, 6 IN Infantry, Sept. 19, 1861. Lieutenant Colonel, 120 IN Infantry, March 1, 1864. Colonel, 120 IN Infantry, Aug. 17, 1864. Commanded 1 Brigade, 1 Division, 23 Army Corps, Department of North Carolina, June 27–Aug. 1, 1865. Resigned Aug. 30, 1865, since "I deem it my duty to myself and my family that I should quit the service and return to civil pursuits." Battle honors: Chickamauga, Atlanta Campaign (Resaca), Franklin, Campaign of the Carolinas (Kinston).

Born: Aug. 10, 1836 Columbus, IN
Died: Nov. 19, 1891 Washington, DC
Education: Graduated Indiana Asbury (now DePauw) University Law School, Greencastle, IN, 1859
Occupation: Lawyer and later U.S. War Department clerk (after 1880)
Miscellaneous: Resided North Vernon, Jennings Co., IN; Columbus, Bartholomew Co., IN; Indianapolis, IN; and Washington, DC. His father, Lieutenant Colonel Hiram Prather (6 IN Infantry), and six brothers also served in the Union army.
Buried: Arlington National Cemetery, Arlington, VA (Section 1, Lot 38-B)
References: Pension File and Military Service File, National Archives. Obituary, *Washington Post,* Nov. 20, 1891. Obituary, *Columbus Herald,* Nov. 21, 1891. Charles C. Briant. *History of the 6th Regiment Indiana Volunteer Infantry, of Both the Three Months' and Three Years' Services.* Indianapolis, IN, 1891. Obituary, *Washington National Tribune,* Nov. 26, 1891. *A Biographical History of Eminent and Self-Made Men of the State of Indiana.* Cincinnati, IN, 1880.

Allen Wiley Prather (courtesy Clark Prather).

John William Ray

Colonel, 49 IN Infantry, Nov. 21, 1861. Described by Brig. Gen. George W. Morgan as "totally unfit to command a regiment in time of war," he was detailed, June 8, 1862, by General Buell for "special duty" at Nashville, TN, since "the condition of the Forty-Ninth Indiana is deplorable, morally and physically." He resigned Oct. 17, 1862, stating as a reason, "Some dissatisfaction in the Regiment has arisen which may possibly impair the efficiency thereof and thereby injure the service, and as I entered the army with the sole, sincere and honest desire to contribute my humble aid in suppressing the unholy rebellion..., my position personally is of too small consideration to present the slightest obstacle to the accomplishment of so great and noble result."

Born: Aug. 15, 1828 Madison, IN
Died: July 27, 1906 Indianapolis, IN
Education: Graduated Indiana Asbury (now DePauw) University, Greencastle, IN, 1848
Occupation: Lawyer and banker
Offices/Honors: U.S. Pension Agent, Indianapolis, IN, 1864–66

John William Ray.

Miscellaneous: Resided Jeffersonville, Clark Co., IN, to 1863; and Indianapolis, IN
Buried: Crown Hill Cemetery, Indianapolis, IN (Section 3, Lot 37)
References: Obituary, *Indianapolis News,* July 28, 1906. John H. B. Nowland. *Sketches of Prominent Citizens of 1876.* Indianapolis, IN, 1877. Pension File and Military Service File, National Archives. Lewis C. Baird. *Baird's History of Clark County, IN.* Indianapolis, IN, 1909. *The War of the Rebellion: A Compilation of the Official Records of the Union and Confederate Armies.* (Series 1, Vol. 16, Part 2, p. 21). Washington, DC, 1886. Charles A. Martin, editor. *DePauw University: Alumnal Register of Officers, Faculties and Graduates, 1837–1900.* Greencastle, IN, 1901.

Hugh B. Reed

Colonel, 44 IN Infantry, Nov. 26, 1861. GSW chest, Shiloh, TN, April 6, 1862. Under arrest for having, through a breakdown in communications, overstayed an August 1862 leave of absence, he resigned Nov. 26, 1862, while awaiting action in his case, claiming "that I have been unjustly treated — all desire to remain longer in the service having been crushed out." Nominated as Brig. Gen., U.S. Volunteers, Nov. 29, 1862. Nomination withdrawn, Feb. 12, 1863. Battle honors: Fort Donelson, Shiloh.
Born: 1818 Zanesville, OH
Died: April 25, 1890 near Somerville, NJ
Education: Attended Ohio Medical College, Cincinnati, OH

Hugh B. Reed (Mark Weldon Collection).

Hugh B. Reed (photograph by Wm. Duncklesburg, Nos. 2 and 3 Phoenix Block, Fort Wayne, Indiana; Mark Weldon Collection).

Occupation: Druggist and farmer in later life
Miscellaneous: Resided Fort Wayne, Allen Co., IN, to 1867; and Somerville, Somerset Co., NJ
Buried: Lindenwood Cemetery, Fort Wayne, IN (Section F, Lot 52)
References: Thomas B. Helm, editor. *History of Allen County, IN.* Chicago, IL, 1880. Obituary, *Fort Wayne Daily Gazette,* April 29, 1890. Pension File and Military Service File, National Archives. Letters Received, Volunteer Service Branch, Adjutant General's Office, File I259(VS)1862, National Archives. John H. Rerick. *The 44th Indiana Volunteer Infantry: History of Its Services in the War of the Rebellion.* LaGrange, IN, 1880.

Nathaniel Pendleton Richmond

2 Lieutenant, Co. E, 13 IN Infantry, April 25, 1861. Acting ADC, Staff of Brig. Gen. William S. Rosecrans, July–Aug. 1861. Discharged for promotion, Aug. 20, 1861. Lieutenant Colonel, 1 WV Cavalry, Sept. 7, 1861. Colonel, 1 WV Cavalry, Oct. 16, 1862. Resigned March 18, 1863, on account of physical disability due to "hemorrhoids, with which he has been afflicted for the past twelve months." Colonel, 1 WV Cavalry, June 12, 1863. Commanded 1 Brigade, 3 Division, Cavalry Corps, Army of the Potomac, July 4–9, 1863. Resigned Nov. 11, 1863, due to injuries to right hip and back caused by fall of his horse at Raccoon Ford, VA, Sept. 16, 1863. Colonel, Howard County Regiment, Indiana Legion, April 1, 1864. *Colonel,* U.S. Veteran Volunteer Infantry, March 6, 1865. Resigned May 29, 1865, since he was "not prepared to pass the examination required in infantry tactics." Battle honors: Gettysburg.

Born: July 26, 1833 Indianapolis, IN
Died: June 28, 1919 Malvern, AR
Education: Attended Brown University, Providence, RI
Occupation: Lawyer and farmer
Offices/Honors: Indiana Senate, 1865–1869. Mayor of Kokomo, IN, 1873–79.
Miscellaneous: Resided Kokomo, Howard Co., IN; and Malvern, Hot Spring Co., AR, after 1882
Buried: Oakridge Cemetery, Malvern, AR (Block 5, Lot 14)
References: Kingman Brothers, compilers. *Combination Atlas Map of Howard County, IN.* Chicago, IL, 1877. Obituary, *Kokomo Daily Tribune,* July 7, 1919. *A Biographical History of Eminent and Self-Made Men of the State of Indiana.* Cincinnati, OH, 1880. Pension File and Military Service File, National Archives. Rebecca A. Shepherd, Charles W. Calhoun, Elizabeth Shanahan-Shoemaker, and Alan F. January, editors. *A Biographical Directory of the Indiana General Assembly.* Vol. 1, 1816–1899. Indianapolis, IN, 1980. Joshua B. Richmond. *The Richmond Family, 1594–1896.* Boston, MA, 1897.

George Washington Riddle

1 Lieutenant, Fredonia Rifles, Crawford County Regiment, IN Legion, Aug. 26, 1861. 1 Lieutenant, Co. H, 49 IN Infantry, Nov. 4, 1861. 1 Lieutenant, Adjutant, 49 IN Infantry, April 20, 1862. Honorably mustered out, Nov. 29, 1864. Captain, Co. D, 144 IN Infantry, Feb. 18, 1865. Colonel, 144 IN Infantry, March 7, 1865. Commanded 1 Brigade, 2 Division, Army of the Shenandoah, Middle Military Division, May–June 1865. Honorably mustered out, Aug. 5, 1865. Battle honors: Champion's Hill.

Born: Dec. 7, 1832 Crawford Co., IN
Died: June 2, 1897 Grantsburg, Crawford Co., IN
Occupation: Farmer and county surveyor
Miscellaneous: Resided Fredonia, Crawford Co., IN
Buried: Riddle Cemetery, Riddle, Crawford Co., IN
References: Pension File and Military Service File, National Archives. *Biographical and Historical Souvenir for the Counties of Clark, Crawford, Harrison, Floyd, Jefferson, Jennings, Scott, and Washington, IN.* Chicago, IL, 1889. Doris Byrd Leistner.

Nathaniel Pendleton Richmond (post-war) (courtesy Howard County Historical Society, Kokomo, Indiana).

George Washington Riddle (courtesy Robert L. Riddle).

Crawford County Indiana Civil War Veterans. New Albany, IN, 2005.

Rufus Robert Roberts

Captain, Newburgh Greys, 3 IN Legion (Warrick and Gibson Counties), Oct. 10, 1861. Colonel, 3 IN Legion (Warrick and Gibson Counties), Nov. 22, 1861.

Born: Nov. 7, 1824 Warrick Co., IN
Died: Jan. 22, 1880 Brazil, IN (killed in coal mine explosion)
Education: Graduated Indiana University, Bloomington, IN, 1846
Occupation: Bank cashier, farmer, and coal mine operator
Miscellaneous: Resided Newburgh, Warrick Co., IN; Evansville, Vanderburgh Co., IN; and Brazil, Clay Co., IN
Buried: Rose Hill Cemetery, Newburgh, IN (Section 1A)
References: Obituary, *Evansville Courier*, Jan. 24, 1880. Theophilus A. Wylie. *Indiana University, Its History from 1820 to 1890*. Indianapolis, IN, 1890. Monte M. Katterjohn. *History of Warrick and Its Prominent People*. Boonville, IN, 1909.

Edward Jones Robinson

1 Lieutenant, Co. D, 54 IN Infantry (3 months), May 29, 1862. Honorably mustered out, Sept. 26, 1862. Assistant Commissary of Prisoners, Camp Morton, Indianapolis, IN, July–Aug. 1863. Colonel, 137 IN Infantry, May 27, 1864. Commanded Post of Tullahoma, TN, June–July 1864. Commanded 2 Brigade, Defenses of the Nashville and Chattanooga Railroad, Department of the Cumberland, Aug. 22–Sept. 21, 1864. Honorably mustered out, Sept. 21, 1864.

Born: Jan. 4, 1817 Pittsburgh, PA
Died: June 26, 1896 Bedford, IN
Occupation: Saw mill operator, railroad agent, and insurance agent
Miscellaneous: Resided Madison, Jefferson Co., IN; Indianapolis, Marion Co., IN; and Bedford, Lawrence Co., IN
Buried: Fairmount Cemetery, Madison, IN
References: Pension File and Military Service File, National Archives. Obituary, *Bedford Mail*, July 3, 1896. Obituary, *Indianapolis Sentinel*, June 27, 1896. Letters Received, Commission Branch, Adjutant General's Office, File R652(CB)1867, National Archives.

David Garland Rose

Colonel, 54 IN Infantry (3 months), June 19, 1862. Commanded Camp Morton Prison, Indianapolis, IN, June–Sept. 1862. Honorably mustered out, Sept. 26, 1862.

Born: 1817? Amherst Co., VA

David Garland Rose (Indiana Historical Society, P0477 [Indiana University Portraits]).

Died: June 8, 1869 Washington, DC
Occupation: Farmer and land speculator
Offices/Honors: Trustee of Indiana University, 1859–61. U.S. Marshal, District of Indiana, 1861–65. Postmaster, Indianapolis, IN, 1866–68.
Miscellaneous: Resided La Porte, La Porte Co., IN; and Indianapolis, IN. Brother-in-law of Colonel John C. Walker (35 IN Infantry).
Buried: Pine Lake Cemetery, La Porte, IN
References: Burton D. Myers. *Trustees and Officers of Indiana University, 1820 to 1950.* Bloomington, IN, 1951. Obituary, *La Porte Weekly Argus,* June 10, 1869. Christine Rose. *Ancestors and Descendants of the Brothers Rev. Robert Rose and Rev. Charles Rose of Colonial Virginia and Wester Alves, Morayshire, Scotland.* San Jose, CA, 1985. George I. Reed, editor. *Encyclopedia of Biography of Indiana.* Chicago, IL, 1895. Hattie Lou Winslow and Joseph R. H. Moore. *Camp Morton, 1861–1865, Indianapolis Prison Camp.* Indianapolis, IN, 1940. Military Service File, National Archives.

Nicholas Randle Ruckle

Ensign, Co. E, 11 IN Infantry (3 months), April 25, 1861. Honorably mustered out, Aug. 4, 1861. 2

Nicholas Randle Ruckle (post-war) (*Commemorative Biographical Record of Prominent and Representative Men of Indianapolis and Vicinity.* Chicago, Illinois, 1908).

Lieutenant, Co. E, 11 IN Infantry (3 years), Aug. 31, 1861. Captain, Co. E, 11 IN Infantry, Dec. 4, 1861. Colonel, 148 IN Infantry, March 3, 1865. Commanded 2 Brigade, District of Middle Tennessee, Department of Tennessee, July 1865. Honorably mustered out, Sept. 5, 1865. Battle honors: Fort Donelson, Port Gibson.
Born: May 8, 1838 Baltimore, MD
Died: May 4, 1900 Indianapolis, IN
Occupation: Printer employed by Indianapolis Journal before war. Printing company superintendent and executive after war.
Offices/Honors: Sheriff of Marion Co., IN, 1870–74. Indianapolis Police Commissioner, 1887–88. Adjutant General of Indiana, 1889–93. Thirty-third degree Scottish Rite Mason.
Miscellaneous: Resided Indianapolis, Marion Co., IN
Buried: Crown Hill Cemetery, Indianapolis, IN (Section 12, Lot 24)
References: *Commemorative Biographical Record of Prominent and Representative Men of Indianapolis and Vicinity.* Chicago, IL, 1908. Jacob P. Dunn. *Indiana and Indianans.* Chicago and New York, 1919. Obituary, *Indianapolis Sentinel,* May 4, 1900. Pension File and Military Service File, National

Nicholas Randle Ruckle (photograph by Davies & Merritt, 26 & 28 West Washington Str., Indianapolis, Indiana).

Archives. Obituary Circular, Whole No. 130, Indiana MOLLUS.

DeWitt Clinton Rugg

Captain, Co. E, 11 IN Infantry (3 months), April 25, 1861. Honorably mustered out, Aug. 4, 1861. Captain, Co. E, 11 IN Infantry (3 years), Aug. 15, 1861. Major, 48 IN Infantry, Jan. 13, 1862. Lieutenant Colonel, 48 IN Infantry, June 17, 1862. GSW left foot, Corinth, MS, Oct. 4, 1862. Resigned April 24, 1863, due to physical disability in consequence of his wound. Colonel, 107 IN Minute Men, July 12, 1863. Honorably mustered out, July 18, 1863. Colonel, City of Indianapolis Regiment, IN Legion, Aug. 14, 1863. Resigned Nov. 7, 1863. Battle honors: Iuka, Corinth.

Born: Sept. 1, 1838 Decatur, IN
Died: May 21, 1918 Hot Springs, AR
Education: Attended Indiana University, Bloomington, IN. Attended U.S. Military Academy, West Point, NY (Class of 1860).
Occupation: School teacher and Deputy Clerk, Indiana Supreme Court, before war. Pension claim agent, farmer, and hotelkeeper after war.
Miscellaneous: Resided Decatur, Adams Co., IN; Indianapolis, Marion Co., IN; Huntsville, Madison Co., AL, 1865–75; and Hot Springs, Garland Co., AR
Buried: Hollywood Cemetery, Hot Springs, AR
References: Pension File and Military Service File, National Archives. Obituary, *Decatur Daily Democrat,* May 25, 1918. Ellen R. Rugg. *The Descendants of John Rugg.* New York City, NY, 1911. Stephen E. Towne, editor. *A Fierce, Wild Joy: The Civil War Letters of Colonel Edward J. Wood, 48th Indiana Volunteer Infantry Regiment.* Knoxville, TN, 2007.

Townsend Ryan

Lieutenant Colonel, 34 IN Infantry, Sept. 21, 1861. Colonel, 34 IN Infantry, Jan. 15, 1862. Facing charges of collusion with the regimental sutler involving the illegal sale of Government horses, he resigned June 14, 1862, due to "long continued ill health, and more particularly, obtuseness of hearing, rendering it dangerous amongst guards and pickets." Surgeon, 54 IN Infantry (one year), April 14, 1863. Honorably mustered out, Dec. 8, 1863.

Born: 1813 Lancaster, PA
Died: Dec. 30, 1879 Anderson, IN
Education: Attended Ohio Medical College, Cincinnati, OH. Attended Jefferson Medical College, Philadelphia, PA.
Occupation: Physician, boot and shoe merchant, and railroad promoter
Offices/Honors: Indiana House of Representatives, 1848–49

Townsend Ryan (post-war) (DeWitt C. Goodrich and Charles R. Tuttle. *An Illustrated History of the State of Indiana.* Indianapolis, Indiana, 1875).

Miscellaneous: Resided Anderson, Madison Co., IN
Buried: West Maplewood Cemetery, Anderson, IN (Northwest Square, Lot 344)
References: DeWitt C. Goodrich and Charles R. Tuttle. *An Illustrated History of the State of Indiana.* Indianapolis, IN, 1875. Pension File and Military Service File, National Archives. Obituary, *Indianapolis Daily Sentinel,* Dec. 31, 1879. Rebecca A. Shepherd, Charles W. Calhoun, Elizabeth Shanahan-Shoemaker, and Alan F. January, editors. *A Biographical Directory of the Indiana General Assembly.* Vol. 1, 1816–1899. Indianapolis, IN, 1980. Letters Received, Volunteer Service Branch, Adjutant General's Office, File R914(VS)1863, National Archives. General W. H. Kemper. *A Medical History of the State of Indiana.* Chicago, IL, 1911. John L. Forkner. *History of Madison County, IN.* Chicago, IL, 1914.

William Lawrence Sanderson

Colonel, 23 IN Infantry, July 29, 1861. Commanded Post of Bolivar, TN, June 1862. Commanded 1 Brigade, 3 Division, Right Wing, 13 Army Corps, Army of the Tennessee, Dec. 1862. Commanded 1 Brigade, 4 Division, 17 Army Corps, Army of the Tennessee, May 26–July 18, 1864. Resigned July 29, 1864, on account of expiration of term of service. Battle honors: Shiloh, Atlanta Campaign (Kenesaw Mountain).

Born: 1813? PA
Died: July 19, 1868 New Albany, IN
Other Wars: Mexican War (Captain, Co. A, 2 IN Infantry)
Occupation: Cabinet maker
Offices/Honors: Mayor of New Albany, IN, 1865–68
Miscellaneous: Resided New Albany, Floyd Co., IN
Buried: Fairview Cemetery, New Albany, IN (Plat 1, Range 5, Lot 1)
References: Pension File and Military Service File, National Archives. Obituary, *New Albany Daily Commercial,* July 21, 1868.

John Smith Scobey

2 Lieutenant, Co. A, 68 IN Infantry, July 14, 1862. Captain, Co. A, 68 IN Infantry, Aug. 13, 1862. Major, 68 IN Infantry, Oct. 21, 1862. Lieutenant Colonel, 68 IN Infantry, June 2, 1863. *Colonel,* 68 IN Infantry, Sept. 21, 1863. Suffering from chronic diarrhea, he resigned Nov. 13, 1863, giving as the reason, "disability to endure the service."
Born: Dec. 2, 1818 Sycamore Twp., Hamilton Co., OH
Died: April 23, 1901 Greensburg, IN
Education: Attended Miami University, Oxford, OH
Occupation: Lawyer and hardware merchant
Offices/Honors: Indiana Senate, 1851–52
Miscellaneous: Resided Greensburg, Decatur Co., IN
Buried: South Park Cemetery, Greensburg, IN (Old Ground, Section 2, Lot 26)
References: *A Biographical History of Eminent and Self-Made Men of the State of Indiana.* Cincinnati, OH, 1880. Pension File and Military Service File, National Archives. Obituary, *Greensburg New Era,* May 1, 1901. Rebecca A. Shepherd, Charles W. Calhoun, Elizabeth Shanahan-Shoemaker, and Alan F. January, editors. *A Biographical Directory of the Indiana General Assembly.* Vol. 1, 1816–1899. Indianapolis, IN, 1980. Lewis A. Harding, editor. *History of Decatur County, Indiana, Its People, Industries and Institutions.* Indianapolis, IN, 1915. *Atlas of Decatur County, Indiana.* Chicago, 1882. Edwin W. High. *History of the 68th Regiment Indiana Volunteer Infantry, 1862–1865.* N.p., 1902.

George H. Scott

1 Sergeant, Co. H, 83 IN Infantry, Sept. 4, 1862. Captain, Co. H, 83 IN Infantry, Nov. 1, 1862. GSW left leg, Vicksburg, MS, May 19, 1863. Major, 83 IN Infantry, May 31, 1864. Lieutenant

John Smith Scobey (post-war) (Edwin W. High. *History of the 68th Regiment Indiana Volunteer Infantry, 1862–1865.* N.p., 1902).

George H. Scott (photograph by J. W. Winder & Co., National Art Palace, 142 Fourth St., bet. Race & Elm, Cincinnati, Ohio; Dennis M. Keesee Collection).

Colonel, 83 IN Infantry, June 1, 1864. *Colonel,* 83 IN Infantry, May 1, 1865. Honorably mustered out, June 2, 1865. Battle honors: Vicksburg Campaign, Atlanta Campaign (Resaca, Kenesaw Mountain), Savannah Campaign.
Born: 1829? Philadelphia, PA
Died: Aug. 19, 1898 Milford, OH
Occupation: Clerk and lawyer before war. Merchant and farmer after war.
Miscellaneous: Resided Lawrenceburg, Dearborn Co., IN, and Cincinnati, OH, to 1872; Holman, Scott Co., IN, 1872-79; Williamsburg, Clermont Co., OH, 1879-95; Terrace Park and Milford, Hamilton Co., OH, 1895-98
Buried: Spring Grove Cemetery, Cincinnati, OH (Section 75, Lot 5, unmarked)
References: Pension File and Military Service File, National Archives. Joseph Grecian. *History of the 83rd Regiment, Indiana Volunteer Infantry, for Three Years with Sherman.* Cincinnati, OH, 1865.

Harvey David Scott

Colonel, Vigo County Regiment, IN Legion, Aug. 15, 1863
Born: Oct. 18, 1819 Milford Center, Union Co., OH
Died: July 12, 1891 Pasadena, CA
Education: Attended Indiana Asbury (now DePauw) University, Greencastle, IN
Occupation: Lawyer and judge
Offices/Honors: Indiana House of Representatives, 1853. U.S. House of Representatives, 1855-57. Vigo County Treasurer, 1859-63. Indiana Senate, 1869, 1871, 1873, and 1875. Circuit Court Judge, 1881-84.
Miscellaneous: Resided Terre Haute, Vigo Co., IN; and Pasadena, Los Angeles Co., CA, after 1887
Buried: Mountain View Cemetery, Altadena, CA (Section A, Row 5, Lot 35)
References: Obituary, *Terre Haute Evening Gazette,* July 13, 1891. Rebecca A. Shepherd, Charles W. Calhoun, Elizabeth Shanahan-Shoemaker, and Alan F. January, editors. *A Biographical Directory of the Indiana General Assembly.* Vol. 1, 1816-1899. Indianapolis, IN, 1980. Hiram W. Beckwith. *History of Vigo and Parke Counties, Together with Historic Notes on the Wabash Valley.* Chicago, IL, 1880. James L. Harrison, compiler. *Biographical Directory of the American Congress, 1774-1949.* Washington, DC, 1950. *Operations of the Indiana Legion and Minute Men, 1863-4. Documents Presented to the General Assembly, with the Governor's Message, Jan. 6, 1865.* Indianapolis, IN, 1865.

Jefferson Kingsley Scott

Captain, Co. K, 7 IN Infantry (3 months), April 25, 1861. Honorably mustered out, Aug. 3, 1861.

Jefferson Kingsley Scott (Craig Dunn Collection).

Lieutenant Colonel, 59 IN Infantry, Feb. 11, 1862. Shell wound head, Champion's Hill, MS, May 16, 1863. *Colonel,* 59 IN Infantry, Aug. 13, 1864. Honorably mustered out, April 10, 1865. Battle honors: Corinth, Vicksburg Campaign (Champion's Hill), Savannah Campaign, Campaign of the Carolinas.
Born: March 27, 1827 Fayette Co., KY
Died: April 5, 1903 Martinsville, IN
Occupation: Tanner and clothing merchant before war. Hotel manager, insurance agent, and accountant after war.
Offices/Honors: Clerk of Morgan County Circuit Court, 1855-59
Miscellaneous: Resided Martinsville, Morgan Co., IN; and Indianapolis, IN
Buried: Hilldale Cemetery, Martinsville, IN
References: *Commemorative Biographical Record of Prominent and Representative Men of Indianapolis and Vicinity.* Chicago, IL, 1908. Pension File and Military Service File, National Archives. H. Engerud, transcriber. *The 1864 Diary of Lt. Col. Jefferson K. Scott, 59th Indiana Infantry.* Bloomington, IN, 1962.

Samuel B. Sering

Colonel, 9 IN Legion (Jefferson County), Aug. 29, 1861. Battle honors: Morgan's Ohio Raid.
Born: July 27, 1820 Madison, IN
Died: June 23, 1889 Madison, IN
Occupation: Pork merchant and later proprietor of extensive lard-oil works
Miscellaneous: Resided Madison, Jefferson Co., IN; and Indianapolis, IN

Buried: Fairmount Cemetery, Madison, IN
References: Obituary, *Madison Courier,* June 24, 1889. Obituary, *Indianapolis Sentinel,* June 26, 1889. *Report of Major General Love of the Indiana Legion.* Indianapolis, IN, 1863. *Operations of the Indiana Legion and Minute Men, 1863–4. Documents Presented to the General Assembly, with the Governor's Message, Jan. 6, 1865.* Indianapolis, IN, 1865. John P. Etter. *The Indiana Legion: A Civil War Militia.* Carmel, IN, 2006.

James Hammond Shannon

Captain, Co. E, 20 IN Infantry, July 22, 1861. Major, 20 IN Infantry, Nov. 1, 1862. Lieutenant Colonel, 20 IN Infantry, April 9, 1863. Resigned June 5, 1863, "varicose veins of my right leg rendering me unfit for duty in the field." Colonel, 138 IN Infantry, May 27, 1864. Honorably mustered out, Sept. 22, 1864. Battle honors: Groveton.
Born: Oct. 9, 1836 Northumberland Co., PA
Died: May 20, 1898 Indianapolis, IN (killed by fall down hotel stairs)
Occupation: Clerk, bookkeeper, and traveling agent
Offices/Honors: La Porte County Clerk, 1865–73
Miscellaneous: Resided La Porte, La Porte Co., IN; Indianapolis, IN; and Chicago, IL

Buried: Pine Lake Cemetery, La Porte, IN
References: Pension File and Military Service File, National Archives. Obituary, *La Porte Daily Herald,* May 21, 1898. Craig L. Dunn. *Harvestfields of Death: The 20th Indiana Volunteers of Gettysburg.* Carmel, IN, 1999. Obituary, *Indianapolis Sentinel,* May 21–22, 1898. Letters Received, Volunteer Service Branch, Adjutant General's Office, File I9(VS)1864, National Archives. Jasper Packard. *History of La Porte County, Indiana, and Its Townships, Towns and Cities.* La Porte, IN, 1876.

Abram Sharra

Sergeant, Co. I, 1 IN Cavalry, July 4, 1861. 2 Lieutenant, Co. I, 1 IN Cavalry, Nov. 1, 1861. Captain, Co. I, 1 IN Cavalry, March 20, 1862. Resigned May 26, 1864, to accept promotion. Lieutenant Colonel, 11 IN Cavalry, June 16, 1864. Commanded 1 Brigade, 5 Division, Cavalry Corps, Military Division of the Mississippi, Jan. 18–Feb. 3, 1865. Colonel, 11 IN Cavalry, May 19, 1865. Commanded 2 Sub-District, District of the Upper Arkansas, Department of the Missouri, July 8–Sept. 6, 1865. Honorably mustered out, Sept. 19, 1865. Battle honors: 2nd Bull Run, Chancellorsville, Gettysburg, Nashville.
Born: Feb. 2, 1840 Westmoreland Co., PA
Died: Oct. 20, 1893 Evansville, IN
Occupation: Railroad conductor
Miscellaneous: Resided Terre Haute, Vigo Co., IN, before war; and Evansville, Vanderburgh Co., IN, after war

James Hammond Shannon (Richard F. Carlile Collection, copied by Richard A. Baumgartner).

Abram Sharra (P. Prescott's New Photograph Gallery, 102 Main Street, Terre Haute, Indiana; John Sickles Collection).

Abram Sharra (left, with Captain Hiram Lindsey) (E. Long, Photographer, Benton Barracks, St. Louis, Missouri).

Buried: Oak Hill Cemetery, Evansville, IN (Section 20, Lot 25)

References: Pension File and Military Service File, National Archives. Obituary, *Evansville Journal*, Oct. 21, 1893. Letters Received, Volunteer Service Branch, Adjutant General's Office, File I304(VS)1864, National Archives. Edmund J. Raus, Jr. *A Generation on the March: The Union Army at Gettysburg*. Gettysburg, PA, 1996.

Thomas Shea

1 Lieutenant, Co. H, 22 IN Infantry, July 15, 1861. Captain, Co. H, 22 IN Infantry, Jan. 3, 1862. Major, 22 IN Infantry, Dec. 6, 1862. GSW neck, Rome, GA, May 17, 1864. GSW left forearm (amputated), Peach Tree Creek, GA, July 19, 1864. Lieutenant Colonel, 22 IN Infantry, Jan. 10, 1865. Colonel, 22 IN Infantry, June 9, 1865. Honorably mustered out, July 24, 1865. Bvt. Captain and Major, USA, March 2, 1867, for gallant and meritorious services in action at Rome, GA. Bvt. Lieutenant Colonel, USA, March 2, 1867, for gallant and meritorious services in the Battle of Peach Tree Creek, GA. Bvt. Colonel, USA, March 2, 1867, for gallant and meritorious services during the war. Battle honors: Pea Ridge, Perryville, Stone's River, Missionary Ridge, Atlanta Campaign (Rome, Peach Tree Creek).

Born: Oct. 6, 1838 Wabash Co., IN
Died: Dec. 3, 1916 Louisville, KY
Occupation: Merchant before war. Regular Army (Lieutenant Colonel, 17 U.S. Infantry, retired Dec. 15, 1870). Advanced to Colonel on the retired list of the Army, April 23, 1904.
Miscellaneous: Resided Lexington, Scott Co., IN; Westport, Oldham Co., KY; and Louisville, KY
Buried: Cave Hill National Cemetery, Louisville, KY (Section E, Grave 4712)
References: Pension File and Military Service File, National Archives. Obituary, *Louisville Courier-Journal*, Dec. 4, 1916. Letters Received, Volunteer Service Branch, Adjutant General's Office, File S2515(VS)1864, National Archives. Randolph V. Marshall. *An Historical Sketch of the 22nd Regiment Indiana Volunteers, from Its Organization to the Close of the War, Its Battles, Its Marches, and Its Hardships, Its Brave Officers and Its Honored Dead.* Madison, IN, 1884. W. R. England. *A Complete Roster of the 22nd Regiment Indiana Infantry.* Seymour, IN, 1901.

Kline Godfrey Shryock

Colonel, 87 IN Infantry, Sept. 1, 1862. Resigned March 21, 1863, since "I am now 53 years of age and the exposure of camp life and night marches so effects (sic) my general health that it renders me totally unable for duty in the field." Colonel, 105 IN Minute Men, July 12, 1863. Honorably mustered out, July 18, 1863. Provost Marshal, 9th District of Indiana, Nov. 21, 1863. Honorably discharged, Oct. 31, 1865. Battle honors: Perryville, Stone's River, Morgan's Ohio Raid.

Born: May 22, 1811 Bedford Co., PA
Died: Dec. 26, 1895 Rochester, IN
Occupation: Lawyer
Offices/Honors: Fulton County Treasurer, 1847–51. Indiana House of Representatives, 1855. Judge of the Court of Common Pleas, 1860–62. Postmaster, Rochester, IN, 1882–86.
Miscellaneous: Resided Rochester, Fulton Co., IN. Uncle of Colonel Alfred B. Wade (73 IN Infantry).
Buried: IOOF Cemetery, Rochester, IN (Section 5, Row 5)
References: Pension File and Military Service File, National Archives. Obituary, *Rochester Weekly Republican*, Jan. 2, 1896. Rebecca A. Shepherd, Charles W. Calhoun, Elizabeth Shanahan-Shoemaker, and Alan F. January, editors. *A Biographical Directory of the Indiana General Assembly.*

Kline Godfrey Shryock (Wm. M. Scott, Photographer, La Porte, Indiana; Craig Dunn Collection).

Vol. 1, 1816–1899. Indianapolis, IN, 1980. Jack K. Overmyer. *A Stupendous Effort: The 87th Indiana in the War of the Rebellion.* Bloomington, IN, 1997. *Operations of the Indiana Legion and Minute Men, 1863–4. Documents Presented to the General Assembly, with the Governor's Message, Jan. 6, 1865.* Indianapolis, IN, 1865.

Lawrence S. Shuler

Captain, Co. A, 4 IN Cavalry, Aug. 1, 1862. Lieutenant Colonel, 4 IN Cavalry, Sept. 4, 1862. GSW head, Mount Washington, KY, Oct. 1, 1862. Colonel, 4 IN Cavalry, Feb. 12, 1863. Laboring from the effects of his wound, he resigned May 16, 1863, due to "partial paralysis of the right side and partial depression on the brain, rendering me totally unfit for the service." Colonel, 103 IN Minute Men, July 10, 1863. Honorably mustered out, July 16, 1863. Battle honors: Mount Washington, Morgan's Ohio Raid.

Born: June 30, 1825 Terre Haute, IN
Died: Dec. 25, 1908 Indianapolis, IN
Occupation: Merchant and trader before war. Boot and shoe manufacturer and Federal Court bailiff after war.
Offices/Honors: Hendricks County Auditor, 1863–67. Warden, Southern Indiana Penitentiary, Jeffersonville, IN, 1869–74.
Miscellaneous: Resided Danville, Hendricks Co., IN; Jeffersonville, Clark Co., IN; and Indianapolis, Marion Co., IN
Buried: Crown Hill Cemetery, Indianapolis, IN (Section 32, Lots 322–323)
References: Pension File and Military Service File, National Archives. Obituary, *Indianapolis News*, Dec. 26, 1908. *Operations of the Indiana Legion and Minute Men, 1863–4. Documents Presented to the General Assembly, with the Governor's Message, Jan. 6, 1865.* Indianapolis, IN, 1865. Richard J. Reid. *Fourth Indiana Cavalry: A History.* Olaton, KY, 1994. John V. Hadley, editor. *History of Hendricks County, Indiana: Her People, Industries and Institutions.* Indianapolis, IN, 1914. "A Painful Reminder of the War," *The Ohio Democrat (New Philadelphia, Ohio)*, Jan. 29, 1880. John P. Etter. *The Indiana Legion: A Civil War Militia.* Carmel, IN, 2006.

Thomas Coleman Slaughter

Colonel, 6 IN Legion (Harrison County), Sept. 24, 1861 (Declined). Major, Judge Advocate, 2 Brigade, IN Legion, Sept. 10, 1864.

Born: Nov. 16, 1820 Harrison Co., IN
Died: Jan. 12, 1879 Corydon, IN
Occupation: Merchant, lawyer, and judge
Offices/Honors: Harrison County Auditor, 1842–47. Circuit Court Judge, 1872–79.
Miscellaneous: Resided Corydon, Harrison Co., IN. Son-in-law of Colonel Lewis Jordan (6 IN Legion).
Buried: Cedar Hill Cemetery, Corydon, IN (Plat 1, Row 12, Grave 210)
References: Obituary, *New Albany Ledger Standard*, Jan. 13, 1879. F. A. Bulleit, compiler. *Illustrated Atlas and History of Harrison County, Indiana.* Corydon, IN, 1906. Interment records, Cedar Hill Cemetery, Corydon, IN. William H. Roose. *Indiana's Birthplace: A History of Harrison County, Indiana.* New Albany, IN, 1911.

James Monroe Smith

Colonel, 52 IN Infantry, Feb. 1, 1862. Resigned June 4, 1862, "in consequence of ill health, which has rendered me unfit for duty since the 28th day of February, and no prospects of getting any better while remaining in the service." Battle honors: Fort Donelson.

Born: March 5, 1821 Moodus, CT
Died: Nov. 15, 1869 Dayton, OH
Occupation: Railroad engineer and superintendent
Miscellaneous: Resided Moodus Middlesex Co., CT; and Dayton, Montgomery Co., OH
Buried: Cedar Hill Cemetery, Hartford, CT (Section 3, Lot 30)
References: Obituary, *Dayton Daily Journal*, Nov. 16, 1869. Military Service File, National Archives.

John Thomas Smith

1 Lieutenant, Co. F, 31 IN Infantry, Sept. 5, 1861. Captain, Co. F, 31 IN Infantry, Jan. 4, 1862. Major, 31 IN Infantry, Dec. 8, 1862. Lieutenant Colonel, 31 IN Infantry, Feb. 11, 1863. Colonel, 31 IN Infantry, July 27, 1863. Resigned March 12, 1865, since "the advanced age of my father and the failure of his health this winter ... creates a pressing necessity for my return home." Battle honors: Fort Donelson, Shiloh, Corinth, Stone's River, Chickamauga, Atlanta Campaign, Nashville.

Born: March 18, 1831 Johnson Co., IN
Died: Feb. 28, 1908 Kingman, Fountain Co., IN
Education: Graduated Indiana Asbury (now DePauw) University, Greencastle, IN, 1860
Occupation: Lawyer, farmer, bee keeper, and Methodist clergyman
Offices/Honors: Greene County Clerk, 1865–70
Miscellaneous: Resided Worthington, Greene Co., IN, 1855–60 and 1870–79; Bloomfield, Greene Co., IN, 1860–70; and Bowling Green, Clay Co., IN, 1879–1908
Buried: Bowling Green Cemetery, Bowling Green, IN
References: Charles Blanchard, editor. *Counties of Clay and Owen, Indiana. Historical and Biographical.* Chicago, IL, 1884. Obituary, *Bloomfield News,* March 13, 1908. Pension File and Military Service File, National Archives. Letters Received, Volunteer Service Branch, Adjutant General's Office, File I572(VS)1864, National Archives. William Travis. *A History of Clay County, Indiana.* New York City, NY, 1909. John Thomas Smith. *A History of the 31st Regiment of Indiana Volunteer Infantry in the War of the Rebellion.* Cincinnati, OH, 1900.

John Thomas Smith (J. W. Campbell, Army Photographer, 20th Army Corps, Army of the Cumberland; courtesy Henry Deeks).

Asbury Earl Steele

Colonel, 34 IN Infantry, Oct. 4, 1861. Resigned Jan. 14, 1862, due to physical disability from inflammatory rheumatism.

Born: Jan. 1, 1814 Mason Co., KY
Died: Sept. 28, 1886 Marion, IN
Occupation: Lawyer and farmer
Offices/Honors: Grant County Clerk, 1845–50. Indiana Senate, 1871 and 1873.
Miscellaneous: Resided Marion, Grant Co., IN
Buried: IOOF (now Estates of Serenity) Cemetery, Marion, IN (Block 5, Lot 12)
References: *A Biographical History of Eminent and Self-Made Men of the State of Indiana.* Cincinnati, OH, 1880. Pension File and Military Service File, National Archives. Rebecca A. Shepherd, Charles W. Calhoun, Elizabeth Shanahan-Shoemaker, and Alan F. January, editors. *A Biographical Directory of the Indiana General Assembly.* Vol. 1, 1816–1899. Indianapolis, IN, 1980. Obituary, *Marion Chronicle,* Oct. 1, 1886. *History of Grant County, IN.* Chicago, IL, 1886. Margaret Steele McGeary. *The House of Steele: Abraham Steele of*

John Thomas Smith (photograph by J. Perry Elliott's City Gallery, No's 8 & 10 East Washington Street, Indianapolis, Indiana; Roger D. Hunt Collection, USAMHI [RG98S-CWP160.31]).

Asbury Earl Steele (from a private collection).

George Kirkpatrick Steele (post-war) (Isaac R. Strouse. *Parke County Indiana Centennial Memorial*. Rockville, Indiana, 1916).

Harford County, Maryland, and Ten Generations of His Descendants. Decorah, IA, 1990.

George Kirkpatrick Steele

Colonel, 43 IN Infantry, Jan. 2, 1862. Resigned Jan. 16, 1862, due to "his advanced age and growing physical infirmities." Commissioner of the Board of Enrollment, 7th District of Indiana, May 1, 1863. Resigned Oct. 9, 1864.

Born: Nov. 25, 1808 near Springfield, OH
Died: May 7, 1879 Terre Haute, IN
Occupation: Farmer, merchant, banker, and railroad promoter
Offices/Honors: Indiana House of Representatives, 1835–37, 1842–43, 1853, 1857. Indiana Senate, 1859 and 1861.
Miscellaneous: Resided Rockville, Parke Co., IN, to 1874; and Terre Haute, Vigo Co., IN, 1874–79
Buried: Rockville Cemetery, Rockville, IN
References: Obituary, *Rockville Republican*, May 14, 1879. *A Biographical History of Eminent and Self-Made Men of the State of Indiana*. Cincinnati, OH, 1880. Rebecca A. Shepherd, Charles W. Calhoun, Elizabeth Shanahan-Shoemaker, and Alan F. January, editors. *A Biographical Directory of the Indiana General Assembly*. Vol. 1, 1816–1899. Indianapolis, IN, 1980. Hiram W. Beckwith. *History of Vigo and Parke Counties, Together with Historic Notes on the Wabash Valley*. Chicago, IL, 1880. Alfred T. Andreas. *Atlas Map of Parke County, Indiana*. Chicago, IL, 1874. Isaac R. Strouse. *Parke County Indiana Centennial Memorial*. Rockville, IN, 1916. William E. McLean. *The 43rd Regiment of Indiana Volunteers. An Historic Sketch of Its Career and Services*. Terre Haute, IN, 1903. Military Service File, National Archives.

James W. Stewart

Captain, Co. E, 2 IN Cavalry, Dec. 7, 1861. Major, 2 IN Cavalry, Nov. 15, 1862. Post Inspector, Camp Nelson, KY, Jan.–Feb. 1864. *Colonel*, 2 IN Cavalry, March 1, 1864. Lieutenant Colonel, 2 IN Cavalry, March 8, 1864. Commanded 2 Brigade, 1 Division, Cavalry Corps, Department of the Cumberland, May 9–26, 1864. Taken prisoner, near Dallas, GA, May 26, 1864. Exchanged Sept. 12, 1864. Honorably mustered out, Oct. 4, 1864. Battle honors: Atlanta Campaign (Dallas).

Born: 1824? IN
Died: Nov. 26, 1865 Terre Haute, IN
Occupation: Merchant and hotel keeper
Miscellaneous: Resided Terre Haute, Vigo Co., IN. Brother of Colonel Robert R. Stewart (11 IN Cavalry).

Buried: Woodlawn Cemetery, Terre Haute, IN (Division 47, Block 27, Lot 12)
References: Pension File and Military Service File, National Archives.

Robert Reed Stewart

Captain, Co. I, 1 IN Cavalry, July 4, 1861. Major, 2 IN Cavalry, Oct. 22, 1861. Lieutenant Colonel, 2 IN Cavalry, April 30, 1862. *Colonel,* 5 IN Cavalry, Oct. 18, 1862. Declined. Taken prisoner Hartsville, TN, Dec. 7, 1862. Confined Libby Prison, Richmond, VA. Paroled April 3, 1863. Colonel, 11 IN Cavalry, Feb. 2, 1864. Commanded Post of Larkinsville, AL, District of Northern Alabama, Department of the Cumberland, June 1864 and Aug.–Sept. 1864. Commanded 1 Brigade, 5 Division, Cavalry Corps, Military Division of the Mississippi, Nov. 27, 1864–Jan. 18, 1865. Commanded 5 Division, Cavalry Corps, Military Division of the Mississippi, Jan. 18–March 3, 1865. Having been in the service "continuously since April 1861 at a great sacrifice of my private and personal interests," and believing "the war virtually at an end," he resigned May 9, 1865, citing "the hardships and exposures incident to field service," which "have wasted my energies and impaired my health," and also the need to settle the estates of his deceased parents and two deceased brothers. Battle honors: Hartsville, Tullahoma Campaign, Nashville.

Robert Reed Stewart.

Born: Nov. 14, 1827 Rockville, IN
Died: Jan. 13, 1873 Terre Haute, IN
Other Wars: Mexican War (Corporal, Co. F, 1 U.S. Dragoons)
Occupation: Fur trader and adventurer before war. Hotel keeper, deputy sheriff, and sealer of weights and measures after war.
Miscellaneous: Resided Terre Haute, Vigo Co., IN. Brother of Colonel James W. Stewart (2 IN Cavalry).
Buried: Woodlawn Cemetery, Terre Haute, IN (Division 47, Block 27, Lot 12)
References: *Report of the 11th Indiana Cavalry Association for 1898.* Anderson, IN, 1898. Jacob P. Dunn. *Indiana and Indianans.* Chicago and New York, 1919. Pension File and Military Service File, National Archives. Letters Received, Volunteer Service Branch, Adjutant General's Office, File I161(VS)1864, National Archives. Obituary, *Terre Haute Daily Express,* Jan. 14, 1873. Obituary, *Terre Haute Daily Journal,* Jan. 14, 1873. John Sickles, "Hoosier Horsemen: Indiana's Cavalry and Mounted Infantry in the Civil War," *Military Images,* Vol. 17, No. 6 (May–June 1996).

Sandford James Stoughton

Major, 44 IN Infantry, Nov. 26, 1861. Lieutenant Colonel, 44 IN Infantry, March 10, 1862. GSW leg, Shiloh, TN, April 7, 1862. Colonel, 100 IN Infantry, Nov. 29, 1862. Having overstayed a sick leave of absence (from June 8, 1863), he returned under arrest, Nov. 9, 1863, and submitted his resignation, claiming that he was "still suffering from neuralgic rheumatism, chronic diarrhea … and with strong symptoms of the return of congestion of the

Robert Reed Stewart (A. S. Morse, Photographer, Department of the Cumberland, Branch of Hd. Qrs., 25 Cedar Street, Nashville, Tennessee; John Sickles Collection).

liver." His resignation was accepted, Jan. 7, 1864, but while recommending its acceptance, Brig. Gen. Hugh Ewing observed, "This officer has been regularly shirking duty." Battle honors: Fort Donelson, Shiloh.

Born: July 21, 1830 St. Lawrence Co., NY
Died: Nov. 29, 1881 Louisburg, Miami Co., KS
Occupation: Lawyer and judge
Offices/Honors: Judge of Common Pleas Court, 1859–60
Miscellaneous: Resided Ligonier, Noble Co., IN; Sturgis, St. Joseph Co., MI, 1866–68; and Ottawa, Franklin Co., KS, 1868–81. In a pension claim affidavit Colonel William C. Williams (44 IN Infantry) described him as "practically worthless as an officer" and as "a man who was utterly destitute of moral principle." Brother of Bvt. Brig. Gen. William L. Stoughton.
Buried: Hope Cemetery, Ottawa, KS (Block 18, Lot 18)
References: *The United States Biographical Dictionary.* Kansas Volume. Chicago and Kansas City, 1879. Pension File and Military Service File, National Archives. Obituary, *Ottawa Daily Republican,* Dec. 1, 1881. John H. Rerick. *The 44th Indiana Volunteer Infantry: History of Its Services in the War of the Rebellion.* LaGrange, IN, 1880. Eli J. Sherlock. *Memorabilia of the Marches and Battles in Which the 100th Regiment of Indiana Infantry Volunteers Took an Active Part, War of the Rebellion, 1861–5.* Kansas City, MO, 1896.

George Ransom Swallow

1 Lieutenant, 7 IN Light Artillery, Dec. 3, 1861. Captain, 7 IN Light Artillery, May 23, 1862. Chief of Artillery, 3 Division, Left Wing, 14 Army Corps, Army of the Cumberland, Dec. 1862. Chief of Artillery, 3 Division, 21 Army Corps, Army of the Cumberland, Jan. 1863 and Sept. 1863. Chief of Artillery, 3 Division, 14 Army Corps, Army of the Cumberland, Oct. 1863–April 1864. Major, 10 IN Cavalry, May 6, 1864. GSW left shoulder, Nashville, TN, Dec. 16, 1864. *Lieutenant Colonel,* 10 IN Cavalry, April 26, 1865. Colonel, 10 IN Cavalry, June 8, 1865. Honorably mustered out, Aug. 31, 1865. Battle honors: Corinth, Stone's River, Chickamauga, Missionary Ridge, Nashville.

Born: Aug. 21, 1839 Roodhouse, Greene Co., IL
Died: July 5, 1936 Denver, CO
Occupation: Banker
Offices/Honors: Treasurer of Colorado, 1885–87
Miscellaneous: Resided Vincennes, Knox Co., IN; Jerseyville, Jersey Co., IL, 1865–73; Trinidad, Las Animas Co., CO, 1873–85; and Denver, CO, after 1885.

George Ransom Swallow (Charles N. Bean, Photographer, Vicksburg City Gallery, Washington Street, Vicksburg, MS; *Companions of the Military Order of the Loyal Legion of the United States.* Second Edition. New York City, 1901).

Buried: Fairmount Cemetery, Denver, CO (Block 32, Lot 2)
References: William H. Powell, editor. *Officers of the Army and Navy (Volunteer) Who Served in the Civil War.* Philadelphia, PA, 1893. Obituary, *Rocky Mountain News,* July 6, 1936. William C. Ferril. *Sketches of Colorado: Being an Analytical Summary and Biographical History of the State of Colorado.* Denver, CO, 1911. Pension File and Military Service File, National Archives. Alice G. Baker. *Genealogy of the Swallow Family, 1666–1910.* White Hall, IL, 1910. *Companions of the Military Order of the Loyal Legion of the United States.* Second Edition. New York City, NY, 1901. Otho H. Morgan. *History of the 7th Independent Battery of Indiana Light Artillery.* Bedford, IN, 1898.

Marsh B. Taylor

Captain, Co. H, 10 IN Infantry, Sept. 18, 1861. Major, 10 IN Infantry, Aug. 16, 1862. Lieutenant Colonel, 10 IN Infantry, Nov. 18, 1862. *Colonel,* 10 IN Infantry, Sept. 21, 1863. Honorably mustered out, Sept. 19, 1864. Colonel, 150 IN Infantry, March 10, 1865. Honorably mustered out, Aug. 5, 1865. Battle honors: Mill Springs, Perryville, Chickamauga, Missionary Ridge, Atlanta Campaign.

William Calvin Linton Taylor

1 Lieutenant, Co. G, 20 IN Infantry, July 22, 1861. Captain, Co. G, 20 IN Infantry, Nov. 20, 1861. Major, 20 IN Infantry, April 9, 1863. Lieutenant Colonel, 20 IN Infantry, June 6, 1863. GSW right arm, Gettysburg, PA, July 2, 1863. Colonel, 20 IN Infantry, July 4, 1863. Honorably mustered out, Sept. 22, 1864. Battle honors: Groveton, Chancellorsville, Gettysburg, Mine Run, Wilderness.

Born: May 22, 1836 Lafayette, IN
Died: Feb. 18, 1901 Lafayette, IN
Education: Graduated Indiana University, Bloomington, IN, 1855
Occupation: Lawyer and judge
Offices/Honors: Judge of Tippecanoe County Circuit Court, 1894–1901
Miscellaneous: Resided Lafayette, Tippecanoe Co., IN; and Bloomington, Monroe Co., IN, 1874–81. Brother of Colonel Marsh B. Taylor (150 IN Infantry).
Buried: Greenbush Cemetery, Lafayette, IN (Division 7, Lot 85)

Marsh B. Taylor (James Birney Shaw. *History of the 10th Regiment Indiana Volunteer Infantry, Three Months and Three Years Organizations.* Lafayette, Indiana, 1912).

Born: March 13, 1835 Lafayette, IN
Died: July 20, 1879 Hagansport, TX
Education: Graduated Indiana Asbury (now DePauw) University, Greencastle, IN, 1855
Other Wars: Taken prisoner and escaped execution during William Walker's filibuster expedition to Nicaragua, 1856–57
Occupation: Lawyer, real estate agent, and boot and shoe merchant. Being "of a roving disposition," he was engaged in his later years in "trading in the West and South."
Miscellaneous: Resided Lafayette, Tippecanoe Co., IN; St. Louis, MO; Omaha, NE; and Hagansport, Franklin Co., TX. Brother of Colonel William C. L. Taylor (20 IN Infantry).
Buried: Place of burial unknown
References: James Birney Shaw. *History of the 10th Regiment Indiana Volunteer Infantry, Three Months and Three Years Organizations.* Lafayette, IN, 1912. Obituary, *Lafayette Daily Journal,* July 29, 1879. Obituary, *Lafayette Daily Courier,* July 28, 1879. Military Service File, National Archives. Charles A. Martin, editor. *DePauw University: Alumnal Register of Officers, Faculties and Graduates, 1837–1900.* Greencastle, IN, 1901.

William Calvin Linton Taylor (photograph by R. A. Lewis, New York; Richard F. Carlile Collection, copied by Richard A. Baumgartner).

References: *Biographical Record and Portrait Album of Tippecanoe County, IN.* Chicago, IL, 1888. Obituary, *Lafayette Daily Call,* Feb. 18, 1901. *A Biographical History of Eminent and Self-Made Men of the State of Indiana.* Cincinnati, OH, 1880. Letters Received, Volunteer Service Branch, Adjutant General's Office, File H1991(VS)1864, National Archives. Craig L. Dunn. *Harvestfields of Death: The 20th Indiana Volunteers of Gettysburg.* Carmel, IN, 1999. Military Service File, National Archives. Theophilus A. Wylie. *Indiana University, Its History from 1820 to 1890.* Indianapolis, IN, 1890. Edmund J. Raus, Jr. *A Generation on the March: The Union Army at Gettysburg.* Gettysburg, PA, 1996.

Hagerman Tripp

Captain, Co. G, 6 IN Infantry (3 months), April 25, 1861. Honorably mustered out, Aug. 2, 1861. Captain, Co. B, 6 IN Infantry (3 years), Sept. 3, 1861. Lieutenant Colonel, 6 IN Infantry, May 20, 1862. GSW left leg, Chickamauga, GA, Sept. 20, 1863. *Colonel,* 6 IN Infantry, Sept. 21, 1863. Discharged "on account of physical disability, from wounds received in action," June 22, 1864. Battle honors: Shiloh, Stone's River, Tullahoma Campaign (Liberty Gap), Chickamauga.

Born: Sept. 16, 1812 Butler Co., OH
Died: Feb. 12, 1891 North Vernon, IN
Occupation: Mill owner, contractor, grain merchant, and farmer
Offices/Honors: U.S. Assessor of Internal Revenue, 1867–73
Miscellaneous: Resided North Vernon, Jennings Co., IN
Buried: Hillcrest Cemetery, North Vernon, IN
References: C. Byron Buckley. *Colonel Hagerman Tripp: His Biography, Civil War Letters, and Diary.* North Vernon, IN, 2004. *A Biographical History of Eminent and Self-Made Men of the State of Indiana.* Cincinnati, OH, 1880. Pension File and Military Service File, National Archives. William Henry Smith, "The Sixth Indiana Regiment, Its Historical Record," *The Indianian,* Vol. 4, No. 5 (Oct. 1899). Charles C. Briant. *History of the 6th Regiment Indiana Volunteer Infantry, of Both the Three Months' and Three Years' Services.* Indianapolis, IN, 1891. William H. Doll. *History of the 6th Regiment Indiana Volunteer Infantry in the Civil War, April 25, 1861, to September 22, 1864.* Columbus, IN, 1903. George L. Randall, compiler. *Tripp Genealogy: Descendants of James, Son of John Tripp.* New Bedford, MA, 1924.

Nelson Trusler

Colonel, 84 IN Infantry, Oct. 4, 1862. Resigned Oct. 19, 1863, "in consequence of general debility resulting from camp diarrhea, accompanied with

Hagerman Tripp (from Coffin Family Album, courtesy Anne Johnson).

Nelson Trusler (post-war) (*A Biographical History of Eminent and Self-Made Men of the State of Indiana.* Cincinnati, Ohio, 1880).

a peculiar irruption affecting the whole surface of his body, resembling elephantiasis." Battle honors: Chickamauga.
Born: Dec. 11, 1823 Franklin Co., IN
Died: Jan. 29, 1880 Indianapolis, IN
Occupation: Lawyer
Offices/Honors: Indiana House of Representatives, 1855. Indiana Secretary of State, 1865–69. U.S. District Attorney for Indiana, 1872–80.
Miscellaneous: Resided Connersville, Fayette Co., IN; and Indianapolis, IN, 1865–80
Buried: City Cemetery, Connersville, IN (Section 2, Lot 113)
References: *A Biographical History of Eminent and Self-Made Men of the State of Indiana.* Cincinnati, OH, 1880. Obituary, *Connersville Examiner*, Feb. 5, 1880. Pension File and Military Service File, National Archives. Rebecca A. Shepherd, Charles W. Calhoun, Elizabeth Shanahan-Shoemaker, and Alan F. January, editors. *A Biographical Directory of the Indiana General Assembly.* Vol. 1, 1816–1899. Indianapolis, IN, 1980. George Hazzard. *Hazzard's History of Henry County, IN, 1822–1906. Military Edition.* New Castle, IN, 1906. Obituary, *New York Times*, Feb. 2, 1880. *History of Fayette County, IN.* Chicago, IL, 1885. *Biographical and Genealogical History of Wayne, Fayette, Union, and Franklin Counties, Indiana.* Chicago, IL, 1899.

William Woodruff Tuley

Major, 7 IN Legion (Floyd County), July 1, 1861. Colonel, 7 IN Legion, Sept. 23, 1861. Resigned Sept. 1862.
Born: Nov. 23, 1825 New Albany, IN
Died: July 25, 1902 Floyd Co., IN
Other Wars: Mexican War (Private, Co. A, 2 IN Infantry)
Occupation: Lawyer and banker
Offices/Honors: Clerk of Indiana General Assembly, 1849–55. Clerk of Floyd County Circuit Court, 1862–71. Indiana House of Representatives, 1883.
Miscellaneous: Resided New Albany, Floyd Co., IN. Brother-in-law of Colonel Thomas D. Sedgewick (2 KY Infantry and 114 USCT).
Buried: Fairview Cemetery, New Albany, IN (Plat 3, Range 8, Lot 17)
References: William F. Tuley. *The Tuley Family Memoirs.* New Albany, IN, 1906. Obituary, *New Albany Daily Ledger*, July 25, 1902. Rebecca A. Shepherd, Charles W. Calhoun, Elizabeth Shanahan-Shoemaker, and Alan F. January, editors. *A Biographical Directory of the Indiana General Assembly.* Vol. 1, 1816–1899. Indianapolis, IN, 1980. *History of the Ohio Falls Cities and Their Counties.* Cleveland, OH, 1882. Mexican War Pension File, National Archives.

William Woodruff Tuley (post-war) (William F. Tuley. *The Tuley Family Memoirs.* New Albany, Indiana, 1906).

John Van Valkenburg

Captain, Co. A, 20 IN Infantry, July 22, 1861. Major, 20 IN Infantry, Dec. 28, 1861. Lieutenant Colonel, 20 IN Infantry, Feb. 16, 1862. GSW right leg, Oak Grove, VA, June 25, 1862. Colonel, 20 IN Infantry, Aug. 30, 1862. Commanded 1 Brigade, 1 Division, 3 Army Corps, Army of the Potomac, Jan.–Feb. 1863. Having made an indiscreet reference to "this nigger administration" in a letter intercepted by Governor Oliver P. Morton, he was dismissed Feb. 10, 1863, for "disloyalty to the Government, and for conduct unbecoming an officer and a gentleman," based on Morton's letter to Secretary of War Stanton describing him as "a traitor of the most villainous character." Despite overwhelming support from fellow officers, he was not reinstated. His dismissal was, however, revoked, April 27, 1866, and he was honorably discharged, to date Feb. 10, 1863. Battle honors: Peninsular Campaign (Oak Grove), Fredericksburg.
Born: July 24, 1822 Exeter, Luzerne Co., PA
Died: Aug. 18, 1883 Huntsville, AL
Other Wars: Private, Co. K, 2 U.S. Artillery, 1839–44
Occupation: Grain merchant before war. Merchant dealing in hardware and agricultural implements after war.
Miscellaneous: Resided Peru, Miami Co., IN; and Huntsville, Madison Co., AL, 1869–83

Buried: Maple Hill Cemetery, Huntsville, AL (Block 13, Row 15)

References: Pension File and Military Service File, National Archives. Letters Received, Volunteer Service Branch, Adjutant General's Office, File W212(VS)1863, National Archives. Craig L. Dunn. *Harvestfields of Death: The 20th Indiana Volunteers of Gettysburg.* Carmel, IN, 1999. Obituary, *Huntsville Weekly Democrat,* Aug. 22, 1883. Obituary, *Huntsville Advocate,* Aug. 22, 1883.

Samuel Colville Vance

Captain, Co. A, 27 MA Infantry, Sept. 20, 1861. Resigned June 16, 1862, "in order to receive my diploma at Amherst College." Major, 70 IN Infantry, Aug. 9, 1862. Resigned April 10, 1863, due to the death of his father, "leaving the affairs of a large family in a deranged condition, and devolving the settlement of the estate upon him." Captain, Co. D, 107 IN Minute men, July 10, 1863. Honorably mustered out, July 18, 1863. Captain, Eighth Ward Guards, City of Indianapolis Regiment, IN Legion, July 10, 1863. Colonel, City of Indianapolis Regiment, IN Legion, April 21, 1864. Colonel, 132

Samuel Colville Vance (center, with Major Hervey Bates, Jr., left, and unidentified officer) (courtesy Stephen B. Rogers).

IN Infantry, May 20, 1864. Commanded Post of Stevenson, AL, July 1864. Honorably mustered out, Sept. 7, 1864. Battle honors: Russellville, KY.

Born: Aug. 22, 1839 Indianapolis, IN

Died: Nov. 3, 1913 Jacksonville, FL

Education: Attended Wabash College, Crawfordsville, IN. Graduated Amherst (MA) College, 1862.

Occupation: Banker, bookseller, and fruit grower

Miscellaneous: Resided Indianapolis, IN; and Jacksonville, Duval Co., FL, 1877–1913

Buried: Crown Hill Cemetery, Indianapolis, IN (Section 8, Lot 1)

References: Pension File and Military Service File, National Archives. Robert S. Fletcher and Malcolm O. Young, editors. *Amherst College. Biographical Record of the Graduates and Non-Graduates.* Centennial Edition, 1821–1921. Amherst, MA, 1927. Letters Received, Volunteer Service Branch, Adjutant General's Office, File I319(VS)1864, National Archives. Samuel Merrill. *The 70th Indiana Volunteer Infantry in the War of the Rebellion.* Indianapolis, IN, 1900. Obituary, *Florida Times-Union,* Nov. 4, 1913. Obituary, *Indianapolis News,* Nov. 4, 1913. Obituary, *Indianapolis Star,* Nov. 5, 1913. Mason W. Tyler. *Recollections of the Civil War.* New York City, NY, 1912.

Samuel Colville Vance (photograph by J. L. Lovell, Amherst, Massachusetts).

Warner Lowder Vestal

Sergeant, Co. A, 7 IN Infantry (3 months), April 24, 1861. Honorably mustered out, Aug. 2, 1861. Corporal, Co. A, 53 IN Infantry, Feb. 19, 1862. Sergeant Major, 53 IN Infantry, April 28, 1862. Captain, Co. A, 53 IN Infantry, June 14, 1862. Major, 53 IN Infantry, Sept. 19, 1863. GSW right leg, Atlanta, GA, July 22, 1864. Lieutenant Colonel, 53 IN Infantry, July 23, 1864. Colonel, 53 IN Infantry, Jan. 31, 1865. Honorably mustered out, July 21, 1865. Battle honors: Atlanta Campaign (Kenesaw Mountain, Atlanta), Campaign of the Carolinas.

Born: Nov. 28, 1839 Guilford Twp., Hendricks Co., IN

Died: Sept. 15, 1910 San Bernardino, CA (committed suicide by gas asphyxiation)

Occupation: Printer and newspaper editor

Offices/Honors: Postmaster, Storm Lake, IA, 1882–85

Miscellaneous: Resided Danville, Hendricks Co., IN; Plainfield, Hendricks Co., IN; Des Moines, Polk Co., IA, 1867–70; Storm Lake, Buena Vista Co., IA, 1870–86; San Diego, CA, 1886–89; and San Bernardino, San Bernardino Co., CA, 1889–1910

Buried: Mountain View Cemetery, San Bernardino, CA (Lotus Lawn, Lot 132)

References: *An Illustrated History of Southern California, Embracing the Counties of San Diego, San Bernardino, Los Angeles and Orange, and the Peninsula of Lower California.* Chicago, IL, 1890. Pension File and Military Service File, National Archives. Obituary, *San Bernardino Daily Sun*, Sept. 16, 1910. Obituary, *Danville Republican*, Sept. 22, 1910. John V. Hadley, editor. *History of Hendricks County, Indiana: Her People, Industries and Institutions.* Indianapolis, IN, 1914. C. H. Wegerslev and Thomas Walpole. *Past and Present of Buena Vista County, Iowa.* Chicago, IL, 1909. Garland A. Haas. *To the Mountain of Fire and Beyond: The 53rd Indiana Regiment from Corinth to Glory.* Carmel, IN, 1997. Letters Received, Volunteer Service Branch, Adjutant General's Office, File V108(VS) 1867, National Archives.

Henry Von Trebra

Lieutenant Colonel, 32 IN Infantry, Aug. 24, 1861. Colonel, 32 IN Infantry, July 18, 1862. Battle honors: Rowlett's Station, Shiloh.

Born: Oct. 28, 1830 Lubben, Prussia

Died: Aug. 6, 1863 Arcola, IL (chronic diarrhea following typhoid fever)

Education: Attended military schools at Potsdam and Berlin, Germany

Occupation: Prussian army officer until 1854 when he came to America. Occupation listed as "match maker" in 1860 census.

Miscellaneous: Resided Arcola, Douglas Co., IL

Buried: Arcola Township Cemetery, Arcola, IL

References: William Sumner Dodge. *History of the Old Second Division, Army of the Cumberland.* Chicago, IL, 1864. Pension File and Military Service File, National Archives. Joseph R. Reinhart, editor. *August Willich's Gallant Dutchmen: Civil War Letters from the 32nd Indiana Infantry.* Kent, OH, 2006. James Barnett, "Willich's Thirty-Second Indiana Volunteers," *Cincinnati Historical Society Bulletin*, Vol. 37, No. 1 (Spring 1979). Michael A. Peake. *Blood Shed in This War: Civil War Illustrations by Captain Adolph Metzner, 32nd Indiana.* Indianapolis, IN, 2010. Thomas M. Eddy. *The Patriotism of Illinois.* Chicago, IL, 1865.

Alfred Bryant Wade

Private, Co. I, 9 IN Infantry (3 months), April 22, 1861. Honorably mustered out, July 29, 1861. 1 Lieutenant, Adjutant, 73 IN Infantry, Aug. 27, 1862. Major, 73 IN Infantry, April 25, 1863. Taken prisoner near Rome, GA, May 3, 1863. Confined Libby Prison, Richmond, VA. Paroled Feb. 26, 1864. Lieutenant Colonel, 73 IN Infantry, July 5, 1864. *Colonel*, 73 IN Infantry, July 6, 1864. Commanded Post of Athens, AL, District of Tennessee, Oct.–Nov. 1864. Commanded 1 Brigade, 4 Division, 20 Army Corps, Army of the Cumberland, Dec. 19–24, 1864. Commanded Post of Larkinsville, AL, District of North Alabama, March–June

Warner Lowder Vestal (as Sergeant, 7 Indiana Infantry, 1861) (Craig Dunn Collection).

Alfred Bryant Wade (Allen Cebula Collection, USAMHI [RG98S-CWP53.99]).

1865. Honorably mustered out, July 1, 1865. Battle honors: Stone's River, Streight's Raid, Athens, AL.
  Born: Dec. 28, 1839 South Bend, IN
  Died: Feb. 27, 1877 near Crum's Point, St. Joseph Co., IN (accidentally drowned while hunting ducks on Kankakee River)
  Education: Attended University of Michigan, Ann Arbor, MI
  Occupation: Lawyer and postmaster
  Offices/Honors: Postmaster, South Bend, IN, 1869–77
  Miscellaneous: Resided South Bend, St. Joseph Co., IN. Nephew of Colonel Kline G. Shryock (87 IN Infantry).
  Buried: City Cemetery, South Bend, IN (Section 3 West, Lot 156)
  References: *History of the 73rd Indiana Volunteers in the War of 1861–65.* Washington, DC, 1909. *History of St. Joseph County, IN.* Chicago, IL, 1880. Obituary, *St. Joseph Valley Register,* March 8, 1877. Obituary, *South Bend Weekly Tribune,* March 3, 1877. *South Bend and the Men Who Have Made It.* South Bend, IN, 1901. Michael P. Downs, transcriber. *The Civil War Diary, Colonel Alfred B. Wade.* Fort Walton Beach, FL, 2009. Pension File and Military Service File, National Archives. Letters Received, Volunteer Service Branch, Adjutant General's Office, Files W494(VS)1864 and W402(VS)1865, National Archives.

John Crawford Walker

Colonel, 35 IN Infantry, Dec. 11, 1861. Having antagonized Governor Oliver P. Morton by refusing to accept officers of the 61st Indiana assigned to his regiment by Morton upon the consolidation of the two regiments, he was discharged, Aug. 6, 1862, at Morton's request upon the Governor's report of the incident to Secretary of War Stanton. In a letter to Major General Halleck he appealed his case, pointing out that he lacked vacancies for these officers and finally imploring, "I appeal to you as the guardian of our army's reputation to rescue my name from unmerited reproach." Halleck took no action except to refer the letter to Morton, who responded, "The vacancy occasioned by his dismissal has been filled, and the regiment, I am well assured, is getting along much better without him than it ever did with him." Becoming a bitter opponent of the war, he was accused in the 1865 treason trial of William A. Bowles, Lambdin P. Milligan, and Stephen Horsey of conspiring with them to "release by force the rebel prisoners" at Camp Morton and other prisons. He escaped prosecution by fleeing to Canada and then to Europe.
  Born: Feb. 11, 1828 Shelbyville, IN
  Died: April 14, 1883 Indianapolis, IN

John Crawford Walker (Frederick Hill Meserve. Historical Portraits, A Part of the Collection of Americana of Frederick Hill Meserve. New York City, 1913–1915; courtesy New York State Library).

John Crawford Walker (post-war) (Berry R. Sulgrove. *History of Indianapolis and Marion County, Indiana.* Philadelphia, Pennsylvania, 1884).

Education: Attended King's College, London, England. Attended Indiana Medical College, La Porte, IN.
Occupation: Newspaper editor before war. Physician after war.
Offices/Honors: Indiana House of Representatives, 1853
Miscellaneous: Resided La Porte, La Porte Co., IN; Europe, 1865–73; Shelbyville, Shelby Co., IN, 1873–79; and Indianapolis, IN, 1879–83. Brother-in-law of Colonel David Garland Rose (54 IN Infantry).
Buried: Crown Hill Cemetery, Indianapolis, IN (Section 21, Lot 22)
References: Berry R. Sulgrove. *History of Indianapolis and Marion County, IN.* Philadelphia, PA, 1884. Obituary, *Indianapolis Times,* April 15, 1883. Rebecca A. Shepherd, Charles W. Calhoun, Elizabeth Shanahan-Shoemaker, and Alan F. January, editors. *A Biographical Directory of the Indiana General Assembly.* Vol. 1, 1816–1899. Indianapolis, IN, 1980. R. French Stone, editor. *Biography of Eminent American Physicians and Surgeons.* Indianapolis, IN, 1894. Military Service File, National Archives. Letters Received, Volunteer Service Branch, Adjutant General's Office, File W725(VS)1862, National Archives. Gilbert R. Tredway. *Democratic Opposition to the Lincoln Administration in Indiana.* Indianapolis, IN, 1973. William L. Burton. *Melting Pot Soldiers: The Union's Ethnic Regiments.* Ames, IA, 1988.

William N. Walker

2 Lieutenant, Co. E, 25 IN Infantry, Aug. 19, 1861. Captain, Co. E, 25 IN Infantry, Oct. 23, 1861. Acting AQM, Staff of Brig. Gen. James C. Veatch, 2 Brigade, 4 Division, District of West Tennessee, Department of the Tennessee, Aug.–Dec. 1862. Acting AQM, District of Memphis (5 Division, 16 Army Corps), Army of the Tennessee, Jan. 24–Oct. 27, 1863. Resigned Jan. 23, 1864, "having been for the past year suffering from disease which has rendered me the greater part of the time unfit for military service." Colonel, 4 IN Legion (Spencer County), June 28, 1864. Resigned Nov. 30, 1864. Battle honors: Fort Donelson, Shiloh, Corinth Campaign (Hatchie Bridge).
Born: May 20, 1831 TN
Died: March 7, 1876 Logansburg, IL
Occupation: Physician
Miscellaneous: Resided Rockport, Spencer Co., IN; Shoals, Martin Co., IN; and Logansburg, Wabash Co., IL
Buried: Warnock Cemetery, Princeton, Gibson Co., IN
References: Pension File and Military Service File, National Archives. Obituary, *Princeton Clarion,* March 9, 1876. John P. Etter. *The Indiana Legion: A Civil War Militia.* Carmel, IN, 2006.

William Robert Wall

1 Lieutenant, Co. I, 8 IN Infantry (3 months), April 25, 1861. Honorably mustered out, Aug. 6, 1861. Captain, Co. B, 8 IN Infantry (3 years), Aug. 25, 1861. Resigned Jan. 17, 1863, being "unable to fill the duties of his office, because of general debility and bronchial irritation." Colonel, Marion County Regiment, IN Legion, Aug. 15, 1863. Captain, Co. B, 9 IN Cavalry, Dec. 10, 1863. Major, 9 IN Cavalry, Dec. 31, 1864. Honorably mustered out, Aug. 28, 1865. Battle honors: Rich Mountain, Pea Ridge.
Born: Feb. 28, 1827 Knoxville, TN
Died: Sept. 4, 1910 Oak Twp., Mills Co., IA
Education: Attended Eclectic Medical Institute, Cincinnati, OH
Other Wars: Mexican War (Private, Co. G, 16 U.S. Infantry)
Occupation: Lawyer before war. Physician and farmer after war.
Miscellaneous: Resided New Palestine, Hancock Co., IN; Livingston, Clark Co., IL; and Folsom, Mills Co., IA, after 1871
Buried: Fairview Cemetery, Council Bluffs, IA
References: *History of Mills County, Iowa.* Des Moines, IA, 1881. Pension File and Military Service File, National Archives. *A Biographical History of Fremont and Mills Counties, Iowa.* Chicago, IL,

William Robert Wall (John Sickles Collection).

1901. Obituary, *Omaha Morning World-Herald*, Sept. 5, 1910.

John Milton Wallace

Adjutant General of Indiana, April 26–May 15, 1861. Colonel, 12 IN Infantry (1 year), May 15, 1861. Resigned Aug. 6, 1861, having "become unable to ride a horse," due to "violent attacks of cramping of stomach and bowels." Additional Paymaster,

John Milton Wallace (*History of Grant County, Indiana*. Chicago, Illinois, 1886).

USA, Aug. 9, 1861. Resigned July 22, 1862, "with the view of offering my services to the Government in the field among the Volunteers of my native state."

Born: Jan. 2, 1822 Brookville, IN
Died: Aug. 27, 1866 Marion, IN
Other Wars: Mexican War (Captain, Co. A, 4 IN Infantry)
Occupation: Lawyer and judge
Offices/Honors: Circuit Court Judge, 1854–60
Miscellaneous: Resided Marion, Grant Co., IN. Uncle of Major Gen. Lew Wallace.
Buried: IOOF (now Estates of Serenity) Cemetery, Marion, IN (Block 3, Lot 17)
References: Pension File and Military Service File, National Archives. *History of Grant County, IN*. Chicago, IL, 1886. George S. Wallace. *Wallace, Genealogical Data Pertaining to the Descendants of Peter Wallace & Elizabeth Woods, His Wife*. Charlottesville, VA, 1927. Letters Received, Commission Branch, Adjutant General's Office, File W293(CB) 1863, National Archives. Sally C. Hogan, editor. *General Reub Williams's Memories of Civil War Times*. Westminster, MD, 2006.

Thomas Webb

2 Lieutenant, Co. G, 70 IN Infantry, Aug. 7, 1862. 1 Lieutenant, Co. G, 70 IN Infantry, Feb. 3, 1863. Resigned June 12, 1863, due to "spinal irritation and chronic rheumatism of eight months duration." Captain, Perry Guards, Marion County Regiment, IN Legion, July 22, 1863. Colonel, Marion County Regiment, IN Legion, June 27, 1864.

Born: Sept. 6, 1828 New Castle, KY
Died: Feb. 16, 1890 Indianapolis, IN
Other Wars: Mexican War (Corporal, Co. D, 4 IN Infantry)
Occupation: Farmer
Miscellaneous: Resided Glenn's Valley, Perry Twp., Marion Co., IN
Buried: Crown Hill Cemetery, Indianapolis, IN (Section 42, Lot 110)
References: Pension File and Military Service File, National Archives. Obituary, *Indianapolis Journal*, Feb. 17–18, 1890. *Operations of the Indiana Legion and Minute Men, 1863–4. Documents Presented to the General Assembly, with the Governor's Message, Jan. 6, 1865*. Indianapolis, IN, 1865.

Samuel Thornton Wells

Captain, Vallonia Rifles, IN Legion, July 9, 1861. Captain, Co. A, 50 IN Infantry, Nov. 4, 1861. Major, 50 IN Infantry, March 1, 1862. Lieutenant Colonel, 50 IN Infantry, Sept. 8, 1862. Taken prisoner and paroled, Munfordville, KY, Sept. 17, 1862. Commanded Post of Lewisburg, AR, Department of Arkansas, Oct. 1863–March 1864. *Colonel*, 50

Samuel Thornton Wells.

IN Infantry, Nov. 19, 1863. Honorably mustered out, May 26, 1865. Battle Honors: Munfordville, Parker's Cross Roads, Camden Expedition (Jenkins' Ferry), Mobile Campaign.
Born: Nov. 4, 1821 Owen Twp., Jackson Co., IN
Died: July 1, 1901 Denver, CO
Education: Attended Indiana University, Bloomington, IN
Other Wars: Mexican War (1 Sergeant, Co. D, 3 U.S. Dragoons)
Occupation: Farmer
Offices/Honors: Sheriff of Jackson Co., IN, 1846. Indiana House of Representatives, 1849–50, 1851–52, and 1877.
Miscellaneous: Resided Vallonia, Jackson Co., IN; and Denver, CO, 1887–1901
Buried: Fairmount Cemetery, Denver, CO (Block 12, Lot 21)
References: *History of Jackson County, IN.* Chicago, IL, 1886. Pension File and Military Service File, National Archives. Rebecca A. Shepherd, Charles W. Calhoun, Elizabeth Shanahan-Shoemaker, and Alan F. January, editors. *A Biographical Directory of the Indiana General Assembly.* Vol. 1, 1816–1899. Indianapolis, IN, 1980. Obituary, *Rocky Mountain News,* July 3, 1901.

Merit C. Welsh

Captain, Clay Guards, IN Legion (Decatur County), July 17, 1861. Captain, Co. D, 7 IN Infantry (3 years), Sept. 1, 1861. Major, 7 IN Infantry, April 23, 1863. Honorably mustered out, Sept. 20, 1864. Colonel, 146 IN Infantry, March 9, 1865. Commanded 1 Brigade, 2 Provisional Division, District of Winchester, Middle Military Department, July 1865. Honorably mustered out, Aug. 31, 1865. Battle honors: Mine Run, Wilderness, Spotsylvania, North Anna, Petersburg Campaign.
Born: May 22, 1825 Napoleon, Ripley Co., IN
Died: Feb. 17, 1913 Greensburg, IN
Other Wars: Mexican War (Private, Co. H, 3 IN Infantry)
Occupation: Grocer and livestock trader before war. Farmer and lawyer after war.
Offices/Honors: Sheriff of Decatur Co., IN, 1884–88
Miscellaneous: Resided Milford, Decatur Co., IN; Adams, Decatur Co., IN; and Greensburg, Decatur Co., IN, 1884–1913
Buried: Milford Cemetery, Milford, IN
References: Lewis A. Harding, editor. *History*

Merit C. Welsh (A. Wilkinson, Photographer, Greensburg, Indiana).

of Decatur County, Indiana, Its People, Industries and Institutions. Indianapolis, IN, 1915. Obituary, *Greensburg Weekly News,* Feb. 21, 1913. Pension File and Military Service File, National Archives. Orville Thomson. *From Philippi to Appomattox: Narrative of the Service of the 7th Indiana Infantry in the War for the Union.* N.p., 1904.

William M. Wheatley

Captain, Indianapolis Union Guards, May 31, 1861. Colonel, 26 IN Infantry, Aug. 30, 1861. Commanded Post of Sedalia, MO, District of Central Missouri, March–May 1862. After being acquitted of all charges in two courts-martial "of a frivolous character," he resigned Sept. 27, 1862, due to "continual sickness in my family." Captain, Co. A, 107 IN Minute Men, July 9, 1863. Honorably mustered out, July 18, 1863. Captain, First Ward Guards, City of Indianapolis Regiment, IN Legion, July 9, 1863. Resigned Sept. 24, 1863.

Born: Oct. 22, 1825 Pittsburgh, PA
Died: Feb. 22, 1917 Los Angeles, CA (killed by street car)
Occupation: Lumber merchant before war. Lumber merchant, insurance adjustor, architect, and contractor after war.
Miscellaneous: Resided Indianapolis, IN, to 1880; Chicago, IL, 1880–98; Livingston, Madison Co., MS; Deadwood, Lawrence Co., SD; and Los Angeles, CA
Buried: Crown Hill Cemetery, Indianapolis, IN (Section 1, Lot 11)
References: Pension File and Military Service File, National Archives. Obituary, *Los Angeles Times,* Feb. 23, 1917. Thomas P. Lowry. *Tarnished Eagles: The Courts-Martial of Fifty Union Colonels and Lieutenant Colonels.* Mechanicsburg, PA, 1997. Court-martial Case Files, 1809–1894, Files KK-165 and MM-2564, National Archives.

John Wheeler

Captain, Co. B, 20 IN Infantry, July 22, 1861. Major, 20 IN Infantry, Feb. 16, 1862. Lieutenant Colonel, 20 IN Infantry, Aug. 30, 1862. Colonel, 20 IN Infantry, Feb. 21, 1863. GSW throat, Gettysburg, PA, July 2, 1863. Battle honors: Groveton, Fredericksburg, Chancellorsville, Gettysburg.

Born: Feb. 6, 1825 New Milford, CT
Died: July 2, 1863 KIA Gettysburg, PA
Occupation: Newspaper editor and farmer
Offices/Honors: Lake County Surveyor, 1853–56
Miscellaneous: Resided Crown Point, Lake Co., IN
Buried: Maplewood Cemetery, Crown Point, IN (Block C, Lot 46)
References: Weston A. Goodspeed and Charles

John Wheeler (Richard F. Carlile Collection, copied by Richard A. Baumgartner).

Blanchard, editors. *Counties of Porter and Lake, Indiana. Historical and Biographical.* Chicago, IL, 1882. David Stevenson. *Indiana's Roll of Honor.* Indianapolis, IN, 1864. Obituary, *Crown Point Register,* July 16 and July 30, 1863. Albert G. Wheeler, Jr., compiler. *The Genealogical and Encyclopedic History of the Wheeler Family in America.* Boston, MA, 1914. Craig L. Dunn. *Harvestfields of Death: The 20th Indiana Volunteers of Gettysburg.* Carmel, IN, 1999. Edmund J. Raus, Jr. *A Generation on the March: The Union Army at Gettysburg.* Gettysburg, PA, 1996. Pension File and Military Service File, National Archives.

Frank Wilcox

Captain, Co. E, 63 IN Infantry, Aug. 14, 1862. Provost Marshal, Post of Indianapolis, IN, July–Oct. 1863. Major, 63 IN Infantry, June 24, 1864. Colonel, 154 IN Infantry, April 17, 1865. Commanded 1 Brigade, 2 Provisional Division, District of Winchester, Middle Military Department, July 31–Aug. 4, 1865. Honorably mustered out, Aug. 4, 1865. Battle honors: Atlanta Campaign, Campaign of the Carolinas.

Born: March 14, 1829 Summit, NJ
Died: March 31, 1917 Champaign, IL
Other Wars: Rogue River Indian War (Private, Oregon Militia, Aug.–Sept. 1853)
Occupation: Involved in varied activities during

his pre-war travels in the Western states. Returned to Covington, IN, in 1860 as the keeper of a livery stable. Real estate agent and mortgage broker after war.

Miscellaneous: Resided Covington, Fountain Co., IN; and Champaign, Champaign Co., IL, 1865–1917

Buried: Mount Hope Cemetery, Urbana, IL (Original Plat, Block 17, Lot 10)

References: *Portrait and Biographical Album of Champaign County, IL.* Chicago, IL, 1887. Robert H. Behrens. *From Salt Fork to Chickamauga: Champaign County Soldiers in the Civil War.* Urbana, IL, 1988. Obituary, *Champaign Daily News,* April 2, 1917. Pension File and Military Service File, National Archives. Letters Received, Volunteer Service Branch, Adjutant General's Office, File W1426(VS) 1865, National Archives.

William M. Wiles

1 Lieutenant, Co. G, 22 IN Infantry, Aug. 15, 1861. Provost Marshal, Staff of Major Gen. William S. Rosecrans, Army of the Mississippi, July 8–Oct. 24, 1862. Captain, Co. G, 22 IN Infantry, July 9, 1862. Provost Marshal General, Department of the Cumberland, Oct. 24, 1862–Feb. 10, 1864. Major,

William M. Wiles (Allen Cebula Collection, USA MHI [RG98S-CWP53.94]).

44 IN Infantry, April 25, 1863. Lieutenant Colonel, 22 IN Infantry, Aug. 5, 1863. *Colonel,* 22 IN Infantry, Feb. 6, 1864. GSW right arm, Rome, GA, May 17, 1864. Honorably mustered out, Jan. 9, 1865. Battle honors: Iuka, Corinth, Stone's River, Tullahoma Campaign, Chickamauga, Atlanta Campaign (Rome).

Born: Aug. 29, 1834 Columbus, IN

Died: March 19, 1880 Indianapolis, IN

Occupation: Druggist, insurance agent, and confectioner

Offices/Honors: U.S. Assessor of Internal Revenue, 1869–73. Indianapolis (IN) City Treasurer, 1877–79.

Miscellaneous: Resided Columbus, Bartholomew Co., IN; Columbia, Maury Co., TN, 1865–66; and Indianapolis, IN, 1866–80

Buried: Crown Hill Cemetery, Indianapolis, IN (Section 25, Lot 244)

References: Pension File and Military Service File, National Archives. Obituary, *Indianapolis Sentinel,* March 20, 1880. John Fitch. *Annals of the Army of the Cumberland.* Philadelphia, PA, 1864. Randolph V. Marshall. *An Historical Sketch of the 22nd Regiment Indiana Volunteers, from Its Organization to the Close of the War, Its Battles, Its Marches, and Its Hardships, Its Brave Officers and Its Honored Dead.* Madison, IN, 1884.

William M. Wiles.

John Fletcher Willey

Captain, Battle Creek Guards, 8 IN Legion (Clark and Scott Counties), June 18, 1862. Colonel, 8 IN Legion (Clark and Scott Counties), Nov. 25, 1862.

Born: June 15, 1809 Cincinnati, OH
Died: April 12, 1899 Monroe Twp., Clark Co., IN
Occupation: Farmer, fruit grower, and Methodist clergyman
Miscellaneous: Resided Monroe Twp., Clark Co., IN; and Flower Gap, Utica Twp., Clark Co., IN
Buried: Union Cemetery, Utica Twp., Clark Co., IN
References: Obituary, *Jeffersonville Evening News,* April 12, 1899. Lewis C. Baird. *Baird's History of Clark County, IN.* Indianapolis, IN, 1909. *History of the Ohio Falls Cities and Their Counties.* Cleveland, OH, 1882. Henry Willey. *Isaac Willey of New London, Conn., and His Descendants.* New Bedford, MA, 1888. *Report of Major General Love of the Indiana Legion.* Indianapolis, IN, 1863. *Operations of the Indiana Legion and Minute Men, 1863–4. Documents Presented to the General Assembly, with the Governor's Message, Jan. 6, 1865.* Indianapolis, IN, 1865.

Hugh T. Williams

Colonel, 11 IN Legion (Ohio County), Sept. 25, 1861. Battle honors: Morgan's Ohio Raid.

Born: May 27, 1812 Breckinridge Co., KY
Died: Dec. 22, 1879 Rising Sun, IN
Education: Graduated Louisville (KY) Medical Institute, 1842
Occupation: Physician and lumber merchant
Offices/Honors: Indiana House of Representatives, 1861
Miscellaneous: Resided Rising Sun, Ohio Co., IN
Buried: Cedar Hedge Cemetery, Rising Sun, IN
References: *A Biographical History of Eminent and Self-Made Men of the State of Indiana.* Cincinnati, OH, 1880. *History of Dearborn, Ohio and Switzerland Counties, Indiana, from Their Earliest Settlement.* Chicago, IL, 1885. Obituary, *Rising Sun Recorder,* Dec. 27, 1879. Rebecca A. Shepherd, Charles W. Calhoun, Elizabeth Shanahan-Shoemaker, and Alan F. January, editors. *A Biographical Directory of the Indiana General Assembly.* Vol. 1, 1816–1899. Indianapolis, IN, 1980. James Sutherland. *Biographical Sketches of the Members of the Forty-First General Assembly of the State of Indiana with That of the State Officers and Judiciary.* Indianapolis, IN, 1861. *Report of Major General Love of the Indiana Legion.* Indianapolis, IN, 1863. *Operations of the Indiana Legion and Minute Men, 1863–4. Documents Presented to the General Assembly, with the Governor's Message, Jan. 6, 1865.* Indianapolis, IN, 1865. John P. Etter. *The Indiana Legion: A Civil War Militia.* Carmel, IN, 2006.

Hugh T. Williams (post-war) (*A Biographical History of Eminent and Self-Made Men of the State of Indiana.* Cincinnati, Ohio, 1880).

John S. Williams

1 Lieutenant, Adjutant, 63 IN Infantry, Dec. 31, 1861. Lieutenant Colonel, 63 IN Infantry, Feb. 21, 1862. Colonel, 63 IN Infantry, Aug. 30, 1862. Commanded Camp Morton Prison, Indianapolis, IN, March 1863. "The precarious condition of my health rendering me wholly unfit for military duty," he resigned June 14, 1863, due to disease of the kidneys and irritation of the prostate gland. Battle honors: 2nd Bull Run.

Born: Dec. 14, 1825 Lockport, NY
Died: Dec. 3, 1900 Lafayette, IN
Education: Attended Genesee Wesleyan Seminary, Lima, NY
Occupation: Lawyer and newspaper editor
Offices/Honors: Mayor of Lafayette, IN, 1856–58. U.S. Internal Revenue Collector, 1866–69. Third Auditor of the U.S. Treasury, 1885–89.
Miscellaneous: Resided Lafayette, Tippecanoe Co., IN
Buried: Springvale Cemetery, Lafayette, IN (Section 14, Lot 75)
References: *A Biographical History of Eminent*

John S. Williams (Gladys A. Lyle Beckwith Collection, USAMHI [RG98S-CWP83.105]).

Samuel J. Williams (Library of Congress [LC-DIG-cwpb-04464]).

and Self-Made Men of the State of Indiana. Cincinnati, OH, 1880. Pension File and Military Service File, National Archives. Obituary, *Lafayette Morning Journal,* Dec. 4, 1900. *Biographical Record and Portrait Album of Tippecanoe County, IN.* Chicago, IL, 1888. Richard P. DeHart, editor. *Past and Present of Tippecanoe County, IN.* Indianapolis, IN, 1909. Obituary Circular, Whole No. 138, Indiana MOLLUS.

Samuel J. Williams

Captain, Co. K, 19 IN Infantry, July 29, 1861. Lieutenant Colonel, 19 IN Infantry, Sept. 18, 1862. Colonel, 19 IN Infantry, Oct. 8, 1862. GSW right breast, Wilderness, VA, May 6, 1864. Battle honors: Fredericksburg, Chancellorsville, Gettysburg, Mine Run, Wilderness.

Born: Oct. 13, 1830 Montgomery Co., VA
Died: May 6, 1864 KIA Wilderness, VA
Occupation: Farmer engaged in warehouse and livestock shipping business
Miscellaneous: Resided Selma, Delaware Co., IN
Buried: White Cemetery, Selma, IN
References: *A Portrait and Biographical Record of Delaware and Randolph Counties, IN.* Chicago, IL, 1894. Theodore T. Scribner. *Indiana's Roll of Honor.* Indianapolis, IN, 1866. Craig L. Dunn. *Iron Men, Iron Will: The Nineteenth Indiana Regiment of the Iron Brigade.* Indianapolis, IN, 1995. Pension File and Military Service File, National Archives.

William C. Williams

Captain, Co. G, 44 IN Infantry, Nov. 22, 1861. Colonel, 44 IN Infantry, Nov. 27, 1862. Taken prisoner, Stone's River, TN, Jan. 2, 1863. Confined Atlanta, GA, and Libby Prison, Richmond, VA. Exchanged May 8, 1863. When he failed to report to his regiment until July 16, 1863, he was arrested and charged with "absence without leave" and also with drunkenness for reporting in a "grossly intoxicated" condition. In a letter of resignation tendered July 22, 1863, he acknowledged his tardiness in reporting, denied the charge of drunkenness, and appealed, "My character will be blighted forever, and no matter how long I may live, the shadow of the awful ruin hanging over me will follow me to my grave, unless I am permitted to save the character I have earned on the battle fields it has been my boast and pride to have fought upon." The order of July 26, 1863, which accepted his resignation and discharged him with the added stigma, "for the good of the service," was finally revoked, July 17, 1868, and he was honorably discharged upon tender of resignation, to date May 12, 1863. Battle honors: Shiloh, Stone's River.

Born: Sept. 9, 1830 near Philadelphia, PA
Died: Jan. 6, 1907 Indianapolis, IN

William C. Williams (Mark Weldon Collection).

Education: Attended Jefferson Medical College, Philadelphia, PA
Occupation: Physician before war. Lawyer and U.S. Pension agency clerk after war.
Offices/Honors: Clerk of Circuit Court, Noble Co., IN, 1867–75
Miscellaneous: Resided Wolf Lake, Noble Co., IN; Albion, Noble Co., IN, 1867–94; and Indianapolis, IN
Buried: Lindenwood Cemetery, Fort Wayne, IN (Section P, Lot 118)
References: *A Biographical History of Eminent and Self-Made Men of the State of Indiana.* Cincinnati, OH, 1880. Pension File and Military Service File, National Archives. Obituary, *Indianapolis News,* Jan. 7, 1907. Obituary, *Fort Wayne Daily News,* Jan. 7, 1907. *Counties of Lagrange and Noble, Indiana. Historical and Biographical.* Chicago, IL, 1882. Weston A. Goodspeed and Charles Blanchard, editors. *Counties of Whitley and Noble, Indiana. Historical and Biographical.* Chicago, IL, 1882. John H. Rerick. *The 44th Indiana Volunteer Infantry: History of Its Services in the War of the Rebellion.* LaGrange, IN, 1880.

John M. Wilson

Captain, Co. B, 13 IN Infantry, April 23, 1861. Major, 13 IN Infantry, May 10, 1862. Lieutenant Colonel, 13 IN Infantry, June 13, 1863. GSW right shoulder, Bermuda Hundred, VA, May 20, 1864. Honorably mustered out, July 2, 1864. Colonel, 155 IN Infantry, April 18, 1865. Commanded District of Delaware and Eastern Shore of Maryland, 8 Army Corps, Middle Department, June 5–Aug. 1, 1865. Honorably mustered out, Aug. 4, 1865. Battle honors: Rich Mountain, Bermuda Hundred.
Born: May 1, 1815 Princeton, IN
Died: March 17, 1876 Indianapolis, IN
Education: Attended Indiana University, Bloomington, IN
Other Wars: Mexican War (Captain, Co. B, 1 IN Infantry)
Occupation: Lawyer
Miscellaneous: Resided Peru, Miami Co., IN
Buried: Mount Hope Cemetery, Peru, IN (Section A, Lot 21)
References: Obituary, *Peru Republican,* March 24, 1876. Arthur L. Bodurtha, editor. *History of Miami County, Indiana.* Chicago and New York, 1914. Military Service File, National Archives. Letters Received, Volunteer Service Branch, Adjutant General's Office, File B1299(VS)1862, National Archives.

William Cochran Wilson

Captain, Co. D, 10 IN Infantry (3 months), April 25, 1861. Major, 10 IN Infantry, May 10, 1861. GSW right leg, Rich Mountain, WV, July 11, 1861. Honorably mustered out, Aug. 6, 1861. Colonel, 40 IN Infantry, Dec. 30, 1861. Resigned March 27, 1862, due to chronic diarrhea. Colonel, 108 IN Minute Men, July 12, 1863. Honorably mustered out, July 18, 1863. Colonel, 135 IN Infantry, May 24, 1864. Commanded Post of Stevenson, AL, District of Tennessee, Aug.–Sept. 1864. Honorably mustered out, Sept. 29, 1864. Battle honors: Rich Mountain.
Born: Nov. 27, 1827 Crawfordsville, IN
Died: Sept. 25, 1891 Lafayette, IN
Education: Graduated Wabash College, Crawfordsville, IN, 1847. Graduated Indiana University Law School, Bloomington, IN, 1849.
Occupation: Lawyer
Offices/Honors: U.S. Assessor of Internal Revenue, 1866–67. Postmaster, Lafayette, IN, 1867–69.
Miscellaneous: Resided Lafayette, Tippecanoe Co., IN
Buried: Greenbush Cemetery, Lafayette, IN (Section 1, Lot 7). Cenotaph in Oak Hill Cemetery, Crawfordsville, IN.
References: Richard P. DeHart, editor. *Past and Present of Tippecanoe County, IN.* Indianapolis, IN, 1909. *Biographical Record and Portrait Album of Tippecanoe County, IN.* Chicago, IL, 1888. *A Biographical History of Eminent and Self-Made Men of*

William Cochran Wilson (post-war) (Album of Portraits of Companions of the Commandery of the State of Ohio MOLLUS. Cincinnati, Ohio, 1893).

the State of Indiana. Cincinnati, OH, 1880. Obituary Circular, Whole No. 38, Indiana MOLLUS. Obituary, *Lafayette Morning Journal,* Sept. 26, 1891. Robert C. Kriebel. *Old Lafayette, 1854–1876: Based Upon Historical Columns from the Pages of the Journal and Courier.* Lafayette, IN, 1990. Charles W. Taylor. *Biographical Sketches and Review of the Bench and Bar of Indiana.* Indianapolis, IN, 1895. *Society of the Army of the Cumberland. Twenty-Second Reunion, Columbus, OH, 1891.* Cincinnati, OH, 1892. *Operations of the Indiana Legion and Minute Men, 1863–4. Documents Presented to the General Assembly, with the Governor's Message, Jan. 6, 1865.* Indianapolis, IN, 1865. Pension File and Military Service File, National Archives. Letters Received, Volunteer Service Branch, Adjutant General's Office, File W560(VS)1862, National Archives.

Edward Jesup Wood

Captain, Co. I, 48 IN Infantry, Jan. 2, 1862. Provost Marshal, Paducah, KY, March–April 1862. Major, 48 IN Infantry, Dec. 4, 1862. Lieutenant Colonel, 48 IN Infantry, April 25, 1863. *Colonel,* 48 IN Infantry, July 12, 1863. Honorably mustered

Edward Jesup Wood (photograph by H. Lazier, Syracuse & Oswego, New York; Craig Dunn Collection).

out, Jan 15, 1865. Battle honors: Iuka, Corinth, Vicksburg Campaign, Missionary Ridge, Savannah Campaign.

Born: Aug. 2, 1834 Marianna, FL
Died: April 9, 1873 Jackson, MI (committed suicide by pistol shot)
Education: Graduated Dartmouth College, Hanover, NH, 1853
Occupation: Lawyer and civil engineer
Offices/Honors: Clerk of Circuit Court, Elkhart Co., IN, 1865–69. Judge of Common Pleas Court, 1870–72.
Miscellaneous: Resided Goshen, Elkhart Co., IN
Buried: Oakwood Cemetery, Syracuse, NY (Section 54, Lot 30)
References: Stephen E. Towne, editor. *A Fierce, Wild Joy: The Civil War Letters of Colonel Edward J. Wood, 48th Indiana Volunteer Infantry Regiment.* Knoxville, TN, 2007. Obituary, *Goshen Times,* April 17, 1873. Pension File and Military Service File, National Archives. Moses T. Runnels. *Memorial Sketches and History of the Class of 1853, Dartmouth College.* Newport, NH, 1895. *Report of the Proceedings of the Society of the Army of the Tennessee at the Eighth Annual Meeting.* Cincinnati, OH, 1877.

Gustavus Adolphus Wood

Major, 15 IN Infantry, June 14, 1861. Lieutenant Colonel, 15 IN Infantry, Oct. 21, 1861. Com-

Gustavus Adolphus Wood (courtesy Bryan Fuxa).

manded 2 Brigade, 1 Division, 21 Army Corps, Army of the Cumberland, Feb. 18–April 13, 1863. Colonel, 15 IN Infantry, March 9, 1863. Taken prisoner, La Vergne, TN, April 10, 1863. Confined Libby Prison, Richmond, VA. Exchanged May 8, 1863. Honorably mustered out, June 25, 1864. Battle honors: Cheat Mountain, Perryville, Stone's River, Missionary Ridge.

Born: Jan. 12, 1825 Galena, Delaware Co., OH
Died: Aug. 11, 1891 Ridgedale, Hamilton Co., TN
Education: Attended Wabash College, Crawfordsville, IN
Other Wars: Mexican War (2 Lieutenant, Co. K, 1 IN Infantry)
Occupation: Lawyer and judge
Offices/Honors: Judge of Court of Common Pleas, Tippecanoe Co., IN, 1854 and 1857–60
Miscellaneous: Resided Lafayette, Tippecanoe Co., IN; and Chattanooga, Hamilton Co., TN, 1865–91
Buried: Chattanooga National Cemetery, Chattanooga, TN (Section U, Site 54-ES)
References: Obituary, *Chattanooga Daily Times*, Aug. 12, 1891. Pension File and Military Service File, National Archives. John Trotwood Moore. *Tennessee, The Volunteer State, 1769–1923*. Chicago, IL, 1923. Richard P. DeHart, editor. *Past and Present of Tippecanoe County, IN*. Indianapolis, IN, 1909. Edward M. Burns. *Historical Sketch of the Or-ganization and Service of the 15th Regiment Indiana Volunteers*. Valparaiso, IN, 1889. Williams T. Blair. *The Michael Shoemaker Book*. Scranton, PA, 1924.

Horatio Woodbury

Colonel, Crawford County Regiment, IN Legion, Oct. 4, 1861. Major, 81 IN Infantry, Aug. 30, 1862. Lieutenant Colonel, 81 IN Infantry, Jan. 18, 1863. Resigned April 30, 1863, since "there exists among the officers of the regiment much ill feeling, discord and strife, which cannot be harmonized while all the present officers remain in the regiment." Colonel, 81 IN Infantry, July 7, 1863 (declined). Battle honors: Perryville, Stone's River.

Born: Aug. 15, 1832 Litchfield, ME
Died: May 4, 1881 New Albany, IN
Occupation: Lawyer
Offices/Honors: Secretary, Wyoming Territory, 1869. U.S. Collector of Internal Revenue, 1870–76.
Miscellaneous: Resided Leavenworth, Crawford Co., IN; and New Albany, Floyd Co., IN, 1870–81
Buried: Fairview Cemetery, New Albany, IN (Plat 4, Range 1, Lot 14)
References: Pension File and Military Service File, National Archives. Obituary, *New Albany Daily Ledger-Standard*, May 4, 1881. Doris Byrd Leistner. *Crawford County Indiana Civil War Veterans*. New Albany, IN, 2005. Hazen H. Pleasant. *A History of Crawford County, IN*. Greenfield, IN, 1926. George W. Morris. *History of the 81st Regiment of Indiana Volunteer Infantry in the Great War of the Rebellion, 1861 to 1865*. Louisville, KY, 1901.

James S. Wright

1 Lieutenant, Co. E, 25 IN Infantry, July 9, 1861. Captain, Co. H, 25 IN Infantry, July 8, 1862. Lieutenant Colonel, 25 IN Infantry, Aug. 21, 1864. *Colonel,* 25 IN Infantry, Jan. 1, 1865. Commanded 3 Brigade, 1 Division, 17 Army Corps, Army of the Tennessee, April 10–12, 1865. Honorably mustered out, July 17, 1865. Battle honors: Corinth Campaign (Hatchie Bridge), Atlanta Campaign, Savannah Campaign, Campaign of the Carolinas (Bentonville).

Born: June 7, 1832 Spencer Co., IN
Died: Feb. 25, 1934 Evansville, IN
Occupation: School teacher before war. Farmer, livestock raiser, flatboat trader, and grocer after war.
Offices/Honors: Indiana House of Representatives, 1865. U.S. Internal Revenue Storekeeper, 1876–77. Commissary General, State of Indiana, 1889–91.
Miscellaneous: Resided Rockport, Spencer Co., IN

Buried: Sunset Hill Cemetery, Rockport, IN (Section 6)

References: *History of Warrick, Spencer and Perry Counties, IN.* Chicago, IL, 1885. Obituary, *Rockport Journal,* March 2, 1934. Rebecca A. Shepherd, Charles W. Calhoun, Elizabeth Shanahan-Shoemaker, and Alan F. January, editors. *A Biographical Directory of the Indiana General Assembly.* Vol. 1, 1816–1899. Indianapolis, IN, 1980. Military Service File, National Archives. Letters Received, Volunteer Service Branch, Adjutant General's Office, File T668(VS)1865, National Archives.

Charles Augustus Zollinger

Private, Co. E, 9 IN Infantry (3 months), April 24, 1861. Honorably mustered out, July 29, 1861. 1 Lieutenant, Co. D, 30 IN Infantry, Sept. 15, 1861. Resigned Feb. 1, 1863, due to "chronic diarrhea at-

Charles Augustus Zollinger (post-war) (William H. Powell, ed. *Officers of the Army and Navy (Volunteer) Who Served in the Civil War.* Philadelphia, Pennsylvania, 1893).

Charles Augustus Zollinger (M. J. Powers, Photographer, Whitehurst Gallery, 434 Pennsylvania Avenue, Washington, DC; Mark Weldon Collection).

tended with pleurisy, which totally incapacitates him from performing his duties." Captain, Co. B, 129 IN Infantry, Jan. 25, 1864. Lieutenant Colonel, 129 IN Infantry, March 21, 1864. Colonel, 129 IN Infantry, June 15, 1864. Honorably mustered out, Aug. 29, 1865. Battle honors: Atlanta Campaign, Franklin, Nashville, Campaign of the Carolinas.

Born: Dec. 9, 1838 Wiesbaden, Germany

Died: Dec. 27, 1893 Fort Wayne, IN

Occupation: Blacksmith before war. Hat merchant, postal clerk and politician after war.

Offices/Honors: Sheriff, Allen Co., IN, 1870–72. Mayor, Fort Wayne, IN, 1873–85 and 1891–93. U.S. Pension Agent, 1885–89.

Miscellaneous: Resided New Haven, Allen Co., IN; Fort Wayne, Allen Co., IN, 1868–85 and 1889–93; and Indianapolis, IN, 1885–89

Buried: Lindenwood Cemetery, Fort Wayne, IN (Section U, Lot 268)

References: *Colonel Charles A. Zollinger: Seven-time Mayor of Fort Wayne.* Fort Wayne, IN, 1963. Obituary, *Fort Wayne Sentinel,* Dec. 28, 1893. Obituary Circular, Whole No. 66, Indiana MOLLUS. *A Biographical History of Eminent and Self-Made Men of the State of Indiana.* Cincinnati, OH, 1880. Thomas B. Helm, editor. *History of Allen County, IN.* Chicago, IL, 1880. William H. Powell, editor. *Officers of the Army and Navy (Volunteer) Who Served in the Civil War.* Philadelphia, PA, 1893. Pension File and Military Service File, National Archives.

Kentucky

Regiments

1st Cavalry

Frank L. Wolford	Oct. 28, 1861	Dismissed March 24, 1864
Silas Adams	June 16, 1864	Mustered out Dec. 31, 1864

2nd Cavalry

Buckner Board	Sept. 9, 1861	Resigned Dec. 25, 1862
Thomas P. Nicholas	Feb. 8, 1863	Resigned Dec. 13, 1863
Elijah S. Watts	Dec. 14, 1863	Resigned Aug. 20, 1864
Owen Starr	May 1, 1865	Mustered out July 17, 1865

3rd Cavalry

James S. Jackson	Dec. 13, 1861	Promoted **Brig. Gen., USV,** July 16, 1862
Eli H. Murray	Oct. 9, 1862	Mustered out July 15, 1865, **Bvt. Brig. Gen.,** USV

4th Cavalry

Jesse Bayles	Dec. 13, 1861	Resigned April 4, 1863
Green Clay Smith	March 15, 1862	Promoted **Brig. Gen., USV,** June 11, 1862
Robert Wickliffe Cooper	May 29, 1863	Mustered out Aug. 21, 1865

5th Cavalry

David R. Haggard	Jan. 1, 1862	Discharged March 24, 1863
William P. Sanders	March 4, 1863	Promoted **Brig. Gen., USV,** Oct. 18, 1863
Oliver L. Baldwin	Jan. 2, 1864	Resigned March 25, 1865

6th Cavalry

Dennis J. Halisy	Sept. 26, 1862	KIA Dec. 31, 1862
Louis D. Watkins	Feb. 1, 1863	Promoted **Brig. Gen., USV,** Sept. 25, 1865

7th Cavalry

Leonidas Metcalfe	Aug. 16, 1862	Commission cancelled
John K. Faulkner	April 3, 1863	Mustered out July 10, 1865

8th Cavalry

James M. Shackelford	Sept. 13, 1862	Promoted **Brig. Gen., USV,** Jan. 2, 1863
Benjamin H. Bristow	April 1, 1863	Mustered out Sept. 23, 1863

9th Cavalry

Richard T. Jacob	Aug. 22, 1862	Mustered out Aug. 21, 1863

10th Cavalry

Joshua Tevis	Sept. 10, 1862	Resigned Nov. 17, 1862
Charles J. Walker	Dec. 12, 1862	Resigned Sept. 1, 1863

11th Cavalry

Alexander W. Holeman	Nov. 19, 1863	Resigned Sept. 20, 1864
Milton Graham	Sept. 20, 1864	Mustered out July 14, 1865

12th Cavalry

Quintus C. Shanks	Oct. 11, 1862	Resigned Feb. 14, 1863
Eugene W. Crittenden	March 20, 1863	Mustered out Aug. 23, 1865

13th Cavalry

James W. Weatherford	Dec. 23, 1863	Mustered out Jan. 10, 1865

14th Cavalry

Henry C. Lilly	Feb. 13, 1863	Mustered out March 24, 1864

15th Cavalry

Regiment not entitled to a colonel since it never attained full strength.

16th Cavalry

Did not complete organization. Consolidated with 12th Cavalry.

17th Cavalry

Samuel F. Johnson	April 25, 1865	Mustered out Sept. 20, 1865

1st Infantry

James V. Guthrie	June 28, 1861	Resigned Dec. 21, 1861
David A. Enyart	Jan. 22, 1862	Mustered out June 18, 1864, **Bvt. Brig. Gen., USV**

2nd Infantry

William E. Woodruff	June 28, 1861	Resigned Jan. 28, 1863
Thomas D. Sedgewick	Jan. 27, 1862	Mustered out June 19, 1864

3rd Infantry

Thomas E. Bramlette	Oct. 8, 1861	Resigned July 13, 1862
William T. Scott	July 14, 1862	Resigned Dec. 7, 1862
Samuel McKee	Dec. 7, 1862	KIA Dec. 31, 1862
William H. Spencer	Jan. 1, 1863	Resigned April 8, 1863
Henry C. Dunlap	April 27, 1863	Mustered out Oct. 13, 1864, **Bvt. Brig. Gen., USV**

4th Infantry/Mounted Infantry

Speed S. Fry	Oct. 9, 1861	Promoted **Brig. Gen., USV,** March 21, 1862
John T. Croxton	May 9, 1862	Promoted **Brig. Gen., USV,** July 30, 1864
Robert M. Kelly	Aug. 25, 1864	Mustered out Aug. 17, 1865

5th Infantry

Lovell H. Rousseau	Sept. 9, 1861	Promoted **Brig. Gen., USV,** Oct. 1, 1861
Harvey M. Buckley	Oct. 5, 1861	Resigned Jan. 26, 1863
William W. Berry	Jan. 27, 1863	Mustered out Sept. 14, 1864

6th Infantry

Walter C. Whitaker	Dec. 24, 1861	Promoted **Brig. Gen., USV,** June 25, 1863
George T. Shackelford	Sept. 1, 1863	Discharged Aug. 22, 1864
Richard C. Dawkins	Sept. 16, 1864	Mustered out Jan. 2, 1865

7th Infantry

Theophilus T. Garrard	Sept. 22, 1861	Promoted **Brig. Gen., USV,** Nov. 29, 1862
Reuben May	May 13, 1863	Mustered out Oct. 5, 1864
George W. Monroe	Dec. 10, 1864	Resigned Sept. 25, 1865, **Bvt. Brig. Gen., USV**

8th Infantry

Sidney M. Barnes	Nov. 25, 1861	Resigned Jan. 11, 1864

9th Infantry

Benjamin C. Grider	Nov. 26, 1861	Resigned Feb. 3, 1863
George H. Cram	March 10, 1863	Mustered out Dec. 15, 1864, **Bvt. Brig. Gen., USV**

10th Infantry

John M. Harlan	Nov. 21, 1861	Resigned March 6, 1863
William H. Hays	March 7, 1863	Mustered out Dec. 6, 1864

11th Infantry

Percival B. Hawkins	Nov. 11, 1861	Resigned June 25, 1863
Smoloff P. Love	July 1, 1863	Mustered out Dec. 17, 1864

12th Infantry

William A. Hoskins	Jan. 31, 1862	Resigned April 16, 1864
Lawrence H. Rousseau	April 21, 1864	Mustered out July 11, 1865

13th Infantry

Edward H. Hobson	Jan. 1, 1862	Promoted **Brig. Gen., USV,** Nov. 29, 1862
William E. Hobson	March 13, 1863	Mustered out Jan. 12, 1865

14th Infantry

Laban T. Moore	Dec. 10, 1861	Resigned Jan. 1, 1862
John C. Cochran	Jan. 16, 1862	Resigned Jan. 12, 1863
George W. Gallup	Jan. 13, 1863	Mustered out Jan. 31, 1865, **Bvt. Brig. Gen., USV**

15th Infantry

Curran Pope	Dec. 14, 1861	Died Nov. 5, 1862
James B. Forman	Nov. 8, 1862	KIA Dec. 31, 1862
Marion C. Taylor	Feb. 25, 1863	Mustered out Jan. 14, 1865

16th Infantry

Charles A. Marshall	Jan. 9, 1862	Resigned May 1, 1862
James W. Craddock	May 5, 1862	Died June 2, 1863
James W. Gault	June 3, 1863	Mustered out Feb. 1, 1865
John S. White	Feb. 22, 1865	Resigned May 12, 1865
John S. Hammer	May 16, 1865	Mustered out July 15, 1865

17th Infantry

John H. McHenry, Jr.	Dec. 31, 1861	Dismissed Dec. 4, 1862
Alexander M. Stout	Dec. 23, 1862	Mustered out Jan. 23, 1865, **Bvt. Brig. Gen., USV**

18th Infantry

William A. Warner	Dec. 2, 1861	Discharged Dec. 18, 1863
Hubbard K. Milward	Dec. 19, 1863	Mustered out July 18, 1865

19th Infantry

William J. Landram	Jan. 2, 1862	Mustered out Jan. 26, 1865, **Bvt. Brig. Gen., USV**

20th Infantry

Sanders D. Bruce	Oct. 1, 1861	Resigned June 30, 1864
Thomas B. Waller	Oct. 5, 1864	Mustered out Jan. 17, 1865

21st Infantry

Ethelbert L. Dudley	Dec. 12, 1861	Died Feb. 20, 1862
Samuel W. Price	Feb. 26, 1862	Mustered out Dec. 9, 1865, **Bvt. Brig. Gen., USV**

22nd Infantry

Daniel W. Lindsey	Jan. 10, 1862	Resigned Oct. 14, 1863
George W. Monroe	Dec. 12, 1863	To 7th Infantry Dec. 10, 1864, **Bvt. Brig. Gen., USV**

23rd Infantry

Marcellus Mundy	Dec. 16, 1861	Resigned Dec. 31, 1863
James C. Foy	March 8, 1864	DOW July 24, 1864
George W. Northup	Nov. 16, 1864	Mustered out Dec. 27, 1865

24th Infantry

Lewis B. Grigsby	Jan. 5, 1862	Resigned July 16, 1863
John S. Hurt	Aug. 20, 1863	Mustered out Jan. 31, 1865

25th Infantry

James M. Shackelford	Jan. 1, 1862	Resigned March 24, 1862, Later **Brig. Gen., USV**

26th Infantry

Stephen G. Burbridge	Aug. 27, 1861	Promoted **Brig. Gen., USV,** June 9, 1862
Cicero Maxwell	June 20, 1862	Resigned Jan. 12, 1865
Thomas B. Fairleigh	Feb. 1, 1865	Mustered out July 10, 1865

27th Infantry

Charles D. Pennebaker	Oct. 5, 1861	Resigned April 10, 1864
John H. Ward	April 14, 1864	Mustered out March 29, 1865

28th Infantry

William P. Boone	Nov. 6, 1861	Resigned June 28, 1864
John Rowan Boone	July 5, 1864	Mustered out Dec. 14, 1865

29th Infantry

Did not complete organization. Consolidated with 6th Cavalry.

30th Infantry

Francis N. Alexander	April 5, 1864	Mustered out April 18, 1865

31st Infantry

Did not complete organization.

32nd Infantry

John J. Landram	Dec. 24, 1862	Resigned Feb. 6, 1863

33rd Infantry

Regiment not entitled to a colonel since it never attained full strength.

34th Infantry

Henry Dent	Oct. 2, 1862	Resigned May 31, 1863
Selby Harney	June 2, 1863	Resigned Dec. 15, 1863
William Y. Dillard	Dec. 26, 1863	Mustered out June 24, 1865

35th Infantry
Edmund A. Starling　　　Oct. 2, 1863　　　Mustered out Dec. 29, 1864

36th Infantry
Did not complete organization. Consolidated with 11th Cavalry and 14th Cavalry.

37th Infantry
Charles S. Hanson　　　Dec. 29, 1863　　　Mustered out March 6, 1865

38th Infantry
Did not complete organization. Consolidated with 12th Cavalry.

39th Infantry
John Dils, Jr.　　　Jan. 21, 1863　　　Dismissed Dec. 10, 1863
David A. Mims　　　Dec. 22, 1863　　　Mustered out Sept. 15, 1865

40th Infantry
Clinton J. True　　　Sept. 29, 1863　　　Mustered out Dec. 30, 1864

41st Infantry
Did not complete organization.

42nd Infantry
Did not complete organization.

43rd Infantry
Did not complete organization. Consolidated with 32nd Infantry.

44th Infantry
Did not complete organization.

45th Infantry
John Mason Brown　　　Dec. 17, 1863　　　Mustered out Dec. 24, 1864

46th Infantry
Did not complete organization.

47th Infantry
Andrew H. Clark　　　Dec. 21, 1863　　　Mustered out Dec. 26, 1864

48th Infantry
Hartwell T. Burge　　　Oct. 15, 1863　　　Mustered out Dec. 19, 1864

49th Infantry
John G. Eve　　　Dec. 14, 1863　　　Mustered out Dec. 26, 1864

50th Infantry
Did not complete organization. Consolidated with 49th Infantry.

51st Infantry
Did not complete organization. Consolidated with 37th Infantry.

52nd Infantry
John H. Grider　　　Feb. 17, 1864　　　Mustered out Jan. 18, 1865

53rd Infantry
Clinton J. True　　　April 17, 1865　　　Mustered out Sept. 15, 1865

54th Infantry
Harvey M. Buckley   Sept. 30, 1864   Mustered out Sept. 1, 1865

55th Infantry
Philip W. Stanhope   Oct. 20, 1864   Commission revoked Jan. 12, 1865
Weden O'Neal   March 23, 1865   Mustered out Sept. 19, 1865

1st Regiment, Capital Guards, Kentucky State Troops
Percival B. Hawkins   July 11, 1864

Police Guard, Kentucky Central Railroad
Bushrod W. Foley   Sept. 17, 1861   Mustered out Dec. 10, 1861

22nd Enrolled Militia
Thomas J. Ewing   May 26, 1864   Mustered out June 28, 1864

36th Enrolled Militia
Edgar A. Keenon   June 8, 1864   Mustered out June 18, 1864

41st Enrolled Militia
Amos Shinkle   Sept. 4, 1862   Mustered out Oct. 4, 1862

42nd Enrolled Militia
Gustavus Artsman   Sept. 2, 1862   Mustered out Oct. 2, 1862

64th Enrolled Militia
John T. Gathright   Sept. 1863

65th Enrolled Militia
Burgess Preston   May 21, 1864   Mustered out June 21, 1864

68th Enrolled Militia
Thomas McKinster   May 21, 1864   Mustered out June 22, 1864

Buckner's Regiment, Kentucky Home Guards
James F. Buckner   Aug. 28, 1861

Rockcastle and Lincoln County Home Guards
James S. Fish   May 7, 1862   Mustered out July 7, 1862

Biographies

Silas Adams

1 Lieutenant, Co. A, 1 KY Cavalry, July 17, 1861. 1 Lieutenant, RQM, 1 KY Cavalry. Oct. 28, 1861. Captain, Co. A, 1 KY Cavalry, June 7, 1862. Lieutenant Colonel, 1 KY Cavalry, Dec. 14, 1862. Taken prisoner, Danville, KY, March 24, 1863. Escaped several days later. Commanded 1 Brigade, 1 Division, Cavalry Corps, Army of the Ohio, Nov. 18, 1863–April 8, 1864. Colonel, 1 KY Cavalry, June 16, 1864. Commanded Independent Brigade, Cavalry Corps, Army of the Ohio, June–Aug. 1864. Honorably mustered out, Dec. 31, 1864. Battle honors: Morgan's Ohio Raid, East Tennessee Campaign, Knoxville Campaign, Atlanta Campaign.

Born: Feb. 9, 1839 Pulaski Co., KY
Died: May 6, 1896 Liberty, KY
Education: Attended Transylvania University, Lexington, KY
Occupation: Lawyer
Offices/Honors: Kentucky House of Representatives, 1869–71 and 1889–93. U.S. House of Representatives, 1893–95.

Silas Adams (post-war) (Z. F. Smith. *History of Kentucky*. Louisville, Kentucky, 1895).

Miscellaneous: Resided Liberty, Casey Co., KY
Buried: Brown Cemetery, near Mount Olive, Casey Co., KY
References: Pension File and Military Service File, National Archives. Obituary, *Louisville Courier-Journal*, May 7, 1896. Z. F. Smith. *History of Kentucky*. Louisville, KY, 1895. Eastham Tarrant. *The Wild Riders of the First Kentucky Cavalry, A History of the Regiment in the Great War of the Rebellion, 1861–1865*. Louisville, KY, 1894. James L. Harrison, compiler. *Biographical Directory of the American Congress, 1774–1949*. Washington, DC, 1950.

Francis N. Alexander

Captain, Co. H, 1 KY Cavalry, Dec. 2, 1861. Colonel, 30 KY Infantry, April 5, 1864. Commanded 2 Brigade, 1 Division, District of Kentucky, 23 Army Corps, Department of the Ohio, Sept.–Oct. 1864. Honorably mustered out, April 18, 1865. Battle honors: Mill Springs.
Born: Feb. 8, 1829 near Monticello, KY
Died: March 17, 1905 Pine Knot, KY
Occupation: Farmer
Miscellaneous: Resided Monticello, Wayne Co., KY; and Pine Knot, McCreary Co., KY
Buried: Alexander Family Cemetery, near Pine Knot, KY
References: Pension File and Military Service File, National Archives. Letters Received, Volunteer Service Branch, Adjutant General's Office, File R684(VS)1864, National Archives. Eastham Tarrant. *The Wild Riders of the First Kentucky Cavalry, A History of the Regiment in the Great War of the Rebellion, 1861–1865*. Louisville, KY, 1894.

Gustavus Artsman

Captain, Artsman's Company, KY Police Guard Infantry, Sept. 19, 1861. Honorably mustered out, Oct. 4, 1861. Colonel, 42 KY Enrolled Militia, Sept. 2, 1862. Honorably mustered out, Oct. 2, 1862. Captain, AQM, USV, Sept. 13, 1864. Honorably mustered out, Aug. 4, 1866.
Born: Oct. 6, 1829 Gera, Germany
Died: Jan. 26, 1902 Newport, KY
Occupation: Lawyer
Offices/Honors: Clerk of Circuit Court, Campbell Co., KY, 1856–62. Master Commissioner, Campbell Co., KY, 1872–92.
Miscellaneous: Resided Alexandria, Campbell Co., KY; and Newport, Campbell Co., KY
Buried: Evergreen Cemetery, Southgate, KY (Section 16, Lot 5)
References: Obituary, *Cincinnati Enquirer*, Jan. 27, 1902. Thomas Speed, Robert M. Kelly, and Alfred Pirtle. *The Union Regiments of Kentucky*. Louisville, KY, 1897. Letters Received, Commission Branch, Adjutant General's Office, File A239(CB) 1866, National Archives. Mary K. Jones. *History of Campbell County, As Read at the Centennial Celebration of 4th of July, 1876*. Newport, KY, 1876.

Oliver Leonard Baldwin

Captain, Co. B, 2 KY Infantry, Feb. 13, 1862. Acting AIG, Staff of Major Gen. William Nelson, 4 Division, Army of the Ohio, July–Sept. 1862. Acting AIG, Staff of Major Gen. Charles C. Gilbert, 3 Corps, Army of the Ohio, Oct.–Nov. 1862. Major, 2 KY Infantry, Jan. 14, 1863. GSW lower jaw, Chickamauga, GA, Sept. 20, 1863. For "gallant services in the field," he was promoted Colonel, 5 KY Cavalry, Jan. 2, 1864. Arrested and anticipating charges for being "disgracefully drunk ... and behaving himself in a boisterous manner" in the City of Savannah, Jan. 9, 1865, he submitted his resignation, Jan. 21, 1865, "deeply humiliated that this thing should have occurred." Later, when no charges were preferred, he attempted, without success, to withdraw his resignation and took a leave of absence, with the explanation, "My health for the past year has been most miserable, and while I am willing to make any necessary sacrifice for the good of the service, yet I deem it just that I should make some effort to preserve the shattered remains of a life which from my earliest manhood has been spent in the service of my country." His resignation

was finally accepted to date, March 25, 1865. Battle honors: Shiloh, Corinth, Richmond, Perryville, Chickamauga, Atlanta Campaign (Jonesborough), Savannah Campaign.
Born: Aug. 5, 1835 Woodford Co., KY
Died: Sept. 30, 1865 Louisville, KY
Occupation: School teacher and Regular Army enlisted man (1 Sergeant, Co. I, 7 U.S. Infantry, 1857–62)
Miscellaneous: Resided New Albany, Floyd Co., IN; and Louisville, KY
Buried: Cave Hill Cemetery, Louisville, KY (Section P, Lot 78)
References: Pension File and Military Service File, National Archives. Letters Received, Volunteer Service Branch, Adjutant General's Office, Files F561(VS)1862 and B2822(VS)1864, National Archives. Obituary, *Louisville Daily Journal*, Oct. 1, 1865. John Wesley and John Calhoun Garr. *Genealogy of the Descendants of John Gar, or More Particularly of His Son, Andreas Gaar*. Cincinnati, OH, 1894.

Sidney Madison Barnes

Colonel, 8 KY Infantry, Nov. 25, 1861. Commanded 3 Brigade, 3 Division, 21 Army Corps, Army of the Cumberland, April 14, 1863–Oct. 9, 1863. Commanded 2 Brigade, 1 Division, 4 Army Corps, Army of the Cumberland, Dec. 8, 1863–Jan. 11, 1864. Resigned Jan. 11, 1864, upon the consolidation of the regiment into a battalion of five companies. Battle honors: Tullahoma Campaign, Chickamauga, Lookout Mountain.
Born: May 10, 1821 Irvine, KY
Died: May 19, 1890 Carthage, MO
Occupation: Lawyer
Offices/Honors: Kentucky House of Representatives, 1848. Kentucky Senate, 1851–53. U.S. District Attorney for New Mexico, 1879–83.
Miscellaneous: Resided Irvine, Estill Co., KY, to 1865; Somerset, Pulaski Co., KY, 1865–71; Little Rock, AR, 1871–79; Santa Fe, NM, 1879–83; and Carthage, Jasper Co., MO, 1883–90
Buried: Fort Smith National Cemetery, Fort Smith, AR (Section 3, Row 1, Grave 1183)
References: Maude Barnes Miller. *Dear Wife: Letters from a Union Colonel*. Ravenna, KY, 2001. Pension File and Military Service File, National Archives. Obituary, *Santa Fe Daily New Mexican*, May 26, 1890. Ralph Barnes, "Col. Sidney Barnes," *Citizen Voice & Times (Irvine, KY)*, July 18, 1996. Elbridge C. Park. *History of Irvine and Estill County, Kentucky*. Lexington, KY, 1906. Thomas J. Wright. *History of the Eighth Regiment Kentucky Vol. Inf., During Its Three Years Campaigns*. St. Joseph, MO, 1880.

Sidney Madison Barnes (post-war) (Maude Barnes Miller. *Dear Wife: Letters from a Union Colonel*. Ravenna, Kentucky, 2001).

Jesse Bayles

Colonel, 4 KY Cavalry, Dec. 13, 1861. Discharged March 15, 1862, upon adverse report of a Board of Examination, which found him "entirely deficient in regard to his duties as commanding officer of a regiment." He was reinstated, May 13, 1862, when the proceedings of the Board were declared void, the Board failing to have the required minimum number of members. Resigned April 4, 1863, "suffering from diabetes of long standing, which has been so much aggravated of late as to render him unfit for the service." In forwarding his resignation, Major Gen. Gordon Granger stated emphatically, "Col. Bayles is in no way fitted for Colonel of a regiment."
Born: Nov. 16, 1801 Monongalia Co., WV
Died: July 17, 1887 Shelbyville, KY
Occupation: Brick maker, contractor, and builder
Offices/Honors: Postmaster, Louisville, KY, 1869
Miscellaneous: Resided Lexington, Fayette Co., KY, to 1852; Louisville, Jefferson Co., KY, 1852–77; and Shelbyville, Shelby Co., KY, after 1877. Uncle of Colonel David Bayles (11 MO Infantry).
Buried: Cave Hill Cemetery, Louisville, KY (Section A, Lot 464)

References: William H. Perrin, J. H. Battle and Gilbert C. Kniffin. *Kentucky: A History of the State.* Louisville and Chicago, 1887. John C. Bayles and G. H. Bayles. *Jesse Bayles: A Partial List of his Descendants.* Morgantown, WV, 1944. Pension File and Military Service File, National Archives. Letters Received, Volunteer Service Branch, Adjutant General's Office, Files C491(VS)1862 and M309(VS)1862, National Archives. Obituary, *Louisville Courier-Journal,* July 19, 1887. William H. Townsend. *Lincoln and His Wife's Home Town.* Indianapolis, IN, 1929.

William Washington Berry

Major, 5 KY Infantry, Sept. 9, 1861. Lieutenant Colonel, 5 KY Infantry, Oct. 5, 1861. GSW left forearm, Stone's River, TN, Dec. 31, 1862. Colonel, 5 KY Infantry, Jan. 27, 1863. Commanded 3 Brigade, 2 Division, 20 Army Corps, Army of the Cumberland, Sept. 20–Oct. 9, 1863. GSW left leg, Orchard Knob, TN, Nov. 23, 1863. GSW right thigh, Missionary Ridge, TN, Nov. 25, 1863. Honorably mustered out, Sept. 14, 1864. Battle honors: Shiloh, Stone's River, Tullahoma Campaign (Liberty Gap), Chickamauga, Missionary Ridge, Atlanta Campaign (Resaca, Pickett's Mills).

Born: Feb. 22, 1836 Harford Co., MD
Died: May 6, 1895 Quincy, IL
Education: Attended Miami University, Oxford, OH
Occupation: Lawyer
Miscellaneous: Resided Louisville, Jefferson Co., KY; Winchester, Scott Co., IL; and Quincy, Adams Co., IL, after 1874

William Washington Berry (post-war) (William B. Hazen. *A Narrative of Military Service.* Boston, Massachusetts, 1885).

Buried: Woodland Cemetery, Quincy, IL (Block 11, Lot 184)
References: Newton Bateman and Paul Selby, editors. *Historical Encyclopedia of Illinois and History of Sangamon County.* Chicago, IL, 1912. William H. Collins and Cicero F. Perry. *Past and Present of the City of Quincy and Adams County, Illinois.* Chicago, IL, 1905. Obituary, *Quincy Daily Journal,* May 6, 1895. "A Soldier and a Man," *Louisville Commercial,* Sept. 10, 1895. Pension File and Military Service File, National Archives. William B. Hazen. *A Narrative of Military Service.* Boston, MA, 1885. Obituary, *Louisville Courier-Journal,* May 7, 1895.

Buckner Board

Colonel, 2 KY Cavalry, Sept. 9, 1861. Resigned Dec. 25, 1862, since "my health and constitution are not good, insufficient ... to stand the exposure of a winter campaign and render efficient service. My business affairs have suffered almost a total annihilation by this war, ... and I am now offered an opportunity for business which will enable me ... to re-establish my business affairs satisfactorily." Battle honors: Perryville.

Born: July 26, 1816 Breckinridge Co., KY
Died: Aug. 16 (or 13), 1866 near Yazoo City, MS
Education: Graduated U.S. Military Academy, West Point, NY, 1838
Occupation: Regular Army (1 Lieutenant, 3 U.S. Artillery, resigned March 31, 1840). Lawyer before war. Merchant and cotton planter after war.
Miscellaneous: Resided Louisville, Jefferson Co., KY, 1842–63; Nashville, TN, 1863–65; and St. Louis, MO, 1865–66
Buried: Place of burial unknown
References: George W. Cullum. *Biographical Register of the Officers and Graduates of the United States Military Academy.* Third Edition. Boston and New York, 1891. Pension File and Military Service File, National Archives. U.S. Military Academy Cadet Application Papers, 1805–1866, National Archives. Ebenezer M. Treman and Murray E. Poole. *History of the Treman, Tremaine, Truman Family in America.* Ithaca, NY, 1901.

John Rowan Boone

1 Lieutenant, Adjutant, 28 KY Infantry, Jan. 3, 1862. Taken prisoner and paroled, Gallatin, TN, Aug. 12, 1862. Acting AAG, Staff of Colonel Sanders D. Bruce, 1 Brigade, 3 Division, Reserve Corps, Army of the Cumberland, March 18–Aug. 27, 1863. Acting AAG, Staff of Brig. Gen. Walter C. Whitaker, 2 Brigade, 1 Division, 4 Army Corps, Army of the Cumberland, Sept.–Dec. 1863. Lieutenant Colonel, 28 KY Infantry, Dec. 18, 1863. GSW right thigh, Kenesaw Mountain, GA, June 27,

William Pennebaker Boone

Colonel, 28 KY Infantry, Nov. 6, 1861. Taken prisoner and paroled, Gallatin, TN, Aug. 12, 1862. Commanded Post of Clarksville, TN, March–April 1863. Commanded Post of Rossville, GA, Jan.–Feb. 1864. Suffering from "fistula in ano," he resigned June 28, 1864, citing "my continued ill health and the probability that, for an indefinite period, I may remain unfit for the service." Battle honors: Dalton.

Born: Oct. 12, 1813 Boone Twp., Harrison Co., IN
Died: Jan. 24, 1875 Louisville, KY
Occupation: Lawyer
Offices/Honors: Kentucky House of Representatives, 1861
Miscellaneous: Resided Louisville, Jefferson Co., KY. Father of Colonel John R. Boone (28 KY Infantry).
Buried: Cave Hill Cemetery, Louisville, KY (Section O, Lot 269)
References: *History of the Ohio Falls Cities and Their Counties.* Cleveland, OH, 1882. Obituary,

John Rowan Boone (post-war) (*History of the Ohio Falls Cities and Their Counties.* Cleveland, Ohio, 1882).

1864. *Colonel,* 28 KY Infantry, July 5, 1864. Commanded 2 Brigade, 2 Division, Central District of Texas, July–Sept. 1865. Commanded Post of Lavaca, TX, Oct.–Dec. 1865. Honorably mustered out, Dec. 14, 1865. Bvt. Colonel, USV, March 13, 1865, for gallant and meritorious services. Battle honors: Lookout Mountain, Atlanta Campaign (Kenesaw Mountain), Franklin, Nashville.

Born: Jan. 27, 1843 Louisville, KY
Died: Nov. 26, 1883 Louisville, KY
Education: Attended Indiana University, Bloomington, IN
Occupation: Lawyer
Miscellaneous: Resided Louisville, Jefferson Co., KY. Son of Colonel William P. Boone (28 KY Infantry).
Buried: Cave Hill Cemetery, Louisville, KY (Section O, Lot 269)
References: *History of the Ohio Falls Cities and Their Counties.* Cleveland, OH, 1882. Obituary, *Louisville Courier-Journal,* Nov. 28, 1883. Hazel A. Spraker, compiler. *The Boone Family: Genealogy and History of the Descendants of George and Mary Boone Who Came to America in 1717.* Rutland, VT, 1922. Military Service File, National Archives. Letters Received, Volunteer Service Branch, Adjutant General's Office, File K917(VS)1865, National Archives.

William Pennebaker Boone (Webster's Photographic Gallery, Louisville, Kentucky; courtesy Henry Deeks).

William Pennebaker Boone (post-war) (*History of the Ohio Falls Cities and Their Counties.* Cleveland, Ohio, 1882).

Louisville Courier-Journal, Jan. 25, 1875. Military Service File, National Archives. Letters Received, Volunteer Service Branch, Adjutant General's Office, File B239(VS)1862, National Archives. Hazel A. Spraker, compiler. *The Boone Family: Genealogy and History of the Descendants of George and Mary Boone Who Came to America in 1717.* Rutland, VT, 1922.

Thomas Elliott Bramlette

Colonel, 3 KY Infantry, Oct. 8, 1861. Commanded Post of Columbia, KY, Dec. 1861. Objecting to the extended detail of a portion of his regiment to serve with an artillery battery from another state, he resigned July 13, 1862, with the declaration, "As a part of my command has been taken from me by detail and transferred to the volunteer service of a different state and in a different arm of the service for an indefinite period, and the right to do so has been affirmed, I cannot with my views of the right conscientiously retain the remnant of command subject to the principle so asserted, exercised, and affirmed."

Born: Jan. 3, 1817 Cumberland Co., KY
Died: Jan. 12, 1875 Louisville, KY
Occupation: Lawyer and judge
Offices/Honors: Kentucky House of Representatives, 1841. Circuit Court Judge, 1856–61. U.S. District Attorney, 1862–63. Declined appointment as Brig. Gen., USV, April 24, 1863. Governor of Kentucky, 1863–67.
Miscellaneous: Resided Columbia, Adair Co., KY; and Louisville, Jefferson Co., KY

Thomas Elliott Bramlette (courtesy Everitt Bowles).

Thomas Elliott Bramlette (as Governor of Kentucky, 1863–67) (The National Archives [B-5907]).

Buried: Cave Hill Cemetery, Louisville, KY (Section P, Lot 244)

References: *Dictionary of American Biography. National Cyclopedia of American Biography. The Biographical Encyclopedia of Kentucky of the Dead and Living Men of the Nineteenth Century.* Cincinnati, OH, 1878. Robert A. Powell. *Kentucky Governors.* Frankfort, KY, 1976. Obituary, *Louisville Courier-Journal,* Jan. 13, 1875. Hambleton Tapp and James C. Klotter, editors. *The Union, the Civil War and John W. Tuttle.* Frankfort, KY, 1980. Military Service File, National Archives. Thomas Speed, Robert M. Kelly, and Alfred Pirtle. *The Union Regiments of Kentucky.* Louisville, KY, 1897. Lewis Collins and Richard H. Collins. *Collins' Historical Sketches of Kentucky. History of Kentucky.* Frankfort, KY, 1966.

Benjamin Helm Bristow

Major, Buckner's Regiment, KY Home Guards, Aug. 28, 1861. Lieutenant Colonel, 25 KY Infantry, Dec. 28, 1861. Injured by bursting of a shell directly over his head, Shiloh, TN, April 6, 1862. Resigned April 15, 1862, upon consolidation of 25 KY with 17 KY Infantry. Lieutenant Colonel, 8 KY Cavalry, Sept. 8, 1862. Colonel, 8 KY Cavalry, April 1, 1863. Commanded Post of Russellville, KY, Aug. 1863. Honorably mustered out, Sept. 23, 1863. Battle honors: Shiloh, Morgan's Ohio Raid.

Benjamin Helm Bristow (Klauber's Photographic Gallery, Louisville, Kentucky; courtesy Special Collections Library, Western Kentucky University [2008.229.73]).

Benjamin Helm Bristow (Klauber's Photographic Gallery, Louisville, Kentucky; courtesy Special Collections Library, Western Kentucky University [2008.229.73]).

Benjamin Helm Bristow (as Secretary of the Treasury, 1874–76) (Brady-Handy Collection, Library of Congress [LC-DIG-cwpbh-03703]).

Born: June 20, 1832 Elkton, KY
Died: June 22, 1896 New York City, NY
Education: Graduated Jefferson College, Canonsburg, PA, 1851
Occupation: Lawyer
Offices/Honors: Kentucky Senate, 1863–65. U.S. District Attorney, 1866–70. U.S. Solicitor-General, 1870–72. U.S. Secretary of the Treasury, 1874–76.
Miscellaneous: Resided Hopkinsville, Christian Co., KY, to 1865; Louisville, Jefferson Co., KY, 1865–78; and New York City, NY, 1878–96
Buried: Woodlawn Cemetery, New York City, NY (Section 98, Oak Hill Plot, Lot 9049)
References: *Memorial of Benjamin Helm Bristow.* Cambridge, MA, 1897. *Dictionary of American Biography.* Ross A. Webb, "Benjamin Helm Bristow, the Man Who Walked in Front of Destiny," *Filson Club History Quarterly*, Vol. 41, No. 2 (April 1967). *National Cyclopedia of American Biography.* Obituary, *New York Times*, June 23, 1896. *Society of the Army of the Cumberland. Twenty-Sixth Reunion, Rockford, IL, 1896.* Cincinnati, OH, 1897. Military Service File, National Archives. Letters Received, Volunteer Service Branch, Adjutant General's Office, File B1996(VS)1864, National Archives. Benjamin Helm Bristow Papers, Manuscript Division, Library of Congress, Washington, DC.

John Mason Brown

Major, 10 KY Cavalry, Oct. 27, 1862. Honorably mustered out, Sept. 17, 1863. Colonel, 45 KY Infantry, Dec. 17, 1863. Commanded 4 Brigade, 1 Division, District of Kentucky, 23 Army Corps, Department of the Ohio, April 26–July 6, 1864. Commanded 2 Brigade, 1 Division, District of Kentucky, 23 Army Corps, Department of the Ohio, July–Nov. 1864. Honorably mustered out, Dec. 24, 1864. Battle honors: Morgan's Raid into Kentucky.
Born: April 26, 1837 Frankfort, KY
Died: Jan. 29, 1890 Louisville, KY
Education: Graduated Yale University, New Haven, CT, 1856
Occupation: Lawyer, historian and man of letters
Miscellaneous: Resided Frankfort, Franklin Co., KY, to 1869; Lexington, Fayette Co., KY, 1869–73; and Louisville, Jefferson Co., KY, 1873–90. Author of several works on the pioneer history of Kentucky. Half-brother of Colonel Benjamin Gratz Brown (4 MO Infantry). Son-in-law of CSA General William Preston. Brother-in-law of Colonel William T. Scott (3 KY Infantry).
Buried: Cave Hill Cemetery, Louisville, KY (Section D, Lot 51)
References: Preston Brown, "John Mason

John Mason Brown (courtesy University of Kentucky Archives [2003AV14-001]).

John Mason Brown (The National Archives [BA-491]).

Brown, 1837–1890, One of the Founders of the Filson Club," *The Filson Club History Quarterly*, Vol. 13, No. 3 (July 1939). J. Stoddard Johnston, editor. *Memorial History of Louisville.* Chicago, IL, 1896. Obituary Circular, Whole No. 171, Ohio MOL-

LUS. Obituary, *Louisville Courier-Journal*, Jan. 30, 1890. *History of the Academic Class of 1856, Yale University, to 1896.* Boston, MA, 1897. Bayless Hardin, "The Brown Family of Liberty Hall," *The Filson Club History Quarterly*, Vol. 16, No. 2 (April 1942). Military Service File, National Archives. Letters Received, Volunteer Service Branch, Adjutant General's Office, File B2488(VS)1864, National Archives.

Sanders Dewees Bruce

Colonel, 20 KY Infantry, Oct. 1, 1861. Commanded 22 Brigade, Army of the Ohio, Jan. 18–Feb. 11, 1862. Commanded 22 Brigade, 4 Division, Army of the Ohio, Feb. 11–April 13, 1862 and Aug. 16–Sept. 29, 1862. Commanded Post of Bowling Green, KY, District of Louisville, Department of the Ohio, May–Nov. 1862. Commanded Post of Russellville, KY, Department of the Ohio, Nov.–Dec. 1862. Commanded Post of Clarksville, TN, Department of the Cumberland, Jan.–June 1863. Commanded 1 Brigade, 3 Division, Reserve Corps, Army of the Cumberland, July 10–Oct. 9, 1863. Commanded Post of Louisville, KY, Jan.–May

Sanders Dewees Bruce (photograph by Webster & Bro., Louisville, Kentucky).

1864. Commanded 1 Brigade, 2 Division, District of Kentucky, 23 Army Corps, Army of the Ohio, April 10–May 1, 1864. Suffering from "functional disease of the heart," he resigned June 30, 1864, citing also the recent loss of his wife, "leaving four small and helpless children with no one to look after or care for them," and his private affairs, which have become "much deranged after three years' neglect." Battle honors: Shiloh.

Born: Aug. 16, 1825 Lexington, KY
Died: Jan. 31, 1902 New York City, NY
Education: Graduated Transylvania University, Lexington, KY, 1846
Occupation: Merchant and horse breeder before war. Author and Editor of the sporting journal, "Turf, Field and Farm," after war.
Miscellaneous: Resided Lexington, Fayette Co., KY; and New York City, NY. A leading authority on the pedigree of thoroughbred horses, he established the well-known "American Stud Book." Brother-in-law of Brig. Gen. John Hunt Morgan, CSA. Brother-in-law of Colonel William A. Warner (18 KY Infantry).

Sanders Dewees Bruce (photograph by Webster & Bro., Louisville, Kentucky; Roger D. Hunt Collection, USAMHI [RG98S-CWP58.48]).

Sanders Dewees Bruce (photograph by Webster & Bro., Louisville, Kentucky; Craig Dunn Collection).

Buried: Lexington Cemetery, Lexington, KY (Section D, Lot 98)
References: Obituary Circular, Whole No. 714, New York MOLLUS. *National Cyclopedia of American Biography.* Charles Morris, editor. *Makers of New York.* Philadelphia, PA, 1895. Obituary, *New York Times,* Feb. 1, 1902. Obituary, *Lexington Morning Herald,* Feb. 1, 1902. Pension File and Military Service File, National Archives. Letters Received, Volunteer Service Branch, Adjutant General's Office, File C1147(VS)1862, National Archives.

Harvey M. Buckley

Lieutenant Colonel, 5 KY Infantry, Aug. 10, 1861. Colonel, 5 KY Infantry, Oct. 5, 1861. Commanded 4 Brigade, 2 Division, Army of the Ohio, July 11–Aug. 10, 1862. Commanded 4 Brigade, 2 Division, 1 Army Corps, Army of the Ohio, Sept.–Nov. 1862. Commanded 3 Brigade, 2 Division, Right Wing, 14 Army Corps, Army of the Cumberland, Nov. 5–Dec. 24, 1862. Anticipating "promotion in the force recently authorized for defense of Kentucky," he resigned Jan. 26, 1863, "for the good of the service, in gaining my assistance in enlisting troops in Kentucky." Colonel, 54 KY Infantry, Sept. 30, 1864. Commanded Provisional Brigade, Military District of Kentucky, Department

Harvey M. Buckley (photograph by Webster & Bro., Louisville, Kentucky).

of the Ohio, Dec. 1864. Honorably mustered out, Sept. 1, 1865. Battle honors: Shiloh, Stoneman's Raid into Southwestern Virginia (Wytheville, Saltville).
Born: 1824? Nicholasville, KY
Died: March 16, 1898 Louisville, KY
Occupation: Lawyer, and in later years Deputy U.S. Marshal, U.S. Customs Storekeeper, and police station keeper
Miscellaneous: Resided New Castle, Henry Co., KY; and Louisville, Jefferson Co., KY, after 1873
Buried: Cave Hill National Cemetery, Louisville, KY (Section B, Grave 4074)
References: Pension File and Military Service File, National Archives. Obituary, *Louisville Courier-Journal,* March 17, 1898.

James Francis Buckner

Colonel, Buckner's Regiment, KY Home Guards, Aug. 28, 1861. Taken prisoner, near Madisonville, KY, Sept. 1861. Confined Columbus, KY. Paroled Nov. 8, 1861.
Born: Sept. 1, 1813 Caroline Co., VA
Died: Aug. 4, 1889 Louisville, KY
Education: Graduated Transylvania University Law School, Lexington, KY, 1836
Occupation: Lawyer
Offices/Honors: Kentucky House of Represen-

tatives, 1839–40, 1842, and 1847. Kentucky Senate, 1855–59. Collector of Internal Revenue, Louisville, KY, 1869–81.

Miscellaneous: Resided Hopkinsville, Christian Co., KY, before war; and Louisville, Jefferson Co., KY, after war

Buried: Cave Hill Cemetery, Louisville, KY (Section P, Lot 897)

References: J. Stoddard Johnston, editor. *Memorial History of Louisville.* Chicago, IL, 1896. Obituary, *Louisville Courier-Journal,* Aug. 5, 1889. Thomas Speed, Robert M. Kelly, and Alfred Pirtle. *The Union Regiments of Kentucky.* Louisville, KY, 1897. William A. Crozier, editor. *The Buckners of Virginia and the Allied Families of Strother and Ashby.* New York City, NY, 1907. Robert M. Kelly, "Holding Kentucky for the Union," *Battles and Leaders of the Civil War,* edited by Robert U. Johnson and Clarence C. Buel. New York City, NY, 1887–88.

Hartwell T. Burge

Chaplain, 3 KY Cavalry, Dec. 13, 1861. Resigned June 23, 1863, to accept promotion. Colonel, 48 KY Infantry, Oct. 15, 1863. Commanded Post of Bowling Green, KY, District of Kentucky, Department of the Ohio, Jan.–March 1864. Commanded Post of Munfordville, KY, District of Kentucky, Department of the Ohio, April–Aug. 1864. Honorably mustered out, Dec. 19, 1864.

Hartwell T. Burge (The Texas Collection, Baylor University, Waco, Texas).

Born: Dec. 23, 1805 Brunswick Co., VA
Died: Aug. 20, 1877 (or 1876) Patoka, IN
Occupation: Methodist clergyman
Miscellaneous: Resided Greenville, Muhlenberg Co., KY, before war; and Louisville, Jefferson Co., KY; Clarksburg (now Odon) Daviess Co., IN; and Patoka, Gibson Co., IN, after war
Buried: Presbyterian Church Cemetery, Patoka, IN
References: Pension File and Military Service File, National Archives. Letters Received, Volunteer Service Branch, Adjutant General's Office, Files S721(VS)1864, B898(VS)1865, and K158(VS)1865, National Archives.

Andrew Hamilton Clark

Captain, Co. D, 7 KY Infantry, Sept. 16, 1861. Taken prisoner and paroled, Richmond, KY, Aug. 30, 1862. Disappointed in not securing a recommendation from Col. Theophilus T. Garrard for promotion within the regiment upon Garrard's promotion to Brig. Gen., he resigned Feb. 22, 1863. In accepting his resignation, brigade commander Brig. Gen. Peter J. Osterhaus commented, "Besides being deficient in military knowledge and spirit, it would appear from the style of his resignation that he is utterly illiterate." Lieutenant Colonel, 47 KY Infantry, Oct. 20, 1863. Colonel, 47 KY Infantry, Dec. 21, 1863. Commanded Post of Camp Nelson (KY), District of Kentucky, 23 Army Corps, Department of the Ohio, April–July 1864. Honorably mustered out, Dec. 26, 1864. Battle honors: Wild Cat Mountain, Richmond.

Born: March 29, 1835 Clay Co., KY
Died: April 12, 1898 Barbourville, KY
Occupation: Farmer before war. Lawyer and judge after war.
Offices/Honors: Kentucky House of Representatives, 1881–82. Serving second term as Circuit Court judge when he died.
Miscellaneous: Resided Booneville, Owsley Co., KY; and Barbourville, Knox Co., KY
Buried: Barbourville Cemetery, Barbourville, KY
References: Charles R. Mitchell, editor. *History and Families, Knox County, Kentucky, 1799–1994.* Paducah, KY, 1994. James L. Clark, "Andrew H. Clark and the Civil War in Kentucky," http://freepages.family.rootsweb.ancestry.com/~kyborn/article42.htm. Pension File and Military Service File, National Archives. Letters Received, Volunteer Service Branch, Adjutant General's Office, File K705(VS)1863, National Archives. Richard D. Sears. *Camp Nelson, Kentucky: A Civil War History.* Lexington, KY, 2002. Obituary, *Stanford Semi-Weekly Interior Journal,* April 15, 1898.

John Carr Cochran

Colonel, 14 KY Infantry, Jan. 16, 1862. Commanded 2 Brigade, 3 Division, Army of Kentucky, Department of the Ohio, Nov. 1862–Jan. 1863. Having "undergone a great deal of fatigue and exposure ... and apprehensive that ... my health might become impaired," he resigned Jan. 12, 1863, "perfectly satisfied that my place can be filled by someone more competent than myself." Battle honors: Cumberland Gap.

Born: May 11, 1824 Flemingsburg, KY
Died: June 18, 1887 Covington, KY
Occupation: Dry goods merchant and fire insurance agent
Miscellaneous: Resided Lexington, Fayette Co., KY; Cincinnati, OH; and Covington, Kenton Co., KY, after 1869
Buried: Lexington Cemetery, Lexington, KY (Section I, Lot 67)
References: Pension File and Military Service File, National Archives. Obituary, *Cincinnati Enquirer,* June 19, 1887. Obituary, *Lexington Daily Press,* June 19, 1887. Letters Received, Volunteer Service Branch, Adjutant General's Office, File K537(VS)1862, National Archives. Ellwood Roberts, editor. *The Dewees Family: Genealogical Data, Biographical Facts and Historical Information.* Norristown, PA, 1905. Death Certificate, City of Covington, KY.

Robert Wickliffe Cooper

Sergeant, Co. K, 20 KY Infantry, Nov. 15, 1861. 2 Lieutenant, Co. H, 20 KY Infantry, Jan. 24, 1862. Acting ADC and Acting AAG, 22 Brigade, 4 Division, Army of the Ohio, Feb.–July 1862. Acting ADC, Staff of Major Gen. William Nelson, 4 Division, Army of the Ohio, July–Sept. 1862. Taken prisoner and paroled, Richmond, KY, Aug. 30, 1862. Lieutenant Colonel, 4 KY Cavalry, April 13, 1863. Colonel, 4 KY Cavalry, May 29, 1863. Badly bruised by horse falling on him, Franklin, TN, June 4, 1863. Commanded 3 Brigade, 1 Division, Cavalry Corps, Army of the Cumberland, Sept.–Oct. 1863. Commanded Union forces, Lexington, KY, June 1864. Commanded Post of Montgomery, AL, April 1865. Commanded Post of Albany, GA, May and July 1865. Honorably mustered out, Aug. 21, 1865. Bvt. Lieutenant Colonel, USA, March 2, 1867, for gallant and meritorious services at the battle of Resaca, GA. Bvt. Colonel, USA, March 2, 1867, for gallant and meritorious services in the capture of Montgomery, AL. Battle honors: Shiloh, Corinth, Richmond, Chickamauga, Morgan's Raid into Kentucky (Cynthiana), Resaca (Oct. 1864), Wilson's Raid (Montgomery).

Born: Oct. 19, 1831 Lexington, KY

Robert Wickliffe Cooper (Roger D. Hunt Collection, USAMHI [RG98S-CWP80.66]).

Died: June 8, 1867 near Fort McPherson, NE (committed suicide by gun shot)
Education: Attended Dickinson College, Carlisle, PA (Class of 1851)
Occupation: Regular Army (Major, 7 U.S. Cavalry, July 28, 1866)
Miscellaneous: Resided Lexington, Fayette Co., KY. Afflicted by alcoholism, he undoubtedly died at his own hand "while in a fit of delirium tremens," but in order to secure a pension for his widow, his record was amended in 1885 to read "died by the hand of person or persons unknown, while in the line of his duty as an officer of the army."
Buried: Lexington Cemetery, Lexington, KY (Section O, Lot 114)
References: Pension File and Military Service File, National Archives. Robert M. Utley, editor. *Life in Custer's Cavalry: Diaries and Letters of Albert and Jennie Barnitz, 1867–1868.* New Haven, CT, 1977. Letters Received, Appointment, Commission and Personal Branch, Adjutant General's Office, File 1990(ACP)1875, National Archives. Letters Received, Volunteer Service Branch, Adjutant General's Office, File P866(VS)1862, National Archives.

James Wesley Craddock

Captain, Co. A, 20 KY Infantry, Nov. 12, 1861. Colonel, 16 KY Infantry, May 5, 1862. Battle honors: Shiloh, Morgan's Second Kentucky Raid.

James Wesley Craddock.

Born: March 7, 1830 Hart Co., KY
Died: June 2, 1863 Louisville, KY (erysipelas)
Other Wars: Mexican War (Corporal, Co. D, 8 U.S. Infantry)
Occupation: Clerk
Miscellaneous: Resided Frankfort, Franklin Co., KY
Buried: Frankfort Cemetery, Frankfort, KY (Section H)
References: Military Service File, National Archives. Obituary, *Frankfort Tri-Weekly Commonwealth,* June 5, 1863. Obituary, *Louisville Daily Democrat,* June 4, 1863. Regular Army Enlistment Papers, 1798–1912, National Archives.

Eugene Wilkinson Crittenden

Captain, 1 U.S. Cavalry, May 7, 1861. Captain, 4 U.S. Cavalry, Aug. 3, 1861. Colonel, 12 KY Cavalry, March 20, 1863. Commanded 4 Brigade, 1 Division, Cavalry Corps, Army of the Ohio, March 1864. Commanded 1 Brigade, 2 Division, Cavalry Corps, Army of the Ohio, April 1864. Commanded Dismounted Cavalry Brigade, 3 Division, 23 Army Corps, Army of the Ohio, June–Aug. 1864. Honorably mustered out of volunteer service, Aug. 23, 1865. Battle honors: Morgan's Ohio Raid, East Tennessee Campaign, Atlanta Campaign.
Born: July 3, 1832 Frankfort, KY
Died: Aug. 1, 1874 Camp Bowie, AZ

Eugene Wilkinson Crittenden (D. H. Anderson, Photographer, Opposite Capitol Hotel, Main Street, Frankfort, Kentucky; Kentucky Historical Society [Crittenden and Starling Album, 2000 PH04]).

Occupation: Regular Army (Major, 5 U.S. Cavalry, July 28, 1866)
Miscellaneous: Resided Frankfort, Franklin Co., KY. Son of Governor and U.S. Senator John J. Crittenden. Step-brother of Major Gen. Thomas L. Crittenden, USA. Step-brother of Major Gen. George B. Crittenden, CSA.
Buried: San Francisco National Cemetery, San Francisco, CA (Section OS, Plot 62, Grave 7). Cenotaph Frankfort Cemetery, Frankfort, KY (Section N, Lot 198).
References: George F. Price. *Across the Continent with the Fifth Cavalry.* New York City, NY, 1883. Dan L. Thrapp. *Encyclopedia of Frontier Biography.* Lincoln, NE, 1991. Obituary, *Weekly Kentucky Yeoman,* Aug. 12, 1874. Pension File and Military Service File, National Archives. Letters Received, Appointment, Commission and Personal Branch, Adjutant General's Office, File 2979(ACP)1874, National Archives. Obituary, *New York Times,* Aug. 6, 1874. Constance Wynn Altshuler. *Cavalry Yellow & Infantry Blue.* Tucson, AZ, 1991. *Record of the Harris Family Descended from John Harris Born 1680 in Wiltshire, England.* Philadelphia, PA, 1903.

Richard C. Dawkins

2 Lieutenant, Co. B, 6 KY Infantry, Sept. 23, 1861. 1 Lieutenant, Co. B, 6 KY Infantry, Jan. 5,

1862. Captain, Co. B, 6 KY Infantry, June 20, 1862. Commanded Provost Guard. 3 Division, 4 Army Corps, Army of the Cumberland, Nov. 1863–Jan. 1864. *Major*, 6 KY Infantry, Jan. 1, 1864. Lieutenant Colonel, 6 KY Infantry, May 11, 1864. *Colonel*, 6 KY Infantry, Sept. 16, 1864. Honorably mustered out, Jan. 2, 1865. Battle honors: Stone's River, Chickamauga.
Born: 1832? KY
Died: April 9, 1881 Decatur, IL
Occupation: Farmer before war. Dentist after war.
Miscellaneous: Resided La Grange, Oldham Co., KY; Chester, Delaware Co., PA; and Decatur, Macon Co., IL
Buried: Rural Cemetery, Chester, PA (Section K, Lots 192–204)
References: Pension File and Military Service File, National Archives. Joseph R. Reinhart. *A History of the 6th Kentucky Volunteer Infantry U.S.: The Boys Who Feared No Noise.* Louisville, KY, 2000. Obituary, *Decatur Daily Republican,* April 9, 1881. Lela W. Prewitt. *The Dawkins and Stewart Families of Virginia and Kentucky.* Fairfield, IA, 1968.

Henry Dent

Lieutenant Colonel, 1 Battalion, Louisville Provost Guard, Sept. 23, 1861. Provost Marshal, Louisville, KY, Sept. 23, 1861. Provost Marshal General of Kentucky, Aug. 9, 1862. Colonel, 34 KY Infantry, Oct. 2, 1862. Possessing a "tubercular disposition," upon his regiment being relieved from provost duty, he resigned May 31, 1863, since "my constitution will not permit me to undergo the fatigues of field and camp duty."
Born: Dec. 25, 1819 Charles Co., MD
Died: May 11, 1877 Rodney, MS
Occupation: Tailor, grocer, and municipal official before war. Salt manufacturer, bank cashier, and city magistrate after war.
Miscellaneous: Resided Louisville, Jefferson Co., KY
Buried: St. Louis Cemetery, Louisville, KY (Section I, Lot 1)
References: *The Biographical Encyclopedia of Kentucky of the Dead and Living Men of the Nineteenth Century.* Cincinnati, OH, 1878. Military Service File, National Archives. Obituary, *Louisville Courier-Journal,* May 13, 1877.

William York Dillard

Captain, Co. A, 1 Battalion, Louisville Provost Guard, Oct. 3, 1861. This organization became Co. A, 34 KY Infantry in Oct. 1862. Major, 34 KY Infantry, Feb. 6, 1863. Lieutenant Colonel, 34 KY Infantry, June 2, 1863. Commanded Post of Glasgow, KY, 1 Division, 23 Army Corps, Department of the Ohio, Aug. 1863. Colonel, 34 KY Infantry, Dec. 26, 1863. Muster as colonel suspended, April 3, 1864, since regiment lacked minimum strength to permit muster of a colonel. The suspension of his muster was, however, cancelled by the Record and Pension Office, Jan. 5, 1903, and his muster as Colonel, 34 KY Infantry, changed to date Feb. 26, 1864. Commanded Post of Cumberland Gap, TN, and also 1 Brigade, 4 Division, 23 Army Corps, Department of the Ohio, May 17–Nov. 29, 1864. Commanded Post of Cumberland Gap, TN, March-May 1865. Honorably mustered out, June 24, 1865. Battle honors: Knoxville Campaign (Rogersville).
Born: 1826? Smith Co., TN
Died: Nov. 18, 1870 Louisville, KY
Other Wars: Mexican War (1 Sergeant, Co. E, 14 U.S. Infantry)
Occupation: Bricklayer
Miscellaneous: Resided Louisville, Jefferson Co., KY
Buried: Cave Hill Cemetery, Louisville, KY (Section M, Range 21, Grave 7, unmarked)
References: Obituary, *Louisville Courier-Journal,* Nov. 19, 1870. Military Service File, National Archives. Letters Received, Volunteer Service Branch, Adjutant General's Office, File K333(VS) 1864, National Archives. Leroy P. Graf, editor. *The Papers of Andrew Johnson.* Vol. 7, 1864–1865. Knoxville, TN, 1986. Register of Enlistments in the United States Army, 1798–1914, National Archives.

John Dils, Jr.

Commissioned as Colonel, 39 KY Infantry, Sept. 1, 1862. Badly injured in fall from his horse, Bull Gap, near Prestonsburg, KY, Dec. 4, 1862. Mustered as Colonel, 39 KY Infantry, Jan. 21, 1863. Dismissed Dec. 10, 1863, for "selling captured property and appropriating proceeds to his own use, using Government transportation for private purposes, improper treatment of a non-commissioned officer whilst the said non-commissioned officer was in the discharge of his duty, and incompetency." In reviewing the case, Judge Advocate General Joseph Holt concluded that "he stands convicted upon the evidence presented of Conduct Unbecoming an Officer and a Gentleman," specifically "gross immorality," a charge not mentioned in the order of dismissal but based upon his "habit of keeping in his camp and quarters a woman of low character with whom he cohabited, at one time sleeping with her in the same room with an officer of his command and his wife."
Born: Sept. 15, 1818 Parkersburg, WV
Died: Aug. 11, 1895 Pikeville, KY
Occupation: Merchant and farmer
Miscellaneous: Resided Pikeville, Pike Co., KY.

John Dils, Jr. (William Ely. *The Big Sandy Valley: History of the People and Country from the Earliest Settlement to the Present Time.* Catlettsburg, Kentucky, 1887).

While a noncombatant civilian in Oct. 1861, he was taken to Libby Prison, Richmond, VA, and confined there for three months.
  Buried: Dils Cemetery, Pikeville, KY
  References: William Ely. *The Big Sandy Valley: History of the People and Country from the Earliest Settlement to the Present Time.* Catlettsburg, KY, 1887. William C. Kozee. *Early Families of Eastern and Southeastern Kentucky.* Baltimore, MD, 1979. Pension File and Military Service File, National Archives. Letters Received, Volunteer Service Branch, Adjutant General's Office, File O811(VS)1863, National Archives. John David Preston. *The Civil War in the Big Sandy Valley of Kentucky.* Second Edition. Baltimore, MD, 2008.

Ethelbert Ludlow Dudley

Colonel, 21 KY Infantry, Dec. 12, 1861
  Born: 1818 Fayette Co., KY
  Died: Feb. 20, 1862 Columbia, KY (typhoid fever)
  Education: Graduated Transylvania University Medical School, Lexington, KY, 1842
  Occupation: Physician and medical college professor
  Miscellaneous: Resided Lexington, Fayette Co., KY. Brother-in-law of Colonel William T. Scott (3 KY Infantry).
  Buried: Lexington Cemetery, Lexington, KY (Section O, Lot 147)

Ethelbert Ludlow Dudley (Library of Congress [LC-DIG-cwpb-06904]).

  References: *The Biographical Encyclopedia of Kentucky of the Dead and Living Men of the Nineteenth Century.* Cincinnati, OH, 1878. Robert Peter. *History of the Medical Department of Transylvania University.* Louisville, KY, 1905. Pension File and Military Service File, National Archives. Dean Dudley. *History of the Dudley Family, with Genealogical Tables, Pedigrees, etc.* Wakefield, MA, 1886–94.

John Gill Eve

Lieutenant Colonel, 49 KY Infantry, Oct. 7, 1863. Colonel, 49 KY Infantry, Dec. 14, 1863. Commanded Camp Burnside, KY, District of Kentucky, 23 Army Corps, Department of the Ohio, March–July 1864. Honorably mustered out, Dec. 26, 1864.
  Born: May 31, 1833 Barbourville, KY
  Died: April 19, 1882 Barbourville, KY
  Education: Attended Western Military Institute, Blue Lick Springs, KY
  Occupation: Lawyer
  Miscellaneous: Resided Barbourville, Knox Co., KY
  Buried: Lexington Cemetery, Lexington, KY (Section O, Lot 38)
  References: John Boyle, compiler. *Boyle Genealogy: John Boyle of Virginia and Kentucky.* St. Louis, MO, 1909. Military Service File, National Archives. Obituary, *Louisville Courier-Journal,* April 21, 1882.

John Gill Eve (James Mullen, Photographer, Magnolia Gallery, No. 52 East Main Street, Lexington, Kentucky; courtesy Everitt Bowles).

Thomas Jackson Ewing

Captain, Co. G, 5 WV Infantry, Sept. 2, 1861. Resigned Jan. 3, 1863, "for the purpose of accepting the lieutenant colonelcy of the 39th KY Vols.," a position he failed to secure. Colonel, 22 KY Enrolled Militia, May 26, 1864. Honorably mustered out, June 28, 1864.

Born: March 10, 1842 Catlettsburg, KY
Died: Feb. 27, 1927 Catlettsburg, KY
Education: Attended Marshall College, Huntington, WV
Occupation: Lawyer and merchant
Miscellaneous: Resided Catlettsburg, Boyd Co., KY
Buried: Chadwick/Ewing Cemetery, near Catlettsburg, KY
References: Pension File and Military Service File, National Archives. William H. Perrin, J. H. Battle and Gilbert C. Kniffin. *Kentucky: A History of the State.* 8th Edition. Louisville and Chicago, 1888. Obituary, *Ashland Daily Independent*, Feb. 28, 1927. William H. Ward, editor. *Records of Members of the Grand Army of the Republic.* San Francisco, CA, 1886. Letters Received, Volunteer Service Branch, Adjutant General's Office, File E285(VS)1864, National Archives.

Thomas Brooks Fairleigh

Captain, Co. G, 26 KY Infantry, Feb. 28, 1862. Major, 26 KY Infantry, May 6, 1862. Lieutenant Colonel, 26 KY Infantry, June 20, 1862. Acting AAG, Staff of Brig. Gen. Stephen G. Burbridge, 1 Division, Army of the Ohio, Aug. 1862. Acting AAG, Staff of Brig. Gen. Horatio P. Van Cleve, 5 Division, 2 Army Corps, Army of the Ohio, Oct. 7–Nov. 26, 1862. Commanded Post of Bowling Green, KY, 2 Division, 23 Army Corps, Department of the Ohio, Aug.–Sept. 1863. Commanded Post of Bowling Green, KY, 1 Division, 23 Army Corps, Department of the Ohio, Oct. 1863–Jan. 1864. Acting AAG, Staff of Brig. Gen. Stephen G. Burbridge, District of Kentucky, 23 Army Corps, Department of the Ohio, March–May 1864. Commanded Post of Louisville, KY, and also 1 Brigade, 2 Division, District of Kentucky, 23 Army Corps, Department of the Ohio, May–Sept. 1864 and Oct. 1864–Jan. 1865. Colonel, 26 KY Infantry, Feb. 1, 1865. Honorably mustered out, July 10, 1865. Battle honors: Shiloh, Campaign of the Carolinas.

Born: Jan. 27, 1837 Brandenburg, KY
Died: Nov. 2, 1890 Louisville, KY
Education: Graduated University of Louisville (KY) Law School, 1858
Occupation: Lawyer
Miscellaneous: Resided Brandenburg, Meade Co., KY; and Louisville, Jefferson Co., KY
Buried: Cave Hill Cemetery, Louisville, KY (Section A, Lot 129, unmarked)
References: J. Stoddard Johnston, editor. *Memorial History of Louisville.* Chicago, IL, 1896.

Thomas Jackson Ewing (post-war) (William H. Perrin, J. H. Battle and Gilbert C. Kniffin. *Kentucky: A History of the State.* 8th Edition. Louisville and Chicago, 1888).

Thomas Brooks Fairleigh (Wm. Bryan, Photographer, Russellville, Kentucky).

John Kavanaugh Faulkner (T. M. Schleier, Photographer, Nashville, Tennessee; courtesy Everitt Bowles).

Obituary, *Louisville Courier-Journal,* Nov. 3, 1890. Pension File and Military Service File, National Archives. William H. Perrin, J. H. Battle, and Gilbert C. Kniffin. *Kentucky: A History of the State.* 8th Edition. Louisville and Chicago, 1888. Otis M. Mather. *Six Generations of LaRues and Allied Families.* Hodgenville, KY, 1921. Letters Received, Volunteer Service Branch, Adjutant General's Office, File F62(VS)1864, National Archives.

John Kavanaugh Faulkner

Major, 7 KY Cavalry, Aug. 16, 1862. Lieutenant Colonel, 7 KY Cavalry, Feb. 6, 1863. Colonel, 7 KY Cavalry, April 3, 1863. GSW right hip, Franklin, TN, June 4, 1863. Commanded 3 Brigade, 1 Division, Cavalry Corps, Army of the Cumberland, July 5–Aug. 10, 1864. Honorably mustered out, July 10, 1865. Battle honors: Hartsville, Franklin, Atlanta Campaign, Lyon's Raid from Paris, TN.

Born: Dec. 27, 1838 Garrard Co., KY

Died: Jan. 7, 1895 Richmond, KY (committed suicide by taking poison)

Education: Graduated Centre College, Danville, KY, 1858

Occupation: Farmer, circuit court clerk, and insurance agent

John Kavanaugh Faulkner (courtesy Henry Deeks).

Offices/Honors: Kentucky House of Representatives, 1863–65. Clerk of Garrard County Circuit Court, 1860, 1874, and 1882. Surveyor of Customs, Louisville, KY, 1883–1885.
Miscellaneous: Resided Lancaster, Garrard Co., KY; Louisville, Jefferson Co., KY; and Richmond, Madison Co., KY
Buried: Paint Lick Cemetery, Paint Lick, Garrard Co., KY
References: *The Biographical Encyclopedia of Kentucky of the Dead and Living Men of the Nineteenth Century*. Cincinnati, OH, 1878. Obituary, *Louisville Courier-Journal*, Jan. 8, 1895. Pension File and Military Service File, National Archives. Obituary, *Richmond Climax*, Jan. 9, 1895. Obituary, *Stanford Semi-Weekly Interior Journal*, Jan. 11, 1895. Letters Received, Volunteer Service Branch, Adjutant General's Office, File F674(VS)1863, National Archives. Thomas Speed, Robert M. Kelly, and Alfred Pirtle. *The Union Regiments of Kentucky*. Louisville, KY, 1897. William Harris Miller. *History and Genealogies of the Families of Miller, Woods, Harris, Wallace, Maupin, Oldham, Kavanaugh, and Brown*. Lexington, KY, 1907.

James Shelby Fish

Colonel, Rockcastle and Lincoln County (KY) Home Guards, May 7, 1862. Honorably mustered out, July 7, 1862.
Born: April 17, 1823 Rockcastle Co., KY
Died: Oct. 13, 1896 Crab Orchard, KY
Occupation: Farmer and surveyor
Miscellaneous: Resided Mount Vernon, Rockcastle Co., KY; and Crab Orchard, Lincoln Co., KY
Buried: Crab Orchard Cemetery, Crab Orchard, KY (Section B)
References: Obituary, *Stanford Semi-Weekly Interior Journal*, Oct. 16, 1896. Jennifer Kidwell Fish, "Descendants of Thomas Fish: Third Generation," http://www.rootsweb.ancestry.com/~kymadiso/research/family/fish/fish/pafg04.htm. Lincoln County Historical Society. *Lincoln County, Kentucky*. Paducah, KY, 2002. Letters Received, Volunteer Service Branch, Adjutant General's Office, File A734(VS) 1863, National Archives. Pension File and Military Service File, National Archives. Shirley Dunn, compiler. *Lincoln County, KY, Marriages 1780–1850 & Tombstone Inscriptions*. St. Louis, MO, 1977.

Bushrod Washington Foley

Colonel, Police Guard, Kentucky Central Railroad, Sept. 17, 1861. Honorably mustered out, Dec. 10, 1861.
Born: 1809 VA
Died: March 16, 1867 Covington, KY
Occupation: Lawyer

Offices/Honors: Mayor of Covington, KY, 1845–60
Miscellaneous: Resided Covington, Kenton Co., KY
Buried: Highland Cemetery, Fort Mitchell, Kenton Co., KY (Section 3, Lots 19–20)
References: Obituary, *Cincinnati Commercial*, March 18, 1867. *Sesqui-Centennial Souvenir Program, City of Covington, KY, 1815–1965*. Covington, KY, 1965. Interment Records, Highland Cemetery, Fort Mitchell, KY.

James Brown Forman

1 Lieutenant, Co. C, 15 KY Infantry, Dec. 14, 1861. Captain, Co. C, 15 KY Infantry, July 13, 1862. Colonel, 15 KY Infantry, Nov. 8, 1862. GSW Stone's River, TN, Dec. 31, 1862. Battle honors: Perryville, Stone's River.

James Brown Forman (Webster & Bro., Photographic Gallery, Louisville, Kentucky; Roger D. Hunt Collection, USAMHI [RG98S-CWP82.32]).

Born: Dec. 12, 1842 Louisville, KY
Died: Dec. 31, 1862 KIA Stone's River, TN
Education: Attended Centre College, Danville, KY
Occupation: Clerk
Buried: Cave Hill Cemetery, Louisville, KY (Section C, Lot 28)
References: Anne Spottswood Dandridge, compiler. *The Forman Genealogy.* Cleveland, OH, 1903. Kirk C. Jenkins. *The Battle Rages Higher: The Union's Fifteenth Kentucky Infantry.* Lexington, KY, 2003. Obituary, *Louisville Journal,* Jan. 15, 1863. Alfred Pirtle, "New Year's Eve on Field of Battle," *Louisville Evening Post,* Dec. 31, 1915. Military Service File, National Archives. *General Catalogue of the Centre College of Kentucky.* Danville, KY, 1890.

James Calvert Foy

Captain, Co. A, 23 KY Infantry, Oct. 21, 1861. Major, 23 KY Infantry, Feb. 27, 1863. Lieutenant Colonel, 23 KY Infantry, April 18, 1863. *Colonel,* 23 KY Infantry, March 8, 1864. Shell wound right thigh, near Vining's Station, GA, July 9, 1864. Battle honors: Chickamauga, Brown's Ferry, Missionary Ridge, Atlanta Campaign (Pickett's Mills, Vining's Station).
Born: Feb. 15, 1826 Washington, DC
Died: July 24, 1864 DOW Marietta, GA
Occupation: Livery stable keeper
Miscellaneous: Resided Covington, Kenton Co., KY
Buried: Linden Grove Cemetery, Covington, KY
References: Ella Foy O'Gorman, compiler. *Descendants of Virginia Calverts.* Los Angeles, CA, 1947. William B. Hazen. *A Narrative of Military Service.* Boston, MA, 1885. Pension File and Military Service File, National Archives.

John Thomas Gathright

Private, Co. A, 22 KY Infantry, Nov. 16, 1861. Quartermaster Sergeant, 22 KY Infantry, Dec. 12, 1861. 1 Lieutenant, Co. H, 22 KY Infantry, May 9, 1862. Captain, Co. H, 22 KY Infantry, July 22, 1862. GSW Chickasaw Bluffs, MS, Dec. 29, 1862. Resigned Feb. 18, 1863, "my protracted ill health having rendered me unfit for duty with no prospect of a speedy recovery." *Colonel,* 64 KY Enrolled Militia, Sept. 1863. Battle honors: Chickasaw Bluffs, Morgan's Raid into Kentucky.
Born: Aug. 11, 1841 Shelby Co., KY
Died: Nov. 24, 1926 Louisville, KY
Occupation: Harness and saddlery manufacturer, and life insurance agent in later life
Offices/Honors: Kentucky Senate, 1879–80. Surveyor of Customs, Louisville, KY, 1885–89.
Miscellaneous: Resided Louisville, Jefferson Co., KY
Buried: Cave Hill Cemetery, Louisville, KY (Section 5, Lot 180)
References: J. Stoddard Johnston, editor. *Memorial History of Louisville.* Chicago, IL, 1896.

James Calvert Foy (William B. Hazen. *A Narrative of Military Service.* Boston, Massachusetts, 1885).

John Thomas Gathright (The Filson Historical Society, Louisville, Kentucky [PC19-0180]).

John Thomas Gathright (William H. Perrin, J. H. Battle, and Gilbert C. Kniffin. *Kentucky: A History of the State*. 8th Edition. Louisville and Chicago, 1888).

William H. Perrin, J. H. Battle, and Gilbert C. Kniffin. *Kentucky: A History of the State*. 8th Edition. Louisville and Chicago, 1888. Pension File and Military Service File, National Archives. *The Biographical Encyclopedia of Kentucky of the Dead and Living Men of the Nineteenth Century*. Cincinnati, OH, 1878. *Biographical Cyclopedia of the Commonwealth of Kentucky*. Chicago and Philadelphia, 1896. Obituary, *Louisville Courier-Journal*, Nov. 25, 1926.

James Washington Gault

Captain, Co. A, 16 KY Infantry, Oct. 5, 1861. Major, 16 KY Infantry, March 15, 1862. Lieutenant Colonel, 16 KY Infantry, July 20, 1862. Colonel, 16 KY Infantry, June 3, 1863. Commanded 1 Brigade, 3 Division, 23 Army Corps, Army of the Ohio, May 26–27, 1864. Honorably mustered out, Feb. 1, 1865. Battle honors: Morgan's Second Kentucky Raid, East Tennessee Campaign, Knoxville Campaign, Atlanta Campaign (Resaca).

Born: Dec. 29, 1828 near Murphysville, KY
Died: April 17, 1896 Murphysville, KY
Education: Attended Medical College of Ohio, Cincinnati, OH
Occupation: Physician
Offices/Honors: Kentucky State Military Agent, Louisville, KY, April 1, 1865–Feb. 15, 1866. Kentucky House of Representatives, 1865–67.
Miscellaneous: Resided Sardis, Mason Co., KY; and Murphysville, Mason Co., KY

James Washington Gault.

Buried: Shannon Methodist Churchyard, Shannon, Mason Co., KY
References: "Col. James Washington Gault," *Bulletin of the Mason County Genealogical Society*. Vol. 9, No. 2, 1991. Obituary, *Maysville Daily Public Ledger*, April 18, 1896. Pension File and Military Service File, National Archives.

Milton Graham

Captain, Co. H, 4 KY Mounted Infantry, Oct. 9, 1861. Discharged Feb. 15, 1862, upon adverse report of a Board of Examination. Captain, Co. D, 11 KY Cavalry, Aug. 17, 1862. Major, 11 KY Cavalry, Sept. 22, 1862. GSW left side chest, near Sevierville, TN, Jan. 28, 1864. Lieutenant Colonel, 11 KY Cavalry, June 10, 1864. *Colonel*, 11 KY Cavalry, Sept. 20, 1864. Honorably mustered out, July 14, 1865. Battle honors: Morgan's Ohio Raid, East Tennessee Campaign, Knoxville Campaign (Maryville), Sevierville.

Born: July 19, 1824 Washington Co., KY
Died: Dec. 14, 1903 Seneca, MO
Occupation: Merchant and farmer
Miscellaneous: Resided Springfield, Washington Co., KY, to 1865; Salvisa, Mercer Co., KY, 1865–67; Green Ridge, Pettis Co., MO; and Seneca, Newton Co., MO, after 1881
Buried: Seneca Cemetery, Seneca, MO (Area D South)
References: Pension File and Military Service

Milton Graham (courtesy University of Kentucky Archives [1997AV30-20]).

File, National Archives. Obituary, *Neosho Times*, Dec. 17, 1903. Letters Received, Volunteer Service Branch, Adjutant General's Office, File G386(VS) 1869, National Archives. Eastham Tarrant. *The Wild Riders of the First Kentucky Cavalry, A History of the Regiment in the Great War of the Rebellion, 1861–1865*. Louisville, KY, 1894.

Benjamin Covington Grider

Colonel, 9 KY Infantry, Nov. 26, 1861. Nominated as Brig. Gen., USV, Nov. 29, 1862. Commanded 1 Brigade, 3 Division, Left Wing, 14 Army Corps, Army of the Cumberland, Dec. 31, 1862–Jan. 9, 1863. Commanded 1 Brigade, 3 Division, 21 Army Corps, Army of the Cumberland, Jan. 9–Feb. 3, 1863. Resigned Feb. 3, 1863, since "the condition of my family and business requires my personal attention." After forwarding his resignation, Major Gen. William S. Rosecrans commented in a telegram to Adjutant General Lorenzo Thomas, "Charges were preferred against him by his superior officers for periodical drunkenness on as well as off duty which would have dismissed him from the service. To save him the disgrace, charges were withdrawn, and I ordered him on duty at Louisville upon his solemn promise of entire reformation. Since then he has violated his promise and been staggering drunk in the presence of his command. When sober he is a gallant and worthy officer. He has been permitted to resign with the hope and belief that he will start on a new career of usefulness out of reach of old temptations." Nomination as Brig. Gen., USV, withdrawn, Feb. 12, 1863. Battle honors: Shiloh, Corinth, Stone's River.

Born: April 10, 1826 Bowling Green, KY
Died: Feb. 9, 1872 Bowling Green, KY
Occupation: Lawyer
Miscellaneous: Resided Bowling Green, Warren Co., KY. His father, U.S. Congressman Henry Grider, Jr., was first cousin of Colonel John Hobson Grider (52 KY Infantry).
Buried: Fairview Cemetery, Bowling Green, KY (Section B, Lot 10)
References: Hecht S. Lackey. *Martin Grider of Pennsylvania and His Descendants, Circa 1731–1978*. Evansville, IN, 1979. Pension File and Military Service File, National Archives. Letters Received, Commission Branch, Adjutant General's Office, File G434(CB)1863, National Archives. *A Memorial and Biographical Record of Kansas City and Jackson County, MO*. Chicago, IL, 1896.

John Hobson Grider

1 Lieutenant, Adjutant, 9 KY Infantry, Nov. 12, 1861. Major, 9 KY Infantry, April 18, 1862. GSW left elbow, Stone's River, TN, Jan. 2, 1863. Lieutenant Colonel, 9 KY Infantry, Feb. 4, 1863. Having entered service with his collection business unsettled, he resigned May 9, 1863, in order to avoid losses that "will cost me all I am worth." In forwarding his resignation, Brig. Gen. Samuel Beatty commented, "He is a very incompetent officer and the service will be benefited by the acceptance of his resignation." Lieutenant Colonel, 52 KY Infantry, Nov. 7, 1863. Colonel, 52 KY Infantry, Feb. 17, 1864. Commanded 2 Brigade, 2 Division, District of Kentucky, 23 Army Corps, Department of the Ohio, July 5–Sept. 12, 1864. Honorably mustered out, Jan. 18, 1865. Battle honors: Shiloh, Stone's River, Morgan's Raid into Kentucky.

Born: Jan. 17, 1822 Bowling Green, KY
Died: May 22, 1884 Bowling Green, KY
Occupation: Constable and collection officer before war. Farmer after war.
Miscellaneous: Resided Bowling Green, Warren Co., KY. First cousin of the father, U.S. Congressman Henry Grider, Jr., of Colonel Benjamin Covington Grider (9 KY Infantry).
Buried: Fairview Cemetery, Bowling Green, KY (Section C, Lot 37)
References: Hecht S. Lackey. *Martin Grider of Pennsylvania and His Descendants, Circa 1731–1978*. Evansville, IN, 1979. Pension File and Military Service File, National Archives. Letters Received, Volunteer Service Branch, Adjutant General's Office, File I418(VS)1863, National Archives.

Lewis Braxton Grigsby

Colonel, 24 KY Infantry, Jan. 5, 1862. Shell wound left side of neck, Shiloh, TN, April 6, 1862.

Commanded 21 Brigade, 6 Division, 2 Army Corps, Army of the Ohio, Oct. 29–Nov. 5, 1862. Commanded 2 Brigade, 1 Division, Left Wing, 14 Army Corps, Army of the Cumberland, Nov. 5–24, 1862. Resigned July 16, 1863, "impelled ... by motives of a purely personal and pecuniary character ... I have in the state of Louisiana ... a large interest in real personal property, which by my immediate personal attention may be saved." Battle honors: Shiloh, Perryville.

Born: 1836 near Winchester, KY
Died: Nov. 3, 1880 Littleton, CO
Education: Attended Bethany (WV) College
Occupation: Lawyer
Miscellaneous: Resided Winchester, Clark Co., KY; and Denver, CO, 1879–80
Buried: Riverside Cemetery, Denver, CO (Block 5, Lot 81, unmarked)
References: Obituary, *Rocky Mountain News*, Nov. 7, 1880. Pension File and Military Service File, National Archives. John A. Joyce. *A Checkered Life.* Chicago, IL, 1883. Research files of Leoneita C. Milner, Dallas, TX.

James Verner Guthrie

Colonel, 1 KY Infantry, June 28, 1861. GSW left hand, Gauley Bridge, WV, July 30, 1861. Resigned Dec. 21, 1861, due to "my continued illness which makes it improbable that I shall soon be able to resume any active command." Battle honors: Gauley Bridge, Morgan's First Kentucky Raid.

Born: Dec. 8, 1809 Pittsburgh, PA
Died: March 8, 1896 Cincinnati, OH
Occupation: Mechanical engineer and steamboat inspector before war. Politician after war.
Offices/Honors: Steamboat inspector, Cincinnati, OH, 1858–67
Miscellaneous: Resided Newport, Campbell Co., KY; Urbana, Champaign Co., OH; and Cincinnati, OH
Buried: Oakdale Cemetery, Urbana, OH (Section 34, Lot 15)
References: Pension File and Military Service File, National Archives. Harriet N. Dunn and Eveline Guthrie Dunn. *Records of the Guthrie Family of Pennsylvania,* *Connecticut, and Virginia.* Chicago, IL, 1898. Laurence R. Guthrie. *American Guthrie and Allied Families.* Chambersburg, PA, 1933. Obituary, *Urbana Citizen and Gazette,* March 12, 1896.

David Rice Haggard

Colonel, 5 KY Cavalry, Jan. 1, 1862. Having been absent many months on sick leave, he was dismissed, Feb. 16, 1863, upon the recommendation of Major Gen. William S. Rosecrans, for "absence without leave." Upon providing evidence that his leave was properly authorized, his dismissal was changed to an honorable discharge, effective March 24, 1863. Having recovered his health, he then appealed to President Lincoln for revocation of the discharge order and for restoration to his command. President Lincoln, in a letter of May 1, 1863,

James Verner Guthrie (pre-war, seated right, with brothers, Robert B., William W., and Presley N. Guthrie, left to right) (Harriet N. Dunn and Eveline Guthrie Dunn. ***Records of the Guthrie Family of Pennsylvania, Connecticut, and Virginia.*** Chicago, Illinois, 1898).

David Rice Haggard (post-war) (David D. Haggard. *History of the Haggard Family in England and America, 1433 to 1899*. Bloomington, Illinois, 1899).

to Major Gen. Rosecrans, recommended his restoration, saying, "He is one of the strongest and most vigorous looking men I have seen, and intimate acquaintances of his, of undoubted veracity, assure me he is really so." By Special Order 255, June 8, 1863, he was "restored to his regiment provided the vacancy has not been filled, evidence of the fact to be obtained from the Governor." Upon learning that Governor James F. Robinson had meanwhile commissioned Captain William P. Sanders as his successor, he lamented, "I suppose I will have to give up my regiment, as my command is tendered and probably accepted by a man who never saw the regiment or spent a dollar in its organization."
Born: 1817? KY
Died: April 29, 1887 Burkesville, KY
Occupation: Physician
Offices/Honors: Kentucky House of Representatives, 1844–47. Kentucky Senate, 1871–75.
Miscellaneous: Resided Burkesville, Cumberland Co., KY
Buried: King/Haggard Cemetery, Burkesville, KY
References: Pension File and Military Service File, National Archives. Letters Received, Volunteer Service Branch, Adjutant General's Office, File C196(VS)1863, National Archives. David D. Haggard. *History of the Haggard Family in England and America, 1433 to 1899*. Bloomington, IL, 1899. "Rice Haggard: Life, Home & Family Burial Plot, 1767–1819," http://www.therestorationmovement.com/haggard.htm. Roy P. Basler, editor. *The Collected Works of Abraham Lincoln*. New Brunswick, NJ, 1953.

Dennis J. Halisy

Colonel, 6 KY Cavalry, Sept. 26, 1862. GSW face, Muldraugh's Hill, near New Market, Marion Co., KY, Dec. 31, 1862, in hand-to-hand conflict with Lieutenant George B. Eastin of John Hunt Morgan's command. Battle honors: Morgan's First Kentucky Raid, Morgan's Second Kentucky Raid (Muldraugh's Hill).
Born: 1828? France
Died: Dec. 31, 1862 KIA near New Market, Marion Co., KY
Education: Graduated Jefferson Medical College, Philadelphia, PA, 1857
Occupation: Physician
Miscellaneous: Resided Manton, Washington Co., KY
Buried: St. Rose Priory Cemetery, near Springfield, KY (unmarked?)
References: Obituary, *Louisville Daily Democrat*, Jan. 11, 1863. *The War of the Rebellion: A Compilation of the Official Records of the Union and Confederate Armies*. (Series 1, Vol. 20, Part 1, pp. 145, 154, 157–158) Washington, DC, 1887. Military Service Record, National Archives. Michael L. and Bettie Anne Cook, editors. *Pioneer History of Washington County, Kentucky*. Owensboro, KY, 1980.

John Shackleford Hammer

2 Lieutenant, Co. B, 16 KY Infantry, Jan. 27, 1862. 1 Lieutenant, Co. B, 16 KY Infantry, July 20, 1862. Taken prisoner and paroled, Lebanon, KY, July 5, 1863. Provost Marshal, Post of Lebanon, KY, Sept.16–Dec. 12, 1863. Captain, Co. B, 16 KY Infantry, July 29, 1864. Lieutenant Colonel, 16 KY Infantry, May 15, 1865. *Colonel*, 16 KY Infantry, May 16, 1865. Honorably mustered out, July 15, 1865. Battle honors: Morgan's Ohio Raid (Lebanon), Franklin.
Born: July 13, 1842 Fleming Co., KY
Died: March 31, 1903 Ada, OK
Occupation: Blacksmith and mechanic before war. Regular Army (1 Lieutenant, 19 U.S. Infantry, honorably discharged Nov. 30, 1870) and Post Trader, Fort Gibson, Indian Territory, 1871–78 and 1881–85.
Offices/Honors: Postmaster, Ardmore, Chickasaw Nation, Indian Territory, 1893–96. U.S. Marshal, Southern District of the Indian Territory, 1897–1901.

John Shackleford Hammer.

Miscellaneous: Resided Flemingsburg, Fleming Co., KY; Ardmore, Carter Co., OK; and Ada, Pontotoc Co., OK

Buried: Rose Hill Cemetery, Ardmore, OK (Section 81)

References: Obituary, *The Daily Ardmoreite*, April 1, 1903. Obituary Circular, Whole No. 267, Kansas MOLLUS. C. W. "Dub" West. *Fort Gibson, Gateway to the West.* Muskogee, OK, 1974. Military Service File, National Archives. Letters Received, Volunteer Service Branch, Adjutant General's Office, File H445(VS)1870, National Archives. Letters Received, Commission Branch, Adjutant General's Office, File H238(CB)1870, National Archives.

Charles S. Hanson

Lieutenant Colonel, 20 KY Infantry, Oct. 1, 1861. Commanded Post of Lebanon, KY, May 28–Aug. 20, 1863. Taken prisoner and paroled, Lebanon, KY, July 5, 1863. Provost Marshal, Louisville, KY, Aug. 20, 1863–Jan. 1, 1864. Colonel, 37 KY Infantry, Dec. 29, 1863. Commanded Sub-District of Southwestern KY, District of Kentucky, 23 Army Corps, Department of the Ohio, Feb. 1864. Commanded 3 Brigade, 1 Division, District of Kentucky, 23 Army Corps, Department of the Ohio, April 13–Oct. 2, 1864. GSW spine and left side and taken prisoner, Saltville, VA, Oct. 2, 1864. Confined Libby Prison, Richmond, VA. Paroled Feb. 22, 1865. Honorably mustered out, March 6,

Charles S. Hanson (E. Polk Johnson. *A History of Kentucky and Kentuckians.* Chicago and New York, 1912).

1865. Battle honors: Shiloh, Corinth, Morgan's Ohio Raid (Lebanon), Morgan's Raid into Kentucky (Cynthiana), Saltville.

Born: Sept. 11, 1829 Winchester, KY

Died: Nov. 8, 1875 Paris, KY

Education: Graduated University of Louisville (KY) Law School, 1851

Occupation: Lawyer

Miscellaneous: Resided Winchester, Clark Co., KY; and Paris, Bourbon Co., KY. Brother of CSA Brig. Gen. Roger W. Hanson.

Buried: Winchester Cemetery, Winchester, KY (Section F)

References: Obituary, *Paris True Kentuckian*, Nov. 10, 1875. E. Polk Johnson. *A History of Kentucky and Kentuckians.* Chicago and New York, 1912. Pension File and Military Service File, National Archives. Letters Received, Volunteer Service Branch, Adjutant General's Office, File H526(VS) 1865, National Archives. Kathryn Owen, compiler. *Civil War Days in Clark County.* N.p., 1963.

John Marshall Harlan

Colonel, 10 KY Infantry, Nov. 21, 1861. Commanded 2 Brigade, 1 Division, 3 Army Corps, Army of the Ohio, Oct. 10–Nov. 5, 1862. Nominated as Brig. Gen., USV, Nov. 29, 1862. Commanded 2 Brigade, 3 Division, Center, 14 Army Corps, Army of the Cumberland, Nov. 5, 1862–

John Marshall Harlan (photograph by Webster & Bro., Louisville, Kentucky; Library of Congress [LC-DIG-cwpb-06960]).

Jan. 9, 1863. Commanded 2 Brigade, 3 Division, 14 Army Corps, Army of the Cumberland, Jan. 9– March 6, 1863. Resigned March 6, 1863, since "the recent sudden death of my father has devolved upon me duties of a private nature which I cannot with propriety neglect." Nomination as Brig. Gen., USV, withdrawn, July 13, 1863. Battle honors: Hartsville, Morgan's Second Kentucky Raid.

Born: June 1, 1833 Boyle Co., KY
Died: Oct. 14, 1911 Washington, DC
Education: Graduated Centre College, Danville, KY, 1850. Attended Transylvania University Law School, Lexington, KY.
Occupation: Lawyer
Offices/Honors: Kentucky Adjutant General, 1855–59. Kentucky Attorney General, 1863–67. Associate Justice, U.S. Supreme Court, 1877–1911.
Miscellaneous: Resided Frankfort, Franklin Co., KY; Louisville, Jefferson Co., KY; and Washington, DC, 1877–1911
Buried: Rock Creek Cemetery, Washington, DC (Section R, Lot 18)

John Marshall Harlan (photograph by Webster & Bro., Louisville, Kentucky; courtesy Henry Deeks).

References: *Dictionary of American Biography.* Loren P. Beth. *John Marshall Harlan: The Last Whig Justice.* Lexington, KY, 1992. Frank B. Latham. *The Great Dissenter: John Marshall Harlan, 1833–1911.* New York City, NY, 1970. Melvin I. Urofsky, editor. *Biographical Encyclopedia of the Supreme Court: The Lives and Legal Philosophies of the Justices.* Washington, DC, 2006. John Marshall Harlan Papers, Manuscript Division, Library of Congress, Washington, DC. Obituary, *New York Times,* Oct. 15, 1911. Pension File and Military Service File, National Archives. Dennis W. Belcher. *The 10th Kentucky Volunteer Infantry in the Civil War: A History and Roster.* Jefferson, NC, 2009. Society of the Army of the Cumberland. *Thirty-Ninth Reunion, Chattanooga, TN, 1911.* Chattanooga, TN, 1912. Alpheus H. Harlan, compiler. *History and Genealogy of the Harlan Family and Particularly of the Descendants of George and Michael Harlan Who Settled in Chester County, PA, 1687.* Baltimore, MD, 1914.

Selby Harney

Major, 1 Battalion, Louisville Provost Guard, Feb. 26, 1862. Provost Marshal, Louisville, KY, Aug. 9, 1862. 1 Battalion, Louisville Provost Guard, consolidated with 34 KY Infantry in Oct. 1862.

Lieutenant Colonel, 34 KY Infantry, Feb. 6, 1863. Colonel, 34 KY Infantry, June 2, 1863. Commanded Post of Glasgow, KY, 2 Division, 23 Army Corps, Department of the Ohio, July 1863. Commanded Post of Morristown, TN, Left Wing Forces in East Tennessee, Department of the Ohio, Oct. 1863. Commanded Post of Tazewell, TN, Left Wing Forces in East Tennessee, Department of the Ohio, Nov.–Dec. 1863. While commending his soldiers as "prompt, active and efficient men, always ready and willing to perform any duty required of them, though at times receiving no rations other than fresh pork and salt," he resigned Dec. 15, 1863, "in justice to them," in order "that a better and more efficient officer be placed in command." Battle honors: Morgan's Ohio Raid, East Tennessee Campaign, Knoxville Campaign (Rogersville).

Born: June 19, 1838 Louisville, KY
Died: May 9, 1893 Louisville, KY
Education: Graduated University of Louisville (KY) Law School, 1858
Occupation: Lawyer
Miscellaneous: Resided Louisville, Jefferson Co., KY
Buried: Cave Hill Cemetery, Louisville, KY (Section E, Lot 25)
References: Obituary, *Louisville Courier-Journal,* May 10, 1893. Pension File and Military Service File, National Archives. William W. Barton and Jean W. Gayle. *Six Wallace Brothers and Their Descendants.* Bountiful, UT, 1996.

Percival (aka Pierce) Butler Hawkins

Colonel, 11 KY Infantry, Nov. 11, 1861. Commanded 14 Brigade, 5 Division, 2 Army Corps, Army of the Ohio, Sept.–Nov. 1862. Commanded Post of Bowling Green, KY, June 1863. Feeling "old and worn down" and "my regiment wasted away through disease and battle," he resigned June 25, 1863, since "my family relations and my business, which has long been neglected, call me to my home." Commissioner, Board of Enrollment, 3 District of Kentucky, July 27–Nov. 12, 1863 and March 28–Aug. 22, 1864. *Colonel,* 1 Regiment, Capital Guards, KY State Troops, July 11, 1864. Battle honors: Shiloh.

Born: Nov. 17, 1817 Spotsylvania Co., VA
Died: March 20, 1893 Bowling Green, KY
Occupation: Lawyer and school teacher before war. Lawyer and pension agent after war.
Offices/Honors: Kentucky House of Representatives, 1850 and 1863–65. Postmaster, Bowling Green, KY, 1870–77.
Miscellaneous: Resided Bowling Green, Warren Co., KY
Buried: Fairview Cemetery, Bowling Green, KY (Section C, Lot 34)

Percival (aka Pierce) Butler Hawkins.

References: Pension File and Military Service File, National Archives. Margaret A. Karsner Murphy, compiler. *The Life and Times of Our Hawkins Family.* N.p., 1988. Letters Received, Volunteer Service Branch, Adjutant General's Office, File W3431(VS)1864, National Archives.

William Hercules Hays

Lieutenant Colonel, 10 KY Infantry, Nov. 13, 1861. Colonel, 10 KY Infantry, March 7, 1863. Commanded 2 Brigade, 3 Division, 14 Army Corps, Army of the Cumberland, Sept. 20, 1863. Commanded 3 Brigade, 3 Division, 14 Army Corps, Army of the Cumberland, Nov. 25, 1863–April 2, 1864. Commanded Post of Ringgold, GA, Sept.–Oct. 1864. Honorably mustered out, Dec. 6, 1864. Battle honors: Hartsville, Morgan's Second Kentucky Raid, Chickamauga, Missionary Ridge, Dalton, Atlanta Campaign (Jonesborough).

Born: Aug. 26, 1820 Washington Co., KY
Died: March 7, 1880 Louisville, KY
Occupation: Lawyer and judge
Offices/Honors: Kentucky House of Representatives, 1861. Kentucky Inspector General, March 22–Nov. 13, 1865. Judge, U.S. District Court, District of Kentucky, 1879–80.
Miscellaneous: Resided Springfield, Washington Co., KY; and Louisville, Jefferson Co., KY

Buried: Springfield Cemetery, Springfield, KY

References: *The Biographical Encyclopedia of Kentucky of the Dead and Living Men of the Nineteenth Century.* Cincinnati, OH, 1878. Obituary, *Louisville Courier-Journal,* March 8, 1880. Dennis W. Belcher. *The 10th Kentucky Volunteer Infantry in the Civil War: A History and Roster.* Jefferson, NC, 2009. Military Service File, National Archives.

William Edward Hobson

Major, 13 KY Infantry, Jan. 1, 1862. Lieutenant Colonel, 13 KY Infantry, Feb. 22, 1863. Colonel, 13 KY Infantry, March 13, 1863. Commanded 1 Brigade, 2 Division, 23 Army Corps, Army of the Ohio, Feb.–March, 1864. Commanded 2 Brigade, 2 Division, 23 Army Corps, Army of the Ohio, June 18–Aug. 15, 1864. Chief of Staff, Staff of Brig. Gen. Milo S. Hascall, 2 Division, 23 Army Corps, Army of the Ohio, Aug.–Sept. 1864. Commanded Post of Bowling Green, KY, Oct.–Nov. 1864. Honorably mustered out, Jan. 12, 1865. Battle honors: Shiloh, Corinth, Morgan's Second Kentucky Raid, East Tennessee Campaign, Knoxville Campaign (Huff's Ferry, Campbell's Station), Atlanta Campaign (Kenesaw Mountain, Peach Tree Creek, Atlanta, Utoy Creek).

Born: Jan. 8, 1844 Bowling Green, KY

Died: Sept. 10, 1909 Bowling Green, KY

Education: Graduated Albany (NY) Law School, 1867

Occupation: Lawyer and farmer

Offices/Honors: Assessor of Internal Revenue, 1869–71. Postmaster, Bowling Green, KY, 1877–85.

William Hercules Hays (courtesy Perry M. Frohne).

William Hercules Hays (courtesy Henry Deeks).

William Edward Hobson (courtesy Special Collections Library, Western Kentucky University [2008.229.81]).

Alexander Wake Holeman

Lieutenant Colonel, 12 KY Cavalry, Nov. 17, 1862. Colonel, 11 KY Cavalry, Nov. 19, 1863. Commanded 1 Brigade, 1 Division, Cavalry Corps, Army of the Ohio, Feb.–March 1864. Commanded 2 Brigade, 2 Division, Cavalry Corps, Army of the Ohio, April 1864. Commanded Independent Brigade, Cavalry Corps, Army of the Ohio, May 1864. Resigned Sept. 20, 1864. Battle honors: Morgan's Second Kentucky Raid, Expedition to Monticello, KY (Horseshoe Bottom, Cumberland River), Atlanta Campaign (Cassville).

Born: Feb. 20, 1827 Frankfort, KY
Died: Oct. 19, 1887 Louisville, KY
Other Wars: Mexican War (Private, Co. C, 1 KY Cavalry). Taken prisoner by the Mexican army, near La Encamacion, Mexico, Jan. 21, 1847, he took two chances in a lottery of death, one for himself and one for a friend, whom he thought less able to risk death. Escaped captivity in July 1847. Took part in William Walker's filibuster expedition to Nicaragua, 1855–56.
Occupation: Merchant and hotel keeper before war. Tobacco inspector and U.S. Internal Revenue official after war.
Miscellaneous: Resided Frankfort, Franklin Co., KY; New Liberty, Owen Co., KY; and Louisville, Jefferson Co., KY, after war

William Edward Hobson (courtesy Special Collections Library, Western Kentucky University [2011.63.15]).

Miscellaneous: Resided Bowling Green, Warren Co., KY. Nephew of Brig. Gen. Edward H. Hobson.
Buried: Fairview Cemetery, Bowling Green, KY (Section A, Lot 45)
References: Arthur J. and Margaret S. Bush. *Black Powder to Black Gold: The Life and Times of William E. Hobson.* N.p., 1990. William H. Perrin, J. H. Battle, and Gilbert C. Kniffin. *Kentucky: A History of the State.* Louisville and Chicago, 1887. Hobson Family Papers, Manuscripts & Folklife Archives, Kentucky Library and Museum, Western Kentucky University, Bowling Green, KY. Pension File and Military Service File, National Archives. Obituary, *Louisville Courier-Journal,* Sept. 11, 1909. *The Biographical Encyclopedia of Kentucky of the Dead and Living Men of the Nineteenth Century.* Cincinnati, OH, 1878.

Alexander Wake Holeman (oil painting in a private collection).

Alexander Wake Holeman (photograph by Webster & Bro., Louisville, Kentucky; courtesy Special Collections Library, Western Kentucky University [2006.181.32]).

Buried: IOOF Cemetery, New Liberty, KY
References: Obituary, *Louisville Courier-Journal*, Oct. 20, 1887. Pension File and Military Service File, National Archives. Henry Watterson, "The Bravest Deed I Ever Knew," *Century Magazine*, Vol. 82, No. 3 (July 1911). Letters Received, Volunteer Service Branch, Adjutant General's Office, File H769(VS)1866, National Archives. Eastham Tarrant. *The Wild Riders of the First Kentucky Cavalry, A History of the Regiment in the Great War of the Rebellion, 1861–1865*. Louisville, KY, 1894.

William Anderson Hoskins

Colonel, 12 KY Infantry, Jan. 31, 1862. Provost Marshal, Post of Tuscumbia, AL, July 1862. Commanded Post of Lebanon, KY, District of Western Kentucky, Department of the Ohio, Dec. 1862–Feb. 1863. Commanded 2 Brigade, Left Wing Forces in East Tennessee, Department of the Ohio, Sept.–Dec. 1863. "Feeling well assured of the fact that another can be found more competent than myself to command the regiment," he resigned April 16, 1864, since "from long neglect of private affairs I have already sustained heavy losses and shall

William Anderson Hoskins.

be pecuniarily ruined unless I immediately devote my personal attention to private business." Battle honors: Mill Springs, Morgan's Second Kentucky Raid (Muldraugh's Hill), Morgan's Ohio Raid, East Tennessee Campaign, Knoxville Campaign.
Born: Nov. 22, 1826 Garrard Co., KY
Died: Oct. 23, 1897 Madisonville, TN
Education: Attended Centre College, Danville, KY
Occupation: Farmer and miner before war. Land speculator and mine operator after war.
Offices/Honors: Kentucky House of Representatives, 1871–73
Miscellaneous: Resided Alpha, Clinton Co., KY; Danville, Boyle Co., KY; Chattanooga, Hamilton Co., TN; and Chilhowee, Blount Co., TN
Buried: Bellevue Cemetery, Danville, KY (Division 4, Section 5, Lot 38)
References: Obituary, *Knoxville Daily Journal*, Oct. 26, 1897. Obituary, *Kentucky Tri-Weekly Advocate*, Oct. 25, 1897. Obituary, *Chattanooga Daily Times*, Oct. 24, 1897. Pension File and Military Service File, National Archives. Eliza A. Herring, "The Hoskins of Kentucky," *The Register of the Kentucky State Historical Society*, Vol. 15, No. 2 (May 1917).

John Smith Hurt

Lieutenant Colonel, 24 KY Infantry, Jan. 5, 1862. Colonel, 24 KY Infantry, Aug. 20, 1863.

Commanded 2 Brigade, 3 Division, 23 Army Corps, Army of the Ohio, May 14–16 and May 18–21, 1864. Honorably mustered out, Jan. 31, 1865. Battle honors: Knoxville Campaign, Atlanta Campaign (Resaca, Kenesaw Mountain).
Born: May 21, 1826 Montgomery Co., KY
Died: Nov. 5, 1905 Mount Sterling, KY
Other Wars: Mexican War (Private, Co. I, 2 KY Infantry)
Occupation: Lawyer
Miscellaneous: Resided Owingsville, Bath Co., KY, to 1889; and Mount Sterling, Montgomery Co., KY, after 1889
Buried: Machpelah Cemetery, Mount Sterling, KY (Section 12)
References: *Biographical Cyclopedia of the Commonwealth of Kentucky.* Chicago and Philadelphia, 1896. H. Levin, editor. *The Lawyers and Lawmakers of Kentucky.* Chicago, IL, 1897. Mary Lee Hurt, compiler. *Family History from Robert Hurt, d. 1583, Ashbourne, Staffordshire, England, Through Leon Jesse Hurt, d. 1956, Barry, Pike County, Illinois, and Family.* Tallahassee, FL, 1985. Edward C. O'Rear. *A History of the Montgomery County Bar.* Frankfort, KY, 1945. John A. Richards. *A History of Bath County, KY.* Yuma, AZ, 1961. William H. Perrin, J. H. Battle and Gilbert C. Kniffin. *Kentucky: A History of the State.* 8th Edition. Louisville and Chicago, 1888. Obituary, *Mount Sterling Advocate,* Nov. 8, 1905. Military Service File, National Archives. John A. Joyce. *A Checkered Life.* Chicago, IL, 1883.

Richard Taylor Jacob

Colonel, 9 KY Cavalry, Aug. 22, 1862. GSW left breast and left arm, near Lawrenceburg, KY, Oct. 8, 1862. Commanded Independent Brigade, District of Western Kentucky, Department of the Ohio, April–June 1863. Honorably mustered out, Aug. 21, 1863. Accused along with Colonel Frank L. Wolford of "making treasonable and seditious speeches, calculated and intended to weaken the power of the Government in its efforts to suppress the rebellion," he was arrested by Major Gen. Stephen G. Burbridge on Nov. 11, 1864, and expelled through the Federal lines under the penalty of death if he returned during the war. In communication with President Lincoln, he demanded a return to his home. Lincoln, recognizing the injustice of his arrest, ordered his unconditional release on Jan. 18, 1865. Battle honors: Lawrenceburg, Expedition to Monticello, KY (Horseshoe Bottom, Cumberland River), Morgan's Ohio Raid.
Born: March 13, 1825 near Goshen, Oldham Co., KY
Died: Sept. 13, 1903 Louisville, KY
Education: Attended Hanover (IN) College

Richard Taylor Jacob.

Other Wars: Mexican War (Captain, California Volunteers)
Occupation: Farmer
Offices/Honors: Kentucky House of Representatives, 1859–61. Lieutenant Governor of Kentucky, 1863–67. Park Commissioner, Louisville, KY, 1895–99.
Miscellaneous: Resided Westport, Oldham Co., KY, to 1891; and Louisville, Jefferson Co., KY, after 1891. Son-in-law of Senator Thomas Hart Benton and brother-in-law of Major Gen. John C. Fremont. His step-sister, Matilda Prather Jacob, married Colonel Curran Pope (15 KY Infantry).
Buried: Cave Hill Cemetery, Louisville, KY (Section 4, Lot 62)
References: *Dictionary of American Biography. The Biographical Encyclopedia of Kentucky of the Dead and Living Men of the Nineteenth Century.* Cincinnati, OH, 1878. J. Stoddard Johnston, editor. *Memorial History of Louisville.* Chicago, IL, 1896. William H. Perrin, J. H. Battle and Gilbert C. Kniffin. *Kentucky: A History of the State.* 6th Edition. Louisville and Chicago, 1887. Obituary, *Louisville Courier-Journal,* Sept. 14, 1903. *Appletons' Cyclopedia of American Biography.* William Kyle Anderson. *Donald Robertson and His Wife, Rachel Rogers, of King and Queen County, Virginia, Their Ancestry and Posterity.* Detroit, MI, 1900. Pension File and Military Service File, National Archives. Letters Received, Volunteer Service Branch, Adjutant General's Office, File B422(VS)1867, National

Archives. Roy P. Basler, editor. *The Collected Works of Abraham Lincoln.* New Brunswick, NJ, 1953.

Samuel F. Johnson

Captain, Co. D, 8 KY Cavalry, Aug. 26, 1862. Honorably mustered out, Sept. 23, 1863. Major, 52 KY Infantry, Nov. 18, 1863. Lieutenant Colonel, 52 KY Infantry, Feb. 17, 1864. Honorably mustered out, Jan. 18, 1865. Colonel, 17 KY Cavalry, April 25, 1865. Commanded 3 Brigade, 2 Division, Department of Kentucky, May–Aug. 1865. Honorably mustered out, Sept. 20, 1865. Battle honors: Lyon's Raid from Paris, TN.

Born: Sept. 9, 1824 Belmont Co., OH
Died: Sept. 22, 1898 Bloomington, IL
Occupation: Methodist clergyman before war. Grocer and farmer after war.
Miscellaneous: Resided Hopkinsville, Christian Co., KY; Russellville, Logan Co., KY; Lincoln, Logan Co., IL, 1866–68; McLean, McLean Co., IL; and Bloomington, McLean Co., IL, after 1875
Buried: Evergreen Memorial Cemetery, Bloomington, IL (Section 14, Lot 49)
References: *History of McLean County, IL.* Chicago, IL, 1879. Obituary, *Bloomington Daily Pantagraph,* Sept. 23, 1898. Pension File and Military Service File, National Archives. Charles M. Meacham. *A History of Christian County, Kentucky, from Oxcart to Airplane.* Nashville, TN, 1930.

Edgar A. Keenon

Colonel, 36 KY Enrolled Militia, June 8, 1864. Honorably mustered out, June 18, 1864. Battle honors: Morgan's Raid into Kentucky.

Born: Aug. 6, 1833 Frankfort, KY
Died: Dec. 4, 1882 Covington, KY
Occupation: Boot and shoe merchant before war. U.S. Internal Revenue official and distillery superintendent after war.
Offices/Honors: U.S. Internal Revenue Storekeeper, Newport, KY, 1877–82
Miscellaneous: Resided Frankfort, Franklin Co., KY; and Covington, Kenton, Co., KY, after 1877. Brother-in-law of Major Gen. John Buford and Brig. Gen. Green Clay Smith. Married Henrietta Duke, a first cousin of CSA Brig. Gen. Basil W. Duke.
Buried: Linden Grove Cemetery, Covington, KY (unmarked)
References: W. M. Paxton. *The Marshall Family.* Cincinnati, OH, 1885. Obituary, *Cincinnati Enquirer,* Dec. 5, 1882. Obituary, *Frankfort Roundabout,* Dec. 9, 1882. Charles and Emily Egbert. *Kith, Kin, Wee Kirk.* Vol. 2. Sadieville, KY, 1995. Stella Pickett Hardy. *Colonial Families of the Southern States of America.* Baltimore, MD, 1958.

Edgar A. Keenon (The Filson Historical Society, Louisville, Kentucky [PC2-0404]).

Robert Morrow Kelly

Captain, Co. K, 4 KY Infantry, Oct. 9, 1861. Major, 4 KY Infantry, March 23, 1862. Acting AIG, Staff of Brig. Gen. John M. Brannan, 3 Division, 14 Army Corps, Army of the Cumberland, Aug.–Sept. 1863. Regiment changed to Mounted Infantry, March 2, 1864. Lieutenant Colonel, 4 KY Mounted Infantry, April 18, 1864. Taken prisoner, near Newnan, GA, July 30, 1864. Confined Charleston, SC. Colonel, 4 KY Mounted Infantry, Aug. 25, 1864. Paroled Sept. 28, 1864. Commanded 1 Brigade, 1 Division, Cavalry Corps, Military Division of the Mississippi, June 1865. Honorably mustered out, Aug. 17, 1865. Battle honors: Mill Springs, Chickamauga, Missionary Ridge, Atlanta Campaign (McCook's Raid), Wilson's Raid.

Born: Sept. 22, 1836 Paris, KY
Died: Dec. 27, 1913 Louisville, KY
Occupation: School teacher and lawyer before war. Lawyer and newspaper editor after war.
Offices/Honors: Collector of Internal Revenue, Lexington, KY, 1867–70. U.S. Pension Agent, 1873–86. Superintendent, Cave Hill National Cemetery, Louisville, KY, at his death.
Miscellaneous: Resided Paris, Bourbon Co., KY, to 1866; Lexington, Fayette Co., KY, 1866–70; and Louisville, Jefferson Co., KY, after 1870

Buried: Cave Hill Cemetery, Louisville, KY (Section 5, Lot 304)

References: J. Stoddard Johnston, editor. *Memorial History of Louisville*. Chicago, IL, 1896. *National Cyclopedia of American Biography*. Obituary Circular, Whole No. 995, Ohio MOLLUS. Pension File and Military Service File, National Archives. Obituary, *Louisville Courier-Journal*, Dec. 28, 1913. Letters Received, Volunteer Service Branch, Adjutant General's Office, File K803(VS) 1865, National Archives. Thomas Speed, Robert M. Kelly, and Alfred Pirtle. *The Union Regiments of Kentucky*. Louisville, KY, 1897. Robert M. Kelly, "Holding Kentucky for the Union," *Battles and Leaders of the Civil War*, edited by Robert U. Johnson and Clarence C. Buel. New York City, NY, 1887–88.

John James Landram

Lieutenant Colonel, 18 KY Infantry, Jan. 20, 1862. GSW ankle, Cynthiana, KY, July 17, 1862. Shell wound face, affecting eyesight in left eye, Richmond, KY, Aug. 30, 1862. Taken prisoner and paroled, Richmond, KY, Aug. 30, 1862. *Colonel*, 32 KY Infantry, Dec. 24, 1862. Resigned Feb. 6, 1863, since "I will hazard the loss of my eyesight by taking the field at present." Battle honors: Morgan's First Kentucky Raid (Cynthiana), Richmond.

Born: Nov. 16, 1826 Gallatin Co., KY

Died: Nov. 13, 1890 Covington, KY

Education: Graduated University of Louisville (KY) Law School, 1859

Other Wars: Mexican War (1 Sergeant, Co. B, 1 KY Cavalry)

Occupation: Lawyer

Offices/Honors: Kentucky House of Representatives, 1851–53. Kentucky Senate, 1863–67. Collector of Internal Revenue, Covington, KY, 1889–90.

Miscellaneous: Resided Warsaw, Gallatin Co., KY; and Covington, Kenton Co., KY, 1889–90

Buried: Warsaw Cemetery, Warsaw, KY

References: Z. F. Smith. *History of Kentucky*. Louisville, KY, 1895. Obituary Circular, Whole No. 239, Ohio MOLLUS. Obituary, *Cincinnati Enquirer*, Nov. 14, 1890. Obituary, *Frankfort Roundabout*, Nov. 15, 1890. Pension File and Military Service File, National Archives. Letters Received, Volunteer Service Branch, Adjutant General's Office, File S42(VS)1863, National Archives.

Top, left: Robert Morrow Kelly (photograph by Carpenter & Mullen, Lexington, Kentucky; courtesy University of Kentucky Archives [1997AV30-03]). *Bottom:* Robert Morrow Kelly (photograph by Webster & Bro., Louisville, Kentucky; Dennis M. Keesee Collection).

John James Landram (post-war) (Z. F. Smith. *History of Kentucky.* Louisville, Kentucky, 1895).

Henry Clay Lilly

Private, Co. F, 14 KY Cavalry, Jan. 2, 1863. Colonel, 14 KY Cavalry, Feb. 13, 1863. Honorably mustered out, March 24, 1864.
  Born: Oct. 8, 1829 KY
  Died: April 17, 1900 Irvine, KY
  Occupation: Lawyer and judge
  Offices/Honors: Kentucky Senate, 1865–69. Circuit Court Judge, 1886–92.
  Miscellaneous: Resided Irvine, Estill Co., KY
  Buried: Old Irvine Cemetery, Irvine, KY
  References: Pension File and Military Service File, National Archives. Obituary, *Richmond Climax,* April 25, 1900. Elbridge C. Park. *History of Irvine and Estill County, Kentucky.* Lexington, KY, 1906. Ellen and Diane Rogers. *Cemetery Records of Estill County, KY.* Baltimore, MD, 1976.

Daniel Weisiger Lindsey

Colonel, 22 KY Infantry, Jan. 10, 1862. Commanded 2 Brigade, 3 Division, Sherman's Expeditionary Force, Dec. 14, 1862–Jan. 4, 1863. Commanded 2 Brigade, 2 Division, 1 Army Corps, Army of the Mississippi, Jan. 4–14, 1863. Commanded 2 Brigade, 9 Division, 13 Army Corps, Army of the Tennessee, Jan 14–Feb. 4, 1863 and May 1–July 28, 1863. Commanded 4 Brigade, 1 Division, 13 Army Corps, Army of the Tennessee, July 28–Aug. 7, 1863. Commanded 4 Brigade, 1 Division, 13 Army Corps, Army of the Gulf, Aug. 7–Sept. 23, 1863. Resigned Oct. 14, 1863, to accept

Henry Clay Lilly (post-war) (photograph by W. E. Singleton & Co., 123 Gay Street, Knoxville, TN; Eastern Kentucky University Special Collections and Archives, Richmond, Kentucky [1986-024-346]).

the position of Inspector General of Kentucky. Battle honors: Cumberland Gap Campaign, Chickasaw Bluffs, Arkansas Post, Vicksburg Campaign (Champion's Hill, Big Black River Bridge, Vicksburg), Jackson Campaign, Morgan's Raid into Kentucky.
  Born: Oct. 4, 1835 Frankfort, KY
  Died: Aug. 4, 1917 Frankfort, KY
  Education: Graduated Kentucky Military Institute, near Frankfort, KY, 1854. Graduated University of Louisville (KY) Law School, 1857.
  Occupation: Lawyer and banker
  Offices/Honors: Kentucky Inspector General, 1863–64. Kentucky Adjutant General, 1864–67.
  Miscellaneous: Resided Frankfort, Franklin Co., KY
  Buried: Frankfort Cemetery, Frankfort, KY (Section G, Lot 434)
  References: William H. Perrin, J. H. Battle and Gilbert C. Kniffin. *Kentucky: A History of the State.* 5th Edition. Louisville and Chicago, 1887. H. Levin, editor. *The Lawyers and Lawmakers of Kentucky.* Chicago, IL, 1897. *The Biographical Encyclo-*

pedia of Kentucky of the Dead and Living Men of the Nineteenth Century. Cincinnati, OH, 1878. Obituary, *Frankfort State Journal,* Aug. 5, 1917. Obituary, *Louisville Courier-Journal,* Aug. 5, 1917. Pension File and Military Service File, National Archives. William H. Powell, editor. *Officers of the Army and Navy (Volunteer) Who Served in the Civil War.* Philadelphia, PA, 1893. Benjamin F. Stevenson. *Letters from the Army.* Cincinnati, OH, 1884.

Smoloff Pallas Love

Lieutenant Colonel, 11 KY Infantry, Nov. 11, 1861. Colonel, 11 KY Infantry, July 1, 1863. Commanded 3 Brigade, 1 Division, Cavalry Corps, Army of the Ohio, Jan.–April 1864. Commanded 1 Brigade, 3 Division, 23 Army Corps, Department of the Ohio, Sept. 22–Oct. 22, 1864. Commanded 2 Brigade, 2 Division, District of Kentucky, 23 Army Corps, Department of the Ohio, Nov. 1–Dec. 17, 1864. Honorably mustered out, Dec. 17, 1864. Battle honors: Shiloh, East Tennessee Campaign, Knoxville Campaign, Atlanta Campaign.

Born: May 10, 1826 Garrard Co., KY
Died: March 26, 1903 Greenville, KY
Other Wars: Mexican War (Private, Co. H, 1 MO Mounted Volunteers)

Left, top: Daniel Weisiger Lindsey (Webster's Photograph Gallery, 475 Main Street, Louisville, Kentucky). *Left, bottom:* Daniel Weisiger Lindsey (as Adjutant General of Kentucky, 1865) (courtesy The Excelsior Brigade, Alexandria, Virginia). *Right, top:* Daniel Weisiger Lindsey (The National Archives [BA-29]).

Smoloff Pallas Love.

Occupation: School teacher and merchant before war. Lawyer and judge after war.
Offices/Honors: Muhlenberg County (KY) Judge, 1866–74
Miscellaneous: Resided South Carrollton, Muhlenberg Co., KY; and Greenville, Muhlenberg Co., KY, after 1866
Buried: Evergreen Cemetery, Greenville, KY
References: *The Biographical Encyclopedia of Kentucky of the Dead and Living Men of the Nineteenth Century.* Cincinnati, OH, 1878. Otto A. Rothert. *A History of Muhlenberg County.* Louisville, KY, 1913. Pension File and Military Service File, National Archives. *Who Was Who in America, 1897–1942.* Chicago, IL, 1942.

Charles Alexander Marshall

Colonel, 16 KY Infantry, Jan. 9, 1862. Resigned May 1, 1862, "my continued ill health (rheumatism) unfitting me for active duty." Battle honors: Ivy Mountain.
Born: May 2, 1809 Washington, KY
Died: Feb. 12, 1896 Washington, KY
Occupation: Farmer
Offices/Honors: Kentucky House of Representatives, 1840 and 1855–59
Miscellaneous: Resided Washington, Mason Co., KY. Nephew of U.S. Supreme Court Chief Justice John Marshall.
Buried: Marshall Family Cemetery, Washington, KY
References: E. Polk Johnson. *A History of Ken-

Charles Alexander Marshall (Webster & Bro. Photographic Gallery, Louisville, Kentucky).

tucky and Kentuckians. Chicago and New York, 1912. *The Biographical Encyclopedia of Kentucky of the Dead and Living Men of the Nineteenth Century.* Cincinnati, OH, 1878. William M. Paxton. *The Paxtons.* Platte City, MO, 1903. William M. Paxton. *The Marshall Family.* Cincinnati, OH, 1885. William E. Connelley and E. M. Coulter. *History of Kentucky.* Chicago and New York, 1922. Obituary, *Maysville Daily Public Ledger,* Feb. 13, 1896. Obituary, *Maysville Evening Bulletin,* Feb. 13, 1896. Pension File and Military Service File, National Archives.

Cicero Maxwell

Lieutenant Colonel, 26 KY Infantry, March 5, 1862. Colonel, 26 KY Infantry, June 20, 1862. Commanded Post of Russellville, KY, District of Western Kentucky, Department of the Ohio, Feb.–March 1863. Commanded Post of Bowling Green, KY, 2 Division, 23 Army Corps, Department of the Ohio, June–Sept. 1863. Commanded District of Southwestern Kentucky, 1 Division, 23 Army Corps, Department of the Ohio, Oct. 1863–Jan. 1864 and March 1864. Commanded 2 Brigade, 2 Division, District of Kentucky, 23 Army Corps, Department of the Ohio, April 10–July 5 and Sept. 12–Nov. 1, 1864. Resigned Jan. 12, 1865, due to "long continued ill health, which is constantly

Cicero Maxwell (Wm. Bryan, Photographer, Russellville, Kentucky).

growing worse, with no prospect of permanent improvement while I remain in the army." Battle honors: Shiloh, Morgan's First Kentucky Raid, Nashville.
Born: Nov. 21, 1831 KY
Died: Feb. 17, 1865 Bowling Green, KY
Occupation: Lawyer
Miscellaneous: Resided Hartford, Ohio Co., KY. His mother-in-law, Sarah Morton, was a sister of Colonel Quintus C. Shanks (12 KY Cavalry).
Buried: Old Hartford Cemetery (also called Old Render), Hartford, KY
References: Pension File and Military Service File, National Archives. Letters Received, Commission Branch, Adjutant General's Office, File M1567(CB)1864, National Archives. McDowell A. Fogle. *Fogle's Papers: A History of Ohio County, Kentucky.* Hartford, KY, 1981. Thomas Speed, Robert M. Kelly, and Alfred Pirtle. *The Union Regiments of Kentucky.* Louisville, KY, 1897.

Reuben May

Lieutenant Colonel, 8 KY Infantry, Jan. 15, 1862. Shell wound abdomen, Stone's River, TN, Jan. 2, 1863. Colonel, 7 KY Infantry, May 13, 1863. Honorably mustered out, Oct. 5, 1864. Battle honors: Stone's River, Vicksburg Campaign, Jackson Campaign.

Reuben May (post-war) (courtesy Dale and Sharon Sternberg).

Born: June 23, 1815 Pike Co., KY
Died: Sept. 26, 1902 near Springville, WI
Occupation: Farmer
Offices/Honors: Wisconsin General Assembly, 1870 and 1872
Miscellaneous: Resided Manchester, Clay Co., KY, before war; and Springville, Vernon Co., WI, after war
Buried: Springville Cemetery, Springville, WI
References: Dale & Sharon Sternberg and Fred T. May. *I Will Uphold the Flag: The Life of Colonel Reuben May, 1815–1902.* Baltimore, MD, 2004. *History of Vernon County, WI.* Springfield, IL, 1884. Obituary, *Vernon County Censor,* Oct. 1, 1902. Pension File and Military Service File, National Archives. Robert C. Dunn, "Typical Southern Homestead of Col. Reuben May Recalls Many Incidents of His Life," *LaCrosse Tribune and Leader Press,* March 29, 1931. *Vernon County Heritage.* Viroqua, WI, 1994. Thomas J. Wright. *History of the Eighth Regiment Kentucky Vol. Inf., During Its Three Years Campaigns.* St. Joseph, MO, 1880. Letters Received, Volunteer Service Branch, Adjutant General's Office, File M1076(VS)1863, National Archives.

John Hardin McHenry, Jr.

Colonel, 17 KY Infantry, Dec. 31, 1861. GSW right arm, Shiloh, TN, April 6, 1862. Dismissed

John Hardin McHenry, Jr. (photograph by Webster & Bro., Louisville, Kentucky; Roger D. Hunt Collection, USAMHI [RG98S-CWP80.67]).

Dec. 4, 1862, for issuing an order to his regiment to return run-away slaves to their owners, in violation of the Additional Article of War, dated March 13, 1862, without first requiring the owners to take an oath that they had neither borne arms against the United States, nor given aid or comfort to the enemy. Battle honors: Fort Donelson, Shiloh, Corinth.

Born: Feb. 21, 1832 Hartford, KY
Died: July 8, 1893 Owensboro, KY
Education: Attended Hanover (IN) College. Attended Centre College, Danville, KY. Attended U.S. Military Academy, West Point, NY (Class of 1855). Graduated University of Louisville (KY) Law School, 1856.
Occupation: Lawyer
Offices/Honors: Postmaster, Owensboro, KY, 1891–93
Miscellaneous: Resided Owensboro, Daviess Co., KY
Buried: Elmwood Cemetery, Owensboro, KY
References: H. Levin, editor. *The Lawyers and Lawmakers of Kentucky.* Chicago, IL, 1897. *Biographical Cyclopedia of the Commonwealth of Kentucky.* Chicago and Philadelphia, 1896. Obituary,

John Hardin McHenry, Jr. (post-war) (H. Levin, ed. *The Lawyers and Lawmakers of Kentucky.* Chicago, Illinois, 1897).

Louisville Courier-Journal, July 9, 1893. Letters Received, Volunteer Service Branch, Adjutant General's Office, File Y107(VS)1863, National Archives. Hugh O. Potter, "Colonel John H. McHenry, Jr., Union Soldier — Owensboro Lawyer," *Filson Club History Quarterly,* Vol. 39, No. 2 (April 1965). "Dismissal of a Union Officer," *New York Times,* Dec. 13, 1862. John Blackburn. *A Hundred Miles, A Hundred Heartbreaks.* N.p., 1972. Military Service File, National Archives. A. V. Phillips. *The Lott Family in America.* Trenton, NJ, 1942. Obituary, *Hartford Republican,* July 14, 1893.

Samuel McKee

Captain, Co. A, 3 KY Infantry, Oct. 8, 1861. Major, 3 KY Infantry, May 6, 1862. Lieutenant Colonel, 3 KY Infantry, July 13, 1862. Colonel, 3 KY Infantry, Dec. 7, 1862. GSW forehead, Stone's River, TN, Dec. 31, 1862. Battle honors: Stone's River.

Born: Nov. 10, 1832 near Lancaster, KY
Died: Dec. 31, 1862 KIA Stone's River, TN
Education: Graduated Centre College, Danville, KY, 1853. Graduated University of Louisville (KY) Law School, 1859.
Occupation: School teacher and lawyer
Miscellaneous: Resided Danville, Boyle Co., KY; and Keokuk, Lee Co., IA
Buried: Cave Hill Cemetery, Louisville, KY (Section E, Lot 111)
References: *General Catalogue of the Centre Col-*

Samuel McKee (William B. Hazen. *A Narrative of Military Service*. Boston, Massachusetts, 1885).

lege of Kentucky. Danville, KY, 1890. Hambleton Tapp and James C. Klotter, editors. *The Union, the Civil War and John W. Tuttle*. Frankfort, KY, 1980. William B. Hazen. *A Narrative of Military Service*. Boston, MA, 1885. George Wilson McKee. *The McKees of Virginia and Kentucky*. Pittsburgh, PA, 1891. Pension File and Military Service File, National Archives.

Thomas McKinster

Captain, Co. D, 14 KY Infantry, Nov. 18, 1861. Resigned June 8, 1862, due to "the enfeebled state of my health which renders me unfit for duty." Colonel, 68 KY Enrolled Militia, May 21, 1864. Honorably mustered out, June 22, 1864.

Born: May 4, 1821 Lawrence Co., KY
Died: April 26, 1881 near Grayson, KY
Occupation: Farmer
Miscellaneous: Resided Louisa, Lawrence Co., KY, to 1872; and Grayson, Carter Co., KY
Buried: Place of burial unknown
References: Pension File and Military Service File, National Archives. Regina Tackett, Patricia Jackson, and Janice Thompson. *History of Lawrence County, KY*. Dallas, TX, 1991. John David Preston. *The Civil War in the Big Sandy Valley of Kentucky*. Second Edition. Baltimore, MD, 2008. Letters Received, Volunteer Service Branch, Adjutant General's Office, File M3640(VS)1864, National Archives.

Top: Leonidas Metcalfe (photograph by Whitaker & Co., No. 814 Chestnut Street, Philadelphia, Pennsylvania; Kentucky Historical Society [Thomas Metcalfe Collection, 89M02]). *Bottom:* Leonidas Metcalfe (courtesy Kalawakua Mayer).

Leonidas Metcalfe

Colonel, 7 KY Cavalry, Aug. 16, 1862. Commission cancelled, Aug. 30, 1862, having left his regiment on the battlefield of Richmond, KY, on Aug. 30, stating that he no longer wished to have any connection with the regiment, due to its disgraceful conduct in the action at Big Hill, KY, on Aug. 23, 1862. Battle honors: Ivy Mountain, Morgan's First Kentucky Raid, Big Hill, Richmond.

Born: March 19, 1819 Nicholas Co., KY
Died: June 7, 1868 Cincinnati, OH
Education: Attended U.S. Military Academy, West Point, NY (Class of 1840)
Other Wars: Mexican War (Captain, 3 KY Infantry)
Occupation: Farmer and commission merchant
Miscellaneous: Resided Headquarters, Nicholas Co., KY; and Cincinnati, OH. Son of former Kentucky Governor Thomas Metcalfe. Killed William T. Casto, former Maysville (KY) mayor, May 8, 1862, in one of the last duels fought in Kentucky.
Buried: Spring Grove Cemetery, Cincinnati, OH (Section 99, Lot 106)
References: J. Winston Coleman, Jr. *Famous Kentucky Duels*. Lexington, KY, 1969. Obituary, *Cincinnati Daily Gazette*, June 9, 1868. Joan W. Conley, compiler. *History of Nicholas County, KY.* Carlisle, KY, 1976. D. Warren Lambert. *When the Ripe Pears Fell: The Battle of Richmond, Kentucky.* Richmond, KY, 1995. B. Kevin Bennett, "The Battle of Richmond, Kentucky: 'A Victory Brilliant and Complete,'" *Blue & Gray Magazine*, Vol. 25, No. 6 (2009). *The War of the Rebellion: A Compilation of the Official Records of the Union and Confederate Armies.* (Series 1, Vol. 16, Part 1, pp. 884–885) Washington, DC, 1886. J. Winston Coleman, Jr. *The Casto-Metcalfe Duel.* Lexington, KY, 1950. Letters Received, Volunteer Service Branch, Adjutant General's Office, File M536(VS)1870, National Archives. Military Service File, National Archives. Thomas Metcalfe Collection, Kentucky Historical Society, Frankfort, KY.

Hubbard Kavanaugh Milward

1 Lieutenant, Adjutant, 18 KY Infantry, Dec. 11, 1861. Major, 18 KY Infantry, Jan. 15, 1863. Lieutenant Colonel, 18 KY Infantry, Feb. 7, 1863. *Colonel*, 18 KY Infantry, Dec. 19, 1863. Commanded Post of Ringgold, GA, May–Aug. 1864 Commanded 3 Brigade, 3 Division, 14 Army Corps, Army of the Cumberland, Oct. 25–Nov. 16, 1864 and March 29–April 9, 1865. Commanded 1 Brigade, 3 Division, 14 Army Corps, Army of the Cumberland, June 9–July 18, 1865. Honorably mustered out, July 18, 1865. Bvt. Colonel, USV, March 13, 1865, for gallantry and good conduct as commander of his regiment. Battle honors: Chickamauga, Atlanta Campaign, Savannah Campaign, Campaign of the Carolinas.

Born: Nov. 23, 1835 Lexington, KY

Hubbard Kavanaugh Milward (photograph by Webster & Bro., Louisville, Kentucky; courtesy Henry Deeks).

Hubbard Kavanaugh Milward (Margaret T. Macdonald Collection, USAMHI [RG98S-CWP131.78]).

Died: April 19, 1892 Lexington, KY
Education: Attended Transylvania University, Lexington, KY
Occupation: Harness maker before war. Journalist, bookkeeper, and merchant after war.
Offices/Honors: Postmaster, Lexington, KY, 1876–87
Miscellaneous: Resided Lexington, Fayette Co., KY; and Louisville, Jefferson Co., KY, 1869–71
Buried: Lexington Cemetery, Lexington, KY (Section R, Lot 5)
References: Margaret T. Macdonald. *The Milward Family of Lexington, KY, 1803–1969.* Dallas, TX, 1970. Robert Peter. *History of Fayette County, KY, with an Outline Sketch of the Blue Grass Region.* Chicago, IL, 1882. *Society of the Army of the Cumberland. Twenty-Fourth Reunion, Cleveland, OH, 1893.* Cincinnati, OH, 1894. Obituary, *Lexington Morning Transcript,* April 20, 1892. Pension File and Military Service File, National Archives. Letters Received, Volunteer Service Branch, Adjutant General's Office, File M2180(VS)1864, National Archives.

David Alexander Mims

Captain, Co. C, 14 KY Infantry, Oct. 25, 1861. Lieutenant Colonel, 39 KY Infantry, Jan. 21, 1863. Colonel, 39 KY Infantry, Dec. 22, 1863. Commanded 2 Brigade, 1 Division, District of Kentucky, 23 Army Corps, Department of the Ohio, June 1864. Commanded Post of Louisa (KY), District of Kentucky, 23 Army Corps, Department of the Ohio, July 1864–Jan. 1865. Commanded Post of Louisa (KY), 1 Division, Department of Kentucky, Feb.–July 1865. Honorably mustered out, Sept. 15, 1865. Battle honors: Morgan's Raid into Kentucky (Cynthiana).
Born: April 18, 1833 Pikeville, KY
Died: Aug. 29, 1901 Garden City, KS
Education: Attended Emory and Henry College, Emory, VA
Occupation: Tanner before war. Saddler, merchant and newspaper editor after war.
Offices/Honors: Register of Deeds, Finney Co., KS, at his death
Miscellaneous: Resided Catlettsburg, Boyd Co., KY, to 1884; and Garden City, Finney Co., KS
Buried: Valley View Cemetery, Garden City, KS (Section C, Lot 331)
References: William E. Connelley. *A Standard History of Kansas and Kansans.* Revised Edition. Chicago, IL, 1919. Katherine K. Powell and Patricia D. Smith, compilers. *Finney County (KS) Obituary Abstracts and Death Notices.* Garden City, KS, 1988. Pension File and Military Service File, National Archives. Obituary, *Garden City Herald,* Aug. 31, 1901. *Semi-centennial Catalogue and Historical Reg-*

David Alexander Mims (post-war) (Donald H. Corson, Jr., Collection, USAMHI [RG98S-CWP 208.9]).

ister of Emory and Henry College, Washington County, VA, 1837–1887. Tazewell Court House, VA, 1887.

Laban Theodore Moore

Colonel, 14 KY Infantry, Dec. 10, 1861. Resigned Jan. 1, 1862.
Born: Jan. 13, 1829 Wayne Co., WV
Died: Nov. 9, 1892 Catlettsburg, KY
Education: Attended Transylvania University Law School, Lexington, KY. Attended Marietta (OH) College.
Occupation: Lawyer
Offices/Honors: U.S. House of Representatives, 1859–61. Kentucky Senate, 1881–83.
Miscellaneous: Resided Louisa, Lawrence Co., KY, to 1863; and Catlettsburg, Boyd Co., KY. Brother-in-law of Bvt. Brig. Gen. George W. Gallup.
Buried: Ashland Cemetery, Ashland, KY (Section 1, Lot 14)
References: H. Levin, editor. *The Lawyers and Lawmakers of Kentucky.* Chicago, IL, 1897. *The Biographical Encyclopedia of Kentucky of the Dead and Living Men of the Nineteenth Century.* Cincinnati, OH, 1878. E. Polk Johnson. *A History of Kentucky and Kentuckians.* Chicago and New York, 1912. William Ely. *The Big Sandy Valley: History of the People and Country from the Earliest Settlement to the Present Time.* Catlettsburg, KY, 1887. Z. F.

Laban Theodore Moore (courtesy Mary Moore Young).

Marcellus Mundy (photograph by Webster & Bro., Louisville, Kentucky; courtesy Henry Deeks).

Smith. *History of Kentucky.* Louisville, KY, 1895. James L. Harrison, compiler. *Biographical Directory of the American Congress, 1774–1949.* Washington, DC, 1950. Obituary, *Mount Sterling Advocate,* Nov. 15, 1892. Jack L. Dickinson. *Wayne County, West Virginia, in the Civil War.* Huntington, WV, 2003. Military Service File, National Archives.

Marcellus Mundy

Colonel, 23 KY Infantry, Dec. 16, 1861. Commanded Post of Pulaski (TN), District of the Ohio, June 1862. Commanded Post of Louisville (KY), District of Western Kentucky, Department of the Ohio, Dec. 1862–Dec. 1863. Suffering from "pulmonary apoplexy of the left lung," he resigned Dec. 31, 1863, "being physically incapable of doing field duty." Battle honors: Morgan's Ohio Raid.

Born: May 16, 1830 Owen County, KY
Died: Feb. 22, 1901 Louisville, KY
Education: Attended Transylvania University, Lexington, KY
Occupation: Lawyer
Miscellaneous: Resided Philadelphia, PA, before war; and Louisville, Jefferson Co., KY, after war
Buried: Cave Hill Cemetery, Louisville, KY (Section 1, Lot 88)
References: Bryan S. Bush, "Marcellus Mundy, 23rd Kentucky: A Colonel with a Conscience," *North South Trader's Civil War,* Vol. 30, No. 6 (2004). Obituary, *Louisville Courier-Journal,* Feb. 23, 1901. Pension File and Military Service File, National Archives. J. Stoddard Johnston, editor. *Memorial History of Louisville.* Chicago, IL, 1896.

Thomas Prather Nicholas

Major, 2 KY Cavalry, Sept. 9, 1861. Colonel, 2 KY Cavalry, Feb. 8, 1863. Resigned Dec. 13, 1863, citing his "incapacity to handle the regiment in the field and control or provide for it in camp," his father's "rapidly failing health," and "two years and three months in the service ... and worn out with the constant anxiety and worry." Battle honors: Stone's River, Tullahoma Campaign, Chickamauga, Chattanooga Campaign.

Born: July 25, 1833 Louisville, KY
Died: Jan. 26, 1870 Louisville, KY
Education: Graduated Yale University, New Haven, CT, 1853. Graduated University of Louisville (KY) Law School, 1856.
Occupation: Lawyer
Miscellaneous: Resided Louisville, Jefferson Co., KY
Buried: Cave Hill Cemetery, Louisville, KY (Section G, Lot 59)
References: Abner L. Train, compiler. *Yale College, Class of 1853.* New Haven, CT, 1883. Obituary, *Louisville Courier-Journal,* Jan. 27 and 29, 1870. Military Service File, National Archives.

George W. Northup

Captain, Co. B, 23 KY Infantry, Dec. 8, 1861. Major, 23 KY Infantry, April 18, 1863. Lieutenant Colonel, 23 KY Infantry, July 28, 1864. Shell wound right hip, near Atlanta, GA, Aug. 1864. *Colonel*, 23 KY Infantry, Nov. 16, 1864. Honorably mustered out, Dec. 27, 1865. Battle honors: Stone's River, Chickamauga, Atlanta Campaign, Franklin, Nashville.

Born: Oct. 1840 OH
Died: May 17, 1906 Dayton, OH
Occupation: Farmer before war. Railroad passenger agent after war.
Miscellaneous: Resided Newport, Campbell Co., KY, to 1867; Louisville, Jefferson Co., KY, 1867–88; Cincinnati, OH, and NHDVS, Dayton, OH, after 1888
Buried: Dayton National Cemetery, Dayton, OH (Section P, Row 24, Grave 15)
References: Pension File and Military Service File, National Archives. Letters Received, Volunteer Service Branch, Adjutant General's Office, File N662(VS)1865, National Archives.

Weden O'Neal

Lieutenant Colonel, 55 KY Infantry, Dec. 27, 1864. Colonel, 55 KY Infantry, March 23, 1865. Honorably mustered out, Sept. 19, 1865.

Born: April 1839 Boone Co., KY
Died: Sept. 10, 1906 near Covington, KY
Education: Attended Transylvania University, Lexington, KY
Occupation: Merchant before war. Lawyer after war.
Offices/Honors: U.S. Marshal, District of Kentucky, 1877
Miscellaneous: Resided Verona, Boone Co., KY, before war; Crittenden, Grant Co., KY, 1865–69; and Covington, Kenton Co., KY, after 1869
Buried: Highland Cemetery, Fort Mitchell, KY (Section 3, Lot 73)
References: Obituary, *Cincinnati Enquirer*, Sept. 11, 1906. William E. Connelley and E. M. Coulter. *History of Kentucky*. Chicago and New York, 1922. Pension File and Military Service File, National Archives. Letters Received, Volunteer Service Branch, Adjutant General's Office, File O683(VS)1865, National Archives.

Charles David Pennebaker

Colonel, 27 KY Infantry, Oct. 5, 1861. Commanded Post of Munfordville (KY), 2 Division, 23 Army Corps, Department of the Ohio, June–Aug. 1863. Commanded 1 Brigade, 4 Division, 23 Army Corps, Department of the Ohio, Oct. 10–Nov. 3, 1863. Commanded 3 Brigade, 1 Division, Cavalry Corps, Department of the Ohio, Nov. 1863–Jan. 1864. Commanded 1 Division, Cavalry Corps, Department of the Ohio, March–April 1864. Resigned April 10, 1864, in order to "accept the agency for the state of Kentucky to be located in Washington to attend to the interests of deceased and discharged soldiers." Battle honors: Corinth, Morgan's Ohio Raid, Knoxville Campaign.

Born: Nov. 3, 1825 Nelson Co., KY
Died: June 21, 1888 Washington, DC
Other Wars: Mexican War (2 Lieutenant, Co. C, 4 KY Infantry)
Occupation: Lawyer and pension claim agent
Offices/Honors: Kentucky House of Representatives, 1857–59. Kentucky Senate, 1859–61. Kentucky State Military Agent, Washington, DC, 1864–65.
Miscellaneous: Resided Louisville, Jefferson Co., KY, before war; and Washington, DC, after war
Buried: Cave Hill Cemetery, Louisville, KY (Section P, Lot 87, unmarked)

George W. Northup (A. S. Morse, Photographer, Department of the Cumberland, Branch of Hd. Qrs., 25 Cedar Street, Nashville, Tennessee).

Charles David Pennebaker (photograph by Webster & Bro., Louisville, Kentucky; courtesy Everitt Bowles).

Charles David Pennebaker (as officer in Kentucky State Guard, 1860) (The Filson Historical Society, Louisville, Kentucky [PC11.0055]).

References: Pension File and Military Service File, National Archives. Obituary, *Louisville Courier-Journal*, June 22, 1888. Obituary, *Washington Evening Star*, June 21, 1888. Letters Received, Volunteer Service Branch, Adjutant General's Office, Files P88(VS)1863 and P1325(VS)1864, National Archives.

Curran Pope

Colonel, 15 KY Infantry, Dec. 14, 1861. Commanded 17 Brigade, 3 Division, Army of the Ohio, March 22–28, 1862. Commanded 17 Brigade, 3 Division, 1 Army Corps, Army of the Ohio, Oct. 8, 1862. GSW right shoulder, Perryville, KY, Oct. 8, 1862. Battle honors: Perryville.

Born: June 30, 1813 Louisville, KY
Died: Nov. 5, 1862 Danville, KY (typhoid fever)
Education: Graduated U.S. Military Academy, West Point, NY, 1834
Occupation: Lawyer
Offices/Honors: Clerk of the Court of Common Pleas, Jefferson Co., KY, 1838–61
Miscellaneous: Resided Louisville, Jefferson Co., KY. Married step-sister, Matilda Prather Jacob, of Colonel Richard T. Jacob (9 KY Cavalry). In a letter of condolence to his widow, Major Gen. William T. Sherman commented, "Among all the men I have ever met in the progress of this unnatural war, I cannot recall one in whose every act and expression was so manifest the good and true

Curran Pope (Roger D. Hunt Collection, USA MHI [RG98S-CWP160.38]).

man; one who so well filled the type of the Kentucky gentleman."

Buried: Cave Hill Cemetery, Louisville, KY (Section G, Lots 64–66)

References: J. Stoddard Johnston, editor. *Memorial History of Louisville*. Chicago, IL, 1896. Kirk C. Jenkins. *The Battle Rages Higher: The Union's Fifteenth Kentucky Infantry*. Lexington, KY, 2003. William H. Perrin, J. H. Battle and Gilbert C. Kniffin. *Kentucky: A History of the State*. 8th Edition. Louisville and Chicago, 1888. Letters Received, Volunteer Service Branch, Adjutant General's Office, File P19(VS)1862, National Archives. George W. Cullum. *Biographical Register of the Officers and Graduates of the United States Military Academy*. Third Edition. Boston and New York, 1891. Nathaniel Field. *A Genealogy of the Pope Family of Kentucky*. Jeffersonville, IN, 1879. Pension File and Military Service File, National Archives.

Burgess Preston

Colonel, 65 KY Enrolled Militia, May 21, 1864. Honorably mustered out, June 21, 1864.

Born: 1817? Floyd Co., KY

Died: Dec. 5, 1875 Johnson Co., KY

Occupation: Farmer

Miscellaneous: Resided Paintsville, Johnson Co., KY

Buried: Place of burial unknown

References: William E. Connelley and E. M. Coulter. *History of Kentucky*. Chicago and New York, 1922. C. Mitchel Hall. *Johnson County Kentucky: A History of the County, and Genealogy of Its People Up to the Year 1927*. Louisville, KY, 1928. C. Mitchel Hall. *Jenny Wiley Country: A History of "Jenny Wiley Country" and Genealogy of Its People Up to the Year 1972*. Kingsport, TN, 1972. John David Preston. *The Civil War in the Big Sandy Valley of Kentucky*. Second Edition. Baltimore, MD, 2008. http://www.suddenlink.net/pages/fpreston/bdnathan.htm.

Lawrence H. Rousseau

Captain, Co. C, 12 KY Infantry, Nov. 3, 1861. Lieutenant Colonel, 12 KY Infantry, Aug. 12, 1862. *Colonel*, 12 KY Infantry, April 21, 1864. Commanded 2 Brigade, 3 Division, 23 Army Corps, Department of North Carolina, June 1865. Honorably mustered out, July 11, 1865. Battle honors: Mill Springs, Atlanta Campaign, Franklin, Nashville, Campaign of the Carolinas.

Born: Nov. 1829 KY

Died: Dec. 1, 1910 Somerset, KY

Other Wars: Mexican War (Private, Co. H, 4 KY Infantry)

Occupation: Hotelkeeper and farmer before war. Lumber merchant, farmer, and insurance agent after war.

Miscellaneous: Resided Creelsboro, Russell Co., KY, to 1871; Edmonton, Metcalfe Co., KY; and Somerset, Pulaski Co., KY

Buried: Somerset City Cemetery, Somerset, KY (Section 4)

References: Pension File and Military Service File, National Archives. Obituary, *Adair County News*, Dec. 7, 1910.

William Thompson Scott

Lieutenant Colonel, 3 KY Infantry, Oct. 8, 1861. Colonel, 3 KY Infantry, July 14, 1862. "In justice to the officers and men I have the honor to command," he resigned Dec. 7, 1862, since "I am satisfied I am not qualified to hold the responsible position of colonel." In forwarding his resignation, Brig. Gen. Milo S. Hascall commented, "He is an excellent officer in some respects and an estimable gentleman, thoroughly loyal, but entirely deficient as a tactician."

Born: June 28, 1833 Lexington, KY

Died: Jan. 2, 1875 Frankfort, KY

Occupation: Trader before war. Farmer after war.

Offices/Honors: Kentucky Paymaster General, 1863–65

William Thompson Scott (photograph by Webster & Bro., Louisville, Kentucky).

William Thompson Scott (photograph by Webster & Bro., Louisville, Kentucky; L. M. Strayer Collection).

Miscellaneous: Resided Lexington, Fayette Co., KY; and Frankfort, Franklin Co., KY. Brother-in-law of Colonel John Mason Brown (45 KY Infantry). Brother-in-law of Colonel Ethelbert L. Dudley (21 KY Infantry).

Buried: Frankfort Cemetery, Frankfort, KY (Section N, Lot 190)

References: Obituary, *Weekly Kentucky Yeoman*, Jan. 6, 1875. Hambleton Tapp and James C. Klotter, editors. *The Union, the Civil War and John W. Tuttle.* Frankfort, KY, 1980. *Biographical Cyclopedia of the Commonwealth of Kentucky.* Chicago and Philadelphia, 1896. Obituary, *Kentucky Gazette*, Jan. 6, 1875. Military Service File, National Archives.

Thomas Duncan Sedgewick

Captain, Co. B, 2 KY Infantry, June 3, 1861. Major, 2 KY Infantry, June 28, 1861. Colonel, 2 KY Infantry, Jan. 27, 1862. Shell wound of thigh, Shiloh, TN, April 7, 1862. Commanded 22 Brigade, 4 Division, Army of the Ohio, April 13–May 30, 1862. Commanded 1 Brigade, 2 Division, 21 Army Corps, Army of the Cumberland, July 15–Aug. 17, 1863. Commanded 1 Brigade, 1 Division, 4 Army Corps, Army of the Cumberland, Oct. 10–Nov. 21, 1863. Honorably mustered out, June 19, 1864. Colonel, 114 USCT, July 3, 1864. Commanded Post of Camp Nelson (KY), District of

Thomas Duncan Sedgewick (Library of Congress [LC-DIG-cwpb-07297]).

Thomas Duncan Sedgewick (photograph by Webster & Bro., Louisville, Kentucky; courtesy Everitt Bowles).

Thomas Duncan Sedgewick (standing, with Colonel David A. Enyart, 1 Kentucky Infantry) (Roger D. Hunt Collection, USAMHI [RG98S-CWP58.45]).

Kentucky, 23 Army Corps, Department of the Ohio, Sept.–Nov. 1864. Commanded 2 Brigade, 1 Division, 25 Army Corps, Department of Virginia, March 3–28, 1865 and April 18–Sept. 22, 1865. Commanded Post of Ringgold Barracks (TX), Department of the Gulf, March–July 1866. Commanded Sub-District of the Rio Grande, Department of the Gulf, Sept.–Dec. 1866. Honorably mustered out, April 2, 1867. Battle honors: Shiloh, Corinth, Stone's River, Chickamauga.

Born: 1837? Louisville, KY
Died: April 26, 1879 New York City, NY (found dead in a city park in an intoxicated condition)
Occupation: Mercantile clerk before war. Chief Clerk, U.S. Corps of Engineers, Louisville, KY, 1869–71. U.S. Treasury Department and U.S. War Department clerk in later years.
Miscellaneous: Resided Louisville, Jefferson Co., KY; New Albany, Floyd Co., IN; and Washington, DC. Brother-in-law of Colonel William W. Tuley (7 IN Legion).
Buried: Cypress Hills National Cemetery, Brooklyn, NY (Section 2, Grave 12172, misidentified as T. B. Sedgwick, removed from City Cemetery, Hart's Island, New York Harbor, June 9, 1941)

References: Obituary, *New Albany Ledger-Standard,* April 28, 1879. Obituary, *New York Times,* April 27, 1879. Obituary, *Louisville Courier-Journal,* April 29, 1879. Letters Received, Volunteer Service Branch, Adjutant General's Office, File S1686(VS)1862, National Archives. Letters Received, Appointment, Commission and Personal Branch, Adjutant General's Office, File 3715(ACP) 1873, National Archives. Pension File and Military Service File, National Archives. Letters Received, Colored Troops Branch, Adjutant General's Office, File F163(CT)1864, National Archives. Richard D. Sears. *Camp Nelson, Kentucky: A Civil War History.* Lexington, KY, 2002. William F. Tuley. *The Tuley Family Memoirs.* New Albany, IN, 1906. http://sedgwick.org/na/families/barnabas1810/sedgwick-thomas1837.html.

George Taliaferro Shackelford

1 Lieutenant, Adjutant, 6 KY Infantry, Dec. 4, 1861. Major, 6 KY Infantry, May 18, 1862. Lieutenant Colonel, 6 KY Infantry, Jan. 1, 1863. Colonel, 6 KY Infantry, Sept. 1, 1863. GSW right arm, Chickamauga, GA, Sept. 19, 1863. Honorably discharged, Aug. 22, 1864, on account of physical disability from wounds received in action. Battle honors: Shiloh, Chickamauga.

Born: Feb. 28, 1837 Springfield, IL

George Taliaferro Shackelford (Landy, Photographer, 68 & 70 Fourth St., opposite Pikes Opera House, Cincinnati, Ohio).

Died: Sept. 21, 1912 Denver, CO

Occupation: Deputy circuit court clerk and Acting Sheriff before war. Farmer and bookkeeper after war. Real estate agent and manager of lubricating oil company after moving to Colorado.

Miscellaneous: Resided Richmond, Madison Co., KY, to 1864; Ironton, Lawrence Co., OH, 1864–67; LaGrange Furnace, Stewart Co., TN, 1867–69; Mount Sterling, Montgomery Co., KY, 1869–82; and Denver, CO, after 1882. Grandfather of Academy Award winning actor Melvyn Douglas.

Buried: Riverside Cemetery, Denver, CO (Block 3, Lot 148)

References: Obituary, *Rocky Mountain News*, Sept. 22, 1912. Pension File and Military Service File, National Archives. Joseph R. Reinhart. *A History of the 6th Kentucky Volunteer Infantry U.S.: The Boys Who Feared No Noise.* Louisville, KY, 2000. Obituary, *Mount Sterling Advocate*, Oct. 2, 1912. Letters Received, Volunteer Service Branch, Adjutant General's Office, File J571(VS)1864, National Archives. William N. Byers. *Encyclopedia of Biography of Colorado; History of Colorado.* Chicago, IL, 1901. http://familytreemaker.genealogy.com/users/s/h/a/William-O-Shackleford/GENE1-0076.html.

Quintus Cincinnatus Shanks

Colonel, 12 KY Cavalry, Oct. 11, 1862. Resigned Feb. 14, 1863, "in consequence of ill health and in consideration of my age (52 years) and feeling confident that a more competent man than myself can be found to assume command of my regiment." Battle honors: Morgan's Second Kentucky Raid.

Born: April 1, 1811 near Shepardsville, KY

Died: July 12, 1900 Hartford, KY

Occupation: Farmer, merchant and public office holder

Offices/Honors: Sheriff, Ohio Co., KY, 1841–47 and 1857–61. Kentucky House of Representatives, 1849. Assistant Assessor of Internal Revenue, 1870.

Miscellaneous: Resided Beaver Dam, Ohio Co., KY; and Hartford, Ohio Co., KY. His sister, Sarah Morton, was mother-in-law of Colonel Cicero Maxwell (26 KY Infantry).

Buried: Oakwood Cemetery, Hartford, KY (Section 2)

References: McDowell A. Fogle. *Fogle's Papers: A History of Ohio County, Kentucky.* Hartford, KY, 1981. Obituary, *Hartford Republican*, July 13, 1900. Pension File and Military Service File, National Archives. Obituary, *Hartford Herald*, July 18, 1900.

Amos Shinkle

Colonel, 41 KY Enrolled Militia, Sept. 4, 1862. Honorably mustered out, Oct. 4, 1862.

Amos Shinkle (post-war) (Louisa J. and Charles L. Abbott. *The Shinkle Genealogy, Comprising the Descendants of Philipp Carl Schenckel, 1717–1897.* Cincinnati, Ohio, 1897).

Born: Aug. 11, 1818 near Higginsport, OH

Died: Nov. 13, 1892 Covington, KY

Occupation: Coal merchant and steamboat builder before war. Banker and philanthropist after war.

Miscellaneous: Resided Covington, Kenton Co., KY. Best known as the prime mover in the construction of the Cincinnati and Covington Suspension Bridge.

Buried: Highland Cemetery, Fort Mitchell, KY (Section 1, Lots 6–11)

References: *Biographical Cyclopedia and Portrait Gallery with an Historical Sketch of the State of Ohio.* Vol. 6. Cincinnati, OH, 1895. Obituary, *Cincinnati Enquirer*, Nov. 14, 1892. *The Biographical Encyclopedia of Kentucky of the Dead and Living Men of the Nineteenth Century.* Cincinnati, OH, 1878. Paul A. Tenkotte and James C. Claypool, editors. *The Encyclopedia of Northern Kentucky.* Lexington, KY, 2009. Louisa J. and Charles L. Abbott. *The Shinkle Genealogy, Comprising the Descendants of Philipp Carl Schenckel, 1717–1897.* Cincinnati, OH, 1897. Robert R. Doherty. *Representative Methodists.* New York City, 1888. John Boh, "The Amos Shinkle Estate," *Papers of the Kenton County Historical Society*, Volume 1, 1990. *Sesqui-Centennial Souvenir Program, City of Covington, KY, 1815–1965.* Covington, KY, 1965.

William H. Spencer

1 Lieutenant, Adjutant, 3 KY Infantry, Oct. 8, 1861. Major, 3 KY Infantry, July 13, 1862. Commanded Post of Louisville (KY), District of Louisville, Department of the Ohio, Sept.–Nov. 1862. Lieutenant Colonel, 3 KY Infantry, Dec. 7, 1862. Colonel, 3 KY Infantry, Jan. 1, 1863. Commanded 1 Brigade, 1 Division, 21 Army Corps, Army of the Cumberland, Jan. 1863. Suffering from "chronic cystitis (inflammation of the urinary bladder) ... for the past six months ... and unable to return to my command," he resigned April 8, 1863, "from a sense of justice to myself, my country, and I believe, the good of the service." Captain, Co. A, 7 VRC, Aug. 13, 1863. Resigned April 18, 1864.

Born: March 9, 1828 Greensburg, KY
Died: Feb. 20, 1898 Lebanon, KY
Other Wars: Mexican War (Private, Co. A, 2 KY Infantry)
Occupation: Druggist and clerk
Miscellaneous: Resided Greensburg, Green Co., KY; Columbia, Adair Co., KY; and Lebanon, Marion Co., KY
Buried: Ryder Cemetery, Lebanon, KY (unmarked)
References: Pension File and Military Service File, National Archives. Hambleton Tapp and James C. Klotter, editors. *The Union, the Civil War and John W. Tuttle.* Frankfort, KY, 1980. Obituary, *Stanford Semi-Weekly Interior Journal*, Feb. 22, 1898.

Philip William Stanhope

Captain, 12 U.S. Infantry, May 14, 1861. GSW left arm and taken prisoner, Gaines' Mill, VA, June 27, 1862. Confined Libby Prison, Richmond, VA. Exchanged Aug. 27, 1862. Assigned by Major Gen. Lewis Wallace to command of volunteer forces (Squirrel Hunters) in defense of Cincinnati, OH, with rank of Brig. Gen., Sept. 1862. Provost Marshal, Staff of Brig. Gen. John J. Abercrombie, June 1864. *Colonel,* 55 KY Infantry, Oct. 20, 1864, under authority from Bvt. Major Gen. Stephen G. Burbridge, commanding Military District of Kentucky, 23 Army Corps, Department of the Ohio. Authority as colonel revoked, Jan. 12, 1865, Governor Bramlette having commissioned Weden O'Neal as colonel of the regiment. Bvt. Major, USA, Aug. 18, 1864, for gallant and meritorious services during the operations on the Weldon Railroad, VA. Bvt. Lieutenant Colonel, USA, Oct. 2, 1864, for gallant and meritorious services in action at Saltville, VA. Battle honors: Peninsular Campaign (Gaines' Mill), Petersburg Campaign (Weldon Railroad), Raid from Kentucky and East Tennessee into Southwestern Virginia (Saltville).

Born: June 4, 1829 Newport, RI

Philip William Stanhope (USAMHI [RG64IS-MOLLUS-PA11.66]).

Died: June 24, 1895 Indianapolis, IN
Occupation: Commission merchant before war. Regular Army (Captain, 12 U.S. Infantry, honorably mustered out, Jan. 1, 1871) and traveling agent after war. Having been mustered out of the service upon "groundless charges," he was, by Act of Congress, appointed Major, U.S. Infantry, on the retired list, May 29, 1879.
Miscellaneous: Resided Cincinnati, OH; and Indianapolis, IN
Buried: Spring Grove Cemetery, Cincinnati, OH (Section 49, Lot 92)
References: Obituary Circular, Whole No. 79, Indiana MOLLUS. Obituary, *Indianapolis Journal*, June 25, 1895. Pension File and Military Service File, National Archives. Philip W. Stanhope. *Official Papers, Letters and Notes, Relating to the War Record of P. W. Stanhope, Major and Brevet Lieutenant Colonel, U.S. Army.* N.p., 1879. Letters Received, Volunteer Service Branch, Adjutant General's Office, Files S2551(VS)1864 and S529(VS)1864, National Archives. Guy V. Henry. *Military Record of Civilian Appointments in the United States Army.* New York City, 1869. John Cornell. *Genealogy of the Cornell Family: Being an Account of the Descendants of Thomas Cornell of Portsmouth, RI.* New York City, 1902.

Edmund Alexander Starling

2 Lieutenant, Co. G, 35 KY Infantry, June 2, 1863. Colonel, 35 KY Infantry, Oct. 2, 1863. Commanded District of Southwestern Kentucky, 1 Division, 23 Army Corps, Department of the Ohio, Feb.–March 1864. Dishonorably mustered out, Jan. 25, 1865, for "violation of Paragraph 89, Mustering Regulations, in transferring men from company to company, thereby fraudulently swelling the ranks to secure improper musters into the service of the United States." Dishonorable muster out revoked, Jan. 31, 1865, "full and satisfactory explanations having been received," and he was honorably mustered out to date Dec. 29, 1864.

Born: Nov. 22, 1826 Logan Co., KY

Died: June 14, 1880 Hopkinsville, KY (assassinated by Jesse Ratcliffe, who had accused him of lying in a speech while campaigning for sheriff)

Occupation: Brick maker and Indian agent before war. Brick maker and deputy sheriff after war.

Offices/Honors: Indian Agent for Oregon Territory, with headquarters at Fort Steilacoom, 1851–52

Miscellaneous: Resided Hopkinsville, Christian Co., KY. First cousin of Major Gen. Irvin McDowell and Colonel John A. McDowell (6 IA Infantry).

Buried: Riverside Cemetery, Hopkinsville, KY (Section B)

References: J. H. Battle and William H. Perrin, editors. *Counties of Todd and Christian, Kentucky, Historical and Biographical.* Chicago and Louisville, 1884. *Family Histories Christian County, KY, 1797–*

Edmund Alexander Starling (seated, with two unidentified soldiers of his regiment) (E. L. Folks, Ambrotypist and Photographist, Hopkinsville, Kentucky; Kentucky Historical Society [Crittenden and Starling Album, 2000PH04]).

1986. Paducah, KY, 1986. Pension File and Military Service File, National Archives. Letters Received, Volunteer Service Branch, Adjutant General's Office, Files F51(VS)1865 and S205(VS)1865, National Archives. Obituary, *Louisville Courier-Journal,* June 15, 1880. Obituary, *Hopkinsville South Kentuckian,* June 15, 1880. Albert Mack Sterling, compiler. *The Sterling Genealogy.* New York City, 1909. Ralph S. and Robert L. Greenlee. *Genealogy of the Greenlee Families in America, Scotland, Ireland and England.* Chicago, IL, 1908. Joseph Sullivant. *A Genealogy and Family Memorial.* Columbus, OH, 1874. Elwood Evans. *History of the Pacific Northwest: Oregon and Washington.* Portland, OR, 1889.

Owen Starr

1 Lieutenant, Co. E, 2 KY Cavalry, Sept. 9, 1861. Captain, Co. C, 2 KY Cavalry, Nov. 22, 1862. Major, 2 KY Cavalry, July 7, 1864. Lieutenant Colonel, 2 KY Cavalry, Oct. 18, 1864. *Colonel,* 2 KY Cavalry, May 1, 1865. Honorably mustered out,

Edmund Alexander Starling (Kentucky Historical Society [Crittenden and Starling Album, 2000 PH04]).

Owen Starr (J. C. Elrod's Gallery, 109 Main St., Louisville, KY, Plain & Painted Photographs).

July 17, 1865. Battle honors: Atlanta Campaign (McCook's Raid), Campaign of the Carolinas.

Born: 1836? KY
Died: Sept. 29, 1897 Marion, IN
Occupation: Mechanic before war. Molder and foundryman after war. Superintendent of stove foundry during residence in St. Louis, MO.
Miscellaneous: Resided Louisville, Jefferson Co., KY; Cincinnati, OH; St. Louis, MO; East Chicago, Lake Co., IN; and NHDVS, Marion, Grant Co., IN, after 1894. Commanded a Fenian army regiment in the Niagara Raid of 1866, culminating in the battle of Ridgeway, June 2, 1866.
Buried: Marion National Cemetery, Marion, IN (Section 1, Grave 281)
References: Pension File and Military Service File, National Archives. Obituary, *Marion Morning News,* Sept. 30, 1897. Historical Register of National Homes for Disabled Volunteer Soldiers, 1866–1938, National Archives. Letters Received, Volunteer Service Branch, Adjutant General's Office, File W175(VS)1867, National Archives. Peter Vronsky. *Ridgeway: The American Fenian Invasion and the 1866 Battle That Made Canada.* Toronto, Canada, 2011.

Marion Cartright Taylor

Captain, Co. A, 15 KY Infantry, Oct. 20, 1861. Acting ADC and Acting AAG, Staff of Major Gen. Lovell H. Rousseau, 1 Division, 14 Army Corps, Army of the Cumberland, Dec. 1862–Feb. 1863. Colonel, 15 KY Infantry, Feb. 25, 1863. Commanded Post of Chattanooga, TN, Dec. 22, 1863–Feb. 15, 1864. GSW Resaca, GA, May 14, 1864. Commanded 1 Brigade, 1 Division, 14 Army Corps, Army of the Cumberland, July 27–Aug. 3, 1864 and Aug. 17–Sept. 20, 1864. Commanded Post of Bridgeport, AL, Oct.–Dec. 1864. Honorably mustered out, Jan. 14, 1865. Battle honors: Stone's River, Tullahoma Campaign, Chickamauga, Missionary Ridge, Atlanta Campaign (Resaca, Jonesborough, Atlanta).

Born: Oct. 30, 1822 Ohio Co., KY
Died: Jan. 4, 1871 Shelbyville, KY
Education: Graduated University of Louisville (KY) Law School, 1849
Other Wars: Took part in the Lopez Cardenas filibuster expedition to Cuba, 1850
Occupation: Lawyer
Offices/Honors: Kentucky House of Representatives, 1853–55
Miscellaneous: Resided Shelbyville, Shelby Co., KY
Buried: Grove Hill Cemetery, Shelbyville, KY
References: *History of Kentucky: The Blue Grass State.* Chicago and Louisville, 1928. Kirk C. Jenkins. *The Battle Rages Higher: The Union's Fifteenth Kentucky Infantry.* Lexington, KY, 2003. *Society of the Army of the Cumberland. Fifth Reunion, Detroit, MI, 1871.* Cincinnati, OH, 1872. John Fitch. *Annals of the Army of the Cumberland.* Philadelphia, PA, 1864. Edna S. Macon, compiler. *Memorials to the Blue and Gray: Commonwealth of Kentucky Civil War Monuments.* Kuttawa, KY, 2011. Military Serv-

Marion Cartright Taylor (courtesy Tennessee State Library and Archives [Gilbert M. L. Johnson Album]).

Joshua Tevis

Colonel, 10 KY Cavalry, Sept. 10, 1862. Resigned Nov. 17, 1862, "in consequence of the request of ten captains in this command and believing that it will promote the best interest of the service." In forwarding the resignation, Major Gen. Gordon Granger commented, "He is no soldier and cannot command his regiment."

Born: June 20, 1826 Shelbyville, KY
Died: Oct. 12, 1900 Fruitvale, CA
Education: Graduated University of Louisville (KY) Law School, 1848
Occupation: Lawyer
Offices/Honors: Kentucky House of Representatives, 1855–57 and 1859–63. U.S. District Attorney, 1863–66.
Miscellaneous: Resided Versailles, Woodford Co., KY; Louisville, Jefferson Co., KY; Exeter, Rockingham Co., NH; and Fruitvale, Alameda Co., CA, after 1880. Brother of millionaire expressman Lloyd Tevis.
Buried: Mountain View Cemetery, Oakland, CA (Plot 14, Lot 203)
References: Obituary, *San Francisco Chronicle*, Oct. 13, 1900. Obituary, *Louisville Courier-Journal*, Oct. 14, 1900. Obituary, *San Francisco Examiner*, Oct. 13, 1900. Obituary, *Oakland Tribune*, Oct. 13, 1900. Military Service File, National Archives.

Clinton Jones True

Captain, Co. C, 20 KY Infantry, Jan. 12, 1862. Resigned June 9, 1863, "in order that I may accept a command in the new troops now being raised by the state of Kentucky." 1 Lieutenant, Adjutant, 45 KY Infantry, June 20, 1863. Colonel, 40 KY Infantry, Sept. 29, 1863. Commanded 2 Brigade, 1 Division, District of Kentucky, 23 Army Corps, Department of the Ohio, April 10–July 6, 1864. Commanded 1 Brigade, 1 Division, District of Kentucky, 23 Army Corps, Department of the Ohio, Oct. 15–Dec. 30, 1864. Honorably mustered out, Dec. 30, 1864. Colonel, 53 KY Infantry, April 17, 1865. Commanded 1 Division, Army of Kentucky, Aug.–Sept. 1865. Honorably mustered out, Sept. 15, 1865. Battle honors: Morgan's Raid into Kentucky.

Born: 1836 NY
Died: Disappeared in British Guiana in the early 1880s. Declared legally dead in 1888.
Occupation: Merchant, foreign service officer, and sugar cane industrialist after 1870
Offices/Honors: U.S. Consul, St. Thomas, West Indies, 1869–70
Miscellaneous: Resided Stillwater, Washington Co., MN; Maysville, Mason Co., KY; and traveling in the West Indies and South America after 1870

Clinton Jones True (courtesy University of Kentucky Archives [PA62M99-002]).

Clinton Jones True (courtesy University of Kentucky Archives [PA62M99-003]).

Buried: Demerara, British Guiana?
References: Clinton Jones True Papers, Special Collections Library, University of Kentucky, Lexington, KY. Letters of Application and Recommendation During the Administration of Ulysses S. Grant, 1869–1877, National Archives. Military Service File, National Archives. Letters Received, Volunteer Service Branch, Adjutant General's Office, File K413(VS)1865, National Archives.

Charles Jones Walker

1 Lieutenant, 2 U.S. Cavalry, Aug. 3, 1861. Captain, 2 U.S. Cavalry, Feb. 15, 1862. Colonel, 10 KY Cavalry, Dec. 12, 1862. Chief of Cavalry, Staff of Major Gen. George L. Hartsuff, 23 Army Corps, Department of the Ohio, May 28–Aug. 11, 1863. Suffering from "a chronic cutaneous affection of the buttocks and other parts which make up the saddle seat," he resigned from volunteer service, Sept. 1, 1863, since "my health ... has been much impaired by exposure in the field" and "my private business renders it necessary." Special Inspector of Cavalry, Department of the Gulf, July 1, 1864–July 25, 1865. Bvt. Major, USA, April 15, 1865, for faithful and meritorious services. Resigned from regular army, July 25, 1865. Battle honors: Glorieta, Carter's Raid into East Tennessee and Southwest Virginia.
Born: 1835 KY

Charles Jones Walker (Brady's National Photographic Portrait Galleries, Broadway & Tenth Street, New York; courtesy The Excelsior Brigade, Alexandria, Virginia).

Charles Jones Walker (as Cadet, U.S. Military Academy, 1857) (U.S. Military Academy Library).

Charles Jones Walker (New Orleans Photographic Co., 57 Camp St., New Orleans, Louisiana; courtesy Henry Deeks).

Died: March 4, 1879 Richmond, KY
Education: Graduated U.S. Military Academy, West Point, NY, 1857
Occupation: Regular Army (Captain, 2 U.S. Cavalry, resigned July 25, 1865). Lawyer and county court clerk after war.
Offices/Honors: County Clerk, Madison Co., KY, 1866–70
Miscellaneous: Resided Richmond, Madison Co., KY
Buried: Richmond Cemetery, Richmond, KY (Section F, Lot 80)
References: *Tenth Annual Reunion of the Association of the Graduates of the United States Military Academy at West Point, NY, June 12, 1879.* New York City, NY, 1879. Obituary, *The Kentucky Register,* March 7, 1879. George W. Cullum. *Biographical Register of the Officers and Graduates of the United States Military Academy.* Third Edition. Boston and New York, 1891. Military Service File, National Archives. Letters Received, Commission Branch, Adjutant General's Office, File W592(CB)1865, National Archives.

Thomas B. Waller

Captain, Co. G, 20 KY Infantry, Jan. 6, 1862. Major, 20 KY Infantry, April 18, 1863. Lieutenant Colonel, 20 KY Infantry, Jan. 15, 1864. *Colonel,* 20 KY Infantry, Oct. 5, 1864. Honorably mustered out, Jan. 17, 1865. Battle honors: Corinth, Morgan's Ohio Raid, Atlanta Campaign.
Born: April 12, 1838 Marshall Co., KY
Died: Aug. 9, 1895 Mayfield, KY
Occupation: Merchant
Miscellaneous: Resided Benton, Marshall Co., KY; Briensburg, Marshall Co., KY; and Mayfield, Graves Co., KY, after 1892
Buried: Maplewood Cemetery, Mayfield, KY (Old Part, Block 12, Lot 11)
References: Obituary, *Mayfield Monitor,* Aug. 14, 1895. Don Simmons. *Marshall County, KY, Newspaper Genealogical Abstracts.* Vol. 2. Melber, KY, 1985. Military Service File, National Archives. Berry Craig, "The Marshall County Wallers Stepped to a Different Drummer," *West Kentucky Journal,* Jan. 27, 2012. J. R. Lemon. *Lemon's Hand Book of Marshall County.* Benton, KY, 1894. William H. Perrin, J. H. Battle and Gilbert C. Kniffin. *Kentucky: A History of the State.* Louisville and Chicago, 1885.

John Hardin Ward

Lieutenant Colonel, 27 KY Infantry, Oct. 5, 1861. *Colonel,* 27 KY Infantry, April 14, 1864. Commanded Post of Munfordville (KY), 2 Division, District of Kentucky, 23 Army Corps, Department of the Ohio, Dec. 1864. Commanded Post of Owensboro (KY), 2 Division, District of Kentucky, 23 Army Corps, Department of the Ohio, Jan. 1865. Commanded 3 Brigade, 2 Division, Department of Kentucky, March 1865. Honorably mustered out, March 29, 1865. Battle honors: Morgan's

John Hardin Ward (photograph by Webster & Bro., Louisville, Kentucky; courtesy Everett Bowles).

John Hardin Ward (post-war) (Album of Portraits of Companions of the Commandery of the State of Ohio MOLLUS. Cincinnati, Ohio, 1893).

Second Kentucky Raid, Knoxville Campaign, Atlanta Campaign.
Born: Nov. 6, 1835 Greensburg, KY
Died: Feb. 27, 1908 Louisville, KY
Occupation: Lawyer and financier
Miscellaneous: Resided Greensburg, Green Co., KY, before war; and Louisville, Jefferson Co., KY, after war. Son of Brig. Gen. William T. Ward.
Buried: Cave Hill Cemetery, Louisville, KY (Section F, Lot 461)
References: J. Stoddard Johnston, editor. *Memorial History of Louisville.* Chicago, IL, 1896. Obituary, *Louisville Courier-Journal,* Feb. 28, 1908. Obituary Circular, Whole No. 763, Ohio MOLLUS. *Society of the Army of the Cumberland. Thirty-Sixth Reunion, Chattanooga, TN, 1908.* Chattanooga, TN, 1909. Letters Received, Volunteer Service Branch, Adjutant General's Office, File W87(VS)1862, National Archives. Military Service File, National Archives.

William Alfred Warner

Colonel, 18 KY Infantry, Dec. 2, 1861. GSW left breast, Richmond, KY, Aug. 30, 1862. Taken prisoner and paroled, Richmond, KY, Aug. 30, 1862. Commanded 2 Brigade, Crook's Division, Department of the Cumberland, April–May 1863. At home suffering from typhoid fever, he was reported as absent without leave and dismissed Dec. 18, 1863, "on account of physical disability, and for absence without leave." His dismissal was revoked, May 21, 1864, and he was honorably discharged on account of physical disability to date Dec. 18, 1863, "in consideration of his valuable services, his high testimonials as an officer, and his severe wounds received in battle." Battle honors: Morgan's First Kentucky Raid, Richmond.
Born: Nov. 7, 1817 Lexington, KY
Died: May 15, 1902 Covington, KY
Occupation: Farmer before war. Farmer, trader and U.S. Internal Revenue official after war.
Offices/Honors: U.S. Internal Revenue Storekeeper, 1879–85
Miscellaneous: Resided Falmouth, Pendleton Co., KY, until 1866; Lafayette Co., MO, 1866–68; Carrollton, Carroll Co., MO, 1868–78; Lexington, Fayette Co., KY, 1878–86; Kansas City, MO, 1886–98; and Covington, Kenton Co., KY, 1898–1902. Brother-in-law of Colonel Sanders D. Bruce (20 KY Infantry).
Buried: Lexington Cemetery, Lexington, KY (Section O, Lot 107)
References: Pension File and Military Service File, National Archives. Obituary, *Lexington Morning Herald,* May 16, 1902. Letters Received, Volunteer Service Branch, Adjutant General's Office, Files M2509(VS)1863 and S23(VS)1864, National Archives. Obituary, *Cincinnati Enquirer,* May 16, 1902. Josiah H. Combs. *Combs: A Study in Comparative Philology and Genealogy.* Pensacola, FL, 1976.

Elijah Searcy Watts

Captain, Co. A, 2 KY Cavalry, Sept. 9, 1861. Major, 2 KY Cavalry, Feb. 1, 1862. Taken prisoner, Bardstown, KY, Oct. 1, 1862. Paroled Oct. 6, 1862. Lieutenant Colonel, 2 KY Cavalry, Dec. 19, 1862. Colonel, 2 KY Cavalry, Dec. 14, 1863. Resigned Aug. 20, 1864, since "my father is getting old ... and needs my services to attend to his affairs at home." Battle honors: Tullahoma Campaign (Liberty Gap, Tullahoma), Dalton, Atlanta Campaign.
Born: Dec. 16, 1836 Bardstown, KY
Died: May 3, 1909 Chicago, IL
Other Wars: Private, Co. C, 1 U.S. Infantry, 1860–61
Occupation: Lawyer, traveling agent, and Post Office Superintendent
Miscellaneous: Resided Bardstown, Nelson Co., KY, before war; Louisville, Jefferson Co., KY; and Chicago, IL
Buried: Cave Hill Cemetery, Louisville, KY (Section P, Lot 221)
References: *Memorials of Deceased Companions of the Commandery of the State of Illinois MOLLUS,*

Elijah Searcy Watts (post-war) (*Memorials of Deceased Companions of the Commandery of the State of Illinois MOLLUS, From July 1, 1901 to Dec. 31, 1911.* Chicago, Illinois, 1912).

from July 1, 1901 to Dec. 31, 1911. Chicago, IL, 1912. Obituary Circular, Whole No. 649, Illinois MOL-LUS. Pension File and Military Service File, National Archives. Obituary, *Louisville Courier-Journal,* May 4, 1909. Elijah S. Watts Papers, 1861–1907, Special Collections, The Filson Historical Society, Louisville, KY. Letters Received, Volunteer Service Branch, Adjutant General's Office, File W1602(VS)1862, National Archives. Obituary, *Chicago Daily Tribune,* May 5, 1909.

James Wallace Weatherford

Major, 8 KY Cavalry, Sept. 8, 1862. Lieutenant Colonel, 13 KY Cavalry, Oct. 7, 1863. Colonel, 13 KY Cavalry, Dec. 23, 1863. Honorably mustered out, Jan. 10, 1865.

Born: Jan. 18, 1837 Lincoln Co., KY
Died: Aug. 17, 1889 Ennis, TX
Occupation: Farmer and banker
Miscellaneous: Resided Bradfordsville, Marion Co., KY, before war; Hustonville, Lincoln Co., KY, 1865–86; and Ennis, Ellis Co., TX, 1886–89
Buried: Myrtle Cemetery, Ennis, TX (Old Addition, Block 5)
References: Pension File and Military Service File, National Archives. Obituary, *Stanford Semi-Weekly Interior Journal,* Aug. 20, 1889.

John Samuel White

1 Lieutenant, Co. A, 16 KY Infantry, Oct. 9, 1861. GSW left foot, Ivy Mountain, KY, Nov. 8, 1861. Captain, Co. A, 16 KY Infantry, March 15, 1862. Major, 16 KY Infantry, June 5, 1863. Provost Marshal, 2 Division, 23 Army Corps, Department of the Ohio, Aug.–Nov. 1863. Lieutenant Colonel, 16 KY Infantry, June 16, 1864. GSW face, Franklin, TN, Nov. 30, 1864. *Colonel,* 16 KY Infantry, Feb. 22, 1865. Resigned May 12, 1865, since "Intelligence has reached me of the death of my brother-in-law, which sad event leaves my sister a widow with five small children, and I consider her claims upon me for advice, assistance and protection paramount to any assistance I can render the country at this stage of the war." Battle honors: Ivy Mountain, Morgan's Second Kentucky Raid, Atlanta Campaign, Franklin, Campaign of the Carolinas.

Born: Jan. 27, 1837 Mason Co., KY
Died: Jan. 17, 1906 Odessa, MO
Occupation: Farmer and stock raiser
Miscellaneous: Resided Sardis, Mason Co., KY, to 1866; Hardin, Ray Co., MO, 1866–72; and Odessa, Lafayette Co., MO, 1872–1906
Buried: Odessa Cemetery, Odessa, MO (Block 2, Lot 272)
References: *History of Lafayette County, MO.* St. Louis, MO, 1881. Obituary, *Odessa Democrat,* Jan. 18, 1906. Pension File and Military Service File, National Archives.

Frank Lane Wolford

Colonel, 1 KY Cavalry, Oct. 28, 1861. GSW left hip and abdomen, Lebanon, TN, May 5, 1862. GSW right leg, near Monticello, KY, June 10, 1863. Commanded Independent Cavalry Brigade, 23 Army Corps, Department of the Ohio, Aug.–Nov. 1863. Commanded 1 Brigade, 1 Division, Cavalry Corps, Army of the Ohio, Nov. 3–18, 1863. Commanded 1 Division, Cavalry Corps, Army of the Ohio, Nov. 18, 1863–March 24, 1864. Having delivered a speech in Lexington, KY, March 10, 1864, in which he denounced President Lincoln as "a tyrant and a usurper" for "overriding all constitutional barriers" in ordering the enlistment of Negro soldiers in Kentucky, he was dismissed March 24, 1864, for "violation of the 5th section of the Rules and Articles of War, in using disrespectful words against the President of the United States, for disloyalty, and for conduct unbecoming an officer and a gentleman." Having continued to make speeches reviling the Lincoln administration, he, along with Lieutenant Governor (and ex–Colonel) Richard T. Jacob, was arrested, Nov. 11, 1864. Detained as a prisoner in Kentucky, he was released more than a month later upon pledging himself to avoid oppos-

Frank Lane Wolford (Peckover's Photograph Gallery, Paris, Kentucky; Library of Congress [LC-DIG-cwpb-07263]).

ters Received, Volunteer Service Branch, Adjutant General's Office, Files W742(VS)1864 and B422 (VS)1867, National Archives. John P. Logan, "Gallant Wolford," *Washington National Tribune,* Nov. 16, 1899. Eastham Tarrant. *The Wild Riders of the First Kentucky Cavalry, A History of the Regiment in the Great War of the Rebellion, 1861–1865.* Louisville, KY, 1894. James L. Harrison, compiler. *Biographical Directory of the American Congress, 1774–1949.* Washington, DC, 1950.

William Elihu Woodruff

Colonel, 2 KY Infantry, June 28, 1861. Taken prisoner, Scarey Creek, WV, July 17, 1861. Confined Libby Prison, Richmond, VA, Charleston, SC, and Columbia, SC. Exchanged April 4, 1862. Nominated as Brig. Gen., USV, June 10, 1862, but not confirmed by Senate. Addressed as Brig. Gen. in an order from Army Headquarters assigning him to duty, Sept. 11, 1862, he sent a letter accepting the position and "did assume the strap and insignia of that rank," only to be informed that the assign-

Frank Lane Wolford (Wm. Garst, Photographer, Danville, Kentucky).

ing U.S. Government policy. By an Act of Congress, approved March 3, 1877, he was "relieved from all the penalties and effects" of the order dismissing him and "restored to all the rights and privileges he would be entitled to had said order not been issued and enforced." Battle honors: Mill Springs, Lebanon, Morgan's First Kentucky Raid, Morgan's Second Kentucky Raid, Monticello, Morgan's Ohio Raid, East Tennessee Campaign, Philadelphia, Knoxville Campaign, Dandridge.

Born: Sept. 2, 1817 near Columbia, KY
Died: Aug. 2, 1895 Columbia, KY
Other Wars: Mexican War (Private, Co. G, 2 KY Infantry)
Occupation: Lawyer
Offices/Honors: Kentucky House of Representatives, 1847 and 1865–67. Kentucky Adjutant General, 1867–68. U.S. House of Representatives, 1883–87.
Miscellaneous: Resided Liberty, Casey Co., KY, to 1879; and Columbia, Adair Co., KY, 1879–95
Buried: Columbia Cemetery, Columbia, KY
References: Hambleton Tapp, "Incidents in the Life of Frank Wolford," *The Filson Club History Quarterly,* Vol. 10, No. 2 (April 1936). Pension File and Military Service File, National Archives. Obituary, *Louisville Courier-Journal,* Aug. 3, 1895. Let-

William Elihu Woodruff (Brady's National Photographic Portrait Galleries, Broadway & Tenth Street, New York; Library of Congress [LC-DIG-cwpb-06513]).

William Elihu Woodruff (as officer in pre-war Marion Rifles) (The Filson Historical Society, Louisville, Kentucky [PC23.0153]).

ment as Brig. Gen. was "premature, the appointment never having been made." Commanded 3 Brigade, 2 Division, Army of Kentucky, Sept. 1862. Commanded 32 Brigade, 9 Division, 3 Army Corps, Army of the Ohio, Oct. 1862. Commanded 9 Division, 3 Army Corps, Army of the Ohio, Oct. 1862. Commanded 3 Brigade, 1 Division, Right Wing, 14 Army Corps, Army of the Cumberland, Dec. 24, 1862–Jan. 9, 1863. Suffering from injuries received at Stone's River and having waited "sufficiently long for justice to be done me," he resigned Jan. 28, 1863, concluding "I have done all a man can in honor do for my country without apparently a recognition of that position to which I am entitled." Battle honors: Stone's River.

Born: June 14, 1827 Louisville, KY
Died: Feb. 5, 1915 Louisville, KY
Other Wars: Mexican War (1 Lieutenant, Co. A, 4 KY Infantry)
Occupation: Lawyer and U.S. Internal Revenue official
Offices/Honors: U.S. Internal Revenue Storekeeper, 1881–93
Miscellaneous: Resided Louisville, Jefferson Co., KY
Buried: Cave Hill Cemetery, Louisville, KY (Section M, Lot 337)
References: Bryan S. Bush, "Brig. Gen. William Woodruff: 'I Have Done All a Man Can,'" *North South Trader's Civil War,* Vol. 26, No. 2 (2000). Obituary, *Louisville Courier-Journal,* Feb. 6, 1915. Pension File and Military Service File, National Archives. Letters Received, Volunteer Service Branch, Adjutant General's Office, File W415(VS) 1862, National Archives. Thomas Speed, Robert M. Kelly, and Alfred Pirtle. *The Union Regiments of Kentucky.* Louisville, KY, 1897. J. Stoddard Johnston, editor. *Memorial History of Louisville.* Chicago, IL, 1896.

Tennessee

Regiments

1st Cavalry

Robert Johnson	Feb. 28, 1862	Resigned May 31, 1864, **Bvt. Brig. Gen., USV**
James P. Brownlow	June 15, 1864	Mustered out April 11, 1865, **Bvt. Brig. Gen., USV**

2nd Cavalry

Daniel M. Ray	Nov. 8, 1862	Resigned Feb. 15, 1864
William F. Prosser	June 26, 1865	Mustered out July 6, 1865

3rd Cavalry

William C. Pickens	Jan. 1, 1863	Mustered out Nov. 21, 1863

3rd West Tennessee Cavalry

William P. Kendrick

4th Cavalry

Richard M. Edwards	Nov. 2, 1863	Mustered out Nov. 24, 1864

5th Cavalry

William B. Stokes	Nov. 15, 1862	Resigned March 10, 1865, **Bvt. Brig. Gen., USV**
Robert Galbraith	May 1, 1865	

6th Cavalry

Fielding Hurst	July 1, 1863	Resigned Jan. 8, 1865
William J. Smith	March 13, 1865	Mustered out July 26, 1865, **Bvt. Brig. Gen., USV**

7th Cavalry

Regiment not entitled to a colonel since it never attained full strength.

8th Cavalry

Jesse H. Strickland	Jan. 30, 1863	Discharged April 1, 1864
Samuel K. N. Patton	April 1, 1864	Mustered out Sept. 11, 1865

9th Cavalry

Joseph H. Parsons	Oct. 1, 1864	Mustered out Sept. 11, 1865

10th Cavalry

Regiment not entitled to a colonel since it never attained full strength.

11th Cavalry
Isham Young	Sept. 25, 1863	Resigned Jan. 6, 1864

12th Cavalry
George Spalding	Feb. 24, 1864	Mustered out Oct. 24, 1865, **Bvt. Brig. Gen., USV**

13th Cavalry
John K. Miller	Oct. 5, 1863	Mustered out Nov. 20, 1865

14th Cavalry
Regiment not entitled to a colonel since it never attained full strength.

1st Light Artillery
Robert Clay Crawford, Jr.	Sept. 10, 1863	Resigned Nov. 20, 1864

1st Infantry
Robert K. Byrd	Sept. 1, 1861	Mustered out Sept. 17, 1864

2nd Infantry
James P. T. Carter	Sept. 28, 1861	Resigned May 2, 1864
James M. Melton	May 2, 1864	Mustered out Oct. 8, 1864

3rd Infantry
Leonidas C. Houk	Feb. 6, 1862	Resigned April 3, 1863
William Cross	June 25, 1863	Mustered out Feb. 23, 1865

4th Infantry
Daniel Stover	Nov. 25, 1862	Resigned Aug. 10, 1864
Thomas H. Reeves	July 29, 1865	Mustered out Aug. 2, 1865

5th Infantry
James T. Shelley	March 6, 1862	Resigned July 22, 1864

6th Infantry
Joseph A. Cooper	May 18, 1862	Promoted **Brig. Gen., USV**, July 30, 1864

7th Infantry
William Clift	March 24, 1862	Resigned Dec. 13, 1862

7th Infantry (1st West Tennessee Infantry)
John A. Rogers	Oct. 10, 1862	Resigned Jan. 16, 1863

8th Infantry
Felix A. Reeve	Sept. 16, 1862	Resigned July 15, 1864

9th Infantry
Did not complete organization.

10th Infantry
Alvan C. Gillem	May 13, 1862	Promoted **Brig. Gen., USV**, Aug. 17, 1863
James W. Scully	June 6, 1864	Mustered out May 25, 1865

11th Infantry
Did not complete organization.

1st Mounted Infantry
Regiment not entitled to a colonel since it never attained full strength.

2nd Mounted Infantry
John Murphy   July 1, 1864   Mustered out Jan. 19, 1865

3rd Mounted Infantry
Robert A. Crawford   Aug. 8, 1864   Mustered out Jan. 4, 1865

4th Mounted Infantry
Joseph H. Blackburn   Feb. 4, 1865   Mustered out Aug. 23, 1865

5th Mounted Infantry
Spencer B. Boyd   Feb. 1, 1865   Mustered out July 17, 1865

6th Mounted Infantry
Regiment not entitled to a colonel since it never attained full strength.

7th Mounted Infantry
James T. Shelley   May 9, 1865   Mustered out July 27, 1865

8th Mounted Infantry
Regiment not entitled to a colonel since it never attained full strength.

1st Regiment, Enrolled Militia, District of Memphis/West Tennessee
John McDonald   Dec. 29, 1863   Promoted Brig. Gen., Enrolled Militia, Jan. 28, 1864
Charles McDonald   July 29, 1864   Died Dec. 12, 1864
Amos P. Curry   Dec. 19, 1864   Regiment disbanded May 8, 1865

2nd Regiment, Enrolled Militia, District of Memphis/West Tennessee
Asa C. Ketchum   Dec. 29, 1863   Resigned Oct. 15, 1864
David Ryan   Oct. 17, 1864   Regiment disbanded May 15, 1865

3rd Regiment, Enrolled Militia, District of Memphis/West Tennessee
Frederick W. Buttinghaus Dec. 29, 1863
Milton T. Williamson   Sept. 21, 1864   Promoted Brig. Gen., Enrolled Militia, Feb. 8, 1865
John S. Lord   April 1, 1865   Regiment disbanded May. 8, 1865

4th Regiment, Enrolled Militia, District of Memphis/West Tennessee
William C. Whitney   Dec. 15, 1864   Regiment disbanded April 12, 1865

1st Regiment, Enrolled Militia (Freedmen), District of Memphis/West Tennessee
Edmund R. Wiley, Jr.   Sept. 6, 1864
Decatur G. Chapin   Jan. 23, 1865   Regiment disbanded May 8, 1865

2nd Regiment, Enrolled Militia (Freedmen), District of Memphis/West Tennessee
Arthur T. Reeve   Dec. 15, 1864   Regiment disbanded April 6, 1865

3rd Regiment, Enrolled Militia (Freedmen), District of Memphis/West Tennessee
Henry Von Heyde   Dec. 19, 1864   Regiment disbanded April 12, 1865

Biographies

Joseph Hayes Blackburn

Captain, Co. A, 5 TN Cavalry, Aug. 30, 1862. GSW left shoulder, Liberty, TN, Jan. 22, 1863. Resigned June 2, 1864, since "I am dissatisfied in this regiment caused by partiality of my superior officers. Also I am desirous to raise a company for another regiment." Lieutenant Colonel, 4 TN Mounted Infantry, Nov. 26, 1864. *Colonel,* 4 TN Mounted Infantry, Feb. 4, 1865. Reprimanded by Major Gen. George H. Thomas for his "highly reprehensible conduct" in an unprovoked attack on CSA Major General Joseph Wheeler in a Nashville hotel, Aug. 21, 1865. Honorably mustered out, Aug. 23, 1865. Battle honors: Liberty, Nashville Campaign.

Born: Jan. 3, 1842 DeKalb Co., TN
Died: May 15, 1913 DeKalb Co., TN
Occupation: Farmer and lawyer
Offices/Honors: U.S. Marshal, Middle District of Tennessee, 1870. Convicted of forgery, he was removed from office, but pardoned by President Grant, May 24, 1875.
Miscellaneous: Resided Liberty, DeKalb Co., TN; and Dowelltown, DeKalb Co., TN. Best known for the capture of the notorious Confederate guerrilla chief, Champ Ferguson, May 28, 1865.
Buried: Salem Baptist Church Cemetery, Liberty, TN
References: *History of Tennessee from the Earliest Times to the Present, Together with an Historical and Biographical Sketch of White, Warren, DeKalb, Coffee and Cannon Counties.* Nashville, TN, 1886. Pension File and Military Service File, National Archives. Thomas G. Webb. *A Bicentennial History of DeKalb County, TN.* Smithville, TN, 1995. Will T. Hale. *History of DeKalb County, TN.* Nashville, TN, 1915. Obituary, *Smithville Review,* May 29, 1913. Letters Received, Volunteer Service Branch, Adjutant General's Office, File P2405(VS)1865, National Archives. John Y. Simon, editor. *The Papers of Ulysses S. Grant.* Vol. 20: Nov. 1, 1869–Oct. 31, 1870. Carbondale, IL, 1995. Leroy P. Graf, editor. *The Papers of Andrew Johnson.* Vol. 7, 1864–1865. Knoxville, TN, 1986. Myers E. Brown II. *Tennessee's Union Cavalrymen.* Charleston, SC, 2008.

Spencer B. Boyd

Lieutenant Colonel, 5 TN Mounted Infantry, Oct. 17, 1864. Colonel, 5 TN Mounted Infantry, Feb. 1, 1865. Honorably mustered out, July 17, 1865.

Joseph Hayes Blackburn (Mabry and Charlton Photograph Album, McClung Historical Collection).

Spencer B. Boyd (courtesy Southeast Tennessee Digital Archive, Cleveland State Community College).

Born: March 18, 1829 Monroe Co., TN
Died: Dec. 19, 1889 Cleveland, TN
Occupation: Farmer, merchant, and lawyer
Offices/Honors: Circuit Court Clerk, Polk Co., TN, 1866–68
Miscellaneous: Resided Benton, Polk Co., TN; and Cleveland, Bradley Co., TN
Buried: Fort Hill Cemetery, Cleveland, TN
References: Patsy L. C. Underhill. *A History and Lineage of the Baldwin, Crox, Eldridge and McClary and Allied Families.* College Park, MD, 1971. Obituary, *Chattanooga Daily Times,* Dec. 20, 1889. Military Service File, National Archives.

Frederick William Buttinghaus

Captain, Co. F, 3 (Memphis) Battalion TN Infantry, CSA, March 12, 1862. Battalion disbanded May 1862, on account of the surrender of Memphis. *Colonel,* 3 Regiment, Enrolled Militia, District of Memphis, Dec. 29, 1863. Described as a "low-flung, dirty foreigner" in a Memphis newspaper editor's letter to Governor Andrew Johnson criticizing the selection of Enrolled Militia officers. Volunteer ADC, Staff of Brig. Gen. Ralph P. Buckland, Oct. 18, 1864.

Born: 1824 (or 1821)? Prussia
Died: Sept. 8, 1888 Memphis, TN
Occupation: Insurance agent and clerk before war. Lawyer after war.
Offices/Honors: Memphis City Recorder, 1864
Buried: Elmwood Cemetery, Memphis, TN (Evergreen Section, Lot 209, unmarked)
References: Leroy P. Graf and Ralph W. Haskins, editors. *The Papers of Andrew Johnson.* Vol. 6, 1862–1864. Knoxville, TN, 1983. Letters Received, Volunteer Service Branch, Adjutant General's Office, File H101(VS)1867, National Archives. J. M. Keating. *History of the City of Memphis and Shelby County, TN.* Syracuse, NY, 1888. Compiled Service Records of Confederate Soldiers Who Served in Organizations from the State of Tennessee, National Archives. Death notice, *Memphis Daily Avalanche,* Sept. 9, 1888.

Robert King Byrd

Colonel, 1 TN Infantry, Sept. 1, 1861. Shell wound left breast, Cumberland Gap, TN, March 1862. Commanded 1 Brigade, 1 Division, 23 Army Corps, Department of the Ohio, July 10–15, 1863. Commanded 1 Division, 23 Army Corps, Department of the Ohio, July 15–Aug. 6, 1863. Commanded 1 Brigade, 4 Division, 23 Army Corps, Department of the Ohio, Aug. 21–Oct. 15, 1863. Commanded 2 Brigade, 1 Division, Cavalry Corps, Army of the Ohio, Nov. 1863. Commanded Post of Kingston, TN, Nov. 1863–May 1864. Commanded 3 Brigade, 3 Division, 23 Army Corps,

Robert King Byrd (The Roane County Heritage Commission).

Army of the Ohio, June 17–Aug. 9, 1864. Honorably mustered out, Sept. 17, 1864. Battle honors: Cumberland Gap, Stone's River, Sanders' Raid in East Tennessee, Morgan's Ohio Raid, East Tennessee Campaign, Knoxville Campaign, Atlanta Campaign.

Born: Nov. 4, 1823 Roane Co., TN
Died: May 2, 1885 Kingston, TN
Other Wars: Mexican War (1 Lieutenant, Co. C, 4 TN Infantry)
Occupation: Farmer and trader
Offices/Honors: Tennessee Senate, 1879–81
Miscellaneous: Resided Houkville, Roane Co., TN; and Kingston, Roane Co., TN
Buried: Bethel Cemetery, Kingston, TN
References: Oliver P. Temple. *Notable Men of Tennessee, from 1833 to 1875, Their Times and Their Contemporaries.* New York City, NY, 1912. Robert M. McBride and Dan M. Robison. *Biographical Directory of the Tennessee General Assembly.* Vol. 2, 1861–1901. Nashville, TN, 1979. Obituary, *Knoxville Daily Chronicle.* May 5, 1885. Pension File and Military Service File, National Archives. Leroy P. Graf and Ralph W. Haskins, editors. *The Papers of Andrew Johnson.* Vol. 5, 1861–1862. Knoxville, TN, 1979. Emma M. Wells. *The History of Roane County, TN, 1801–1870.* Chattanooga, TN, 1927.

James Patton Taylor Carter

Colonel, 2 TN Infantry, Sept. 28, 1861. Commanded 1 Brigade, 1 Division, 23 Army Corps, Department of the Ohio, July 15–Aug.6, 1863. Commanded 3 Brigade, 4 Division, 23 Army Corps, Department of the Ohio, Sept. 10–Nov. 3, 1863. Commanded 2 Division, Cavalry Corps, Army of the Ohio, Nov. 1863. Resigned May 2, 1864, since "I have become ... a supernumerary officer in the service of the United States" due to "the capture of about three-fourths of my command." Battle honors: Carter's Raid into East Tennessee and Southwest Virginia, Scott's Raid in Eastern Kentucky, East Tennessee Campaign (Blue Springs), Rogersville, Knoxville Campaign.

Born: July 30, 1822 Elizabethton, TN
Died: Sept. 29, 1869 Rancho Francisco, Sonora, Mexico
Education: Attended Washington (TN) College
Occupation: Iron manufacturer
Offices/Honors: Secretary of State, Arizona Territory, 1866–69. Acting Governor, Arizona Territory, 1868–69.
Miscellaneous: Resided Elizabethton, Carter Co., TN; and Tucson, Pima Co., AZ. Brother of Major Gen. Samuel P. Carter.
Buried: Place of burial unknown
References: John S. Goff, "Colonel James P. T. Carter of Carter County," *Tennessee Historical Quarterly*, Vol. 26, No. 4 (Winter 1967). John S. Goff. *The Secretaries, United States Attorneys, Marshals, Surveyors General and Superintendents of Indian Affairs, 1863–1912.* Cave Creek, AZ, 1988. Eddie M. Nikazy. *Forgotten Soldiers: History of the 2nd Tennessee Volunteer Infantry Regiment (USA), 1861–1865.* Bowie, MD, 1996. Samuel W. Scott and Samuel P. Angel. *History of the 13th Regiment Tennessee Volunteer Cavalry, U.S.A.* Philadelphia, PA, 1903. Obituary, *Tucson Weekly Arizonan*, Oct. 9, 1869. Mildred Kozsuch. *Historical Reminiscences of Carter County, TN.* Johnson City, TN, 1985. Military Service File, National Archives. Leroy P. Graf and Ralph W. Haskins, editors. *The Papers of Andrew Johnson.* Vol. 5, 1861–1862. Knoxville, TN, 1979. Richard N. Current. *Lincoln's Loyalists: Union Soldiers from the Confederacy.* Boston, 1992. Letters Received, Volunteer Service Branch, Adjutant General's Office, File J2(VS)1862, National Archives.

Decatur G. Chapin

Private, Co. K, 12 IL Infantry, Sept. 1, 1862. Quartermaster Sergeant, 12 IL Infantry, Sept. 3, 1862. Commissary Sergeant, 12 IL Infantry, March 1, 1863. 1 Lieutenant, Co. B, 55 USCT, May 21, 1863. Detached as *Major*, 2 Regiment, Enrolled Militia (Freedmen), District of West Tennessee, Dec. 8, 1864. Detached as *Colonel*, 1 Regiment, Enrolled Militia (Freedmen), District of West Tennessee, Jan. 23, 1865. Regiment disbanded, May 8, 1865. Reassigned as Acting AQM, Engineer De-

James Patton Taylor Carter (post-war) (courtesy Arizona Capitol Museum).

Decatur G. Chapin (J. W. Taft, Artist, Oak Gallery, 282½ Main St., Memphis, Tennessee; Roger D. Hunt Collection, USAMHI [RG98S-CWP207.79]).

partment, District of West Tennessee, May 22, 1865. Suffering from "chronic bronchitis, hepatization of the lower lobe of the right lung, and slight ulceration of the left lung," he resigned Sept. 12, 1865, "on account of physical disability contracted while in the service of the United States Army."

Born: 1821 NY
Died: Feb. 5, 1874 Galena, IL
Occupation: Machinist and foundryman
Miscellaneous: Resided Dubuque, Dubuque Co., IA; and Galena, Jo Daviess Co., IL. Brother-in-law of Brig. Gen. Augustus L. Chetlain.
Buried: Greenwood Cemetery, Galena, IL (Division 2, Lot 24)
References: Obituary, *Galena Weekly Gazette*, Feb. 13, 1874. Letters Received, Colored Troops Branch, Adjutant General's Office, File C90(CT)1863, National Archives. Pension File and Military Service File, National Archives. Letters Received, Volunteer Service Branch, Adjutant General's Office, File H101(VS)1867, National Archives.

William Clift

Colonel, 7 TN Infantry, March 24, 1862. Described by Major Gen. Horatio G. Wright as "moving about at will, acknowledging no control, and rendering little or no service; and ... entirely incompetent for the position he holds," he was mustered out of the service, Dec. 13, 1862, his authority as colonel being revoked. Placed in charge of the courier line between Knoxville and Chattanooga, he was taken prisoner, Oct. 24, 1863, by a Confederate raiding party commanded by his son, Moses H. Clift. Confined at Atlanta, GA, he escaped Jan. 5, 1864, and after twenty days travel reached the Union lines.

Born: Dec. 5, 1795 Greene Co., TN
Died: Feb. 17, 1886 Hamilton Co., TN
Occupation: Farmer and lumber merchant
Miscellaneous: Resided Soddy, Hamilton Co., TN; and Sale Creek, Hamilton Co., TN
Buried: Soddy Presbyterian Cemetery, Soddy, TN
References: Oliver P. Temple. *Notable Men of Tennessee, from 1833 to 1875, Their Times and Their Contemporaries*. New York City, NY, 1912. Obituary, *Chattanooga Daily Times*, Feb. 18, 1886. Pension File and Military Service File, National Archives. Letters Received, Volunteer Service Branch, Adjutant General's Office, File C1366(VS)1862, National Archives. Zella Armstrong. *History of Hamilton County and Chattanooga, TN.* Chattanooga, TN, 1931. Clift Family Papers, Tennessee State Library and Archives, Nashville, TN. J. S. Hurlburt. *History of the Rebellion in Bradley County, East Tennessee*. Indianapolis, IN, 1866.

Robert A. Crawford

Chief of Secret Police in East Tennessee, by command of Major Gen. Burnside, Nov. 10, 1863. Served as Colonel and Chief of Scouts, March–April 1864. *Colonel,* 3 TN Mounted Infantry, Aug. 8, 1864. Honorably mustered out, Jan. 4, 1865.

Born: April 19, 1819 Greene Co., TN
Died: July 17, 1883 Washington, DC
Occupation: Lawyer
Miscellaneous: Resided Greeneville, Greene Co., TN; and Washington, DC, 1867–83
Buried: Congressional Cemetery, Washington, DC (Range 97, Site 315)
References: Obituary, *Washington National Republican*, July 18, 1883. Leroy P. Graf and Ralph W. Haskins, editors. *The Papers of Andrew Johnson*. Vol. 6, 1862–1864. Knoxville, TN, 1983. Pension File, National Archives. Letters Received, Volunteer Service Branch, Adjutant General's Office, File F572(VS)1864, National Archives.

Robert Clay Crawford, Jr.

1 Sergeant, Co. F, 64 IL Infantry, Dec. 31, 1861. *Captain,* Co. K, 26 MO Infantry, March 30, 1862. Taken prisoner Lockridge's Mill, TN, May 5, 1862. Confined Madison, GA. Paroled Oct. 12, 1862.

William Clift (Zella Armstrong. *History of Hamilton County and Chattanooga, Tennessee.* Chattanooga, Tennessee, 1931).

Captain, Co. B, 5 TN Infantry, Feb. 10, 1863. Captain, 1 Independent Battery, TN Light Artillery (later Battery B, 1 Battalion, TN Light Artillery), April 16, 1863. GSW left leg, Irvine, KY, July 30, 1863. Colonel, 1 TN Light Artillery, Sept. 10, 1863. Lieutenant Colonel, 1 Battalion, TN Light Artillery, Nov. 1, 1863. Held appointments as prospective colonel of two USCT regiments while recruiting colored troops in 1864. Described by Reuben D. Mussey, Commissioner for the Organization of U.S. Colored Troops, as "not a gentleman and I believe ... wholly unscrupulous," he was dismissed Nov. 20, 1864, for receiving from enlisted men of his command "a large amount of the signed and unsigned bank notes of the Branch Bank of Tennessee at Rogersville ... falsely pretending that he wished to and would destroy the said notes" ... and then applying "the same to his own use and benefit." His dismissal was "disapproved" and his resignation accepted to date Nov. 20, 1864, by order of President Andrew Johnson, Nov. 16, 1865. Battle honors: Scott's Raid in Eastern Kentucky (Irvine).

Born: Dec. 8, 1825 Rogersville, TN
Died: June 23, 1907 Hampton, VA
Education: Attended U.S. Military Academy, West Point, NY (Class of 1854)
Other Wars: Mexican War (Private, Co. D, 4 TN Infantry)
Occupation: Serving in the 1850s with Narciso Lopez in Cuba and William Walker in Nicaragua, he acquired a reputation as a soldier of fortune, a reputation further enhanced by his service in the Mexican Liberal Army in 1865 and later in the Egyptian army. Employed as a surveyor in Utah, 1858–61. Described as a chemist in the 1870 census, as an author in the 1900 census, and as a scientist when he entered the Hampton (VA) Soldiers Home in 1901.
Miscellaneous: Resided Rogersville, Hawkins Co., TN; Bensalem, Bucks Co., PA (1866); Chestertown, Kent Co., MD (1870); and Hampton (VA) Soldiers Home, 1901–07
Buried: Hampton National Cemetery, Hampton, VA (Section B, Grave 9349)
References: Pension File and Military Service File, National Archives. Letters Received, Volunteer Service Branch, Adjutant General's Office, Files C1398(VS)1862 and C681(VS)1863, National Archives. Sheila W. Johnston, compiler. *The Blue and Gray from Hawkins County, TN, 1861–1865*. Rogersville, TN, 1995. Leroy P. Graf and Ralph W. Haskins, editors. *The Papers of Andrew Johnson*. Vol. 6, 1862–1864. Knoxville, TN, 1983. Leroy P. Graf, editor. *The Papers of Andrew Johnson*. Vol. 7, 1864–1865. Knoxville, TN, 1986. Theodore C. Tracie. *Annals of the 19th Ohio Battery Volunteer Artillery*. Cleveland, OH, 1878. "Crawford Pasha," *Louisville Courier-Journal*, Sept. 5, 1877. Letters Received, Colored Troops Branch, Adjutant General's Office, Files M437(CT)1864 and M438(CT) 1864, National Archives.

William Cross

Private, Co. H, 1 TN Infantry, Aug. 21, 1861. Major, 3 TN Infantry, Feb. 15, 1862. Colonel, 3 TN Infantry, June 25, 1863. Commanded 3 Brigade (1 East Tennessee Brigade), 3 Division, 12 Army Corps, Army of the Cumberland, (temporarily assigned to 2 Division, 23 Army Corps, Army of the Ohio), Feb. 6–March 7, 1864. Suffered head injury from bursting of a shell, Pine Mountain, GA, May 27, 1864. Honorably mustered out, Feb. 23, 1865. Battle honors: Richmond, Chickamauga Campaign, Atlanta Campaign (Resaca, Pine Mountain), Nashville.

Born: Nov. 18, 1841 near Clinton, Anderson Co., TN
Died: Feb. 1, 1898 Ball Camp, TN
Occupation: Farmer. In later years held positions in the post office, police department, and fire department of Knoxville, TN.
Offices/Honors: Chief of Knoxville (TN) Fire Department, 1894–96
Miscellaneous: Resided Robertsville, Anderson Co., TN; Ball Camp, Knox Co., TN: and Knoxville, Knox Co., TN
Buried: Liberty Cemetery, near Clinton, Anderson Co., TN
References: Pension File and Military Service File, National Archives. Obituary, *Knoxville Daily Journal*, Feb. 2, 1898. Leroy P. Graf and Ralph W. Haskins, editors. *The Papers of Andrew Johnson*. Vol. 5, 1861–1862. Knoxville, TN, 1979. Walter Lynn Bates, "Southern Unionists: A Socio-Economic Examination of the Third East Tennessee Volunteer Infantry Regiment, U.S.A., 1862–1865," *Tennessee Historical Quarterly*, Vol. 50, No. 4 (Winter 1991).

Amos P. Curry

Private, Co. A, 13 IL Infantry, May 24, 1861. 2 Lieutenant, Co. B, Bowen's Battalion MO Cavalry, Aug. 1, 1861. Accidental GSW left ankle, Rolla, MO, Sept. 10, 1861. Captain, Co. B, 9 MO Cavalry, Oct. 1, 1862. Captain, Co. B, 10 MO Cavalry, Dec. 4, 1862. Honorably mustered out, Aug. 5, 1864. Colonel, 1 Regiment, Enrolled Militia, District of West Tennessee, Dec. 19, 1864. Regiment disbanded, May 8, 1865. Battle honors: Brice's Cross Roads.

Born: July 8, 1834 Bangor, ME
Died: June 9, 1901 Spokane, WA
Occupation: Grocer before war. Commission

Amos P. Curry (post-war) (*History of the Arkansas Valley, Colorado.* Chicago, Illinois, 1881).

merchant, railroad contractor, mine operator, and real estate agent after war.
Offices/Honors: Sheriff of Shelby Co., TN, 1867–73. Brig. Gen., Washington National Guard, 1889–95.
Miscellaneous: Resided Dixon, Lee Co., IL, to 1864; Memphis, Shelby Co., TN, 1864–73; Little Rock, Pulaski Co., AR, 1873–78; Leadville, Lake Co., CO, 1878–83; and Spokane, Spokane Co., WA, 1883–1901
Buried: Fairmount Memorial Park, Spokane, WA
References: Jonathan Edwards. *An Illustrated History of Spokane County, State of Washington.* San Francisco, 1900. *History of the Arkansas Valley, Colorado.* Chicago, 1881. Obituary, *Spokane Spokesman-Review,* June 10, 1901. Pension File and Military Service File, National Archives. Letters Received, Volunteer Service Branch, Adjutant General's Office, File H101(VS)1867, National Archives.

Richard Mitchel Edwards

Appointed Captain, Commissary of Subsistence, USV, June 30, 1862, he acted as such on the staff of Brig. Gen. James G. Spears until July 24, 1862, when he received authority from Governor Andrew Johnson to organize a regiment of cavalry. Organization of the regiment (4 TN Cavalry) was not completed, however, until Nov. 24, 1864, at which time the strength of the regiment was reduced below the minimum required by law for muster of a colonel. To complete his record and to "enable him to liquidate obligations that he actually incurred in the organization of this regiment," he was, by War Department Special Orders No. 549, Oct. 16, 1865, mustered into service as Colonel, 4 TN Cavalry, to date Nov. 2, 1863, and honorably mustered out, to date Nov. 24, 1864.
Born: Dec. 31, 1822 Roane Co., TN
Died: Jan. 19, 1907 Johnson City, TN
Other Wars: Mexican War (Corporal, Co. C, 5 TN Infantry)
Occupation: Lawyer
Offices/Honors: Tennessee House of Representatives, 1861–62
Miscellaneous: Resided Cleveland, Bradley Co., TN
Buried: Fort Hill Cemetery, Cleveland, TN
References: Robert M. McBride and Dan M. Robison. *Biographical Directory of the Tennessee General Assembly.* Vol. 2, 1861–1901. Nashville, TN, 1979. Roy G. Lillard, editor. *History of Bradley County, TN.* Cleveland, TN, 1976. *The Heritage of Bradley County, TN, 1836–1998.* Waynesville, NC, 1998. Letters Received, Volunteer Service Branch, Adjutant General's Office, File K554(VS)1863, National Archives. Pension File and Military Service File, National Archives. *History of Tennessee from the Earliest Times to the Present, Together with an Historical and Biographical Sketch of Thirty East Tennessee Counties.* Nashville, TN, 1887. Obituary, *Chattanooga Daily Times,* Jan. 22, 1907. Alexander Eckel. *History of the 4th TN Cavalry: U.S.A., War of the Rebellion, 1861–65.* Johnson City, TN, 2001. Leroy P. Graf and Ralph W. Haskins, editors. *The Papers of Andrew Johnson.* Vol. 6, 1862–1864. Knoxville, TN, 1983.

Robert Galbraith

2 Lieutenant, Co. C, 5 TN Cavalry, July 25, 1862. Captain, Co. C, 5 TN Cavalry, Sept. 2, 1862. Major, 5 TN Cavalry, Nov. 24, 1862. Lieutenant Colonel, 5 TN Cavalry, Feb. 11, 1863. Commanded Post of Shelbyville, TN, Sept.–Oct. 1863. Amid regimental dissension triggered by his competition with Colonel William B. Stokes for control of the regiment, he resigned March 11, 1864, "for the purpose of tranquilizing the affairs of this regiment." Colonel, 5 TN Cavalry, May 1, 1865. The War Department refused to allow his muster as colonel since his earlier resignation had been accepted "for the good of the service." Battle honors: Tullahoma Campaign (Shelbyville), Wheeler and Roddey's Raid (Farmington).
Born: 1836 Shelbyville, TN
Died: March 30, 1881 Shelbyville, TN
Occupation: Merchant, bookkeeper and clerk
Offices/Honors: Tennessee House of Representatives, 1867–69

Robert Galbraith (John Sickles Collection).

Miscellaneous: Resided Shelbyville, Bedford Co., TN
Buried: Old City Cemetery, Shelbyville, TN
References: Robert M. McBride and Dan M. Robison. *Biographical Directory of the Tennessee General Assembly.* Vol. 2, 1861–1901. Nashville, TN, 1979. Pension File and Military Service File, National Archives. Letters Received, Volunteer Service Branch, Adjutant General's Office, File G251(VS) 1864, National Archives. Obituary, *Nashville Daily American,* March 31, 1881. Myers E. Brown II. *Tennessee's Union Cavalrymen.* Charleston, SC, 2008.

Leonidas Campbell Houk

1 Lieutenant, RQM, 1 TN Infantry, Sept. 1, 1861. Colonel, 3 TN Infantry, Feb. 6, 1862. Resigned April 3, 1863, due to physical disability from erysipelas and hemorrhage of the lungs and also the need to care for his family "banished from their home in East Tennessee." Battle honors: Cumberland Gap Campaign (London).
Born: June 8, 1836 near Boyd's Creek, Sevier Co., TN
Died: May 25, 1891 Knoxville, TN (accidental poisoning with arsenic)
Occupation: Lawyer and judge
Offices/Honors: Circuit Court Judge, 1866–70. Tennessee House of Representatives, 1873–75. U.S. House of Representatives, 1879–91.
Miscellaneous: Resided Clinton, Anderson Co.,

Leonidas Campbell Houk (post-war) (Library of Congress [LC-USZ62-104347]).

TN, to 1870; Knoxville, Knox Co., TN, 1870–78; and Washington, DC, 1878–91
Buried: Old Gray Cemetery, Knoxville, TN (Lot 424)
References: *Dictionary of American Biography.* William S. Speer, compiler. *Sketches of Prominent Tennesseans.* Nashville, TN, 1888. Oliver P. Temple. *Notable Men of Tennessee, from 1833 to 1875, Their Times and Their Contemporaries.* New York City, NY, 1912. *Memorial Addresses on the Life and Character of Leonidas Campbell Houk, A Representative from Tennessee.* Washington, DC, 1892. Obituary, *Knoxville Weekly Tribune,* May 27, 1891. *Society of the Army of the Cumberland. Twenty-Second Reunion, Columbus, OH, 1891.* Cincinnati, OH, 1892. Carroll Van West, editor-in-chief. *The Tennessee Encyclopedia of History & Culture.* Nashville, TN, 1998. Robert M. McBride and Dan M. Robison. *Biographical Directory of the Tennessee General Assembly.* Vol. 2, 1861–1901. Nashville, TN, 1979. James L. Harrison, compiler. *Biographical Directory of the American Congress, 1774–1949.* Washington, DC, 1950. Pension File and Military Service File, National Archives. Walter Lynn Bates, "Southern Unionists: A Socio-Economic Examination of the Third East Tennessee Volunteer Infantry Regiment, U.S.A., 1862–1865," *Tennessee Historical Quarterly,* Vol. 50, No. 4 (Winter 1991).

Fielding Jackson Hurst

Arrested and imprisoned at least three times for pro–Union activities between June 1861 and Feb. 1862. Commissioned Colonel, 6 TN Cavalry, Aug.

11, 1862. Mustered as colonel, July 1, 1863. Commanded 2 Brigade, 1 Cavalry Division, 16 Army Corps, Army of the Tennessee, Aug. 20–Sept. 20, 1863. Suffering from "the effects of scurvy ... contracted while a prisoner in the hands of the rebels," he resigned Jan. 8, 1865, "being in bad health and physically unfit for the service." Battle honors: Chalmers' Raid (Collierville), Forrest's Expedition into West Tennessee and Kentucky (Bolivar).

Born: 1810 Claiborne Co., TN
Died: April 3, 1882 near Rose Creek, TN
Occupation: Lawyer, farmer, and merchant
Offices/Honors: Tennessee Senate, 1865. Circuit Court Judge, 1865–69. U.S. Internal Revenue Collector, 1869–71.
Miscellaneous: Resided Purdy, McNairy Co., TN; and Rose Creek, McNairy Co., TN
Buried: Mount Gilead Baptist Cemetery, near Rose Creek, McNairy Co., TN
References: Kevin D. McCann. *Hurst's Wurst: Colonel Fielding Hurst and the Sixth Tennessee Cavalry, U.S.A.* Dickson, TN, 2007. Gary Blankinship, "Colonel Fielding Hurst and the Hurst Nation," *West Tennessee Historical Society Papers*, Vol. 34 (1980). Robert M. McBride and Dan M. Robison. *Biographical Directory of the Tennessee General Assembly.* Vol. 2, 1861–1901. Nashville, TN, 1979. http://hurstnation.com. W. Clay Crook, "Hurst!," *Confederate Veteran*, March–April 1992. Pension File and Military Service File, National Archives. http://tennesseeencyclopedia.net/entry.php?rec=1616.

Fielding Jackson Hurst.

William Patrick Kendrick (aka Kindrick)

Colonel, 3 West TN Cavalry, date unknown. Taken prisoner Corinth, MS, June 10, 1863. Confined Libby Prison, Richmond, VA. Participated in the famous Libby Prison Tunnel escape, Feb. 9, 1864. Best known for his Feb. 21, 1864 letter to President Abraham Lincoln advising him of the "condition of my fellow officers at Libby Prison, Richmond, VA, and the extreme suffering of our enlisted men on Belle Isle (that rebel hell)."

Born: April 1, 1826 Tazewell Co., VA
Died: March 18, 1864 Clifton, TN
Occupation: Lawyer
Offices/Honors: Tennessee House of Representatives, 1857–59
Miscellaneous: Resided Waynesboro, Wayne Co., TN
Buried: Family Cemetery, North High Street, Waynesboro, TN
References: Robert M. McBride and Dan M. Robison. *Biographical Directory of the Tennessee General Assembly.* Vol. 1, 1796–1861. Nashville, TN, 1975. Pension File and Military Service File, National Archives. *The War of the Rebellion: A Compilation of the Official Records of the Union and Confederate Armies.* (Series 2, Vol. 6, pp. 966, 977–978). Washington, DC, 1899. http://biffle.org/fgs-elizabethbifflekindrick.html. *History of Tennessee from the Earliest Times to the Present, Together with an Historical and Biographical Sketch of Lawrence, Wayne, Perry, Hickman, and Lewis Counties.* Nashville, TN, 1886. James Gindlesperger. *Escape from Libby Prison.* Shippensburg, PA, 1995.

Asa Calkins Ketchum

Captain, Co. B, 15 TN Infantry, CSA, May 17, 1861. Date of discharge unknown. Colonel, 2 Regiment, Enrolled Militia, District of Memphis, Dec. 29, 1863. Resigned Oct. 15, 1864.

Born: June 4, 1820 Cortland Co., NY
Died: Dec. 8, 1881 Chautauqua Springs, KS
Occupation: Lawyer and judge
Offices/Honors: Wisconsin General Assembly, 1854
Miscellaneous: Resided Portage, Columbia Co., WI; Memphis, Shelby Co., TN; Marble Hill, Bollinger Co., MO; St. Louis, MO; Columbus, Cherokee Co., KS; and Neodesha, Wilson Co., KS
Buried: Chautauqua Springs, Chautauqua Co., KS
References: Robert P. Addleman. *Ketchum-McCorkell Pioneers: Midwestern Families of Lillias Jacinth Burton.* Apollo, PA, 1993. Letters Received, Volunteer Service Branch, Adjutant General's Office, File H101(VS)1867, National Archives.

Asa Calkins Ketchum (courtesy Robert P. Addleman).

http://ketchum.bobaddleman.com. Leroy P. Graf and Ralph W. Haskins, editors. *The Papers of Andrew Johnson.* Vol. 6, 1862–1864. Knoxville, TN, 1983. Compiled Service Records of Confederate Soldiers Who Served in Organizations from the State of Tennessee, National Archives.

John Smith Lord

Sergeant Major, 113 IL Infantry, Oct. 1, 1862. 1 Lieutenant, Adjutant, 113 IL Infantry, July 27, 1863. Acting AAG, Post of Corinth, MS, Oct. 26, 1863. Acting AAG, 2 Brigade, District of Memphis, Jan. 27, 1864. Acting AAG, 1 Brigade, District of Memphis, June 22, 1864. Acting AAG, Post and Defenses of Memphis, District of West Tennessee, Jan. 26, 1865. Detached as *Colonel*, 3 Regiment, Enrolled Militia, District of West Tennessee, April 1, 1865. Regiment disbanded, May 8, 1865. Honorably mustered out (113 IL Infantry), June 20, 1865.

Born: Nov. 5, 1837 Lyme, CT
Died: Dec. 22, 1911 Springfield, IL
Education: Graduated University of Michigan, Ann Arbor, MI, 1861
Occupation: Real estate and insurance agent, coal mine operator, and state and federal government official
Offices/Honors: Secretary of Bureau of Illinois

John Smith Lord (A. Pattiani, Photographer, No. 75 Lake Street, Chicago, Illinois; courtesy The Gilder Lehrman Institute of American History [GLC05111.02.0914]).

Labor Statistics, 1882–93. Chief of Population Division, 12th U.S. Census, 1900–1901. Deputy Collector, U.S. Internal Revenue Service, 1901–11.

Miscellaneous: Resided Henry, Marshall Co., IL, to 1861; Chicago, IL, 1861–72; Green River, Henry Co., IL, 1872–79; Davenport, Scott Co., IA, 1879–82; and Springfield, Sangamon Co., IL, 1882–1911

Buried: Oak Ridge Cemetery, Springfield, IL (Block 10, Lot 282)

References: Henry M. Utley and Byron M. Cutcheon, compilers. *The Class of Sixty-One, University of Michigan, and Something About What "the Boys" Have Been Doing During Forty Years from 1861 to 1901.* Detroit, MI, 1902. Pension File and Military Service File, National Archives. Obituary, *Illinois State Register,* Dec. 23, 1911. Obituary, *Illinois State Journal,* Dec. 23, 1911. Letters Received, Volunteer Service Branch, Adjutant General's Office, Files L15(VS)1864, L1126(VS)1864, L148 (VS)1865, and L608(VS)1865, National Archives. Theodore R. Chase. *The Michigan University Book: 1844–1880.* Detroit, MI, 1881. Kenneth Lord, compiler. *Genealogy of the Descendants of Thomas Lord,*

Charles McDonald (oil painting; courtesy Tennessee State Museum [83.109.1]).

John Smith Lord (post-war) (Henry M. Utley and Byron M. Cutcheon, comps. *The Class of Sixty-One, University of Michigan, and Something About What "the Boys" Have Been Doing During Forty Years from 1861 to 1901.* Detroit, Michigan, 1902).

an Original Proprietor and Founder of Hartford, CT, in 1636. New Haven, CT, 1946.

Charles McDonald

Captain, Co. C, 8 MO Infantry, June 13, 1861. Acting AAG, Staff of Brig. Gen. Morgan L. Smith, 1 Brigade, 5 Division, District of Memphis, Army of West Tennessee, July 27, 1862. Captain, AAG, USV, Staff of Brig. Gen. David Stuart, 2 Division, 15 Army Corps, Army of the Tennessee, Dec. 23, 1862. Resigned Aug. 18, 1863, since "business of a peculiar private nature (already long delayed) now demands my earliest personal attention and ... my health has been very much impaired for the past three months." *Lieutenant Colonel,* 1 Regiment, Enrolled Militia, District of Memphis, Dec. 29, 1863. *Colonel,* 1 Regiment, Enrolled Militia, District of Memphis, July 29, 1864. Battle honors: Fort Donelson, Arkansas Post.

Born: Feb. 10, 1838 NY
Died: Dec. 12, 1864 Memphis, TN (killed by accidental fall of his horse during a review of his regiment)
Occupation: Wholesale grocer

Miscellaneous: Resided St. Louis, MO; and Memphis, Shelby Co., TN. Brother of Colonel John McDonald (1 Regiment, Enrolled Militia, District of Memphis).
Buried: Elmwood Cemetery, Memphis, TN (Chapel Hill Section, Lot 24, unmarked)
References: Pension File and Military Service File, National Archives. Letters Received, Commission Branch, Adjutant General's Office, File M439(CB)1863, National Archives. Letters Received, Volunteer Service Branch, Adjutant General's Office, File H101(VS)1867, National Archives. Leroy P. Graf and Ralph W. Haskins, editors. *The Papers of Andrew Johnson.* Vol. 6, 1862–1864. Knoxville, TN, 1983.

John McDonald

Captain, Co. A, 8 MO Infantry, June 12, 1861. Major, 8 MO Infantry, July 4, 1861. Sentenced by general court martial, May 4, 1862, to be dismissed for using "grossly insulting, obscene and abusive language" toward Lt. Col. James Peckham. Although the sentence was remitted upon appealing to the clemency of Major Gen. Halleck, he resigned May 26, 1862, "with a view of entering the service in another quarter." *Colonel,* 1 Regiment, Enrolled Militia, District of Memphis, Dec. 29, 1863. *Brig. Gen.,* Enrolled Militia, District of Memphis, Jan. 28, 1864. Resigned July 23, 1864. Battle honors: Fort Donelson.

Born: Feb. 22, 1831 Rochester, NY
Died: Jan. 20, 1912 Chicago, IL

John McDonald (post-war) (John McDonald. *Secrets of the Great Whiskey Ring: And Eighteen Months in the Penitentiary.* St. Louis, Missouri, 1880).

Occupation: Livery stable keeper and steamboat operator before war. Pension claim agent and real estate broker after war.

Offices/Honors: Supervisor of U.S. Internal Revenue, 1869–75

Miscellaneous: Resided St. Louis, MO; Chicago, IL; and Green Lake, Green Lake Co., WI. Brother of Colonel Charles McDonald (1 Regiment, Enrolled Militia, District of Memphis). One of the organizers of the Great Whiskey Ring, he was convicted and served eighteen months in the Missouri Penitentiary before being pardoned by President Grant on his last day in office.

Buried: Dartford Cemetery, Green Lake, WI

References: Lawrence O. Christensen, William E. Foley, Gary R. Kremer, and Kenneth H. Winn, editors. *Dictionary of Missouri Biography.* Columbia, MO, 1999. Obituary, *Ripon Commonwealth,* Jan. 26, 1912. Pension File and Military Service File, National Archives. Robert W. and Emma B. Heiple. *A Heritage History of Beautiful Green Lake, WI.* Green Lake, WI, 1977. Obituary, *Chicago Daily Tribune,* Jan. 21, 1912. John McDonald. *Secrets of the Great Whiskey Ring: And Eighteen Months in the Penitentiary.* St. Louis, MO, 1880. Lucius E. Guese, "St. Louis and the Great Whisky Ring," *Missouri Historical Review,* Vol. 36, No. 2 (Jan. 1942). Leroy P. Graf and Ralph W. Haskins, editors. *The Papers of Andrew Johnson.* Vol. 6, 1862–1864. Knoxville, TN, 1983. Letters Received, Volunteer Service Branch, Adjutant General's Office, File H101(VS) 1867, National Archives.

James Marion Melton

Captain, Co. B, 2 TN Infantry, Aug. 20, 1861. Major, 2 TN Infantry, April 1, 1862. Lieutenant Colonel, 2 TN Infantry, Oct. 18, 1862. Colonel, 2 TN Infantry, May 2, 1864. Honorably mustered out, Oct. 8, 1864. Battle honors: Stone's River, Morgan's Ohio Raid.

Born: March 26, 1832 Morgan Co., TN
Died: Feb. 1, 1923 Knoxville, TN
Occupation: Farmer before war. Lumber merchant after war.

Offices/Honors: Sheriff, Morgan Co., TN, 1856–58. County court clerk, Morgan Co., TN, 1858–61. Tennessee House of Representatives, 1865–67. Tennessee Senate, 1873–75. Collector of U.S. Internal Revenue, 1879–85.

Miscellaneous: Resided Wartburg, Morgan Co., TN, to 1870; Kingston, Roane Co., TN; Eureka Springs, Carroll Co., AR; and Knoxville, Knox Co., TN

Buried: Bethel Cemetery, Kingston, TN
References: Robert M. McBride and Dan M. Robison. *Biographical Directory of the Tennessee General Assembly.* Vol. 2, 1861–1901. Nashville, TN, 1979. Obituary, *Knoxville Journal and Tribune,* Feb. 2, 1923. Eddie M. Nikazy. *Forgotten Soldiers: History of the 2nd Tennessee Volunteer Infantry Regiment (USA), 1861–1865.* Bowie, MD, 1996. Pension File and Military Service File, National Archives. James D. Richardson. *Tennessee Templars.* Nashville, TN, 1883.

John Kelly Miller

Colonel, 13 TN Cavalry, Oct. 5, 1863. Commanded 3 Brigade, 4 Division, Cavalry Corps, De-

John Kelly Miller.

John Kelly Miller (Samuel W. Scott and Samuel P. Angel. *History of the 13th Regiment Tennessee Volunteer Cavalry, U.S.A.* Philadelphia, Pennsylvania, 1903).

partment of the Cumberland, April–June 1864. Commanded Post of Gallatin, TN, District of Tennessee, Department of the Cumberland, July–Aug. 1864. Commanded Brigade of Governor's Guard, Department of the Cumberland, Aug. 1864–Jan. 1865. Commanded 3 Brigade, Cavalry Division, District of East Tennessee, Department of the Cumberland, March–July 1865. Tried by court martial for "forging and counterfeiting a signature ... for the purpose of obtaining payment of a false claim," he was found not guilty of that charge, but found guilty of the accompanying charge of "conduct to the prejudice of good order and military discipline" and dismissed Nov. 20, 1865. The findings and sentence of the court martial were, however, disapproved, by order of President Andrew Johnson, Jan. 13, 1866, and he was honorably mustered out to date Nov. 20, 1865. Battle honors: Operations in East Tennessee (Greeneville), Breckinridge's Advance into East Tennessee (Bull's Gap), Expedition into Southwestern Virginia and Western North Carolina (Wytheville, Salisbury).

Born: April 5, 1828 Carter Co., TN
Died: July 10, 1903 Elizabethton, TN

Occupation: Wagon maker before war. Farmer, merchant, and county court clerk after war.
Offices/Honors: Sheriff, Carter Co., TN, 1860–63. Collector of U.S. Internal Revenue, 1871–75. Tennessee Senate, 1879–81.
Miscellaneous: Resided Elizabethton, Carter Co., TN, to 1878; Johnson City, Washington Co., TN, 1878–80; Erwin, Unicoi Co., TN; and Bristol, Sullivan Co., TN
Buried: Highland Cemetery, Elizabethton, TN
References: *Carter County, Tennessee, and Its People, 1796–1993.* Elizabethton, TN, 1993. Robert M. McBride and Dan M. Robison. *Biographical Directory of the Tennessee General Assembly.* Vol. 2, 1861–1901. Nashville, TN, 1979. Samuel W. Scott and Samuel P. Angel. *History of the 13th Regiment Tennessee Volunteer Cavalry, U.S.A.* Philadelphia, PA, 1903. Pension File and Military Service File, National Archives. Obituary, *Knoxville Journal and Tribune*, July 11, 1903. Letters Received, Volunteer Service Branch, Adjutant General's Office, File M639(VS)1867, National Archives.

John Murphy

Private and Corporal, Co. G, 4 U.S. Cavalry, Aug. 25, 1855. 1 Lieutenant, Adjutant, 5 TN Cav-

John Murphy (Giers & Co., National Portrait Gallery and Dealers in Photographic Materials, 42 & 44 Union St., Nashville, Tennessee).

alry, Aug. 31, 1862. Major, 5 TN Cavalry, Feb. 13, 1863. Resigned Oct. 13, 1863, since "I cannot in my opinion render efficient service to the regiment, and I find that all my efforts to promote the discipline of the regiment are fruitless." Resignation revoked, Nov. 1, 1863. On detached service with Governor's Guard, Nov. 1863–April 1864. Commanded Post of Clifton, TN, March–April 1864. Lieutenant Colonel, 2 TN Mounted Infantry, May 16, 1864. Colonel, 2 TN Mounted Infantry, July 1, 1864. Honorably mustered out, Jan. 19, 1865. Battle honors: Bradyville (TN).
Born: 1837? Abbeyfeale, County Limerick, Ireland
Died: Feb. 26, 1871 Trinidad, CO
Occupation: Regular Army (1 Lieutenant, 4 U.S. Cavalry, resigned July 31, 1869, while awaiting trial on charges of "Conduct unbecoming an officer and a gentleman, Positive and willful disobedience of orders, and Drunkenness on duty")
Miscellaneous: Resided Dubuque, Dubuque Co., IA, before war; Gallatin, Sumner Co., TN, and Pueblo, Pueblo Co., CO, after war
Buried: Place of burial unknown
References: Letters Received, Commission Branch, Adjutant General's Office, File M519(CB) 1866, National Archives. Military Service File, National Archives. http://trees.ancestry.com/tree/8947993/person/-871016185. Obituary, *Colorado Chieftain,* March 2, 1871. Leroy P. Graf and Ralph W. Haskins, editors. *The Papers of Andrew Johnson.* Vol. 6, 1862–1864. Knoxville, TN, 1983.

Joseph H. Parsons

Colonel, 9 TN Cavalry, Oct. 1, 1864. Sentenced by General Court Martial, Oct. 10, 1865, to be hanged for ordering the killing of John A. Thornhill, Captain, Co. B, 9 TN Cavalry, who had previously assaulted him. Sentence remitted in full, "in consideration of the high social and military standing of Colonel Parsons and of his long, faithful and valuable services to the Government during the rebellion, and the numerous and strong recommendations of the Court which tried him, to the mercy of the reviewing authority, based as they state on their conviction that 'he was actuated by no malice or hatred, but simply by a sincere though mistaken idea that the fatal act was necessary for the safety of himself and friends.'" In reviewing the proceedings of the court, Major Gen. George Stoneman commented, "Society lost nothing in Thornhill's death, and justice will be satisfied by sparing Parsons' life." Honorably mustered out, to date Sept. 11, 1865. Battle honors: Operations in East Tennessee (Morristown), Breckinridge's Advance into East Tennessee (Bull's Gap).
Born: Feb. 4, 1823 Rogersville, TN
Died: Nov. 27–Dec. 3, 1888 Fabius, AL
Other Wars: Mexican War (Private, Co. D, 4 TN Infantry)
Occupation: Lawyer and school teacher
Offices/Honors: Tennessee House of Representatives, 1849–51
Miscellaneous: Resided Maryville, Blount Co., TN; Knoxville, Knox Co., TN; Pana, Christian Co., IL (1869); and Fabius, Jackson Co., AL, 1880–88
Buried: Place of burial unknown
References: Pension File and Military Service File, National Archives. Robert M. McBride and Dan M. Robison. *Biographical Directory of the Tennessee General Assembly.* Vol. 1, 1796–1861. Nashville, TN, 1975. Obituary, *Stevenson Chronicle,* Dec. 4, 1888. Letters Received, Volunteer Service Branch, Adjutant General's Office, Files T251(VS) 1864 and P3319(VS)1865, National Archives. Court-martial Case Files, 1809–1894, File MM-3016, National Archives. Leroy P. Graf and Ralph W. Haskins, editors. *The Papers of Andrew Johnson.* Vol. 6, 1862–1864. Knoxville, TN, 1983.

Samuel Kelsey Nelson Patton

Colonel, 8 TN Cavalry, April 1, 1864. Commanded Post of Gallatin (TN), District of Tennessee, Department of the Cumberland, Aug.–Sept. 1864. Sentenced by court martial, Aug. 18, 1865, to be reprimanded upon "various charges of a serious character," he was released from arrest and restored to duty when the sentence was disapproved by Major Gen. Alvan C. Gillem, with the comment, "The Court in finding the accused guilty of a specification embodying a grave charge, but attaching no criminality thereto, have added a novel clause to the annals of Military Courts." Honorably mustered out, Sept. 11, 1865. Battle honors: Operations in East Tennessee (Morristown), Breckinridge's Advance into East Tennessee (Bull's Gap), Expedition from East Tennessee into Southwestern Virginia (Kingsport).
Born: March 6, 1816 Jonesborough, TN
Died: Feb. 3, 1886 Meadow Brook, Washington Co., TN
Occupation: Merchant, farmer and iron manufacturer before war. Farmer after war.
Offices/Honors: Tennessee House of Representatives, 1861–63 and 1866–67. Tennessee Senate, 1873–75.
Miscellaneous: Resided Jonesborough, Washington Co., TN; Kingsport, Sullivan Co., TN; and Haws Crossroads, Washington Co., TN
Buried: Fall Branch Methodist Churchyard, Fall Branch, Washington Co., TN
References: Pension File and Military Service File, National Archives. Robert M. McBride and

Samuel Kelsey Nelson Patton (T. H. Smiley's Photograph Gallery, Opposite Custom House, Gay Street, Knoxville, Tennessee).

Dan M. Robison. *Biographical Directory of the Tennessee General Assembly.* Vol. 2, 1861–1901. Nashville, TN, 1979. Leroy P. Graf, editor. *The Papers of Andrew Johnson.* Vol. 7, 1864–1865. Knoxville, TN, 1986. Court-martial Case Files, 1809–1894, File MM-3351, National Archives. Obituary, *Jonesborough Herald and Tribune,* Feb. 4, 1886.

William Cowan Pickens

Saber wound left forearm, while leading a band of bridge burners in an attempt to burn the Strawberry Plains (TN) bridge over the Holston River, Nov. 8, 1861. Major, 6 TN Infantry, May 2, 1862. Resigned Aug. 22, 1862. Colonel, 3 TN Cavalry, Jan. 1, 1863. Honorably mustered out, Nov. 21, 1863, as a supernumerary officer, his regiment lacking sufficient strength to entitle it to an officer of the grade of colonel. Battle honors: Stone's River.
  Born: March 7, 1825 Sevier Co., TN
  Died: April 8, 1872 near Maryville, TN
  Occupation: Farmer
  Offices/Honors: Sheriff, Sevier Co., TN, 1851–52. Blount County (TN) Clerk, 1864–67.
  Miscellaneous: Resided Boyd's Creek, Sevier Co., TN; and Maryville, Blount Co., TN
  Buried: Eusebia Presbyterian Churchyard, Prospect, Blount Co., TN
  References: Nellie P. Anderson. *The John Pickens Family.* Rockford, TN, 1951. Obituary, *Knoxville Daily Chronicle,* April 10, 1872. Pension File and Military Service File, National Archives. Charles S. McCammon. *Loyal Mountain Troopers: The Second and Third Tennessee Volunteer Cavalry in the Civil War.* Maryville, TN, 1992. Leroy P. Graf and Ralph W. Haskins, editors. *The Papers of Andrew Johnson.* Vol. 6, 1862–1864. Knoxville, TN, 1983. Letters Received, Volunteer Service Branch, Adjutant General's Office, File T595(VS)1863, National Archives. Oliver P. Temple. *East Tennessee and the Civil War.* Cincinnati, OH, 1899.

William Farrand Prosser

Quartermaster Sergeant, Palmer's Independent Co. (Anderson Troop), PA Cavalry, Nov. 30, 1861. Taken prisoner en route Huntsville, AL, June 1862. Paroled August 1862. Acting 2 Lieutenant, Co. E, 15 PA Cavalry, Dec. 28, 1862. Major, 2 TN Cavalry, March 31, 1863. *Lieutenant Colonel,* 2 TN Cavalry, March 26, 1864. Commanded 1 Brigade, 4 Cavalry Division, Department of the Cumberland, Aug. 1864 and Oct. 1864. *Colonel,* 2 TN Cavalry, June 26, 1865. Honorably mustered out, July 6, 1865. Battle honors: Shiloh, Stone's River, Meridian Expedition (Okolona), Wheeler's Raid to North Georgia and East Tennessee, Forrest's Raid into Northern Alabama and Middle Tennessee

William Farrand Prosser (U.S. House of Representatives, 1869) (Brady-Handy Photograph Collection, Library of Congress [LC-DIG-cwpbh-00353]).

William Farrand Prosser (post-war) (Review of Reviews Collection, USAMHI [RG490S-R of R.120]).

(Athens), Operations in North Georgia and North Alabama (Decatur).
Born: March 16, 1834 Williamsport, PA
Died: Sept. 23, 1911 Seattle, WA
Occupation: School teacher and California miner before war. Civil engineer, real estate agent, and capitalist after war.
Offices/Honors: Tennessee House of Representatives, 1867–69. U.S. House of Representatives, 1869–71. Postmaster, Nashville, TN, 1871–74. Special Agent, U.S. Land Office, 1879–85. Seattle City Treasurer, 1908–10. One of the founders of the Washington State Historical Society.
Miscellaneous: Resided Nashville, Davidson Co., TN, to 1879; North Yakima, Yakima Co., WA; and Seattle, King Co., WA
Buried: Lake View Cemetery, Seattle, WA (Lot 279A)
References: *A Volume of Memoirs and Genealogy of Representative Citizens of the City of Seattle and County of King, Washington.* New York and Chicago, 1903. Elwood Evans. *History of the Pacific Northwest: Oregon and Washington.* Portland, OR, 1889. Obituary, *Seattle Post-Intelligencer,* Sept. 24, 1911. William Horatio Barnes. *The Forty-First Congress of the United States, 1869–71.* New York, 1872. Robert M. McBride and Dan M. Robison. *Biographical Directory of the Tennessee General Assembly.* Vol. 2, 1861–1901. Nashville, TN, 1979. James L. Harrison, compiler. *Biographical Directory of the American Congress, 1774–1949.* Washington, DC, 1950. Obituary Circular, Whole No. 197, Washington MOLLUS. Pension File and Military Service File, National Archives. Letters Received, Volunteer Service Branch, Adjutant General's Office, File G635(VS)1865, National Archives. Charles S. McCammon. *Loyal Mountain Troopers: The Second and Third Tennessee Volunteer Cavalry in the Civil War.* Maryville, TN, 1992.

Daniel Mack Ray

1 Lieutenant, Adjutant, 3 TN Infantry, Feb. 10, 1862. Colonel, 2 TN Cavalry, Nov. 8, 1862. Commanded 3 Brigade, 1 Cavalry Division, Department of the Cumberland, Feb.–April 1863. Commanded 2 Brigade, 1 Division, Cavalry Corps, Army of the Cumberland, Sept.–Oct. 1863. Resigned Feb. 15, 1864, since "my business is [in] such a condition that I am compelled to attend to it." Battle honors: Stone's River, Franklin, Tullahoma Campaign, Chickamauga.
Born: March 27, 1833 Yancey Co., NC
Died: April 7, 1913 Yates Center, KS
Occupation: School teacher before war. Farmer and real estate agent after war.
Offices/Honors: Woodson County (KS) Surveyor for twelve years
Miscellaneous: Resided Sevierville, Sevier Co., TN, before war; Arcola, Douglas Co., IL, 1864–

Daniel Mack Ray (post-war) (L. Wallace Duncan and Charles F. Scott, eds. ***History of Allen and Woodson Counties, Kansas.*** Iola, Kansas, 1901).

67; Loda, Iroquois Co., IL, 1867–70; Everett Twp., Woodson Co., KS, 1870–82; Yates Center, Woodson Co., KS, after 1882

Buried: Yates Center Cemetery, Yates Center, KS (Section 11, Lot 49)

References: Pension File and Military Service File, National Archives. L. Wallace Duncan and Charles F. Scott, editors. *History of Allen and Woodson Counties, KS.* Iola, KS, 1901. Charles S. McCammon. *Loyal Mountain Troopers: The Second and Third Tennessee Volunteer Cavalry in the Civil War.* Maryville, TN, 1992. Leroy P. Graf and Ralph W. Haskins, editors. *The Papers of Andrew Johnson.* Vol. 5, 1861–1862. Knoxville, TN, 1979.

Arthur Tappan Reeve

Private, Co. K, 7 KS Cavalry, Nov. 12, 1861. Hospital Steward, 7 KS Cavalry, Sept. 16, 1862. Captain, Co. D, 55 USCT, May 21, 1863. Detached as *Lieutenant Colonel*, 1 Regiment, Enrolled Militia (Freedmen), District of Memphis, Sept. 21, 1864. Detached as *Colonel*, 2 Regiment, Enrolled Militia (Freedmen), District of West Tennessee, Dec. 15, 1864–April 6, 1865. Major, 88 USCT, April 7, 1865. Resigned Dec. 4, 1865, since "I entered the service with a desire and intention to remain only so long as the country might need my services and still desire to return to my family and private business so soon as my services may be no longer needed which time I trust is already at hand." Battle honors: Brice's Cross Roads.

Born: Dec. 18, 1835 New Lyme, Ashtabula Co., OH

Died: Oct. 25, 1889 Washington, DC

Occupation: Lawyer, real estate agent, and U.S. Government agent in Quartermaster General's Office

Offices/Honors: Franklin County (IA) Treasurer, 1869–73. Chief of the Seed Division, U.S. Agriculture Department, at his death.

Miscellaneous: Resided Maysville, Franklin Co., IA; Hampton, Franklin Co., IA; and Washington, DC

Buried: Hampton Cemetery, Hampton, IA

References: *History of Franklin and Cerro Gordo Counties, IA.* Springfield, IL, 1883. *The United States Biographical Dictionary and Portrait Gallery of Eminent and Self-Made Men.* Iowa Volume. Chicago and New York, 1878. Obituary, *Washington Post,* Oct. 26, 1889. Pension File and Military Service File, National Archives. Letters Received,

Officers of the 55 USCT, including Arthur Tappan Reeve (No. 3, upper left).

Colored Troops Branch, Adjutant General's Office, File R84(CT)1865, National Archives. Letters Received, Volunteer Service Branch, Adjutant General's Office, File H101(VS)1867, National Archives.

Felix Alexander Reeve

Colonel, 8 TN Infantry, Sept. 16, 1862. Commanded 1 Brigade, 3 Division, 23 Army Corps, Department of the Ohio, Jan. 16–April 3, 1864. Resigned July 15, 1864, on account of physical disability due to chronic inflammation of the bladder, chronic laryngitis, and an attack of dysentery. Battle honors: Atlanta Campaign (Resaca, Kenesaw Mountain).

Born: Sept. 4, 1836 Cocke Co., TN
Died: Nov. 15, 1920 Washington, DC
Occupation: Lawyer
Offices/Honors: Solicitor of the U.S. Treasury, 1893–97. Assistant Solicitor of the U.S. Treasury, 1886–93 and 1897–1920.
Miscellaneous: Resided Greeneville, Greene Co., TN; Knoxville, Knox Co., TN, 1873–79; and Washington, DC, after 1879
Buried: Arlington National Cemetery, Arlington, VA (Section 3, Lot 1718)
References: *The Union Army.* Vol. 8 (Washington, DC, Edition). Madison, WI, 1908. William H. Powell, editor. *Officers of the Army and Navy (Volunteer) Who Served in the Civil War.* Philadelphia, PA, 1893. Obituary, *Washington Evening Star,* Nov. 16, 1920. *Who Was Who in America, 1897–1942.* Chicago, 1942. Obituary, *Knoxville Journal and Tribune,* Nov. 16, 1920. Pension File and Military Service File, National Archives. Letters Received, Volunteer Service Branch, Adjutant General's Office, File O340(VS)1862, National Archives.

Thomas Hansel Reeves

Private, Co. F, 2 TN Infantry, Nov. 19, 1861. Despite assurances that he had proper authority to return to East Tennessee to recruit a company of volunteers, he was reported for desertion, Aug. 25, 1862, a charge not removed until Nov. 10, 1864, when he was mustered out to date April 30, 1862. 1 Lieutenant, Co. D, 4 TN Infantry, Feb. 19, 1863. Captain, Co. D, 4 TN Infantry, May 29, 1863. Taken prisoner and paroled, McMinnville, TN, Oct. 3, 1863. Acting AIG, 1 Brigade, 3 Division, 23 Army Corps, Department of the Ohio, Feb.–March 1864. Major, 4 TN Infantry, Aug. 10, 1864. Lieutenant Colonel, 4 TN Infantry, May 31, 1865. *Colonel,* 4 TN Infantry, July 29, 1865. Honorably mustered out, Aug. 2, 1865. Bvt. Major, USA, March 2, 1867, for faithful and meritorious services during the war. Bvt. Lieutenant Colonel, USA,

Felix Alexander Reeve (post-war) (William H. Powell, ed. *Officers of the Army and Navy (Volunteer) Who Served in the Civil War.* Philadelphia, Pennsylvania, 1893).

Thomas Hansel Reeves (as Captain, 39 U.S. Infantry, 1867) (courtesy Tennessee State Library and Archives [wash089]).

March 2, 1867, for faithful and meritorious services during the war. Battle honors: Wheeler and Roddey's Raid (McMinnville).

Born: Feb. 24, 1843 Iredell Co., NC
Died: Aug. 26, 1926 Johnson City, TN
Occupation: Regular Army (Captain, 39 U.S. Infantry, retired June 5, 1868), lawyer, and farmer
Offices/Honors: U.S. Marshal, Eastern District of Tennessee, 1881–85
Miscellaneous: Resided Fall Branch, Washington Co., TN; Jonesborough, Washington Co., TN; Knoxville, Knox Co., TN; Morristown, Hamblen Co., TN; and Johnson City, Washington Co., TN
Buried: Maple Lawn Cemetery, Jonesborough, TN (unmarked?)
References: *History of Tennessee from the Earliest Times to the Present, Together with an Historical and Biographical Sketch of Thirty East Tennessee Counties.* Nashville, TN, 1887. Obituary, *Jonesborough Herald and Tribune,* Sept. 1, 1926. Military Service File, National Archives. Letters Received, Appointment, Commission, and Personal Branch, Adjutant General's Office, File 1260(ACP)1873, National Archives. Letters Received, Volunteer Service Branch, Adjutant General's Office, File P1725(VS)1866, National Archives. Eddie M. Nikazy. *Forgotten Soldiers: History of the 4th Tennessee Volunteer Infantry Regiment (USA), 1863–1865.* Bowie, MD, 1995. Obituary, *Knoxville Journal,* Aug. 28, 1926. Leroy P. Graf and Ralph W. Haskins, editors. *The Papers of Andrew Johnson.* Vol. 6, 1862–1864. Knoxville, TN, 1983.

John A. Rogers

Colonel, 1 West TN Infantry (also known as 7 TN Infantry), Oct. 10, 1862. Accused of "inexperience and incompetency and utter unfitness for the command of anything military" for his conduct at Humboldt, TN, Dec. 20, 1862, he resigned Jan. 16, 1863. Battle honors: Forrest's Expedition into West Tennessee (Humboldt).

Born: 1824? NC
Died: June 18, 1890 Dresden, TN
Occupation: Lawyer
Offices/Honors: Circuit Court Judge, 1868–70
Miscellaneous: Resided Dresden, Weakley Co., TN
Buried: Place of burial unknown
References: Obituary, *Nashville American,* June 19, 1890. Pension File and Military Service File, National Archives. Letters Received, Volunteer Service Branch, Adjutant General's Office, File 199(VS)1878, National Archives. Leroy P. Graf and Ralph W. Haskins, editors. *The Papers of Andrew Johnson.* Vol. 5, 1861–1862. Knoxville, TN, 1979. *The War of the Rebellion: A Compilation of the Official Records of the Union and Confederate Armies.* (Series 1, Vol. 17, Part 1, p. 565). Washington, DC, 1886. *History of Tennessee from the Earliest Times to the Present, Together with an Historical and Biographical Sketch of Gibson, Obion, Dyer, Weakley, and Lake Counties.* Nashville, TN, 1887.

David Ryan

1 Lieutenant, Co. E, 8 IA Infantry, Sept. 4, 1861. Taken prisoner Shiloh, TN, April 6, 1862. Confined Libby Prison, Richmond, VA; Montgomery, AL; and Macon, GA. Paroled Oct. 12, 1862. Captain, Co. E, 8 IA Infantry, July 4, 1863. Detached as *Colonel,* 2 Regiment, Enrolled Militia, District of Memphis and District of West Tennessee, Oct. 17, 1864–May 15, 1865. Honorably mustered out (8 IA Infantry), Feb. 23, 1865. Battle honors: Shiloh.

Born: March 15, 1840 Hebron, Washington Co., NY
Died: June 19, 1905 Des Moines, IA
Education: Attended Iowa Central University, Pella, IA
Occupation: Lawyer and judge
Offices/Honors: Iowa House of Representatives, 1866–68. District Court Judge, 1887–99.
Miscellaneous: Resided Prairie City, Jasper Co.,

David Ryan (Anna Howell Clarkson. *A Beautiful Life and Its Associations.* New York, 1899).

IA; Newton, Jasper Co., IA; and Des Moines, Polk Co., IA

Buried: Woodland Cemetery, Des Moines, IA (Block 19, Lot 71)

References: Benjamin F. Gue. *Biographies and Portraits of the Progressive Men of Iowa, Leaders in Business, Politics and the Professions, Together with an Original and Authentic History of the State.* Des Moines, IA, 1899. Obituary, *Des Moines Register and Leader,* June 21, 1905. Obituary Circular, Whole No. 252, Iowa MOLLUS. Anna Howell Clarkson. *A Beautiful Life and Its Associations.* New York, 1899. Pension File and Military Service File, National Archives. Letters Received, Volunteer Service Branch, Adjutant General's Office, Files R1563(VS)1864 and H101(VS)1867, National Archives.

James Wall Scully

Private, Corporal and Sergeant, Battery K, 1 U.S. Artillery, Sept. 20, 1856–Sept. 20, 1861. 1 Lieutenant, RQM, 10 TN Infantry, July 14, 1862. Lieutenant Colonel, 10 TN Infantry, Aug. 21, 1863. Colonel, 10 TN Infantry, June 6, 1864. Honorably mustered out, May 25, 1865. Bvt. Major, USA, Sept. 27, 1865, for gallant and meritorious services in the battle of Mill Springs, KY. Bvt. Lieutenant Colonel, USA, Sept. 27, 1865, for gallant and meritorious services in the battle of Shiloh, TN. Bvt. Colonel, USA, Sept. 27, 1865, for gallant and meritorious services in the battle of Nashville, TN. Battle honors: Mill Springs, Shiloh, Nashville.

Born: Feb. 19, 1837 Enisnag, County Kilkenny, Ireland

Died: June 1, 1918 Atlanta, GA

James Wall Scully (Massachusetts MOLLUS Collection, USAMHI [Vol. 112, p. 5795]).

James Wall Scully (T. M. Schleier, Photographer, Nashville, Knoxville & Chattanooga, Tennessee).

Education: Attended St. Kieran's College, Kilkenny, Ireland

Other Wars: Spanish American War (Transport Service)

Occupation: Regular Army (Colonel, Assistant Quartermaster General, Feb. 4, 1898. Retired Nov. 1, 1900. Advanced to Brig. Gen. on retired list, April 23, 1904)

Miscellaneous: Resided Atlanta, Fulton Co., GA

Buried: West View Cemetery, Atlanta, GA (Section 4, Lot 12 1/2, Grave 4)

References: *National Cyclopedia of American Biography.* William H. Powell and Edward Shippen, editors. *Officers of the Army and Navy (Regular) Who Served in the Civil War.* Philadelphia, 1892. Anthony McCan, "James Wall Scully — A Kilkenny Soldier in the American Civil War," *The Irish Sword: The Journal of the Military History Society of Ireland,* Vol. 23, No. 91 (Summer 2002). Arline Scully, "James Wall Scully, Brigadier General, United States Army," *Journal of the American Irish Historical Society,* Vol. 29 (1930–31). Obituary, *Atlanta Constitution,* June 2, 1918. Pension File and Military Service File, National Archives. Letters Received, Appointment, Commission, and Personal Branch, Adjutant General's Office, File 2809(ACP) 1877, National Archives. Leroy P. Graf and Ralph W. Haskins, editors. *The Papers of Andrew Johnson.* Vol. 6, 1862–1864. Knoxville, TN, 1983.

James Thomas Shelley

Major, 1 TN Infantry, Sept. 1, 1861. Colonel, 5 TN Infantry, March 6, 1862. Provost Marshal, Post of Loudon, TN, Feb. 1864. Although he submitted his resignation, April 15, 1864, in order to "take charge of a boat on the (Tennessee) River in Government employ, that I may be near my family to provide for their wants," his resignation was not accepted until July 22, 1864. While considering his resignation, Brig. Gen. Jacob D. Cox commented, "I have no wish that it should be revoked," citing "the embarrassment which had arisen on the question of brigade commanders, Col. Shelley being one of the oldest regimental officers, but not having the requisite qualifications to command a brigade." Colonel, 7 TN Mounted Infantry, May 9, 1865. Honorably mustered out, July 27, 1865. Battle honors: Cumberland Gap Campaign, Chickamauga Campaign, Atlanta Campaign (Resaca).

Born: Feb. 25, 1827 Columbiana, Shelby Co., AL

Died: Jan. 3, 1891 Rockwood, TN

Occupation: Merchant and county court clerk before war. Farmer, clerk and master in chancery, and justice of the peace after war.

Offices/Honors: Roane County Court Clerk, 1860–61

Miscellaneous: Resided Post Oak Springs, Roane Co., TN; Kingston, Roane Co., TN; and Rockwood, Roane Co., TN. Son of Lt. Col. Jacob D. Shelley, 11 Battalion, LA Infantry, CSA.

Buried: Chattanooga National Cemetery, Chattanooga, TN (Section U, Site 8-SS)

References: Pension File and Military Service File, National Archives. Robert K. Cannon. *Volunteers for Union and Liberty: History of the 5th TN Infantry, U.S.A. 1862–1865*. Knoxville, TN, 1995. Letters Received, Volunteer Service Branch, Adjutant General's Office, File F785(VS)1865, National Archives. Emma M. Wells. *The History of Roane County, TN, 1801–1870*. Chattanooga, TN, 1927. Leroy P. Graf and Ralph W. Haskins, editors. *The Papers of Andrew Johnson*. Vol. 5, 1861–1862. Knoxville, TN, 1979.

Daniel Stover

Colonel, 4 TN Infantry, Nov. 25, 1862. Suffering from "phthisis pulmonalis contracted by exposure whilst lying out in the mountains of East Tennessee," he resigned Aug. 10, 1864.

Born: Nov. 14, 1826 Carter Co., TN

Died: Dec. 18, 1864 Nashville, TN

Occupation: Farmer

Miscellaneous: Resided Elizabethton, Carter

James Thomas Shelley (The Roane County Heritage Commission).

Daniel Stover (Thomas J. Merritt's Photograph Galleries, Nashville, Tennessee; courtesy Tennessee State Library and Archives [25498]).

Co., TN. Son-in-law of President Andrew Johnson.
Buried: Fitzsimmons Cemetery, Elizabethton, TN
References: *Carter County, Tennessee, and Its People, 1796–1993.* Elizabethton, TN, 1993. Pension File and Military Service File, National Archives. Eddie M. Nikazy. *Forgotten Soldiers: History of the 4th Tennessee Volunteer Infantry Regiment (USA), 1863–1865.* Bowie, MD, 1995. Leroy P. Graf and Ralph W. Haskins, editors. *The Papers of Andrew Johnson.* Vol. 6, 1862–1864. Knoxville, TN, 1983.

Jesse Hartley Strickland

Colonel, 8 TN Cavalry (originally 5 East TN Cavalry), Jan. 30, 1863. "Having been seen drunk in cars with a number of soldiers," his authority to raise a regiment was revoked, Oct. 19, 1863. The order of revocation was rescinded, Dec. 14, 1863, upon receipt of letters "from generals and officers of less rank testifying to my sobriety." However, when the organization of the regiment was completed by consolidation with the 10 East TN Cavalry, he was honorably discharged, April 1, 1864, as a supernumerary officer. Despite numerous claims in his later years, he never received any compensation for his fourteen months' service, although he did succeed in getting a pension by an Act of Congress, which also confirmed his muster as colonel. By Act of Congress, May 25, 1900, his widow, Corinne, finally received $2,865.81 in compensation for his services.
Born: Nov. 1827 Philadelphia, PA
Died: March 27, 1899 Washington, DC
Occupation: According to his obituary, he was an officer in U.S. Marine Corps before war, but his name does not appear on any list of Marine Corps officers. Merchant, postal clerk, and U.S. Inspector of Steam Vessels after war.
Miscellaneous: Resided Nashville, Davidson Co., TN; Brooklyn, NY; and Washington, DC. Son of the prominent architect William Strickland, designer of the Tennessee State Capitol building.
Buried: Arlington National Cemetery, Arlington, VA (Section 1, Lot 1246)
References: Obituary, *Washington Post*, March 28, 1899. Obituary, *Washington Evening Star*, March 28, 1899. Pension File and Military Service File, National Archives. Letters Received, Volunteer Service Branch, Adjutant General's Office, File P120(VS)1863, National Archives. Leroy P. Graf and Ralph W. Haskins, editors. *The Papers of Andrew Johnson.* Vol. 5, 1861–1862. Knoxville, TN, 1979. Leroy P. Graf and Ralph W. Haskins, editors. *The Papers of Andrew Johnson.* Vol. 6, 1862–1864. Knoxville, TN, 1983. Agnes A. Gilchrist. *William Strickland, Architect and Engineer, 1788–1854.* New York, 1969.

Henry Von Heyde

Captain, Co. H, 2 WI Cavalry, Jan. 25, 1862. Resigned June 2, 1863, "on account of property confiscated from me during the revolution in Germany, 1848–49, which by virtue of a decree sent my relations, will be given back to me, provided I do personally appear." Captain, Co. L, 4 WI Cavalry, April 13, 1864. Resigned Nov. 3, 1864, "on account of ill health received on an expedition to Clinton, LA, on the 27th day of August, 1864, by a sunstroke." Colonel, 3 Regiment, Enrolled Militia (Freedmen), District of West Tennessee, Dec. 19, 1864. Regiment disbanded, April 12, 1865.
Born: April 1820 Prussia
Died: Jan. 16, 1892 Chicago, IL
Occupation: Saloon keeper and clerk
Miscellaneous: Resided Portage, Columbia Co., WI, before war; Columbus, Franklin Co., OH; Albany, NY; and Chicago, IL, after war
Buried: Graceland Cemetery, Chicago, IL (Bellevue Section, Lot 168, unmarked)
References: Pension File and Military Service File, National Archives. Letters Received, Volunteer Service Branch, Adjutant General's Office, Files W851(VS)1864 and H101(VS)1867, National Archives. Michael J. Martin. *A History of the 4th*

Henry Von Heyde (G. W. Davis, Photographer, No. 250 South High Street, Columbus, Ohio).

Wisconsin Infantry and Cavalry in the Civil War. New York, 2006.

William Clifford Whitney

2 Lieutenant, Battery G, 2 IL Light Artillery, Oct. 5, 1861. 1 Lieutenant, Battery G, 2 IL Light Artillery, Dec. 31, 1861. Honorably mustered out, Feb. 22, 1863. Private, Battery D, 1 IL Light Artillery, Dec. 29, 1863. 2 Lieutenant, Battery D, 1 IL Light Artillery, Jan. 27, 1864. Captain, Co. L, 7 U.S. Colored Heavy Artillery, July 8, 1864. Detached as *Colonel,* 4 Regiment, Enrolled Militia, District of West Tennessee, Dec. 15, 1864. Regiment disbanded, April 12, 1865. Detached as *Colonel,* 2 Regiment (Freedmen), Enrolled Militia, District of West Tennessee, April 20, 1865. Regiment disbanded, May 8, 1865. Captain, Co. B, 11 USCT, May 8, 1865. Honorably mustered out, Jan. 12, 1866.

Born: Jan. 3, 1828 Dexter, ME
Died: June 16, 1907 Cawker City, KS
Occupation: Express man before war. Farmer, hotelkeeper and municipal official after war.
Offices/Honors: Postmaster, Cawker City, KS, 1884–88 and 1889–94
Miscellaneous: Resided Boston, MA; New Milford, Winnebago Co., IL; and Cawker City, Mitchell Co., KS, after 1871
Buried: Prairie Grove Cemetery, Cawker City, KS
References: *The United States Biographical Dictionary.* Kansas Volume. Chicago and Kansas City, 1879. Pension File and Military Service File, National Archives. Obituary, *Cawker City Public Record,* June 20, 1907. George A. Gray, compiler. *The Descendants of George Holmes of Roxbury, 1594–1908.* Boston, 1908. Letters Received, Colored Troops Branch, Adjutant General's Office, File W554(CT)1864, National Archives. Letters Received, Volunteer Service Branch, Adjutant General's Office, File H101(VS)1867, National Archives.

Edmund Roberts Wiley, Jr.

1st Lieutenant, Adjutant, 62 IL Infantry, July 1, 1862. Adjutant, Post of Jackson, TN, March 16, 1863. Acting AAG, 3 Brigade, 3 Division, 16 Army Corps, Army of the Tennessee, April 19, 1863. Major, 61 USCT, June 30, 1863. Detached as *Colonel,* 1 Regiment, Enrolled Militia (Freedmen), District of West Tennessee, Sept. 6, 1864. Assigned to recruiting service, Jan. 10, 1865. Colonel, 88 USCT, Aug. 10, 1865. Lieutenant Colonel, 3 U.S. Colored Heavy Artillery, Jan. 4, 1866. Honorably mustered out, April 30, 1866. Battle honors: Holly Springs.

Born: June 20, 1833 New York City, NY
Died: Nov. 2, 1917 Little Rock, AR
Education: Attended Illinois College, Jacksonville, IL

William Clifford Whitney (seated right, with 1 Lieutenant James M. Vaughan, seated left, and 2 Lieutenant John C. Malloy, Co. L, 7 U.S. Colored Heavy Artillery) (J. W. Taft, Artist, Oak Gallery, 282½ Main St., Memphis, Tennessee).

Edmund Roberts Wiley, Jr.

Occupation: Lawyer and journalist
Offices/Honors: Arkansas County (AR) Clerk, 1867–71. Arkansas Legislature, 1871–72. Sheriff of Arkansas Co., AR, 1872–74. U.S. Internal Revenue Storekeeper, 1878–86.
Miscellaneous: Resided Springfield, Sangamon Co., IL; DeWitt, Arkansas Co., AR; Atlanta, Logan Co., IL; and Little Rock, Pulaski Co., AR
Buried: Oakland Cemetery, Little Rock, AR (Lilac Street, Lot 14)
References: John Carroll Power. *History of the Early Settlers of Sangamon County, IL.* Springfield, IL, 1876. *Catalogue of Phi Alpha Society, Illinois College, 1845–1890.* Jacksonville, IL, 1890. Pension File and Military Service File, National Archives. Obituary, *Arkansas Gazette,* Nov. 3, 1917. Letters Received, Colored Troops Branch, Adjutant General's Office, Files W852(CT)1864 and R84(CT) 1865, National Archives. Letters Received, Volunteer Service Branch, Adjutant General's Office, File H101(VS)1867, National Archives.

Milton T. Williamson

2 Lieutenant, Co. C, 72 OH Infantry, Oct. 29, 1861. 1 Lieutenant, Co. C, 72 OH Infantry, Feb. 13, 1862. 1 Lieutenant, Acting ADC, Staff of Brig. Gen. James W. Denver, 3 Brigade, 5 Division,

Milton T. Williamson (standing second from right, with Brig. Gen. Ralph P. Buckland, seated, and officers of his staff, including 1 Lieutenant Orin O. England, Captain Andrew Nuhfer, 1 Lieutenant Eugene A. Rawson, and Captain Henry W. Buckland, left to right) (Sandusky County Kin Hunters Collection, USAMHI [RG98S-CWP144.16]).

Army of the Tennessee, May 16, 1862. 1 Lieutenant, Acting ADC, Staff of Brig. Gen. Ralph P. Buckland, 1 Brigade, 3 Division, 15 Army Corps, Army of the Tennessee, May 21, 1863. GSW left thigh, Vicksburg, MS, May 31, 1863. Detached as *Colonel*, 3 Regiment, Enrolled Militia, District of Memphis, Sept. 21, 1864. Honorably mustered out (72 OH Infantry), Oct. 28, 1864. Brig. Gen., Enrolled Militia, District of West Tennessee, Feb. 8, 1865. Enrolled Militia disbanded, May 8, 1865. Bvt. Captain, USV, March 13, 1865, for faithful and meritorious services. Battle honors: Shiloh, Corinth, Vicksburg Campaign.

Born: April 28, 1828 Butler Co., OH

Died: June 1, 1902 Memphis, TN

Occupation: Lawyer and dry goods merchant before war. Lawyer, map publisher and real estate agent after war.

Offices/Honors: Tennessee House of Representatives, 1873–75. U.S. Marshal, Western District of Tennessee, 1878–85.

Miscellaneous: Resided Cincinnati, OH, before war; and Memphis, Shelby Co., TN, after war

Buried: Elmwood Cemetery, Memphis, TN (Turley Section, Lot 595)

References: Obituary, *Memphis Commercial Appeal*, June 2, 1902. Robert M. McBride and Dan M. Robison. *Biographical Directory of the Tennessee General Assembly*. Vol. 2, 1861–1901. Nashville, TN, 1979. Perre Magness. *Elmwood 2002: In the Shadows of the Elms*. Memphis, TN, 2001. Pension File and Military Service File, National Archives. Letters Received, Volunteer Service Branch, Adjutant General's Office, File H101(VS)1867, National Archives.

Isham Young

1 Sergeant, Co. I, 1 TN Infantry, Aug. 20, 1861. 1 Lieutenant, Co. I, 1 TN Infantry, March 1, 1862. Captain, Co. I, 1 TN Infantry, June 6, 1862. Lieutenant Colonel, 8 TN Infantry, May 15, 1863. Colonel, 11 TN Cavalry, Sept. 25, 1863. "Unable to perform the duties of an officer in consequence of having preliminary symptoms of fever," he resigned Jan. 6, 1864, commenting "I am anxiously solicited by all to return home, which I desire to do at once."

Born: June 13, 1839 near Kingston, Roane Co., TN

Died: Aug. 23, 1889 Knoxville, TN (fatally injured in railroad accident)

Occupation: Farmer before war. Railroad conductor and dry goods merchant after war.

Offices/Honors: Sheriff of Roane Co., TN, 1864–66. Chairman of Knoxville Board of Public Works, 1886–89.

Miscellaneous: Resided Kingston, Roane Co., TN; and Knoxville, Knox Co., TN. Son of Lieutenant Colonel Freemorton Young, 5 TN Infantry.

Buried: Old Gray Cemetery, Knoxville, TN (Lot 878)

References: *History of Tennessee from the Earliest Times to the Present, Together with an Historical and Biographical Sketch of Thirty East Tennessee Counties*. Nashville, TN, 1887. Obituary, *Knoxville Journal*, Aug. 24, 1889. "The Flat Gap Horror—An 1889 Knoxville Tragedy," *The Tennessee Genealogical Magazine*, Vol. 47, No. 3 (Fall 2000). Pension File and Military Service File, National Archives. James D. Richardson. *Tennessee Templars*. Nashville, TN, 1883.

BIBLIOGRAPHY

Books

Abbott, Louisa J., and Charles L. Abbott. *The Shinkle Genealogy, Comprising the Descendants of Philipp Carl Schenckel, 1717–1897*. Cincinnati: Press of Curts & Jennings, 1897.

Addleman, Robert P. *Ketchum-McCorkell Pioneers: Midwestern Families of Lillias Jacinth Burton*. Apollo, PA: Closson Press, 1993.

Albjerg, Victor Lincoln. *Richard Owen, Scotland 1810, Indiana 1890*. Lafayette, IN: Archives of Purdue, 1946.

Allison, Nathaniel T. *History of Cherokee County, Kansas, and Representative Citizens*. Chicago: Biographical, 1904.

Altshuler, Constance Wynn. *Cavalry Yellow & Infantry Blue*. Tucson: Arizona Historical Society, 1991.

The Alumni and Former Student Catalogue of Miami University, 1809–1892. Oxford, OH: Press of the Oxford News, 1892.

Anderson, Edward. *Camp Fire Stories: A Series of Sketches of the Union Army in the Southwest*. Chicago: Star, 1896.

Anderson, Nellie P. *The John Pickens Family*. Rockford, TN: S. B. Newman, 1951.

Anderson, William Kyle. *Donald Robertson and His Wife, Rachel Rogers, of King and Queen County, Virginia, Their Ancestry and Posterity*. Detroit: Winn and Hammond, 1900.

Andreas, Alfred T. *Atlas Map of Parke County, IN*. Chicago: A. T. Andreas, 1874.

_____. *History of Chicago from the Earliest Period to the Present Time*. Chicago: A. T. Andreas, 1884–86.

_____. *History of the State of Kansas*. Chicago: A. T. Andreas, 1883.

Andrews, Elliott M. *The Descendants of Lieutenant John Andrews*. Lee, ME: E. M. Andrews, 1962.

Annual Reunion of the Fifth Indiana Cavalry Association. Indianapolis: Association, 1883–1919.

Appletons' Cyclopedia of American Biography.

Armstrong, Zella. *History of Hamilton County and Chattanooga, TN*. Chattanooga: Lookout, 1931.

Atlas of Decatur County, Indiana. Chicago: J. H. Beers, 1882.

Atlas of Johnson County, Indiana. Chicago: J. H. Beers, 1881.

Baird, Lewis C. *Baird's History of Clark County, IN*. Indianapolis: B. F. Bowen, 1909.

Baird, William Raimond. *Betas of Achievement*. New York City: Beta, 1914.

Baker, Alice G. *Genealogy of the Swallow Family, 1666–1910*. White Hall, IL: Pearce Brothers, 1910.

Baldwin, Charles C. *The Baldwin Genealogy from 1500 to 1881*. Cleveland: Leader Printing, 1881.

Barnes, James A., James R. Carnahan, and Thomas H. B. McCain. *The 86th Regiment Indiana Volunteer Infantry. A Narrative of Its Services in the Civil War of 1861–1865*. Crawfordsville, IN: Journal, 1895.

Barnes, William Horatio. *The Forty-First Congress of the United States, 1869–71*. New York: W. H. Barnes, 1872.

Bartholomew, Henry S. K. *Pioneer History of Elkhart County, Indiana, with Sketches and Stories*. Goshen, IN: Goshen Printery, 1930.

Barton, William W., and Jean W. Gayle. *Six Wallace Brothers and Their Descendants*. Bountiful, UT: Family History, 1996.

Basler, Roy P., ed. *The Collected Works of Abraham Lincoln*. New Brunswick, NJ: Rutgers University Press, 1953.

Bateman, Newton, and Paul Selby, eds. *Historical Encyclopedia of Illinois and History of Sangamon County*. Chicago: Munsell, 1912.

Battle, J. H., and William H. Perrin, eds. *Counties of Todd and Christian, Kentucky, Historical and Biographical*. Chicago and Louisville: F. A. Battey, 1884.

Baxter, Nancy Niblack. *Gallant Fourteenth: The Story of an Indiana Civil War Regiment*. Traverse City, MI: Pioneer Study Center Press, 1980.

Bayles, John C., and G. H. Bayles. *Jesse Bayles: A Partial List of His Descendants*. Morgantown, WV: John C. Bayles, 1944.

Beatty, John. *The Citizen-Soldier; or, Memoirs of a Volunteer*. Cincinnati: Wilstach, Baldwin, 1879.

Beckwith, Hiram W. *History of Fountain County, Together with Historic Notes on the Wabash Valley*. Chicago: H. H. Hill and N. Iddings, 1881.

_____. *History of Vigo and Parke Counties, Together*

with *Historic Notes on the Wabash Valley*. Chicago: H. H. Hill and N. Iddings, 1880.

Behrens, Robert H. *From Salt Fork to Chickamauga: Champaign County Soldiers in the Civil War*. Urbana: Urbana Free Library, 1988.

Belcher, Dennis W. *The 10th Kentucky Volunteer Infantry in the Civil War: A History and Roster*. Jefferson, NC: McFarland, 2009.

Beth, Loren P. *John Marshall Harlan: The Last Whig Justice*. Lexington: University Press of Kentucky, 1992.

Biographical and Genealogical History of Cass, Miami, Howard and Tipton Counties, IN. Chicago: Lewis, 1898.

Biographical and Genealogical History of Wayne, Fayette, Union, and Franklin Counties, IN. Chicago: Lewis, 1899.

Biographical and Historical Record of Kosciusko County, IN. Chicago: Lewis, 1887.

Biographical and Historical Record of Putnam County, IN. Chicago: Lewis, 1887.

Biographical and Historical Souvenir for the Counties of Clark, Crawford, Harrison, Floyd, Jefferson, Jennings, Scott, and Washington, IN. Chicago: John M. Gresham, 1889.

Biographical Cyclopedia and Portrait Gallery with an Historical Sketch of the State of Ohio. Vol. 3. Cincinnati: Western Biographical, 1884.

Biographical Cyclopedia and Portrait Gallery with an Historical Sketch of the State of Ohio. Vol. 6. Cincinnati: Western Biographical, 1895.

Biographical Cyclopedia of the Commonwealth of Kentucky. Chicago and Philadelphia: John M. Gresham, 1896.

The Biographical Encyclopedia of Kentucky of the Dead and Living Men of the Nineteenth Century. Cincinnati: J. M. Armstrong, 1878.

A Biographical History of Eminent and Self-Made Men of the State of Indiana. Cincinnati: Western Biographical, 1880.

A Biographical History of Fremont and Mills Counties, Iowa. Chicago: Lewis, 1901.

Biographical History of Page County, Iowa. Chicago: Lewis & Dunbar, 1890.

Biographical History of Tippecanoe, White, Jasper, Newton, Benton, Warren and Pulaski Counties, IN. Chicago: Lewis, 1899.

Biographical Memoirs of Greene County, IN, with Reminiscences of Pioneer Days. Indianapolis: B. F. Bowen, 1908.

Biographical Memoirs of Huntington County, IN. Chicago: B. F. Bowen, 1901.

Biographical Record and Portrait Album of Tippecanoe County, IN. Chicago: Lewis, 1888.

Biographical Record of Bartholomew and Jackson Counties, IN. Indianapolis: B. F. Bowen, 1904.

Black, Glenn A. *Down Through the Years: A History of Newburgh Lodge No. 174, F. & A. M., Newburgh, IN*. Franklin, IN: Indiana Freemasons, 1955.

Blackburn, John. *A Hundred Miles, A Hundred Heartbreaks*. N.p.: John Blackburn, 1972.

Blair, Williams T. *The Michael Shoemaker Book*. Scranton, PA: International Text Book Press, 1924.

Blanchard, Charles, ed. *Counties of Clay and Owen, Indiana. Historical and Biographical*. Chicago: F. A. Battey, 1884.

_____, ed. *Counties of Howard and Tipton, Indiana. Historical and Biographical*. Chicago: F. A. Battey, 1883.

_____, ed. *Counties of Morgan, Monroe and Brown, Indiana. Historical and Biographical*. Chicago: F. A. Battey, 1884.

Bodenhamer, David J., and Robert G. Barrows, eds. *The Encyclopedia of Indianapolis*. Bloomington: Indiana University Press, 1994.

Bodurtha, Arthur L., ed. *History of Miami County, Indiana*. Chicago and New York: Lewis, 1914.

Boyle, John, comp. *Boyle Genealogy: John Boyle of Virginia and Kentucky*. St. Louis: Perrin & Smith Printing, 1909.

Bradsby, Henry C. *History of Vigo County, IN*. Chicago: S. B. Nelson, 1891.

Brant, Jefferson E. *History of the 85th Indiana Volunteer Infantry, Its Organization, Campaigns and Battles*. Bloomington: Cravens Brothers, 1902.

Briant, Charles C. *History of the 6th Regiment Indiana Volunteer Infantry, of Both the Three Months' and Three Years' Services*. Indianapolis: W. B. Burford, 1891.

Bridge, Carolyn S. *These Men Were Heroes Once: The 69th Indiana Volunteer Infantry*. West Lafayette, IN: Twin Publications, 2005.

Brooks, Lewis. *Lewis Brooks, Soldier and Citizen*. N.p., 1907.

Brooks, Thomas J., comp. *The Brooks and Houghton Families Descended from Hannah Chute Poor*. N.p., 1909.

Brown, Cyrus H., comp. *Genealogical Record of Nathaniel Babcock, Simeon Main, Isaac Miner, Ezekiel Main*. Boston: Everett Press, 1909.

Brown, Edmund R. *The 27th Indiana Volunteer Infantry in the War of the Rebellion*. Monticello, IN: Edmund R. Brown, 1899.

Brown, J. Willard. *The Signal Corps, U.S.A., in the War of the Rebellion*. Boston: U.S. Veteran Signal Corps Association, 1896.

Brown, Myers E., II. *Tennessee's Union Cavalrymen*. Charleston: Arcadia, 2008.

Brummett, Dianne, and Donna Kuhlman, eds. *City Cemetery Records of Columbus, IN*. Columbus, IN: Bartholomew County Genealogical Society, 1991.

Buckley, C. Byron. *Colonel Hagerman Tripp: His Biography, Civil War Letters, and Diary*. North Vernon, IN: C. Byron Buckley, 2004.

Bulleit, F. A., comp. *Illustrated Atlas and History of Harrison County, Indiana*. Corydon, IN: F. A. Bulleit, 1906.

Burgess, Joe H. *Hamilton County and the Civil War*. N.p., 1967.

Burns, Edward M. *Historical Sketch of the Organization*

and Service of the 15th Regiment Indiana Volunteers. Valparaiso, IN: Edward M. Burns, 1889.

Burton, William L. *Melting Pot Soldiers: The Union's Ethnic Regiments.* Ames: Iowa State University Press, 1988.

Bush, Arthur J., and Margaret S. Bush. *Black Powder to Black Gold: The Life and Times of William E. Hobson.* N.p.: A. J. and M. S. Bush, 1990.

Byers, William N. *Encyclopedia of Biography of Colorado; History of Colorado.* Chicago: Century Publishing and Engraving, 1901.

Cannon, Robert K. *Volunteers for Union and Liberty: History of the 5th TN Infantry, U.S.A. 1862–1865.* Knoxville: Bohemian Brigade, 1995.

Carter County, Tennessee, and Its People, 1796–1993. Elizabethton: Carter County History Book Committee, 1993.

Cary, Seth C. *John Cary, The Plymouth Pilgrim.* Boston: S. C. Cary, 1911.

Catalogue of Phi Alpha Society, Illinois College, 1845–1890. Jacksonville, IL: Phi Alpha Society, 1890.

Chase, Theodore R. *The Michigan University Book: 1844–1880.* Detroit: Richmond, Backus, 1881.

Childress, Nancy Porter. *The Main Tree II: The Descendants of John Main of North Yarmouth, ME.* Phoenix: N. P. Childress, 1995.

Christensen, Lawrence O., William E. Foley, Gary R. Kremer, and Kenneth H. Winn, eds. *Dictionary of Missouri Biography.* Columbia: University of Missouri Press, 1999.

Clarkson, Anna Howell. *A Beautiful Life and Its Associations.* New York: Historical Department of Iowa, 1899.

Claybaugh, Joseph. *History of Clinton County, IN.* Indianapolis: A. W. Bowen, 1913.

Clifton, Thomas A., ed. *Past and Present of Fountain and Warren Counties, Indiana.* Indianapolis: B. F. Bowen, 1913.

Coleman, J. Winston, Jr. *The Casto-Metcalfe Duel.* Lexington, KY: Winburn Press, 1950.

———. *Famous Kentucky Duels.* Lexington, KY: Henry Clay Press, 1969.

Collins, Lewis, and Richard H. Collins. *Collins' Historical Sketches of Kentucky: History of Kentucky.* Frankfort: Kentucky Historical Society, 1966.

Collins, William H., and Cicero F. Perry. *Past and Present of the City of Quincy and Adams County, Illinois.* Chicago: S. J. Clarke, 1905.

Colonel Charles A. Zollinger: Seven-time Mayor of Fort Wayne. Fort Wayne: Public Library of Fort Wayne and Allen County, 1963.

Colonel Sion S. Bass, 1827–1862. Fort Wayne: Public Library of Fort Wayne and Allen County, 1954.

Combs, Josiah H. *Combs: A Study in Comparative Philology and Genealogy.* Pensacola: N. K. Combs, 1976.

Commemorative Biographical Record of Prominent and Representative Men of Indianapolis and Vicinity. Chicago: J. H. Beers, 1908.

Companions of the Military Order of the Loyal Legion of the United States, 2d ed. New York: L. R. Hamersly, 1901.

Comstock, Daniel W. *Ninth Cavalry. 121st Regiment Indiana Volunteers.* Richmond, IN: J. M. Coe, 1890.

Conley, Joan W., comp. *History of Nicholas County, KY.* Carlisle: Nicholas County Historical Society, 1976.

Connelley, William E. *A Standard History of Kansas and Kansans,* rev. ed. Chicago: Lewis, 1919.

———, and E. M. Coulter. *History of Kentucky.* Chicago and New York: American Historical Society, 1922.

Cook, Michael L., and Bettie Anne Cook, eds. *Pioneer History of Washington County, Kentucky.* Owensboro: Cook and McDowell Publications, 1980.

Coons, John W., comp. *Indiana at Shiloh.* Indianapolis: Indiana Shiloh National Park Commission, 1904.

Cornell, John. *Genealogy of the Cornell Family: Being an Account of the Descendants of Thomas Cornell of Portsmouth, RI.* New York: Press of T. A. Wright, 1902.

Counties of Lagrange and Noble, Indiana. Historical and Biographical. Chicago: F. A. Battey, 1882.

Counties of Warren, Benton, Jasper and Newton, Indiana. Historical and Biographical. Chicago: F. A. Battey, 1883.

Craine, J. Robert T., comp. *The Ancestry and Posterity of Matthew Clarkson (1664–1702).* N.p., 1971.

Craven, Hervey. *A Brief History of the 89th Indiana Volunteer Infantry.* Wabash, IN: Monson-Corrie, 1899.

Crist, Leander M. *History of Boone County, IN.* Indianapolis: A. W. Bowen, 1914.

Crozier, William A., ed. *The Buckners of Virginia and the Allied Families of Strother and Ashby.* New York: Genealogical Association, 1907.

Cullum, George W. *Biographical Register of the Officers and Graduates of the U.S. Military Academy,* 3d ed. Boston: Houghton, Mifflin, 1891.

Cumback, Will, and J. B. Maynard, eds. *Men of Progress Indiana.* Indianapolis: Indianapolis Sentinel, 1899.

Current, Richard N. *Lincoln's Loyalists: Union Soldiers from the Confederacy.* Boston: Northeastern University Press, 1992.

Dandridge, Anne Spottswood, comp. *The Forman Genealogy.* Cleveland: Forman-Bassett-Hatch, 1903.

DeHart, Richard P., ed. *Past and Present of Tippecanoe County, IN.* Indianapolis: B. F. Bowen, 1909.

De la Hunt, Thomas J. *Perry County: A History.* Indianapolis: W. K. Stewart, 1916.

Demmon, Isaac N., ed. *General Catalogue of Officers and Students University of Michigan, 1837–1911.* Ann Arbor: Ann Arbor Press, 1912.

Dickinson, Jack L. *Wayne County, West Virginia, in the Civil War.* Huntington, WV: J. L. Dickinson, 2003.

Doane, Alfred A., comp. *The Doane Family.* Boston: A. A. Doane, 1902.

Dodge, William Sumner. *History of the Old Second Division, Army of the Cumberland*. Chicago: Church & Goodman, 1864.

Doherty, Robert R. *Representative Methodists*. New York: Phillips & Hunt, 1888.

Doll, William H. *History of the 6th Regiment Indiana Volunteer Infantry in the Civil War, April 25, 1861, to September 22, 1864*. Columbus, IN: Republican Print, 1903.

Downs, Michael P., trans. *The Civil War Diary, Colonel Alfred B. Wade*. Fort Walton Beach, FL: James K. Baughman, 2009.

Drury, Augustus W. *History of the City of Dayton and Montgomery County, Ohio*. Chicago and Dayton: S. J. Clarke, 1909.

Dudley, Dean. *History of the Dudley Family, with Genealogical Tables, Pedigrees, etc*. Wakefield, MA: Dean Dudley, 1886–94.

Dufour, Perret. *The Swiss Settlement of Switzerland County, IN*. Indianapolis: Indiana Historical Commission, 1925.

Duncan, L. Wallace, and Charles F. Scott, eds. *History of Allen and Woodson Counties, KS*. Iola, KS: Iola Register, 1901.

Dunn, Craig L. *Harvestfields of Death: The 20th Indiana Volunteers of Gettysburg*. Carmel: Guild Press of Indiana, 1999.

———. *Iron Men, Iron Will: The Nineteenth Indiana Regiment of the Iron Brigade*. Indianapolis: Guild Press of Indiana, 1995.

Dunn, Harriet N., and Eveline Guthrie Dunn. *Records of the Guthrie Family of Pennsylvania, Connecticut, and Virginia*. Chicago: H. N. and S. L. Dunn, 1898.

Dunn, Jacob Piatt. *Greater Indianapolis: The History, the Industries, the Institutions, and the People of a City of Homes*. Chicago: Lewis, 1910.

———. *Indiana and Indianans*. Chicago and New York: American Historical Society, 1919.

Dunn, Shirley, comp. *Lincoln County, KY, Marriages 1780–1850 & Tombstone Inscriptions*. St. Louis: D. A. Griffith, 1977.

Dyer, Frederick H. *A Compendium of the War of the Rebellion*. Des Moines: Dyer, 1908.

Eckel, Alexander. *History of the 4th TN Cavalry: U.S.A., War of the Rebellion, 1861–65*. Johnson City, TN: Overmountain Press, 2001.

Eddy, Ruth S. D., comp. *The Eddy Family in America*. Boston: Eddy Family Association, 1930.

Eddy, Thomas M. *The Patriotism of Illinois*. Chicago: Clarke, 1865.

Edgar, John F. *Pioneer Life in Dayton and Vicinity, 1796–1840*. Dayton: W. J. Shuey, 1896.

Edwards, Jonathan. *An Illustrated History of Spokane County, State of Washington*. San Francisco: W. H. Lever, 1900.

Egbert, Charles, and Emily Egbert. *Kith, Kin, Wee Kirk*, Vol. 2. Sadieville, KY: C. and E. Egbert, 1995.

Ehrmann, Bess V. *Back Trails of Indiana*. New York: Horizon House, 1943.

———. *The Missing Chapter in the Life of Abraham Lincoln*. Chicago: W. M. Hill, 1938.

Elliott, Joseph P. *History of Evansville and Vanderburgh County, IN*. Evansville: Keller Printing, 1897.

Ely, William. *The Big Sandy Valley: History of the People and Country from the Earliest Settlement to the Present Time*. Catlettsburg, KY: Central Methodist, 1887.

Engerud, H., trans. *The 1864 Diary of Lt. Col. Jefferson K. Scott, 59th Indiana Infantry*. Bloomington: Monroe County Civil War Centennial Commission, 1962.

England, W. R. *A Complete Roster of the 22nd Regiment Indiana Infantry*. Seymour: Indiana Reform School Press, 1901.

Espy, Florence M. *History and Genealogy of the Espy Family in America*. Fort Madison, IA: Pythian Printing, 1905.

Etter, John P. *The Indiana Legion: A Civil War Militia*. Carmel, IN: Hawthorne, 2006.

Evans, Elwood. *History of the Pacific Northwest: Oregon and Washington*. Portland: North Pacific History, 1889.

Fairbanks, Lorenzo S. *Genealogy of the Fairbanks Family in America, 1633–1897*. Boston: American Printing and Engraving, 1897.

Faller, Phillip E. *The Indiana Jackass Regiment in the Civil War: A History of the 21st Infantry/1st Heavy Artillery Regiment, with a Roster*. Jefferson, NC: McFarland, 2013.

Family Histories Christian County, KY, 1797–1986. Paducah: Turner, 1986.

Ferril, William C. *Sketches of Colorado: Being an Analytical Summary and Biographical History of the State of Colorado*. Denver: Western Press Bureau, 1911.

Field, Nathaniel. *A Genealogy of the Pope Family of Kentucky*. Jeffersonville, IN: Evening News Print, 1879.

Fitch, John. *Annals of the Army of the Cumberland*. Philadelphia: J. B. Lippincott, 1864.

Fitch, Roscoe C., comp. *History of the Fitch Family, 1400–1930*. Haverhill, MA: Record, 1930.

Fletcher, Robert S., and Malcolm O. Young, eds. *Amherst College. Biographical Record of the Graduates and Non-Graduates*, centennial ed., 1821–1921. Amherst: Amherst College, 1927.

Floyd, David B. *History of the 75th Regiment of Indiana Infantry Volunteers, Its Organization, Campaigns, and Battles (1862–65)*. Philadelphia: Lutheran Publication Society, 1893.

Fogle, McDowell A. *Fogle's Papers: A History of Ohio County, Kentucky*. Hartford, KY: McDowell Publications, 1981.

Foote, H. S., ed. *Pen Pictures from the Garden of the World, or Santa Clara County, CA*. Chicago: Lewis, 1888.

Forkner, John L. *History of Madison County, IN*. Chicago: Lewis, 1914.

Foster, John W. *Diplomatic Memoirs*. Boston: Houghton, Mifflin, 1909.

———. *War Stories for My Grandchildren*. Washington, DC: Riverside Press, 1918.
Fox, Henry C. *Memoirs of Wayne County and the City of Richmond, IN*. Madison, WI: Western Historical Association, 1912.
Fulfer, Richard J. *A History of the Trials and Hardships of the 24th Indiana Volunteer Infantry*. Indianapolis: Indianapolis Printing, 1913.
Funk, Arville L. *The Morgan Raid in Indiana and Ohio (1863)*. Corydon, IN: ALFCO Publications, 1978.
Gaff, Alan D. *On Many a Bloody Field: Four Years in the Iron Brigade*. Bloomington: Indiana University Press, 1996.
Gage, Moses D. *From Vicksburg to Raleigh; or, A Complete History of the 12th Regiment Indiana Volunteer Infantry*. Chicago: Clarke, 1865.
Garr, John Wesley, and John Calhoun Garr. *Genealogy of the Descendants of John Gar, or More Particularly of His Son, Andreas Gaar*. Cincinnati: John W. Garr, 1894.
A Genealogical and Biographical Record of Decatur County, IN. Chicago: Lewis, 1900.
A Genealogy of the King Family. Buffalo: American Heraldic Society, 1930.
General Catalogue of the Alumni of Hanover College, 1833–1883. Hanover, IN: Alumni Association, 1883.
General Catalogue of the Centre College of Kentucky. Danville: Kentucky Advocate Printing, 1890.
Gilbert, Arlan K. *Hillsdale Honor: The Civil War Experience*. Hillsdale, MI: Hillsdale College Press, 1994.
Gilchrist, Agnes A. *William Strickland, Architect and Engineer, 1788–1854*. New York: Da Capo Press, 1969.
Gindlesperger, James. *Escape from Libby Prison*. Shippensburg, PA: Burd Street Press, 1995.
Goff, John S. *The Secretaries, United States Attorneys, Marshals, Surveyors General and Superintendents of Indian Affairs, 1863–1912*. Cave Creek, AZ: Black Mountain Press, 1988.
Goodrich, DeWitt C., and Charles R. Tuttle. *An Illustrated History of the State of Indiana*. Indianapolis: Richard S. Peale, 1875.
Goodspeed, Weston A., and Charles Blanchard, eds. *Counties of Porter and Lake, Indiana. Historical and Biographical*. Chicago: F. A. Battey, 1882.
———, and ———, eds. *Counties of Whitley and Noble, Indiana. Historical and Biographical*. Chicago: F. A. Battey, 1882.
Gracie, Archibald. *The Truth About Chickamauga*. Boston: Houghton Mifflin, 1911.
Graf, Leroy P., ed. *The Papers of Andrew Johnson*, Vol. 7, 1864–1865. Knoxville: University of Tennessee Press, 1986.
———, and Ralph W. Haskins, eds. *The Papers of Andrew Johnson*, Vol. 5, 1861–1862. Knoxville: University of Tennessee Press, 1979.
———, and ———, eds. *The Papers of Andrew Johnson*, Vol. 6, 1862–1864. Knoxville: University of Tennessee Press, 1983.
Graham, John. *Our Graham Family History*. Woodbridge, VA: John Graham, 1992.
Gray, George A., comp. *The Descendants of George Holmes of Roxbury, 1594–1908*. Boston: David Clapp, 1908.
Grecian, Joseph. *History of the 83rd Regiment, Indiana Volunteer Infantry, for Three Years with Sherman*. Cincinnati: John F. Uhlhorn, 1865.
Greene, George E. *History of Old Vincennes and Knox County, IN*. Chicago: S. J. Clarke, 1911.
Greenlee, Ralph S., and Robert L. Greenlee. *Genealogy of the Greenlee Families in America, Scotland, Ireland and England*. Chicago: R. S. and R. L. Greenlee, 1908.
Gregory, Grant, comp. *Ancestors and Descendants of Henry Gregory*. Provincetown, MA: Grant Gregory, 1938.
Gresham, Matilda. *Life of Walter Quintin Gresham*. Chicago: Rand, McNally, 1919.
Griswold, Bert J. *The Pictorial History of Fort Wayne, IN*. Chicago: Robert O. Law, 1917.
Grose, William. *The Story of the Marches, Battles and Incidents of the 36th Regiment Indiana Volunteer Infantry*. New Castle, IN: Courier Company Press, 1891.
Gue, Benjamin F. *Biographies and Portraits of the Progressive Men of Iowa, Leaders in Business, Politics and the Professions, Together with an Original and Authentic History of the State*. Des Moines: Conaway & Shaw, 1899.
Guthrie, Laurence R. *American Guthrie and Allied Families*. Chambersburg, PA: Kerr Printing, 1933.
Haas, Garland A. *To the Mountain of Fire and Beyond: The 53rd Indiana Regiment from Corinth to Glory*. Carmel, IN: Guild Press of Indiana, 1997.
Hadley, John V., ed. *History of Hendricks County, Indiana: Her People, Industries and Institutions*. Indianapolis: B. F. Bowen, 1914.
Haggard, David D. *History of the Haggard Family in England and America, 1433 to 1899*. Bloomington, IL: Corn Belt Printing & Stationery, 1899.
Haimbaugh, Frank D., ed. *History of Delaware County, IN*. Indianapolis: Historical, 1924.
Hale, Will T. *History of DeKalb County, TN*. Nashville: Paul Hunter, 1915.
Hall, C. Mitchel. *Jenny Wiley Country: A History of "Jenny Wiley Country" and Genealogy of Its People Up to the Year 1972*. Kingsport, TN: Kingsport Press, 1972.
———. *Johnson County, Kentucky: A History of the County, and Genealogy of Its People Up to the Year 1927*. Louisville: Standard Press, 1928.
Hamilton, Louis H., and William Darroch, eds. *Standard History of Jasper and Newton Counties, IN*. Chicago and New York: Lewis, 1916.
Hardacre, F. C., comp. *Historical Atlas of Knox County, IN*. Vincennes, IN: F. C. Hardacre, 1903.
Harden, Samuel, and D. Spahr, comp. *Early Life and Times in Boone County, Indiana*. Indianapolis: Carlon & Hollenbeck, 1887.

Harding, Lewis A., ed. *History of Decatur County, Indiana, Its People, Industries and Institutions*. Indianapolis: B. F. Bowen, 1915.

Hardy, Stella Pickett. *Colonial Families of the Southern States of America*. Baltimore: Southern Book, 1958.

Harlan, Alpheus H., comp. *History and Genealogy of the Harlan Family and Particularly of the Descendants of George and Michael Harlan Who Settled in Chester County, PA, 1687*. Baltimore: Lord Baltimore Press, 1914.

Harrison, James L., comp. *Biographical Directory of the American Congress, 1774–1949*. Washington, DC: Government Printing Office, 1950.

Hartpence, William R. *History of the 51st Indiana Veteran Volunteer Infantry*. Cincinnati: Robert Clarke, 1894.

Hayes, A. B., and Sam D. Cox. *History of the City of Lincoln, Nebraska*. Lincoln: State Journal, 1889.

Hazen, William B. *A Narrative of Military Service*. Boston: Ticknor, 1885.

Hazzard, George. *Hazzard's History of Henry County, IN, 1822–1906. Military Edition*. New Castle, IN: George Hazzard, 1906.

Heiple, Robert W., and Emma B. Heiple. *A Heritage History of Beautiful Green Lake, WI*. Green Lake: Robert W. Heiple, 1977.

Heitman, Francis B. *Historical Register and Dictionary of the United States Army*. Washington, DC: Government Printing Office, 1903.

Helm, Thomas B. *History of Delaware County, IN*. Chicago: Kingman Brothers, 1881.

_____. *History of Hamilton County, IN*. Chicago: Kingman Brothers, 1880.

_____. *History of Wabash County, IN*. Chicago: John Morris, 1884.

_____, ed. *History of Allen County, IN*. Chicago: Kingman Brothers, 1880.

_____, ed. *History of Cass County, IN*. Chicago: Brant & Fuller, 1886.

Henry, Guy V. *Military Record of Civilian Appointments in the United States Army*. New York: Carleton, 1869.

The Heritage of Bradley County, TN, 1836–1998. Waynesville, NC: Bradley County Heritage Book Committee, 1998.

Hicks, Lewis W., comp. *The Biographical Record of the Class of 1870 Yale College*. Boston: Thomas Todd, 1911.

High, Edwin W. *History of the 68th Regiment Indiana Volunteer Infantry, 1862–1865*. N.p.: Sixty-eighth Indiana Infantry Association, 1902.

History of the 73rd Indiana Volunteers in the War of 1861–65. Washington, DC: Carnahan Press, 1909.

History of the Academic Class of 1856, Yale University, to 1896. Boston: Class of 1856, 1897.

History of Adams County, IL. Chicago: Murray, Williamson & Phelps, 1879.

History of the Arkansas Valley, Colorado. Chicago: O. L. Baskin, 1881.

History of Clinton County, IN. Chicago: Inter-state, 1886.

History of Dearborn, Ohio and Switzerland Counties, Indiana, from Their Earliest Settlement. Chicago: Weakley, Harraman, 1885.

History of DeKalb County, IN. Indianapolis: B. F. Bowen, 1914.

History 88th Indiana Volunteers Infantry. Engagements, Chronology, Roster. Fort Wayne, IN: W. D. Page, 1895.

History of Fayette County, IN. Chicago: Warner, Beers, 1885.

History of the 46th Regiment Indiana Volunteer Infantry, September 1861–September 1865. Logansport, IN: Press of Wilson, Humphreys, 1888.

History of Franklin and Cerro Gordo Counties, IA. Springfield, IL: Union, 1883.

History of Grant County, IN. Chicago: Brant & Fuller, 1886.

History of Greene and Sullivan Counties, IN. Chicago: Goodspeed Brothers, 1884.

History of Hendricks County, IN. Chicago: Inter-state, 1885.

History of Huntington County, IN, From the Earliest Time to the Present. Chicago: Brant & Fuller, 1887.

History of Jackson County, IN. Chicago: Brant & Fuller, 1886.

History of Jasper County, MO. Des Moines: Mills, 1883.

History of Kentucky: The Blue Grass State. Chicago and Louisville: S. J. Clarke, 1928.

History of Knox and Daviess Counties, IN. Chicago: Goodspeed, 1886.

History of Lafayette County, MO. St. Louis: Missouri Historical, 1881.

History of Lawrence and Monroe Counties, Indiana. Their People, Industries and Institutions. Indianapolis: B. F. Bowen, 1914.

History of Lawrence, Orange and Washington Counties, IN. Chicago: Goodspeed Brothers, 1884.

History of McLean County, IL. Chicago: W. LeBaron, Jr., 1879.

History of Miami County, Indiana. Chicago: Brant & Fuller, 1887.

History of Mills County, Iowa. Des Moines: State Historical, 1881.

History of Montana, 1739–1885. Chicago: Warner, Beers, 1885.

History of Posey County, IN. Chicago: Goodspeed, 1886.

History of St. Joseph County, IN. Chicago: Chas. C. Chapman, 1880.

History of Saline County, MO. St. Louis: Missouri Historical, 1881.

History of Steuben County, IN. Chicago: Inter-state, 1885.

History of Tennessee from the Earliest Times to the Present, Together with an Historical and Biographical Sketch of Gibson, Obion, Dyer, Weakley, and Lake Counties. Nashville: Goodspeed, 1887.

History of Tennessee from the Earliest Times to the Present, Together with an Historical and Biographical Sketch of Lawrence, Wayne, Perry, Hickman, and Lewis Counties. Nashville: Goodspeed, 1886.

History of Tennessee from the Earliest Times to the Present, Together with an Historical and Biographical Sketch of Thirty East Tennessee Counties. Nashville: Goodspeed, 1887.

History of Tennessee from the Earliest Times to the Present, Together with an Historical and Biographical Sketch of White, Warren, DeKalb, Coffee and Cannon Counties. Nashville: Goodspeed, 1886.

History of the Ohio Falls Cities and Their Counties. Cleveland: L. A. Williams, 1882.

History of Vanderburgh County, IN. Madison, WI: Brant & Fuller, 1889.

History of Vernon County, WI. Springfield, IL: Union, 1884.

History of Warrick, Spencer and Perry Counties, IN. Chicago: Goodspeed Brothers, 1885.

History of Wayne County, IN. Chicago: Inter-state, 1884.

Hogan, Sally C., ed. *General Reub Williams's Memories of Civil War Times.* Westminster, MD: Heritage Books, 2006.

Holloway, Lisabeth M. *Medical Obituaries: American Physicians' Biographical Notices in Selected Medical Journals Before 1907.* New York: Garland, 1981.

Holton, David Parsons, and Mrs. Frances K. (Forward) Holton. *Winslow Memorial. Family Records of Winslows and Their Descendants in America, with the English Ancestry as Far as Known. Kenelm Winslow.* New York: D. P. Holton, 1877–88.

Horrall, Spillard F. *History of the 42nd Indiana Volunteer Infantry.* Chicago: Donohue & Henneberry, 1892.

Hunt, Jeffrey W. *The Last Battle of the Civil War: Palmetto Ranch.* Austin: University of Texas Press, 2002.

Hurd, D. Hamilton, comp. *History of Bristol County, MA.* Philadelphia: J. W. Lewis, 1883.

Hurlburt, J. S. *History of the Rebellion in Bradley County, East Tennessee.* Indianapolis: Downey & Brouse, 1866.

Hurt, Mary Lee, comp. *Family History from Robert Hurt, d. 1583, Ashbourne, Staffordshire, England, Through Leon Jesse Hurt, d. 1956, Barry, Pike County, Illinois, and Family.* Tallahassee: M. L. Hurt, 1985.

Illustrated Album of Biography of Pope and Stevens Counties, MN. Chicago: Alden, Ogle, 1888.

An Illustrated History of Southern California, Embracing the Counties of San Diego, San Bernardino, Los Angeles and Orange, and the Peninsula of Lower California. Chicago: Lewis, 1890.

Indiana at Chickamauga, 1863–1900. Report of Indiana Commissioners Chickamauga National Military Park. Indianapolis: W. B. Burford, 1901.

Jenkins, Kirk C. *The Battle Rages Higher: The Union's Fifteenth Kentucky Infantry.* Lexington: University Press of Kentucky, 2003.

Johnson, Allen, and Dumas Malone, eds. *Dictionary of American Biography.* New York: Scribner's, 1964.

Johnson, E. Polk. *A History of Kentucky and Kentuckians.* Chicago and New York: Lewis, 1912.

Johnston, J. Stoddard, ed. *Memorial History of Louisville.* Chicago: American Biographical, 1896.

Johnston, Sheila W., comp. *The Blue and Gray from Hawkins County, TN, 1861–1865.* Rogersville: Hawkins County Genealogical and Historical Society, 1995.

Jones, Mary K. *History of Campbell County, As Read at the Centennial Celebration of 4th of July, 1876.* Newport, KY, 1876.

Jones, Wilbur D., Jr. *Giants in the Cornfield: The 27th Indiana Infantry.* Shippensburg, PA: White Mane, 1997.

Joyce, John A. *A Checkered Life.* Chicago: S. P. Rounds, 1883.

Katterjohn, Monte M. *History of Warrick and Its Prominent People.* Boonville, IN: Crescent Publication, 1909.

Keating, J. M. *History of the City of Memphis and Shelby County, TN.* Syracuse: D. Mason, 1888.

Kemper, General W. H. *A Medical History of the State of Indiana.* Chicago: American Medical Association Press, 1911.

_____, ed. *A Twentieth Century History of Delaware County, IN.* Chicago: Lewis, 1908.

Kerwood, Asbury L. *Annals of the 57th Regiment Indiana Volunteers, Marches, Battles, and Incidents of Army Life.* Dayton: W. J. Shuey, 1868.

King, Cameron H. *The King Family of Suffield, CT.* San Francisco, CA: Press of Walter N. Brunt, 1908.

King, James L., ed. *History of Shawnee County, Kansas, and Representative Citizens.* Chicago: Richmond & Arnold, 1905.

Kingman Brothers, comp. *Combination Atlas Map of Boone County, IN.* Chicago: Kingman Brothers, 1878.

_____, comp. *Combination Atlas Map of Cass County, IN.* Chicago: Kingman Brothers, 1878.

_____, comp. *Combination Atlas Map of Grant County, IN.* Chicago: Kingman Brothers, 1877.

_____, comp. *Combination Atlas Map of Howard County, IN.* Chicago: Kingman Brothers, 1877.

_____, comp. *Combination Atlas Map of Kosciusko County, IN.* Chicago: Kingman Brothers, 1879.

Kingsbury, George W. *History of Dakota Territory.* Chicago: S. J. Clarke, 1915.

Kirkpatrick, Ralph D. *Local History and Genealogy Abstracts from Marion, Indiana Newspapers, 1865–1870.* Bowie, MD: Heritage Books, 2001.

Koontz, Lowell L. *History of the Descendants of John Koontz.* Parsons, WV: McClain Printing, 1979.

Kozee, William C. *Early Families of Eastern and Southeastern Kentucky.* Baltimore: Genealogical, 1979.

Kozsuch, Mildred. *Historical Reminiscences of Carter County, TN.* Johnson City, TN: Overmountain Press, 1985.

Kriebel, Robert C. *Old Lafayette, 1854–1876: Based*

Upon Historical Columns from the Pages of the Journal and Courier. Lafayette, IN: Tippecanoe County Historical Association, 1990.

Kuhbander, Rita Espy, and William G. Espy. *The Espy-Espey Genealogy Book.* Baltimore: Gateway Press, 1987.

Lackey, Hecht S. *Martin Grider of Pennsylvania and His Descendants, Circa 1731–1978.* Evansville: Unigraphic, 1979.

Lambert, D. Warren. *When the Ripe Pears Fell: The Battle of Richmond, Kentucky.* Richmond: Madison County Historical Society, 1995.

Lang, George, Raymond L. Collins, and Gerard F. White, comp. *Medal of Honor Recipients, 1863–1994.* New York: Facts on File, 1995.

Latham, Frank B. *The Great Dissenter: John Marshall Harlan, 1833–1911.* New York: Cowles Book, 1970.

Leach, Josiah G. *History of the Bringhurst Family with Notes on the Clarkson, DePeyster, and Boude Families.* Philadelphia: J. B. Lippincott, 1901.

Leffel, John C., ed. *History of Posey County, IN.* Chicago: Standard, 1913.

Leistner, Doris Byrd. *Crawford County Indiana Civil War Veterans.* New Albany, IN: D. B. Leistner, 2005.

Lemon, J. R. *Lemon's Hand Book of Marshall County.* Benton, KY: J. R. Lemon, 1894.

Leonard, William P. *History and Directory of Posey County.* Evansville: A. C. Isaacs, 1882.

Levin, H., ed. *The Lawyers and Lawmakers of Kentucky.* Chicago: Lewis, 1897.

Lewis, Audree S. *Cemeteries of Steuben County, Indiana.* N.p.: A. S. Lewis, 1990.

Lillard, Roy G., ed. *History of Bradley County, TN.* Cleveland: Bradley County Chapter, East Tennessee Historical Society, 1976.

Lincoln County Historical Society. *Lincoln County, Kentucky.* Paducah: Turner, 2002.

Link, Paxson R. *The Link Family.* Paris, IL, 1951.

Liston-Griswold, Mattie, comp. *Tracy Genealogy: Ancestors and Descendants of Thomas Tracy of Lenox, Massachusetts.* Kalamazoo: Doubleday Brothers, 1900.

Locke, Norma Paden Heskett, Elona Paden Bruce, Merrill Paden, Elsie Paden Beavers, and Esther Paden Birk Osborn. *Peden-Paden Family History.* Wichita: Paden Five, 2003.

Lord, Kenneth, comp. *Genealogy of the Descendants of Thomas Lord, an Original Proprietor and Founder of Hartford, CT, in 1636.* New Haven: Tuttle, Morehouse & Taylor, 1946.

Lowry, Thomas P. *Tarnished Eagles: The Courts-Martial of Fifty Union Colonels and Lieutenant Colonels.* Mechanicsburg, PA: Stackpole Books, 1997.

Lucas, Daniel R. *New History of the 99th Indiana Infantry.* Rockford, IL: Horner Printing, 1900.

Lyon, Sidney Elizabeth, ed. *Lyon Memorial: Families of Connecticut and New Jersey.* Detroit: William Graham Printing, 1907.

MacDonald, Margaret Read. *Scipio, Indiana: Threads from the Past.* Fairfield, WA: Ye Galleon Press, 1988.

Macdonald, Margaret T. *The Milward Family of Lexington, KY, 1803–1969.* Dallas: M. T. Macdonald, 1970.

Macon, Edna S., comp. *Memorials to the Blue and Gray: Commonwealth of Kentucky Civil War Monuments.* Kuttawa, KY: McClanahan Publishing House, 2011.

Magee, Benjamin F. *History of the 72nd Indiana Volunteer Infantry of the Mounted Lightning Brigade.* Lafayette, IN: S. Vater, 1882.

Magness, Perre. *Elmwood 2002: In the Shadows of the Elms.* Memphis: Elmwood Cemetery, 2001.

Major General Henry W. Lawton of Fort Wayne, Indiana. Fort Wayne: Public Library of Fort Wayne and Allen County, 1954.

Marshall, Randolph V. *An Historical Sketch of the 22nd Regiment Indiana Volunteers, from Its Organization to the Close of the War, Its Battles, Its Marches, and Its Hardships, Its Brave Officers and Its Honored Dead.* Madison, IN: Courier, 1884.

Martin, Charles A., ed. *DePauw University: Alumnal Register of Officers, Faculties and Graduates, 1837–1900.* Greencastle, IN: DePauw University, 1901.

Martin, Else. *Cemeteries of Jackson County, Mississippi: A Requiem.* Pascagoula, MS: Jackson County Historical and Genealogical Society, 2008.

Martin, Michael J. *A History of the 4th Wisconsin Infantry and Cavalry in the Civil War.* New York: Savas Beatie, 2006.

Mather, Otis M. *Six Generations of LaRues and Allied Families.* Hodgenville, KY, 1921.

Maxwell, W. J., comp. *The Catalogue of the Phi Delta Theta Fraternity.* 8th ed. New York: R. L. Polk, 1918.

McBride, John R. *History of the 33rd Indiana Veteran Volunteer Infantry.* Indianapolis: W. B. Burford, 1900.

McBride, Robert M., and Dan M. Robison. *Biographical Directory of the Tennessee General Assembly*, Vol. 1, 1796–1861. Nashville: Tennessee Historical Commission, 1975.

_____, and _____. *Biographical Directory of the Tennessee General Assembly*, Vol. 2, 1861–1901. Nashville: Tennessee Historical Commission, 1979.

McCammon, Charles S. *Loyal Mountain Troopers: The Second and Third Tennessee Volunteer Cavalry in the Civil War.* Maryville, TN: Blount County Genealogical and Historical Society, 1992.

McCann, Kevin D. *Hurst's Wurst: Colonel Fielding Hurst and the Sixth Tennessee Cavalry, U.S.A.* Dickson, TN: McCann, 2007.

McConnell, Darlene. *Posey Troops, 1861–1865. An Indiana Border County in the Great Rebellion.* Mount Vernon, IN: Darlene McConnell, 1999.

McDonald, John. *Secrets of the Great Whiskey Ring: And Eighteen Months in the Penitentiary.* St. Louis: W. S. Bryan, 1880.

McGeary, Margaret Steele. *The House of Steele: Abraham Steele of Harford County, Maryland, and Ten Generations of His Descendants.* Decorah, IA: Anundsen, 1990.

McKee, George Wilson. *The McKees of Virginia and Kentucky.* Pittsburgh, PA: J. B. Richards, 1891.

McLean, William E. *The 43rd Regiment of Indiana Volunteers. An Historic Sketch of Its Career and Services.* Terre Haute: C. W. Brown, 1903.

Meacham, Charles M. *A History of Christian County, Kentucky, from Oxcart to Airplane.* Nashville: Marshall & Bruce, 1930.

Memorial Addresses on the Life and Character of Leonidas Campbell Houk, A Representative from Tennessee. Washington, DC: Government Printing Office, 1892.

A Memorial and Biographical Record of Kansas City and Jackson County, MO. Chicago: Lewis, 1896.

Memorial of Benjamin Helm Bristow. Cambridge: Cambridge University Press, 1897.

Memorial Record of Northeastern Indiana. Chicago: Lewis, 1896.

Memorials of Deceased Companions of the Commandery of the State of Illinois MOLLUS, from July 1, 1901 to Dec. 31, 1911. Chicago: Illinois Commandery MOLLUS, 1912.

Merrill, Samuel. *The 70th Indiana Volunteer Infantry in the War of the Rebellion.* Indianapolis: Bowen-Merrill, 1900.

Miller, Maude Barnes. *Dear Wife: Letters from a Union Colonel.* Ravenna, KY: Estill County Historical and Genealogical Society, 2001.

Miller, William Harris. *History and Genealogies of the Families of Miller, Woods, Harris, Wallace, Maupin, Oldham, Kavanaugh, and Brown.* Lexington, KY: Transylvania, 1907.

Mitchell, Charles R., ed. *History and Families, Knox County, Kentucky, 1799–1994.* Paducah: Turner, 1994.

Montague, William L., ed. *Biographical Record of the Alumni of Amherst College, During Its First Half Century, 1821–1871.* Amherst: J. E. Williams, 1883.

Moore, Frank, ed. *The Rebellion Record: A Diary of American Events.* Vol. 5. New York: G. P. Putnam, 1864.

Moore, John Trotwood. *Tennessee, The Volunteer State, 1769–1923.* Chicago: S. J. Clarke, 1923.

Morford, Wanda L. *Switzerland County, Indiana, Cemetery Inscriptions, 1817–1985.* Cincinnati: W. L. Morford, 1986.

Morgan, Otho H. *History of the 7th Independent Battery of Indiana Light Artillery.* Bedford, IN: Press of the Democrat, 1898.

Morris, Charles, ed. *Makers of New York.* Philadelphia: L. R. Hamersly, 1895.

Morris, George W. *History of the 81st Regiment of Indiana Volunteer Infantry in the Great War of the Rebellion, 1861 to 1865.* Louisville: Franklin Printing, 1901.

Morrow, Jackson. *History of Howard County, IN.* Indianapolis: B. F. Bowen, 1910.

Mullen, Andrew. *Col. Bernard F. Mullen, Commander of the 35th Indiana Volunteers, 1st Irish Regiment, Civil War.* Celina, OH: Andrew Mullen, 1968.

Mullins, Michael A. *The Fremont Rifles: A History of the 37th Illinois Veteran Volunteer Infantry.* Wilmington: Broadfoot, 1990.

Munson, Myron A. *The Munson Record, 1637–1887: A Genealogical and Biographical Account of Captain Thomas Munson and His Descendants.* New Haven: Munson Association, 1895.

Murphy, Margaret A. Karsner, comp. *The Life and Times of Our Hawkins Family.* N.p.: M. A. K. Murphy, 1988.

Myers, Burton D. *Trustees and Officers of Indiana University, 1820 to 1950.* Bloomington: Indiana University Press, 1951.

National Cyclopedia of American Biography. New York: James T. White, 1898–1926.

Nikazy, Eddie M. *Forgotten Soldiers: History of the 4th Tennessee Volunteer Infantry Regiment (USA), 1863–1865.* Bowie, MD: Heritage Books, 1995.

_____. *Forgotten Soldiers: History of the 2nd Tennessee Volunteer Infantry Regiment (USA), 1861–1865.* Bowie, MD: Heritage Books, 1996.

Nowland, John H. B. *Sketches of Prominent Citizens of 1876.* Indianapolis: Tilford & Carlon, 1877.

Oakey, Charles C. *Greater Terre Haute and Vigo County Closing the First Century's History of City and County.* Chicago and New York: Lewis, 1908.

Official Army Register of the Volunteer Force of the United States Army for the Years 1861, '62, '63, '64, '65. 8 Vol. Washington, DC: Government Printing Office, 1865–1867.

O'Gorman, Ella Foy, comp. *Descendants of Virginia Calverts.* Los Angeles: E. F. O'Gorman, 1947.

Operations of the Indiana Legion and Minute Men, 1863–4. Documents Presented to the General Assembly, with the Governor's Message, Jan. 6, 1865. Indianapolis: W. R. Holloway, 1865.

O'Rear, Edward C. *A History of the Montgomery County Bar.* Frankfort: E. C. O'Rear, 1945.

Overmyer, Jack K. *A Stupendous Effort: The 87th Indiana in the War of the Rebellion.* Bloomington: Indiana University Press, 1997.

Owen, Kathryn, comp. *Civil War Days in Clark County.* N.p.: Kathryn Owen, 1963.

Packard, Jasper. *History of La Porte County, Indiana, and Its Townships, Towns and Cities.* La Porte, IN: S. E. Taylor, 1876.

Page, Oliver O. *A Short Account of the Family of Ormsby of Pittsburgh.* Albany: Munsell's, 1892.

Park, Elbridge C. *History of Irvine and Estill County, Kentucky.* Lexington: University Press of Kentucky, 1906.

Paxton, William M. *The Marshall Family.* Cincinnati: Robert Clarke, 1885.

_____. *The Paxtons.* Platte City, MO: Landmark Print, 1903.

Peake, Michael A. *Blood Shed in This War: Civil War Illustrations by Captain Adolph Metzner, 32nd Indiana.* Indianapolis: Indiana Historical Society Press, 2010.

Peddycord, Will F. *History of the 74th Regiment In-*

diana Volunteer Infantry. Warsaw, IN: Smith Printery, 1913.
Perrin, William H., J. H. Battle, and Gilbert C. Kniffin. *Kentucky: A History of the State*. Louisville and Chicago: F. A. Battey, 1885.
_____, _____ and _____. *Kentucky: A History of the State*. Louisville and Chicago: F. A. Battey, 1887.
_____, _____ and _____. *Kentucky: A History of the State*. 5th ed. Louisville and Chicago: F. A. Battey, 1887.
_____, _____ and _____. *Kentucky: A History of the State*. 6th ed. Louisville and Chicago: F. A. Battey, 1887.
_____, _____ and _____. *Kentucky: A History of the State*. 8th ed. Louisville and Chicago: F. A. Battey, 1888.
Perry, Henry F. *History of the 38th Regiment Indiana Volunteer Infantry*. Palo Alto, CA: F. A. Stuart, 1906.
Perry, Oran. *Recollections of the Civil War*, 2d ed. Indianapolis: Historical Bureau of the Indiana Library and Historical Department, 1928.
Peter, Robert. *History of Fayette County, KY, With an Outline Sketch of the Blue Grass Region*. Chicago: O. L. Baskin, 1882.
_____. *History of the Medical Department of Transylvania University*. Louisville: J. P. Morton, 1905.
Phillips, A. V. *The Lott Family in America*. Trenton, NJ: A. V. Phillips, 1942.
Piatt, Emma C. *History of Piatt County, Illinois*. Chicago: Shepard & Johnston, 1883.
Pickerill, William N. *History of the 3rd Indiana Cavalry*. Indianapolis: Aetna Printing, 1906.
_____, comp. *Indiana at the Fiftieth Anniversary of the Battle of Gettysburg*. Indianapolis: Indiana Gettysburg Anniversary Commission, 1913.
Pictorial and Biographical Memoirs of Elkhart and St. Joseph Counties, Indiana. Chicago: Goodspeed Brothers, 1893.
Pictorial and Biographical Memoirs of Indianapolis and Marion County, IN. Chicago: Goodspeed Brothers, 1893.
Pictorial and Genealogical Record of Greene County, MO. Chicago: Goodspeed Brothers, 1893.
Platter, the Rev. David Edwin. *A History of the Platter Family from About Year 1600 to the Present Time*. Cleveland: D. E. Platter, 1919.
Pleasant, Hazen H. *A History of Crawford County, IN*. Greenfield, IN: William Mitchell Printing, 1926.
Pope, Charles Henry, comp. *The Haverhill Emersons*. Boston: Murray and Emery, 1913.
Portrait and Biographical Album of Champaign County, IL. Chicago: Chapman Brothers, 1887.
Portrait and Biographical Record of Boone and Clinton Counties, IN. Chicago: A. W. Bowen, 1895.
A Portrait and Biographical Record of Boone, Clinton and Hendricks Counties, IN. Chicago: A. W. Bowen, 1895.
A Portrait and Biographical Record of Delaware and Randolph Counties, IN. Chicago: A. W. Bowen, 1894.
Portrait and Biographical Record of Lee County, IL. Chicago: Biographical, 1892.
Portrait and Biographical Record of Madison and Hamilton Counties, IN. Chicago: Biographical, 1893.
Portrait and Biographical Record of Montgomery, Parke and Fountain Counties, IN. Chicago: Chapman Brothers, 1893.
Powell, Jehu Z., ed. *History of Cass County, IN*. Chicago and New York: Lewis, 1913.
Powell, Katherine K., and Patricia D. Smith, comps. *Finney County (KS) Obituary Abstracts and Death Notices*. Garden City, KS: P. D. and Stanley C. Smith, 1988.
Powell, Robert A. *Kentucky Governors*. Frankfort: Kentucky Images, 1976.
Powell, William H. *Records of Living Officers of the United States Army*. Philadelphia: L. R. Hamersly, 1890.
_____, ed. *Officers of the Army and Navy (Volunteer) Who Served in the Civil War*. Philadelphia: L. R. Hamersly, 1893.
_____, and Edward Shippen, eds. *Officers of the Army and Navy (Regular) Who Served in the Civil War*. Philadelphia: L. R. Hamersly, 1892.
Power, John C., ed. *Directory and Soldiers' Register of Wayne County, IN*. Richmond, IN: W. H. Lanthurn, 1865.
Power, John Carroll. *History of the Early Settlers of Sangamon County, IL*. Springfield, IL: Edwin A. Wilson, 1876.
Pressler, Larry. *U.S. Senators from the Prairie*. Vermillion, SD: Dakota Press, 1982.
Preston, John David. *The Civil War in the Big Sandy Valley of Kentucky*, 2d ed. Baltimore: Gateway Press, 2008.
Prewitt, Lela W. *The Dawkins and Stewart Families of Virginia and Kentucky*. Fairfield, IA: L. W. Prewitt, 1968.
Price, George F. *Across the Continent with the Fifth Cavalry*. New York: D. Van Nostrand, 1883.
Proceedings of the 8th Annual Reunion of the 9th Indiana Veteran Volunteer Infantry Association, Held at Logansport, IN, August 26–27, 1891.
Proceedings of the 18th Annual Reunion of the 9th Indiana Veteran Volunteer Infantry Association, Held at Logansport, IN, October 7–8, 1904.
Puntenney, George H. *History of the 37th Regiment of Indiana Infantry Volunteers*. Rushville, IN: Jacksonian Book and Job Department, 1896.
Randall, George L., comp. *Tripp Genealogy: Descendants of James, Son of John Tripp*. New Bedford, MA: Vining Press, 1924.
Raus, Edmund J., Jr. *A Generation on the March: The Union Army at Gettysburg*. Gettysburg: Thomas Publications, 1996.
Record of the Harris Family Descended From John Harris Born 1680 in Wiltshire, England. Philadelphia: Press of George F. Lasher, 1903.
Reed, George I., ed. *Encyclopedia of Biography of In-*

diana. Chicago: Century Publishing and Engraving, 1895.

Reed, George Leffingwell, ed. *Alumni Record Dickinson College*. Carlisle, PA: Dickinson College, 1905.

Reid, Richard J. *Fourth Indiana Cavalry: A History*. Olaton, KY: R. J. Reid, 1994.

Reinhart, Joseph R. *A History of the 6th Kentucky Volunteer Infantry U.S.: The Boys Who Feared No Noise*. Louisville: Beargrass Press, 2000.

_____, ed. *August Willich's Gallant Dutchmen: Civil War Letters from the 32nd Indiana Infantry*. Kent: Kent State University Press, 2006.

Report of the Adjutant General of the State of Indiana. 8 Vol. Indianapolis: Alexander H. Conner, State Printer, 1865–1869.

Report of the Adjutant General of the State of Kentucky, 1861–1866, 2 vols. Frankfort: John. H. Harney, Public Printer, 1866–67.

Report of the Adjutant General of the State of Tennessee, of the Military Forces of the State from 1861 to 1865. Nashville: S. C. Mercer, State Printer, 1866.

Report of Major General Love of the Indiana Legion. Indianapolis: J. J. Bingham, 1863.

Report of the 11th Indiana Cavalry Association for 1898. Anderson, IN: Benham Printery, 1898.

Report of the Proceedings of the Society of the Army of the Tennessee at the Eighth Annual Meeting. Cincinnati: Published by the Society, 1877.

Rerick, John H. *The 44th Indiana Volunteer Infantry: History of Its Services in the War of the Rebellion*. LaGrange, IN: J. H. Rerick, 1880.

Richards, John A. *A History of Bath County, KY*. Yuma: Southwest Printers, 1961.

Richardson, James D. *Tennessee Templars*. Nashville: R. H. Howell, 1883.

Richmond, Joshua B. *The Richmond Family, 1594–1896*. Boston: J. B. Richmond, 1897.

Ritter, Charles F., and Jon L. Wakelyn. *American Legislative Leaders, 1850–1910*. Westport, CT: Greenwood Press, 1989.

Roberts, Ellwood, ed. *The Dewees Family: Genealogical Data, Biographical Facts and Historical Information*. Norristown, PA: W. H. Roberts, 1905.

Robinson, Doane. *History of South Dakota*. Logansport, IN: B. F. Bowen, 1904.

Rogers, Ellen, and Diane Rogers. *Cemetery Records of Estill County, KY*. Baltimore: Gateway Press, 1976.

Rogers, James T. *Col. Lewis Brooks: A Tribute*. N.p., 1915.

Roose, William H. *Indiana's Birthplace: A History of Harrison County, Indiana*. New Albany, IN: Tribune, 1911.

Rose, Christine. *Ancestors and Descendants of the Brothers Rev. Robert Rose and Rev. Charles Rose of Colonial Virginia and Wester Alves, Morayshire, Scotland*. San Jose: Rose Family Association, 1985.

Rose, Theodore C., comp. *The Tousey Family in America*. Elmira, NY: Osborne Press, 1916.

Rothert, Otto A. *A History of Muhlenberg County*. Louisville: J. P. Morton, 1913.

Rowell, John W. *Yankee Artillerymen: Through the Civil War with Eli Lilly's Indiana Battery*. Knoxville: University of Tennessee Press, 1975.

Royalty, James H. *History of the Town of Remington and Vicinity*. Logansport, IN: Wilson, Humphreys, 1894.

Royse, Lemuel W. *A Standard History of Kosciusko County, IN*. Chicago: Lewis, 1919.

Rugg, Ellen R. *The Descendants of John Rugg*. New York: F. H. Hitchcock, 1911.

Runnels, Moses T. *Memorial Sketches and History of the Class of 1853, Dartmouth College*. Newport, NH: Barton & Wheeler, 1895.

Sanford, Washington L. *History of 14th Illinois Cavalry and the Brigades to Which It Belonged*. Chicago: R. R. Donnelley & Sons, 1898.

Scott, Reuben B. *The History of the 67th Regiment Indiana Infantry Volunteers, War of the Rebellion*. Bedford, IN: Herald Print, 1892.

Scott, Samuel W., and Samuel P. Angel. *History of the 13th Regiment Tennessee Volunteer Cavalry, U.S.A*. Philadelphia: P. W. Ziegler, 1903.

Scribner, Theodore T. *Indiana's Roll of Honor*. Indianapolis: A. D. Streight, 1866.

Sears, Richard D. *Camp Nelson, Kentucky: A Civil War History*. Lexington: University Press of Kentucky, 2002.

Semi-Centennial Catalogue and Historical Register of Emory and Henry College, Washington County, VA, 1837–1887. Tazewell Court House, VA: Clinch Valley News Print, 1887.

Sesqui-Centennial Souvenir Program, City of Covington, KY, 1815–1965. Covington: T. & W. Printing, 1965.

Sexton, Naomi K. *The Hoosier Journal of Ancestry: Jennings County Special*, no. 1–3. Little York, IN: N. K. Sexton, 1987–92.

Shaw, Archibald, ed. *History of Dearborn County, IN*. Indianapolis: B. F. Bowen &, 1915.

Shaw, James Birney. *History of the 10th Regiment Indiana Volunteer Infantry, Three Months and Three Years Organizations*. Lafayette, IN: Burt-Hayward, 1912.

Shelby County in the Civil War. Shelbyville, IN: Shelby County Civil War Centennial Committee, 1961.

Shepherd, Rebecca A., Charles W. Calhoun, Elizabeth Shanahan-Shoemaker, and Alan F. January, eds. *A Biographical Directory of the Indiana General Assembly*, Vol. 1, 1816–1899. Indianapolis: Indiana Historical Bureau, 1980.

Sherlock, Eli J. *Memorabilia of the Marches and Battles in Which the 100th Regiment of Indiana Infantry Volunteers Took an Active Part, War of the Rebellion, 1861–5*. Kansas City: Gerard-Woody Printing, 1896.

Simmons, Don. *Marshall County, KY, Newspaper Genealogical Abstracts*, Vol. 2. Melber, KY: Simmons Historical Publications, 1985.

Simon, John Y., ed. *The Papers of Ulysses S. Grant*, Vol. 4: January 8–March 31, 1862. Carbondale: Southern Illinois University Press, 1972.

_____, ed. *The Papers of Ulysses S. Grant*, Vol. 20:

November 1, 1869–October 31, 1870. Carbondale: Southern Illinois University Press, 1995.
Smith, Barbara A., comp. *The Civil War Letters of Col. Elijah H. C. Cavins, 14th Indiana.* Owensboro, KY: Cook-McDowell Publications, 1981.
Smith, John Thomas. *A History of the 31st Regiment of Indiana Volunteer Infantry in the War of the Rebellion.* Cincinnati: Western Methodist Book Concern, 1900.
Smith, Z. F. *History of Kentucky.* Louisville: Prentice Press, 1895.
Snepp, Daniel W. *John W. Foster: Evansville's Distinguished Citizen.* N.p.: D. W. Snepp, 1975.
Society of the Army of the Cumberland. Fifth Reunion, Detroit, MI, 1871. Cincinnati: Robert Clarke, 1872.
Society of the Army of the Cumberland. Thirty-Ninth Reunion, Chattanooga, TN, 1911. Chattanooga: MacGowan-Cooke Printing, 1912.
Society of the Army of the Cumberland. Thirty-Sixth Reunion, Chattanooga, TN, 1908. Chattanooga: MacGowan-Cooke Printing, 1909.
Society of the Army of the Cumberland. Twenty-Eighth Reunion, Detroit, MI, Sept. 26 and 27, 1899. Cincinnati: Robert Clarke, 1900.
Society of the Army of the Cumberland. Twenty-First Reunion, Toledo, OH, 1890. Cincinnati: Robert Clarke, 1891.
Society of the Army of the Cumberland. Twenty-Fourth Reunion, Cleveland, OH, 1893. Cincinnati: Robert Clarke, 1894.
Society of the Army of the Cumberland. Twenty-Second Reunion, Columbus, OH, 1891. Cincinnati: Robert Clarke, 1892.
Society of the Army of the Cumberland. Twenty-Sixth Reunion, Rockford, IL, 1896. Cincinnati: Robert Clarke, 1897.
South Bend and the Men Who Have Made It. South Bend: Tribune Printing, 1901.
Souvenir and Official Program 19th Annual Encampment, Department of Indiana, GAR and Auxiliary Societies, Columbus, IN, May 17–20, 1898. Louisville: Courier-Journal Job Printing, 1898.
Speed, Thomas, Robert M. Kelly, and Alfred Pirtle. *The Union Regiments of Kentucky.* Louisville: Courier-Journal Job Printing, 1897.
Speer, William S., comp. *Sketches of Prominent Tennesseans.* Nashville: Albert B. Tavel, 1888.
Spraker, Hazel A., comp. *The Boone Family: Genealogy and History of the Descendants of George and Mary Boone Who Came to America in 1717.* Rutland, VT: Tuttle, 1922.
Stanhope, Philip W. *Official Papers, Letters and Notes, Relating to the War Record of P. W. Stanhope, Major and Brevet Lieutenant Colonel, U.S. Army.* N.p.: P. W. Stanhope, 1879.
Stein, Theodore. *Historical Sketch of the German-English Independent School of Indianapolis.* Indianapolis: Cheltenham-Aetna Press, 1913.
Stephens, John H. *History of Miami County Illustrated.* Peru, IN: John H. Stephens Publishing House, 1896.

Sterling, Albert Mack, comp. *The Sterling Genealogy.* New York: Grafton Press, 1909.
Sternberg, Dale, Sharon Sternberg and Fred T. May. *I Will Uphold the Flag: The Life of Colonel Reuben May, 1815–1902.* Baltimore: Gateway Press, 2004.
Stevenson, Benjamin F. *Letters from the Army.* Cincinnati: W. E. Dibble, 1884.
Stevenson, David. *Indiana's Roll of Honor.* Indianapolis: David Stevenson, 1864.
Stevenson, Kenyon. *A History of the William Carroll Family of Allegany County, NY.* York, PA: York Printing, 1929.
Stewart, J. Adger. *Descendants of Valentine Hollingsworth, Sr.* Louisville: J. P. Morton, 1925.
Stone, R. French, ed. *Biography of Eminent American Physicians and Surgeons.* Indianapolis: Carlon & Hollenbeck, 1894.
Stormont, Gilbert R., comp. *History of the 58th Regiment of Indiana Volunteer Infantry, Its Organization, Campaigns and Battles, from 1861 to 1865.* Princeton, IN: Press of the Clarion, 1895.
Strouse, Isaac R. *Parke County Indiana Centennial Memorial.* Rockville, IN: Rockville Chautauqua Association, 1916.
Sulgrove, Berry R. *History of Indianapolis and Marion County, IN.* Philadelphia: L. H. Everts, 1884.
Sullivant, Joseph. *A Genealogy and Family Memorial.* Columbus: Ohio State Journal Book and Job Rooms, 1874.
Sutherland, James. *Biographical Sketches of the Members of the Forty-First General Assembly of the State of Indiana with That of the State Officers and Judiciary.* Indianapolis: Indianapolis Journal, 1861.
Tackett, Regina, Patricia Jackson, and Janice Thompson. *History of Lawrence County, KY.* Dallas: Curtis Media Corp., 1991.
Tapp, Hambleton, and James C. Klotter, eds. *The Union, the Civil War and John W. Tuttle.* Frankfort: Kentucky Historical Society, 1980.
Tarrant, Eastham. *The Wild Riders of the First Kentucky Cavalry, A History of the Regiment in the Great War of the Rebellion, 1861–1865.* Louisville: Press of R. H. Carothers, 1894.
Taylor, Charles W. *Biographical Sketches and Review of the Bench and Bar of Indiana.* Indianapolis: Bench and Bar, 1895.
Temple, Oliver P. *East Tennessee and the Civil War.* Cincinnati: Robert Clarke, 1899.
_____. *Notable Men of Tennessee, from 1833 to 1875, Their Times and Their Contemporaries.* New York: Cosmopolitan Press, 1912.
Tenkotte, Paul A., and James C. Claypool, eds. *The Encyclopedia of Northern Kentucky.* Lexington: University Press of Kentucky, 2009.
Tennesseans in the Civil War, 2 vols. Nashville: Civil War Centennial Commission, 1964–65.
Tenth Annual Reunion of the Association of the Graduates of the United States Military Academy at West Point, NY, June 12, 1879. New York: D. Van Nostrand, 1879.

Thompson, Donald E., comp. *Indiana Authors and Their Books, 1967–1980.* Crawfordsville, IN: Wabash College, 1981.

Thomson, Orville. *From Philippi to Appomattox: Narrative of the Service of the 7th Indiana Infantry in the War for the Union.* N.p.: Orville Thomson, 1904.

Thrapp, Dan L. *Encyclopedia of Frontier Biography,* 3 vols. Lincoln: University of Nebraska Press, 1991.

Towne, Stephen E., ed. *A Fierce, Wild Joy: The Civil War Letters of Colonel Edward J. Wood, 48th Indiana Volunteer Infantry Regiment.* Knoxville: University of Tennessee Press, 2007.

Townsend, Edna W., compiler and ed. *Griswold Family: England-America.* Middleboro, MA: Griswold Family Association of America, 1978.

Townsend, William H. *Lincoln and His Wife's Home Town.* Indianapolis: Bobbs-Merrill, 1929.

Tracie, Theodore C. *Annals of the 19th Ohio Battery Volunteer Artillery.* Cleveland: J. B. Savage, 1878.

Train, Abner L., comp. *Yale College, Class of 1853.* New Haven: Press of Tuttle, Morehouse & Taylor, 1883.

Travis, William. *A History of Clay County, IN.* New York and Chicago: Lewis, 1909.

Tredway, Gilbert R. *Democratic Opposition to the Lincoln Administration in Indiana.* Indianapolis: Indiana Historical Bureau, 1973.

Treman, Ebenezer M., and Murray E. Poole. *History of the Treman, Tremaine, Truman Family in America.* Ithaca: Press of the Ithaca Democrat, 1901.

Tucker, Ebenezer. *History of Randolph County, IN.* Chicago: A. L. Kingman, 1882.

Tuley, William F. *The Tuley Family Memoirs.* New Albany, IN: W. J. Hedden, 1906.

Tyler, Mason W. *Recollections of the Civil War.* New York: G. P. Putnam's Sons, 1912.

Underhill, Patsy L. C. *A History and Lineage of the Baldwin, Crox, Eldridge and McClary and Allied Families.* College Park, MD: Patsy L. C. Underhill, 1971.

The Union Army. 8 Vol. Madison, WI: Federal, 1908.

The United States Biographical Dictionary. Kansas Volume. Chicago and Kansas City: S. Lewis, 1879.

The United States Biographical Dictionary and Portrait Gallery of Eminent and Self-Made Men, Iowa Vol. Chicago and New York: American Biographical, 1878.

University of Pennsylvania: Biographical Catalogue of the Matriculates of the College. Philadelphia: Society of the Alumni, 1894.

Upham, Warren, and Mrs. Rose Barteau Dunlap, comp. *Minnesota Biographies, 1655–1912. Minnesota Historical Society Collections,* Vol. 14. St. Paul: Minnesota Historical Society, 1912.

Urofsky, Melvin I., ed. *Biographical Encyclopedia of the Supreme Court: The Lives and Legal Philosophies of the Justices.* Washington, DC: CQ Press, 2006.

Utley, Henry M., and Byron M. Cutcheon, comp. *The Class of Sixty-One, University of Michigan, and Something About What "the Boys" Have Been Doing During Forty Years from 1861 to 1901.* Detroit: John Bornman & Son, 1902.

Utley, Robert M., ed. *Life in Custer's Cavalry: Diaries and Letters of Albert and Jennie Barnitz, 1867–1868.* New Haven: Yale University Press, 1977.

Valley of the Upper Maumee River with Historical Account of Allen County and the City of Fort Wayne, Indiana. Madison, WI: Brant & Fuller, 1889.

Van West, Carroll, ed.-in-chief. *The Tennessee Encyclopedia of History & Culture.* Nashville: Rutledge Hill Press, 1998.

Vernon County Heritage. Viroqua, WI: Vernon County Historical Society, 1994.

Versailles, Elizabeth S., comp. *Hathaways of America.* Northampton, MA: Gazette Printing, 1970.

Vohland, Mabel. *Christopher and Esther Leaming and Their Descendants.* Gibbon, NE: Mabel Vohland, 1977.

A Volume of Memoirs and Genealogy of Representative Citizens of the City of Seattle and County of King, Washington. New York and Chicago: Lewis, 1903.

Vronsky, Peter. *Ridgeway: The American Fenian Invasion and the 1866 Battle That Made Canada.* Toronto: Allen Lane Canada, 2011.

Wallace, George S. *Wallace, Genealogical Data Pertaining to the Descendants of Peter Wallace & Elizabeth Woods, His Wife.* Charlottesville: Michie, 1927.

War Letters of Aden G. Cavins Written to His Wife Matilda Livingston Cavins. Evansville: Rosenthal-Kuebler Printing, 1907.

The War of the Rebellion: A Compilation of the Official Records of the Union and Confederate Armies. Washington, DC: Government Printing Office, 1880–1901.

Ward, William H., ed. *Records of Members of the Grand Army of the Republic.* San Francisco: H. S. Crocker, 1886.

Webb, Thomas G. *A Bicentennial History of DeKalb County, TN.* Smithville, TN: Bradley Printing, 1995.

Weesner, Clarkson W., ed. *History of Wabash County, Indiana.* Chicago and New York: Lewis, 1914.

Wegerslev, C. H., and Thomas Walpole. *Past and Present of Buena Vista County, Iowa.* Chicago: S. J. Clarke, 1909.

Weik, Jesse W. *Weik's History of Putnam County, IN.* Indianapolis: B. F. Bowen, 1910.

Welcher, Frank J., and Larry G. Ligget. *Coburn's Brigade: 85th Indiana, 33rd Indiana, 19th Michigan, and 22nd Wisconsin in the Western Civil War.* Carmel: Guild Press of Indiana, 1999.

Wells, Emma M. *The History of Roane County, TN, 1801–1870.* Chattanooga: Lookout, 1927.

West, C. W. "Dub." *Fort Gibson, Gateway to the West.* Muskogee: Muskogee, 1974.

Wheeler, Albert G., Jr., comp. *The Genealogical and Encyclopedic History of the Wheeler Family in America.* Boston: American College of Genealogy, 1914.

White, Edward, ed. *Evansville and Its Men of Mark.* Evansville: Historical, 1873.

Who Was Who in America, 1897–1942. Chicago: A. N. Marquis, 1942.

Who Was Who in America: Historical Volume, 1607–1896. Chicago: A. N. Marquis, 1963.

Willey, Henry. *Isaac Willey of New London, Conn., and His Descendants.* New Bedford, MA: Henry Willey, 1888.

Williamson, David. *The 47th Indiana Volunteer Infantry: A Civil War History.* Jefferson, NC: McFarland, 2012.

Winslow, Hattie Lou, and Joseph R. H. Moore. *Camp Morton, 1861–1865, Indianapolis Prison Camp.* Indianapolis: Indiana Historical Society, 1940.

Wise, Jennings C. *The Military History of the Virginia Military Institute from 1839 to 1865.* Lynchburg: J. P. Bell, 1915.

Woollen, William W. *Biographical and Historical Sketches of Early Indiana.* Indianapolis: Hammond, 1883.

Wright, Thomas J. *History of the Eighth Regiment Kentucky Vol. Inf., During Its Three Years Campaigns.* St. Joseph, MO: St. Joseph Steam Printing, 1880.

Wylie, Theophilus A. *Indiana University, Its History from 1820 to 1890.* Indianapolis: William B. Burford, 1890.

Young, Andrew W. *History of Wayne County, Indiana.* Cincinnati: Robert Clarke, 1872.

Zinn, Jack. *The Battle of Rich Mountain.* Parsons, WV: McClain Printing, 1971.

Articles in Periodicals and Newspapers

Barnes, Ralph. "Col. Sidney Barnes." *Citizen Voice & Times* (Irvine, KY), July 18, 1996.

Barnett, James. "Willich's Thirty-Second Indiana Volunteers." *Cincinnati Historical Society Bulletin*, Vol. 37, No. 1 (Spring 1979).

Bates, Walter Lynn. "Southern Unionists: A Socio-Economic Examination of the Third East Tennessee Volunteer Infantry Regiment, U.S.A., 1862–1865." *Tennessee Historical Quarterly*, Vol. 50, No. 4 (Winter 1991).

Beck, Elias W. H. "Letters of a Civil War Surgeon." *Indiana Magazine of History*, Vol. 27, No. 2 (June 1931).

Bennett, B. Kevin. "The Battle of Richmond, Kentucky: 'A Victory Brilliant and Complete.'" *Blue & Gray Magazine*, Vol. 25, No. 6 (2009).

Boh, John. "The Amos Shinkle Estate." *Papers of the Kenton County Historical Society*, Volume 1 (1990).

Boomhower, Ray E. "Destination Indiana: Col. William Jones: Friend of Lincoln." *Traces of Indiana and Midwestern History*, Vol. 4, No. 4 (Fall 1992).

Brown, Preston. "John Mason Brown, 1837–1890, One of the Founders of the Filson Club." *The Filson Club History Quarterly*, Vol. 13, No. 3 (July 1939).

Bush, Bryan S. "Brig. Gen. William Woodruff: 'I Have Done All a Man Can.'" *North South Trader's Civil War*, Vol. 26, No. 2 (2000).

_____. "Marcellus Mundy, 23rd Kentucky: A Colonel with a Conscience." *North South Trader's Civil War*, Vol. 30, No. 6 (2004).

"Col. James Washington Gault." *Bulletin of the Mason County (KY) Genealogical Society*, Vol. 9, No. 2, 1991.

"Col. Lamson Paralyzed." *Washington Morning Times*, June 25, 1897.

Craig, Berry. "The Marshall County Wallers Stepped to a Different Drummer." *West Kentucky Journal*, Jan. 27, 2012.

"Crawford Pasha." *Louisville Courier-Journal*, Sept. 5, 1877.

Crook, W. Clay. "Hurst!" *Confederate Veteran*, March-April 1992.

"Dismissal of a Union Officer." *New York Times*, Dec. 13, 1862.

Dunn, Robert C. "Typical Southern Homestead of Col. Reuben May Recalls Many Incidents of His Life." *LaCrosse Tribune and Leader Press*, March 29, 1931.

"The Flat Gap Horror—An 1889 Knoxville Tragedy." *The Tennessee Genealogical Magazine*, Vol. 47, No. 3 (Fall 2000).

Goff, John S. "Colonel James P. T. Carter of Carter County." *Tennessee Historical Quarterly*, Vol. 26, No. 4 (Winter 1967).

Guese, Lucius E. "St. Louis and the Great Whisky Ring." *Missouri Historical Review*, Vol. 36, No. 2 (Jan. 1942).

Hardin, Bayless. "The Brown Family of Liberty Hall." *The Filson Club History Quarterly*, Vol. 16, No. 2 (April 1942).

Herring, Eliza A. "The Hoskins of Kentucky." *The Register of the Kentucky State Historical Society*, Vol. 15, No. 2 (May 1917).

"Hon. William Jones." *Rockport Weekly Democrat*, Feb. 19, 1876.

"Howard County's Ranking Civil War Soldiers." *Kokomo Tribune*, centennial ed., Oct. 30, 1950.

Hubbard, Paul, and Christine Lewis, eds. "'Give Yourself No Trouble About Me': The Shiloh Letters of George W. Lennard." *Indiana Magazine of History*, Vol. 76, No. 1 (March 1980).

Immel, Mary Blair, comp. "Family Records of Civil War Colonel, Gold Rusher, Horse Thief Detective, and Prosperous Farmer, James McMannomy." *The Hoosier Genealogist*, Vol. 44, No. 1 (Spring 2004).

Kelly, Robert M. "Holding Kentucky for the Union." *Battles and Leaders of the Civil War*, edited by Robert U. Johnson and Clarence C. Buel. New York: Century, 1887–88.

Lamb, J. J. "The 'Preacher Regiment' from Indiana: The 57th Indiana Infantry." *Civil War: The Magazine of the Civil War Society*, Vol. 12 (March 1988).

"Letters from Civil War Soldiers to a Relative in Sullivan County, 1862–1866." *The Observer: A Publication of the Sullivan County Historical Society*, Vol. 21, No. 1 (Jan.-Feb. 2001) and Vol. 23, Issue 1 (Jan.-Feb. 2003).

Logan, John P. "Gallant Wolford." *Washington National Tribune*, Nov. 16, 1899.

McCan, Anthony. "James Wall Scully—A Kilkenny Soldier in the American Civil War." *The Irish Sword: The Journal of the Military History Society of Ireland*, Vol. 23, No. 91 (Summer 2002).

McCormick, Mike. "Wabash Valley Profiles: Robert N. Hudson." *Terre Haute Tribune-Star*, Sept. 18, 1999.

"One Day a Year for the Sons of Erin; First Indianapolis Observance in 1864." *Indianapolis News*, March 11, 1922.

Ossad, Steven L. "Henry Ware Lawton: Flawed Giant and Hero of Four Wars." *Army History: The Professional Bulletin of Army History*, PB 20-06-1, No. 63 (Winter 2007).

"A Painful Reminder of the War." *The Ohio Democrat* (New Philadelphia, Ohio), Jan. 29, 1880.

Pirtle, Alfred. "New Year's Eve on Field of Battle." *Louisville Evening Post*, Dec. 31, 1915.

Potter, Hugh O. "Colonel John H. McHenry, Jr., Union Soldier—Owensboro Lawyer." *Filson Club History Quarterly*, Vol. 39, No. 2 (April 1965).

Robertson, Robert S. "Address Delivered Before the Lawton Memorial Meeting." *Addresses, Memorials, and Sketches*. Published by the Maumee Valley Pioneer Association, Toledo, OH, 1900.

Scully, Arline. "James Wall Scully, Brigadier General, United States Army." *Journal of the American Irish Historical Society*, Vol. 29 (1930–31).

Seigel, Peggy. "Charles Case: A Radical Republican in the Irrepressible Conflict." *Indiana Magazine of History*, Vol. 107, No. 4 (Dec. 2011).

Sickles, John. "Hoosier Horsemen: Indiana's Cavalry and Mounted Infantry in the Civil War." *Military Images*, Vol. 17, No. 6 (May-June 1996).

Smith, William Henry. "The Sixth Indiana Regiment, Its Historical Record." *The Indianian*, Vol. 4, No. 5 (Oct. 1899).

Snow, Richard F. "American Characters: Henry Ware Lawton." *American Heritage*, Vol. 33, No. 3 (April/May 1982).

"A Soldier and a Man." *Louisville Commercial*, Sept. 10, 1895.

Tapp, Hambleton. "Incidents in the Life of Frank Wolford." *The Filson Club History Quarterly*, Vol. 10, No. 2 (April 1936).

Tarbell, Ida M. "Abraham Lincoln: Indiana Reminiscences of Lincoln." *McClure's Magazine*, Vol. 6, No. 1 (December 1895).

"A Tyrannous Colonel Rebuked." *New York Daily Tribune*, Feb. 19, 1862.

Watterson, Henry. "The Bravest Deed I Ever Knew." *Century Magazine*, Vol. 82, No. 3 (July 1911).

Webb, Ross A. "Benjamin Helm Bristow, the Man Who Walked in Front of Destiny." *Filson Club History Quarterly*, Vol. 41, No. 2 (April 1967).

Manuscript Sources

Death Certificates, City of Covington, KY.
The Filson Historical Society, Special Collections, Louisville, KY.
    Elijah S. Watts Papers, 1861–1907.
Indiana Historical Society
    Col. Bernard F. Mullen Family Materials, 1834–1893 (Collection SC 2807).
    McLaughlin-Jordan Family Papers, 1841–1915 (Collection SC 1030).
Interment Records, Cedar Hill Cemetery, Corydon, IN.
Interment Records, Greendale Cemetery, Lawrenceburg, IN.
Interment Records, Highland Cemetery, Fort Mitchell, KY.
Interment Records, Oak Hill Cemetery, Evansville, IN.
Interment Records, Riverview Cemetery, Aurora, IN.
Kentucky Historical Society, Frankfort, KY.
    Thomas Metcalfe Collection.
Library of Congress
    Benjamin Helm Bristow Papers.
    John Marshall Harlan Papers.
Military Order of the Loyal Legion of the United States (MOLLUS)
    Obituary Circulars of various State Commanderies.
National Archives
    Compiled Service Records of Confederate Soldiers Who Served in Organizations from the State of Tennessee (Record Group 109).
    Court-martial Case Files, 1809–1894 (Record Group 153).
    Dispatches from U.S. Consuls in Manzanillo, Mexico (Record Group 59).
    Historical Register of National Homes for Disabled Volunteer Soldiers, 1866–1938 (Record Group 15).
    Letters of Application and Recommendation During the Administration of Ulysses S. Grant, 1869–1877 (Record Group 59).
    Letters Received, Adjutant General's Office (Record Group 94).
    Letters Received, Appointment, Commission and Personal Branch, Adjutant General's Office (Record Group 94).
    Letters Received, Colored Troops Branch, Adjutant General's Office (Record Group 94).
    Letters Received, Commission Branch, Adjutant General's Office (Record Group 94).
    Letters Received, Volunteer Service Branch, Adjutant General's Office (Record Group 94).
    Military Service Files (Record Group 94).
    Pension Files (Record Group 15).
    Register of Enlistments in the United States Army, 1798–1914 (Record Group 94).
    Regular Army Enlistment Papers, 1798–1912 (Record Group 94).
    U.S. Census Records (Record Group 29).

U.S. Military Academy Cadet Application Papers, 1805–1866 (Record Group 94).
Research files of Leoneita C. Milner, Dallas, TX.
Research files of Robert A. Goelzer, Jr., courtesy of John A. Stovall.
Tennessee State Library and Archives, Nashville, TN.
  Clift Family Papers.
U.S. Military Academy Library.
  Cullum File.
University of Kentucky, Special Collections Library, Lexington, KY.
  Clinton Jones True Papers.
Western Kentucky University, Manuscripts & Folklife Archives, Kentucky Library and Museum, Bowling Green, KY.
  Hobson Family Papers.

Internet Sources

http://biffle.org/fgs-elizabethbifflekindrick.html.
http://familytreemaker.genealogy.com/users/s/h/a/William-O-Shackleford/GENE1-0076.html.
http://www.findagrave.com.
http://freepages.history.rootsweb.ancestry.com/~indiana42nd/JAMES_G_JONES_BIO.htm.
http://hurstnation.com.
http://ketchum.bobaddleman.com.
James L. Clark, "Andrew H. Clark and the Civil War in Kentucky," *http://freepages.family.rootsweb.ancestry.com/~kyborn/article42.htm.*
"Rice Haggard: Life, Home & Family Burial Plot, 1767–1819," *http://www.therestorationmovement.com/haggard.htm.*
Jennifer Kidwell Fish, "Descendants of Thomas Fish: Third Generation," *http://www.rootsweb.ancestry.com/~kymadiso/research/family/fish/fish/pafg04.htm.*
http://sedgwick.org/na/families/barnabas1810/sedgwick-thomas1837.html.
http://www.suddenlink.net/pages/fpreston/bdnathan.htm.
http://tennesseeencyclopedia.net/entry.php?rec=1616.
http://trees.ancestry.com/tree/1090618/person/-1999448652.
http://trees.ancestry.com/tree/15478846/person/269005268.
http://trees.ancestry.com/tree/17161688/person/538989107.
http://trees.ancestry.com/tree/8947993/person/-871016185.

Newspapers

Adair County (KY) *News*
Andrew County (MO) *Republican*
Arkansas Gazette (Little Rock)
Ashland Daily (KY) *Independent*
Atlanta Constitution
Aurora (IN) *Commercial*
Bedford (IN) *Daily Mail*
Bedford (IN) *Mail*
Bloomfield (IN) *News*
Bloomington (IL) *Daily Pantagraph*
Bloomington (IN) *Evening World*
Boston Globe
Brownstown (IN) *Banner*
Cannelton (IN) *Enquirer*
Carthage (MO) *Evening Press*
Cawker City (KS) *Public Record*
Champaign Daily News
Chattanooga Daily Times
Chicago Daily Inter Ocean
Chicago Daily Tribune
Cincinnati Commercial
Cincinnati Daily Commercial
Cincinnati Daily Gazette
Cincinnati Enquirer
Colorado Chieftain (Pueblo)
Columbus (IN) *Daily Herald*
Columbus (IN) *Herald*
Columbus Evening Republican
Connersville (IN) *Examiner*
Connersville (IN) *Weekly Times*
Corydon (IN) *Democrat*
Covington (IN) *Republican*
Crawfordsville (IN) *Daily Argus News*
Crown Point (IN) *Register*
The Daily Ardmoreite (OK)
Danville (IN) *Republican*
Daviess County (IN) *Democrat*
Dayton Daily Journal
Decatur (IN) *Daily Democrat*
Decatur (IL) *Daily Republican*
The Decatur Press (Greensburg, IN)
Des Moines Register and Leader
Dixon (IL) *Evening Telegraph*
Evansville Courier
Evansville Daily Journal
Evansville Journal
Evansville Journal-News
Florida Times-Union (Jacksonville)
Fort Wayne Daily Gazette
Fort Wayne Daily News
Fort Wayne Daily Sentinel
Fort Wayne Journal-Gazette
Fort Wayne News
Fort Wayne Sentinel
Fort Worth (TX) *Daily Gazette*
Frankfort (IN) *Crescent-News*
Frankfort (IN) *News*
Frankfort (KY) *Roundabout*
Frankfort (KY) *State Journal*
Frankfort (KY) *Tri-Weekly Commonwealth*
Franklin (IN) *Republican*
Galena (IL) *Weekly Gazette*
Garden City (KS) *Herald*
Goshen (IN) *Times*
Goshen (IN) *Weekly Democrat*
Greencastle (IN) *Banner*
Greencastle (IN) *Banner Times*
Greencastle (IN) *Times*
Greensburg (IN) *New Era*
Greensburg (IN) *Weekly News*
Hartford (KY) *Herald*

Hartford (KY) *Republican*
Hendricks County (IN) *Union*
Hopkinsville (KY) *South Kentuckian*
Huntington (IN) *Daily News-Democrat*
Huntsville Advocate
Huntsville Weekly Democrat
Illinois State Journal (Springfield)
Illinois State Register (Springfield)
Indianapolis Daily Sentinel
Indianapolis Journal
Indianapolis News
Indianapolis Sentinel
Indianapolis Star
Indianapolis Times
Jackson (OH) *Standard*
Jasper County (IN) *Democrat*
Jeffersonville (IN) *Evening News*
Jonesborough (TN) *Herald and Tribune*
Kentucky Gazette (Lexington)
The Kentucky Register (Richmond)
Kentucky Tri-Weekly Advocate (Danville)
Knightstown (IN) *Banner*
Knoxville Daily Chronicle
Knoxville Daily Journal
Knoxville Journal
Knoxville Journal and Tribune
Knoxville Weekly Tribune
Kokomo (IN) *Daily Tribune*
Kokomo (IN) *Gazette Tribune*
Kokomo (IN) *Weekly Tribune*
Lafayette (IN) *Daily Call*
Lafayette (IN) *Daily Courier*
Lafayette (IN) *Daily Journal*
Lafayette (IN) *Morning Journal*
La Porte (IN) *Daily Herald*
La Porte (IN) *Weekly Argus*
Lawrenceburg (IN) *Democratic Register*
Lawrenceburg (IN) *Register*
Lebanon (IN) *Patriot*
Lebanon (IN) *Pioneer*
Lexington Daily Press
Lexington Morning Herald
Lexington Morning Transcript
Logansport (IN) *Daily Journal*
Los Angeles Daily Times
Los Angeles Times
Louisville Commercial
Louisville Courier-Journal
Louisville Daily Democrat
Louisville Daily Journal
Louisville Journal
Madison (IN) *Courier*
Madison (IN) *Daily Evening Courier*
Marion (IN) *Chronicle*
Marion (IN) *Morning News*
Martin County (IN) *Tribune*
Martinsville (IN) *Republican*
Mayfield (KY) *Monitor*
Maysville (KY) *Daily Public Ledger*
Maysville (KY) *Evening Bulletin*

Memphis Commercial Appeal
Memphis Daily Avalanche
Mobile Daily Register
Morris (MN) *Sun*
Mount Sterling (KY) *Advocate*
Mount Vernon (IN) *Western Star*
Nashville American
Nashville Daily American
Neosho (MO) *Times*
New Albany (IN) *Daily Commercial*
New Albany (IN) *Daily Ledger*
New Albany (IN) *Daily Ledger-Standard*
New Albany (IN) *Ledger-Standard*
New Castle (IN) *Courier*
New York Times
New York Tribune
Noblesville (IN) *Democrat*
North Platte (NE) *Semi-Weekly Tribune*
Norton's Union Intelligencer (Dallas)
Oakland Tribune
Odessa (MO) *Democrat*
Omaha Morning World-Herald
Oskaloosa (IA) *Herald*
Ottawa (KS) *Daily Republican*
Paris True Kentuckian
Peru (IN) *Daily Chronicle*
Peru (IN) *Republican*
Piatt County (IL) *Herald*
Placerville (CA) *Mountain Democrat*
Portland Morning Oregonian
Princeton (IN) *Clarion*
Quincy (IL) *Daily Journal*
Richmond (KY) *Climax*
Richmond (IN) *Evening Item*
Richmond (IN) *Item*
Ripon (WI) *Commonwealth*
Rising Sun (IN) *Recorder*
Rochester (IN) *Weekly Republican*
Rockport (IN) *Journal*
Rockport (IN) *Weekly Democrat*
Rockville (IN) *Republican*
Rocky Mountain News (Denver)
St. Joseph Valley Register (South Bend, IN)
St. Louis Globe Democrat
San Antonio Express
San Bernardino Daily Sun
San Francisco Call
San Francisco Chronicle
San Francisco Examiner
Santa Barbara Weekly Press
Santa Fe Daily New Mexican
Seattle Post-Intelligencer
The Shelby News (Shelbyville, KY)
Shelbyville (IN) *Democrat*
Shenandoah (IA) *World*
Smithville (TN) *Review*
South Bend (IN) *National Union*
South Bend (IN) *Weekly Tribune*
Spokane Spokesman-Review
Springfield (MO) *Daily Leader*

Stanford (KY) *Semi-Weekly Interior Journal*
Stevenson (AL) *Chronicle*
Tagliche Evansville (IN) *Union*
Terre Haute Daily Express
Terre Haute Daily Journal
Terre Haute Evening Gazette
Terre Haute Express
Terre Haute Tribune
Terre Haute Tribune-Star
Topeka Daily Capital
Topeka State Journal
Tucson Weekly Arizonan
Urbana (OH) *Citizen and Gazette*
Vernon County (WI) *Censor*

Vevay (IN) *Reveille*
Vincennes (IN) *Capital*
Vincennes (IN) *Weekly Western Sun*
Vinita (OK) *Indian Chieftain*
Wabash (IN) *Plain Dealer*
Warsaw (IN) *Daily Times*
Washington Evening Star
Washington National Republican
Washington National Tribune
Washington Post
Weekly Kentucky Yeoman (Frankfort)
Winchester (IN) *Herald*
Winfield (KS) *Daily Courier*

INDEX

Numbers in ***bold italics*** indicate pages with illustrations.

Abercrombie, John J. 39, 187
Adams, Silas 135, 140, *141*
Adams, Will A. 14
Aldrich, Simeon C. 7, *16, 17*
Alexander, Francis N. 138, 141
Alexander, Jesse Ianthus 9, *17*
Ammen, Jacob 66
Anderson, Edward 4, 17, *18*
Anderson, Oliver P. 10, 18, *19*
Andrews, Albert Shaw 6, *19*
Anthony, DeWitt C. 9
Artsman, Gustavus 140, 141

Babbitt, George Seymour 6, 19, *20*
Baird, John Pearson 10, *20*
Baker, Conrad 3, *21*
Baker, Myron H. 10, *21*
Baldwin, Oliver Leonard 135, 141
Baldwin, Philemon Prindle 4, *22*
Barnes, Sidney Madison 137, *142*
Barter, Richard Fulton 12, 22, *23*
Bass, Sion St. Clair 6, *23, 24*
Bates, Daniel Francis 14, 24
Bates, Hervey, Jr. *121*
Bayles, David 142
Bayles, Jesse 135, 142
Beatty, John 69
Beatty, Samuel 59, 160
Belknap, David S. *42*
Bennett, Thomas W. 9, *94*
Benton, Thomas Hart 169
Benton, William P. 4
Berry, William Washington 136, *143*
Bickle, William A. 9, 24, 75
Biddle, James 3, 9
Bingham, Judson D. 66
Bingham, Newton 8, *24*
Bisch, Victor 14, 25
Blackburn, Joseph Hayes 199, *200*
Blake, John Wesley 7, *25*, 26
Blake, William Howard 4, 25, *26*
Blanche, Willis 8, *26*
Blythe, James E. 14, 27
Board, Buckner 135, 143
Boone, John Rowan 138, 143, *144*

Boone, William Pennebaker 138, *144, 145*
Bowden, Doil R. 5, *27*
Bowles, William A. 123
Boyd, Spencer B. 199, *200*
Brady, Thomas J. 12, 13
Bramlette, Thomas Elliott 136, *145*, 187
Brannan, John M. 170
Braxton, Hiram Francis 12, 27
Briant, Cyrus E. 11, *28*
Bridgland, John Alexander 3, 28
Bringhurst, Thomas Hall 8, 28, *29*
Bristow, Benjamin Helm 135, *146*
Brooks, Lewis 10, *30, 41*
Brown, Benjamin Gratz 147
Brown, John Mason 139, *147*, 184
Brown, Kennedy 15, *30*
Brown, William Lyons 6, *31*, 93
Browne, Thomas M. 3
Brownlow, James P. 197
Bruce, Sanders Dewees 138, 143, *148, 149*, 193
Buckland, Henry W. *222*
Buckland, Ralph P. 201, *222*, 223
Buckley, Harvey M. 136, 140, *149*
Buckner, James Francis 140, 149
Budd, Casper 16, 31, *32*
Buell, Don Carlos 75, 90, 103
Buell, George P. 9
Buford, John 170
Burbridge, Stephen G. 40, 138, 155, 169, 187
Burge, George W. 12, *32*
Burge, Hartwell T. 139, *150*
Burgess, James 13, 32
Burkam, Joseph Hayes 15, 33
Burnett, Henry L. *94*
Burnside, Ambrose E. 203
Burton, James Ellis 7, *33*
Butler, Thomas H. 3
Buttinghaus, Frederick William 199, 201
Byrd, Robert King 198, *201*

Caldwell, William Wallace 10, 33
Cameron, Robert A. 7

Carey, Oliver Hazard Perry 7, 14, *34*
Carr, Henry Montgomery 9, 35
Carroll, William B. 5, *35*
Carter, James Patton Taylor 198, *202*
Carter, Samuel P. 202
Carter, Scott 3, 36
Carter, William H. *98*
Case, Charles 11, 13, *36, 37*
Casto, William T. 178
Catterson, Robert F. 11
Cavins, Aden Gainey 11, *37*
Chapin, Decatur G. 199, *202*
Chapman, Charles Warner 10, *38*
Chapman, George H. 3
Chetlain, Augustus L. 203
Clark, Andrew Hamilton 139, 150
Clark, John Gilkeson 6, *39*
Clay, Cassius M. 75
Clift, Moses H. 203
Clift, William 198, *203*
Coburn, John 7
Cochran, John Carr 137, 151
Colgrove, Silas 6, *94*
Comparet, John Marcellus 13, 39
Conover, Robert 5, 12, 39
Coons, John 5, *40*
Cooper, Joseph A. 198
Cooper, Robert Wickliffe 135, *151*
Cox, Jacob D. 219
Craddock, James Wesley 137, 151, *152*
Cram, George H. 137
Crane, Alexander Baxter 10, *40*
Crawford, Robert A. 199, 203
Crawford, Robert Clay, Jr. 198, 203
Crittenden, Eugene Wilkinson 136, *152*
Crittenden, George B. 152
Crittenden, John J. 152
Crittenden, Thomas L. 152
Crittenden, Thomas T. 4, 22
Crooks, John Wilson 14, 41
Cross, William 198, 204
Croxton, John T. 136
Cruft, Charles 6, 36, 49

243

Index

Culbertson, James Lowery 10, *41*
Curry, Amos P. 199, 204, *205*
Curtis, James F. 7, 41, *42*

Davis, Jefferson C. 6
Dawkins, Richard C. 136, 152
DeHart, Richard P. 13, *94*
Denby, Charles 10, *42*, 50
Denny, William N. 8, 43
Dent, Henry 138, 153
Denver, James W. 222
Deweese, John T. 3
Dick, George F. 10
Dillard, William York 138, 153
Dils, John, Jr. 139, 153, *154*
Doan, Thomas 11, *43*
Dobbs, Cyrus Johnson 5, *44*
Dodge, Joseph B. 6, 44, *45*
Douglas, Melvyn 186
Dudley, Ethelbert Ludlow 138, *154*, 184
Duke, Basil W. 170
Duke, Henrietta 170
Dulles, John Foster 51
Dumont, Ebenezer 4
Dunham, Cyrus Livingston 8, *45*
Dunlap, Henry C. 136
Dunn, David Maxwell 6, *46*
Dunn, William McKee 46

Eastin, George B. 162
Eddy, Norman 8, 46, *47*
Edwards, Richard Mitchel 197, 205
Emerson, Frank 9, 47
England, Orin O. *222*
Enyart, David A. 136, *185*
Erdelmeyer, Francis 7, 47, *48*
Espy, Harvey (aka Henry) Jefferson 9, *48*
Eve, John Gill 139, 154, *155*
Ewing, Hugh 117
Ewing, Thomas Jackson 140, *155*

Fairbanks, William Henry 14, 49
Fairleigh, Thomas Brooks 138, 155, *156*
Farrar, Josiah 11, *49*
Faulkner, John Kavanaugh 135, *156*
Ferguson, Champ 200
Fish, James Shelby 140, 157
Fitch, Graham Newell 8, 12, 42, 49, *50*, 88
Fitton, Henry F. *98*
Foley, Bushrod Washington 140, 157
Forman, James Brown 137, *157*
Foster, John Watson 9, 13, *50*
Foster, Robert S. 5
Fournier, Charles Theodore 15, 51
Fowler, Alexander 11, *51*
Foy, James Calvert 138, *158*
Frémont, John C. 65, 169
Fry, Speed S. 136

Galbraith, Robert 197, 205, *206*
Gallup, George W. 137, 179
Garrard, Theophilus T. 137, 150
Garrett, John M. 16, 52
Garver, William 11, *52*
Gathright, John Thomas 140, *158*, *159*
Gault, James Washington 137, *159*
Gavin, James 4, 10, 12, 13, 52, *53*
Gazlay, Carter 7, 53
Gilbert, Charles C. 141
Gillem, Alvan C. 198, 212
Gleason, Newell 11
Goelzer, Augustus 9, 53
Gooding, Michael 6, *54*
Graham, Felix William 3, 54
Graham, Milton 136, 159, *160*
Granger, Gordon 54, 142, 189
Grant, Ulysses S. 82, 200, 210
Gray, Isaac Pusey 3, 12, *55*
Gregory, Benjamin Moore 11, 15, 55, *56*
Gregory, Samuel Oscar 6, *56*
Gresham, Walter Q. 8, 19
Grider, Benjamin Covington 137, 160
Grider, Henry, Jr. 160
Grider, John Hobson 139, 160
Griffin, Daniel F. 7
Grigsby, Lewis Braxton 138, 160
Grill, John Frederick 13, 56, *57*
Griswold, Whedon Wyllys 14, *57*
Grose, William 7, 100
Grover, Ira G. 4
Guthrie, James Verner 136, *161*
Guthrie, Presley N. *161*
Guthrie, Robert B. *161*
Guthrie, William W. *161*

Hackleman, Pleasant A. 5
Haggard, David Rice 135, 161, *162*
Halisy, Dennis J. 135, 162
Halleck, Henry W. 123, 209
Hallowell, James Reed 6, *58*
Hamilton, Orville S. 10, 58
Hammer, John Shackleford 137, 162, *163*
Hammond, John W. 9, *59*
Hanson, Charles S. 139, *163*
Hanson, Roger W. 163
Harlan, John Marshall 137, 163, *164*
Harney, Selby 138, 164
Harrison, Benjamin 9
Harrison, Thomas J. 3
Harrow, William 5, 67, 68
Hartsuff, George L. 191
Hascall, Milo S. 5, 166, 183
Hathaway, Gilbert 10, 59, *60*
Hawkins, Percival (aka Pierce) Butler 137, 140, *165*
Hays, Benjamin F. 4, *60*
Hays, William Hercules 137, 165, *166*
Hazzard, George Whitfield 7, *61*

Healey, Joshua 14, 61, *62*
Heath, Albert 11, *62*, *63*, *94*
Hendricks, John Abram 15, *63*
Hendricks, William 63
Heustis, Zephaniah 15, 63
Hines, Cyrus Cooke 8, *64*
Hobson, Edward H. 137, 167
Hobson, William Edward 137, *166*, *167*
Hodges, Joseph C. *42*
Holeman, Alexander Wake 136, *167*, *168*
Hollingsworth, William E. 14, *64*
Holt, Joseph 34, 153
Horsey, Stephen 123
Hoskins, William Anderson 137, *168*
Houk, Leonidas Campbell 198, *206*
Houston, Sampson McMillan 16, 64
Hovey, Alvin P. 6, 14, 56, 67
Hudson, Robert Noble 3, 13, *65*
Hull, James Standiford 7, 65
Humphrey, George 11, 13, *66*
Hunter, Morton C. 10
Hurst, Fielding Jackson 197, 206, *207*
Hurt, John Smith 138, 168

Ingram, John Nelson 15, 66

Jackson, George Washington 3, 12, 66, *67*, *79*
Jackson, James S. 135
Jacob, Matilda Prather 169, 182
Jacob, Richard Taylor 135, *169*, 182, 194
James, Enoch Randolph 14, 67
Johnson, Andrew 204, 205, 211, 220
Johnson, Gilbert M.L. 4
Johnson, Robert 197
Johnson, Ruel Milton 11, *68*
Johnson, Samuel F. 136, 170
Johnson, Thomas 9, 69
Johnston, Samuel M. 15, 69
Jones, Fielder A. 3
Jones, James Garrard 7, *69*
Jones, Robert Barclay 7, *70*
Jones, William 8, 70, *71*
Jordan, Lewis 15, *71*, 113

Kearny, Philip 31
Keeney, Harris 15, 71
Keenon, Edgar A. 140, *170*
Keigwin, James 8, 15, *72*
Keith, John Alexander 4, 72, *73*
Kellams, Gideon R. 7, *73*
Kelly, Robert Morrow 136, 170, *171*
Kendrick, William Patrick 197, 207
Ketchum, Asa Calkins 199, 207, *208*
Kimball, Nathan 5
King, Edward Augustine 9, 73, *74*

Index

Kise, Reuben C. 12, 74
Kise, William Coalbaugh 5, 12, *74*
Knefler, Frederick 10
Koontz, Jacob Harvey 15, 74, *75*
Korff, Hermann Jacob 9, 75

Lambertson, Samuel 12, 16, 75, *76*
Lamson, Horace P. 3, 76
Landram, John James 138, 171, *172*
Landram, William J. 137
Lawrence, John Henry 5, *76, 77*
Lawton, Henry Ware 6, *77, 78*
Leaming, Henry 7, 78
Leeper, James 8, 78
Lennard, George Washington 8, 78, *79*
Lilly, Eli 3, *79*
Lilly, Henry Clay 136, *172*
Lincoln, Abraham 161, 169, 194, 207
Lindley, John M. 5
Lindsey, Daniel Weisiger 138, 172, *173*
Lindsey, Hiram *112*
Link, William Hardy 5, *80*
Logan, Newton A. 6, 80
Lopez, Narciso 204
Lord, John Smith 199, *208, 209*
Love, Smoloff Pallas 137, 173, *174*
Lucas, Thomas J. 5, *94*
Lyon, Virgil H. 15, 80, *81*

Macauley, Daniel 5
Maginness, Edmund Ayres 15, 81
Mahan, John Riley 12, 81, *82*
Main, Zalmon Smith 8, *82*
Major, John Crittenden 7, *83*
Malick, Washington 15, 83
Malloy, John C. *221*
Mann, John Albert 14, 84
Mansfield, Fielding 8, 84
Mansfield, John Lutz 8, *84*
Manson, Mahlon D. 4
Marshall, Charles Alexander 137, *174*
Marshall, John 174
Martin, Roger 9, *85*
Mason, Charles Holland 15, 85
Mathey, Edward G. 18
Matson, Courtland Cushing 3, 85, *86*
Maxwell, Cicero 138, 174, *175,* 186
May, Reuben 137, *175*
McClure, William Simrall 3, *86*
McCook, Edward M. 3
McDonald, Charles 199, *209,* 210
McDonald, John 199, 209, *210*
McDowell, Irvin 188
McDowell, John A. 188
McGinnis, George F. 5
McGraw, John S. 8, *87*
McHenry, John Hardin, Jr. 137, 175, *176*
McHolland, David Armstrong 8, *87*

McIntire, William T.B. 7, 88
McKee, Samuel 136, 176, *177*
McKinster, Thomas 140, 177
McLaughlin, John Alexander 8, *88*
McLean, William Edward 7, 88, *89, 94*
McMannomy, James 9, 89
McMillan, James W. 6
McMullen, John William Thomas 8, 89
McNaught, Thomas A. 9
McQuiston, John C. 12
Mehringer, John 11
Melton, James Marion 198, 210
Meredith, Solomon 5
Metcalfe, Leonidas 135, *177*
Metcalfe, Thomas 178
Miller, Abram O. 9
Miller, John F. 6
Miller, John Kelly 198, *210, 211*
Miller, Martin Boots 10, 90
Milligan, Lambdin P. 94, 123
Milroy, Robert H. 4
Milward, Hubbard Kavanaugh 137, *178*
Mims, David Alexander 139, *179*
Monroe, George W. 137, 138
Moody, Gideon Curtis 4, *90*
Moore, Laban Theodore 137, 179, *180*
Moore, Ranna Stevens 10, 91
Morgan, George W. 103
Morgan, John Hunt 148, 162
Morgan, John T. 15, 91
Morgan, Thomas 10, *91*
Morgan, William H. 6
Morrison, Robert Gilbert 7, *92*
Morton, Oliver P. 82, 88, 120, 123
Morton, Sarah 175, 186
Mulky, James Boleyn 16, 92
Mullen, Bernard Francis 7, 92, *93*
Mundy, Marcellus 138, *180*
Murphy, John 199, *211*
Murray, Charles Dennis 11, 93, *94*
Murray, Eli H. 135
Mussey, Reuben D. 204

Neff, Andrew J. 10
Nelson, William 141, 151
Nicholas, Thomas Prather 135, 180
Nichols, Thomas 15, *94*
Northup, George W. 138, *181*
Nuhfer, Andrew *222*

O'Brien, William 10, *95*
O'Neal, Weden 140, 181, 187
Ormsby, Oliver 15, 95
Orr, John M. 13, 95, *96*
Orr, William 6, *96*
Osborn, John 6, 96
Osterhaus, Peter J. 150
Owen, Alfred Dale 10, *41, 97,* 98
Owen, David Dale 97, 98
Owen, Eugene F. *98*

Owen, Richard 9, 97, *98*
Owen, Robert Dale 98

Pace, Thomas Newsom 4, 98
Packard, Jasper 13
Palmer, John J. *98*
Parrish, Charles S. 13
Parsons, Joseph H. 197, 212
Pattison, Thomas 5, 98, *99*
Patton, David Henry 7, *99*
Patton, Samuel Kelsey Nelson 197, 212, *213*
Pearson, Charles Dewey 16, 100
Peckham, James 209
Peden, Milton 14, *100*
Pennebaker, Charles David 138, 181, *182*
Perry, Oran 9, *101*
Pettit, John Upfold 10, 101, *102*
Pickens, William Cowan 197, 213
Platter, John Andrew 3, 15, *102*
Pleasanton, Alfred 36
Polk, John Robert 4, 102
Pope, Curran 137, 169, *182*
Post, Philip Sidney 46
Prather, Allen Wiley 12, *103*
Prather, Hiram 103
Preston, Burgess 140, 183
Preston, William 147
Price, Samuel W. 138
Prosser, William Farrand 197, *213, 214*

Ratcliffe, Jesse 188
Rawson, Eugene A. *222*
Ray, Daniel Mack 197, *214*
Ray, John William 8, 103, *104*
Reed, Hugh B. 7, *104*
Reeve, Arthur Tappan 199, *215*
Reeve, Felix Alexander 198, *216*
Reeves, Thomas Hansel 198, *216*
Reynolds, Joseph J. 4
Richmond, Nathaniel Pendleton 16, *105*
Riddle, George Washington 14, 105, *106*
Roberts, Rufus Robert 14, 106
Robinson, Edward Jones 13, 106
Robinson, James F. 162
Robinson, Milton S. 10
Rogers, John A. 198, 217
Rose, David Garland 8, *106,* 124
Rosecrans, William S. 25, 34, 46, 105, 128, 160, 161, 162
Rousseau, Lawrence H. 137, 183
Rousseau, Lovell H. 136, 189
Ruckle, Nicholas Randle 14, *107*
Ruger, Thomas H. 61
Rugg, DeWitt Clinton 12, 15, 108
Ryan, David 199, *217*
Ryan, Townsend 7, *108*

Sanders, William P. 135, 162
Sanderson, William Lawrence 6, 108

Index

Scobey, John Smith 9, *109*
Scott, George H. 10, *109*
Scott, Harvey David 16, 110
Scott, Jefferson Kingsley 9, *110*
Scott, William Thompson 136, 147, 154, *183*, *184*
Scribner, Benjamin F. 7, 15, 81
Scully, James Wall 198, *218*
Sedgewick, Thomas Duncan 120, 136, *184*, *185*
Sering, Samuel B. 15, 110
Shackelford, George Taliaferro 136, *185*
Shackelford, James M. 135, 138
Shanks, John P.C. 3
Shanks, Quintus Cincinnatus 136, 175, 186
Shannon, James Hammond 13, *111*
Sharra, Abram 4, *111*, *112*
Shea, Thomas 6, 112
Shelley, Jacob D. 219
Shelley, James Thomas 198, 199, 218, *219*
Sherman, William T. 182
Shinkle, Amos 140, *186*
Shryock, Kline Godfrey 11, 12, 112, *113*, 123
Shuler, Lawrence S. 3, 11, 113
Shunk, David 4
Slack, James R. 8
Slaughter, Thomas Coleman 15, 71, 113
Smith, Green Clay 135, 170
Smith, James Monroe 8, 113
Smith, John Thomas 6, *114*
Smith, Morgan L. 209
Smith, Samuel E. *42*
Smith, William J. 197
Spalding, George 198
Spears, James G. 205
Spencer, William H. 136, 187
Spicely, William T. 6, 27
Spooner, Benjamin J. 10, *94*
Stanhope, Philip William 140, *187*
Stanton, Edwin M. 120, 123
Starling, Edmund Alexander 139, *188*
Starr, Owen 135, 188, *189*
Steele, Asbury Earl 7, 114, *115*
Steele, George Kirkpatrick 7, *115*
Stevens, Ambrose A. *94*
Stewart, James W. 3, 115, 116
Stewart, Robert Reed 3, 4, 115, *116*
Stiles, Israel N. 9
Stokes, William B. 197, 205

Stoneman, George 39, 212
Stoughton, Sandford James 11, 116
Stoughton, William L. 117
Stout, Alexander M. 137
Stover, Daniel 198, *219*
Streight, Abel D. 8
Strickland, Jesse Hartley 197, 220
Strickland, William 220
Stuart, David 209
Sullivan, Jeremiah C. 5
Suman, Isaac C.B. 4
Swallow, George Ransom 4, *117*

Tassin, Augustus G. 7
Taylor, Marion Cartright 137, 189, *189*
Taylor, Marsh B. 5, 14, 117, *118*
Taylor, William Calvin Linton 6, *118*
Tevis, Joshua 136, 190
Tevis, Lloyd 189
Thomas, DeWitt C. 11
Thomas, George H. 90, 200
Thomas, Lorenzo 160
Thornhill, John A. 212
Tripp, Hagerman 4, *119*
True, Clinton Jones 139, *190*
Trusler, Nelson 10, *119*
Tucker, John W. *41*
Tuley, William Woodruff 15, *120*, 185

Vail, Jacob G. 5
Vance, Samuel Colville 13, 15, *121*
Van Cleve, Horatio P. 155
Van Valkenburg, John 6, 120
Vaughan, James M. 221
Veatch, James C. 6, 124
Vestal, Warner Lowder 8, *122*
Von Heyde, Henry 199, *220*
Von Trebra, Henry 7, 122

Wade, Alfred Bryant 10, 112, 122, *123*
Wagner, George D. 5, 25
Walker, Charles Jones 136, *191*
Walker, John Crawford 7, 107, *123*, *124*
Walker, William 118, 167, 204
Walker, William N. 14, 124
Wall, William Robert 16, 124, *125*
Wallace, John Milton 5, *125*
Wallace, Lewis 5, 75, 125, 187
Waller, Thomas B. 138, 192
Ward, John Hardin 138, *192*

Ward, William T. 193
Warner, William Alfred 137, 148, 193
Washburn Henry D. 5
Wass, Ansel D. *94*
Watkins, Louis D. 135
Watts, Elijah Searcy 135, *193*
Weatherford, James Wallace 136, 194
Webb, Thomas 16, 125
Wells, Samuel Thornton 8, 125, *126*
Welsh, Merit C. 14, *126*
Wheatley, William M. 6, 127
Wheeler, John 6, *127*
Wheeler, Joseph 200
Whitaker, Walter C. 136, 143
White, John Samuel 137, 194
Whitney, William Clifford 199, *221*
Wilcox, Frank 14, 127
Wilder, John T. 5
Wiles, William M. 6, *128*
Wiley, Edmund Roberts, Jr. 199, 221, *222*
Willey, John Fletcher 15, 129
Williams, Hugh T. 15, *129*
Williams, John S. 9, 129, *130*
Williams, Reuben 5, *94*
Williams, Samuel J. 5, *130*
Williams, William C. 7, 117, 130, *131*
Williamson, Milton T. 199, *222*
Willich, August 6
Wilson, John M. 14, 131
Wilson, William Cochran 7, 12, 13, 131, *132*
Wolfe, Edward H. 8
Wolford, Frank Lane 135, 169, *194*, *195*
Wood, Edward Jesup 8, *132*
Wood, Gustavus Adolphus 5, 132, *133*
Wood, Thomas J. 73, 78
Woodbury, Horatio 10, 15, 133
Woodruff, William Elihu 136, *195*, *196*
Wright, Horatio G. 203
Wright, James S. 6, 133

Young, Freemorton 223
Young, Isham 198, 223

Zollinger, Charles Augustus 13, *134*

www.ingramcontent.com/pod-product-compliance
Lightning Source LLC
Chambersburg PA
CBHW081549300426
44116CB00015B/2808